Praise for *Black Wave*

'[A] blistering account . . . Ghattas knows how to tell a cracking story . . . *Black Wave* is a *cri de coeur*, an action-packed modern history written with the pace of a detective thriller'

Justin Marozzi, *The Sunday Times*

'The publication of *Black Wave* could not be better timed . . . A fascinating . . . highly readable tale'

James Barr, 'Book of the Week', *The Times*

'Wonderfully readable . . . Whatever happens next in this long-running, oppressive and dangerous Middle Eastern drama, *Black Wave* will be a vivid, indispensable guide to the story so far'

Ian Black, 'Book of the Week', *Observer*

'Profoundly moving . . . There is a simmering anger not far below the surface of [this] book. It is a gripping tale. It is a tract for our times. Read and weep. But also, like Ghattas, allow yourself to hope'

John Jenkins, *New Statesman*

'A timely and welcome guide . . . Well-researched and elegantly written, *Black Wave* focuses on the lives of a number of key individuals – from guerrilla fighters, revolutionary clerics and spy chiefs to Sufi leaders and journalists'

Financial Times

'Sweeping and authoritative'   ***New York Times***

'Skilfully written and scrupulously researched, *Black Wave* is an essential book in understanding the origins of the modern conflicts in the Middle East'

Lawrence Wright, Pulitzer Prize-winning author of *The Looming Tower*

'The book is packed with accounts of ambition, treachery and cruelty – with a wealth of historical detail down to the hour of the day . . . [Ghattas] serves up a wealth of human interest wrapped in ambience and atmosphere'

Wall Street Journal

'A brilliant book, written with verve and style. It is not just essential reading, but thoroughly riveting as well. I could not put it down'

Peter Frankopan, author of *The Silk Roads*

'In this ambitious and highly readable book, Kim Ghattas tells the story of how Middle Eastern political and religious leaders betrayed their people. Her bold thesis that the events of 1979 scattered the seeds of destruction is revelatory and original'

Lindsey Hilsum, International Editor, Channel 4 News
and author of *In Extremis: The Life of War Correspondent Marie Colvin*

'Vivid reporting, deep analysis. This is a fascinating and important book ... *Black Wave* is essential reading if you want to understand why the region slid into religious extremism and blood-soaked sectarianism'

Jeremy Bowen, BBC Middle East Editor
and author of *The Arab Uprisings*

'Reveals in masterful detail the rivalry between Saudi Arabia and Iran, and its pernicious effect on the wider region from 1979 to the present day – a sharp and sobering analysis, beautifully written'
Zeid Ra'ad al Hussein, former UN High Commissioner for Human Rights

'A brilliant piece of work. Ghattas reveals how the competition between Tehran and Riyadh led to the instrumentalization of Islam to destroy cosmopolitanism, force women to veil, and to mobilize sectarian extremists'
Emma Sky, Senior Fellow at Yale University's Jackson Institute and author
of *In a Time of Monsters*

'Kim Ghattas portrays the last four decades across the Middle East as a kind of Islamic Dark Ages, a world dimmed behind a curtain of violence, misogyny, and religious extremism. In exploring how this blackness came to be, she both reminds us of a brighter past and holds out the possibility of a future of light. It's a powerful and important book'
Anne-Marie Slaughter, CEO of the New America Foundation

'Brutally honest, perfectly researched and brilliantly written ... A must-read for outsiders and people in the region'
Marwen Muasher, Vice President for Studies at the Carnegie Endowment
for International Peace and former Minister of Foreign Affairs of Jordan

BLACK WAVE

Saudi Arabia, Iran and
the Rivalry That Unravelled
the Middle East

KIM GHATTAS

WILDFIRE

First published in 2020 by
Wildfire
an imprint of HEADLINE PUBLISHING GROUP

First published in paperback in 2021 by
WILDFIRE
an imprint of HEADLINE PUBLISHING GROUP

Cataloguing in Publication Data is available from the British Library

ISBN 978 1 4722 7113 6

Printed and bound in Great Britain by Clays Ltd, Elcograf S.p.A.

Headline's policy is to use papers that are natural, renewable and recyclable products
and made from wood grown in well-managed forests and other controlled sources.
The logging and manufacturing processes are expected to conform to the
environmental regulations of the country of origin.

HEADLINE PUBLISHING GROUP
An Hachette UK Company
Carmelite House
50 Victoria Embankment
London EC4Y 0DZ

www.headline.co.uk
www.hachette.co.uk

In memory of my father,
who told me so many stories about before.

Where they make a wasteland, they call it peace.
—*Agricola*, Tacitus (Roman senator, d. AD 120)

CONTENTS

PART III REVENGE

NOTE ON NAMES AND SPELLINGS

I have used the most common spellings for well-known names and terms in Arabic, Persian, and Urdu. In other cases, I have used my own transliterations. Translations of Arabic newspaper headlines and text as well as of some of the poetry are my own. Wherever similar concepts exist across the three cultures I cover, I have indicated their equivalent in Arabic.

For the concept of the Guardianship of the Jurist introduced by Khomeini, which is mentioned repeatedly, I have used the Arabic transliteration *wilayat al-faqih* (rather than the Persian *velayat-e faqih*) throughout the book to avoid confusion. In Arabic, both *ibn* and *bin* can be translated as "son of." I have used both depending on the most common usage (Mohammad bin Salman versus Abdelaziz ibn Saud). The name Muhammad can also be transliterated *as* Mohammad and I have used both depending on the most widespread usage or the preference expressed by characters in the book. I have chosen to refer to many of the central characters by their first names to distinguish them from prominent or historical figures.

PEOPLE

Lebanon

Hussein al-Husseini: Shia politician and speaker of parliament during the 1980s

Musa Sadr: Iranian Shia cleric, moved to Lebanon in 1959, disappeared in Libya in 1978

Hani Fahs: Shia cleric, lived in Iran 1979–86; supporter, then critic, of the revolution

Badia Fahs: daughter of Hani and journalist, lived in Iran as a student

Sobhi Tufayli: founding member of Hezbollah

Hassan Nasrallah: secretary-general of Hezbollah since 1992

Rafiq Hariri: billionaire politician and three-time prime minister, assassinated in 2005

Iran

Mahmoud Ahmadinejad: president 2005–13

Masih Alinejad: journalist and activist

Abolhassan Banisadr: leftist nationalist and first president after the revolution

Mehdi Bazergan: founding member of the Liberation Movement of Iran (LMI), first prime minister after the revolution

Mohammad Beheshti: loyal Khomeinist and founder of the Islamic Republican Party

Mostafa Chamran: key member of the LMI, first defense minister of revolutionary Iran

Sadegh Ghotbzadeh: key member of the LMI
Mohammad Khatami: president 1997–2005
Mohsen Sazegara: student activist with the LMI, founding member of
    Revolutionary Guards (IRGC)
Ebrahim Yazdi: key member of the LMI, first foreign minister after the
    revolution

Saudi Arabia

Sami Angawi: architect and founder of the Hajj Research Center
Abdelaziz bin Baz: powerful cleric, vice rector of Medina University in
    the 1960s, grand mufti of the kingdom 1993–99
Sofana Dahlan: lawyer and descendant of nineteenth-century mufti
    Ahmad ibn Zayni Dahlan
Turki al-Faisal: intelligence chief 1979–2001
Muhammad ibn Saud: founder of the Al-Saud dynasty in the eighteenth
    century
Muhammad ibn Abdelwahhab: ultra-fundamentalist orthodox preacher
    in the eighteenth century, ally of Muhammad ibn Saud
Mohammad bin Salman: crown prince since 2017 and defense minister
    since 2015, son of King Salman
Abdelaziz ibn Saud: founder of Kingdom of Saudi Arabia, ruled 1932–53
Faisal ibn Saud: third king of Saudi Arabia, assassinated 1975

Iraq

Saddam Hussein: president 1979–2003
Mohammad Baqer al-Hakim: Iranian ayatollah in exile in Iran
    1980–2003, assassinated in Iraq in 2003
Atwar Bahjat: Iraqi journalist, assassinated 2006
Abdulmajid al-Khoei: Shia cleric, exiled in 1991, assassinated in 2003
Mohammad Taqi al-Khoei: Shia cleric, killed in 1994
Jawad al-Khoei: Shia cleric, son of Mohammad Taqi, exiled in 1991,
    returned to Iraq in 2010
Mohammad Baqer al-Sadr: ayatollah executed by Saddam in 1980,
    founder of Islamist Shia Da'wa Party
Moqtada al-Sadr: cleric and founder of the Mahdi army

Syria

Hafez al-Assad: president 1970–2000
Bashar al-Assad: son of Hafez, president since 2000

Yassin al-Haj Saleh: student communist activist jailed in 1980, Syria's
   leading intellectual since 2000
Samira al-Khalil: activist and Yassin's wife, kidnapped by militants in
   2013
Sa'id Hawwa: key ideologue of the Syrian Muslim Brotherhood
Zahran Alloush: leader of Islamist rebel group Jaysh al-Islam, killed in
   2015

Pakistan

Zulfiquar Ali Bhutto: prime minister 1973–77
Benazir Bhutto: daughter of Zulfiquar, prime minister 1988–90, 1993–96,
   assassinated 2007
Mehtab Channa Rashdi: television anchor
Faiz Ahmed Faiz: one of the most celebrated poets in the Urdu language
Arif Hussaini: Shia cleric, supporter of Khomeini
Zia ul-Haq: president 1978–88
Ehsan Elahi Zaheer: Sunni religious scholar, author of anti-Shia books

Egypt

Gamal Abdel Nasser: president 1954–70
Nasr Abu Zeid: secular professor of Arabic literature and Islamic studies
Farag Foda: secular intellectual, assassinated in 1992
Nageh Ibrahim: Islamist student activist, founding member of Gama'a
   Islamiyya
Hosni Mubarak: president 1981–2011
Ahmed Naji: journalist and novelist
Anwar Sadat: president of Egypt assassinated in 1981
Ebtehal Younes: professor of French literature and wife of Nasr Abu Zeid
Ayman al-Zawahiri: leader of Islamic Jihad in Egypt, number two in
   al-Qaeda

Others

Yasser Arafat: chairman, Palestinian Liberation Organization
Issam Berqawi, aka Abu Muhammad al-Maqdissi: Jordanian Salafist,
   mentor of Abu Musab al-Zarqawi
Muammar al-Gaddafi: ruler of Libya 1970–2011

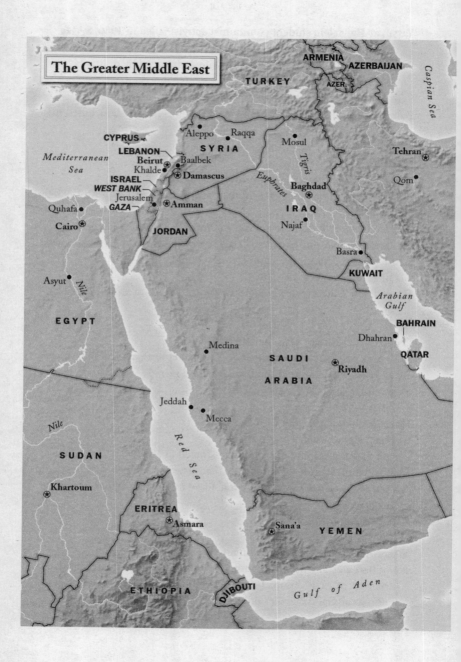

The Greater Middle East

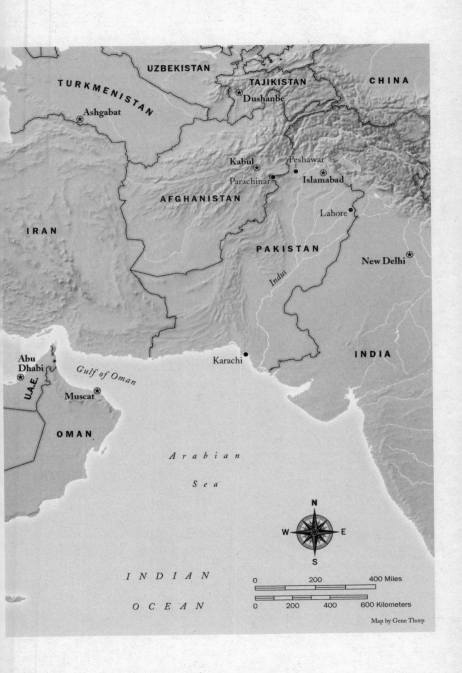

Map by Gene Thorp

BLACK WAVE

INTRODUCTION

"What happened to us?" The question haunts us in the Arab and Muslim world. We repeat it like a mantra. You will hear it from Iran to Syria, from Saudi Arabia to Pakistan, and in my own country of Lebanon. For us, the past is a different country, one that is not mired in the horrors of sectarian killings; a more vibrant place, without the crushing intolerance of religious zealots and seemingly endless, amorphous wars. Though the past had coups and wars too, they were contained in time and space, and the future still held much promise. "What happened to us?" The question may not occur to those too young to remember a different world, or whose parents did not tell them of a youth spent reciting poetry in Peshawar, debating Marxism late into the night in the bars of Beirut, or riding bicycles to picnic on the banks of the Tigris River in Baghdad. The question may also surprise those in the West who assume that the extremism and the bloodletting of today were always the norm.

Although this book journeys into the past, it is not driven by wistful nostalgia about a halcyon world. My aim was to understand when and why things began to unravel, and what was lost, slowly at first and then with unexpected force. There are many turning points in the Middle East's modern history that could explain how we ended up in these depths of despair. Some people will identify the end of the Ottoman Empire and the fall of the last Islamic caliphate after World War I as the moment when the Muslim world lost its way; or they will see the creation of Israel in 1948 and the defeat of the Arabs in the subsequent Six-Day War of 1967 as the first fissure in the collective Arab psyche. Others will skip directly to the US invasion of Iraq in 2003 and point to the aftermath as the final paroxysm of conflicts dating back millennia: Sunnis and Shias killing each other, Saudi Arabia and Iran locked in a fight to the death. They will insist that both the killings and the rivalry are inevitable and eternal. Except for the "inevitable and eternal" part, none of these explanations is wrong, but none, on its own, paints a complete picture.

Trying to answer the question "What happened to us?" led me to the fateful year of 1979. Three major events took place in that same year, almost independent of one another: the Iranian Revolution; the siege of the Holy Mosque in Mecca by Saudi zealots; and the Soviet invasion of Afghanistan, the first battleground for *jihad* in modern times, an effort supported by the United States. The combination of all three was toxic, and nothing was ever the same again. From this noxious brew was born the Saudi-Iran rivalry, a destructive competition for leadership of the Muslim world, in which both countries wield, exploit, and distort religion in the more profane pursuit of raw power. That is the constant from 1979 onward, the torrent that flattens everything in its path.

Nothing has changed the Arab and Muslim world as deeply and fun-damentally as the events of 1979. Other pivotal moments undid alliances, started or ended wars, or saw the birth of a new political movement. But the radical legacy of 1979 did all this and more: it began a process that trans-formed societies and altered cultural and religious references. The dynamics unleashed in 1979 changed who we are and hijacked our collective memory.

The year 1979 and the four decades that followed are the story at the heart of this book. The Saudi-Iran rivalry went beyond geopolitics, descend-ing into an ever-greater competition for Islamic legitimacy through reli-gious and cultural domination, changing societies from within—not only in Saudi Arabia and Iran, but throughout the region. While many books explore the Iranian Revolution, few look at how it rippled out, how the Arab and Sunni world reacted and interacted with the momentous event. All the way to Pakistan, the ripples of the rivalry reengineered vibrant, plu-ralistic countries and unleashed sectarian identities and killings that had never defined us in the past. While Pakistan is geographically located on the Indian subcontinent, its modern history is closely linked to the trends that unfolded in the Middle East, and the country features prominently in this narrative. Across this Greater Middle East, the rise of militancy and the rise of cultural intolerance happened in parallel and often fed into each other.

Everywhere I went to conduct interviews for this book, from Cairo to Baghdad, from Tehran to Islamabad, I was met with a flood of emotions when I asked people about the impact the year 1979 had on their lives. I felt I was conducting national or regional therapy, sitting in people's living rooms and studies: everyone had a story about how 1979 had wrecked their lives, their marriage, their education, including those born after that year. Although this is neither a work of historical scholarship nor an academic study, it is more than a reported narrative: I dug deep into archives, pored over thousands of newspapers, interviewed dozens of people, and built a virtual library of the history of those four decades. The result is a new reading of known events, some forgotten, some overlooked, most heretofore seen in isolation. Brought together, spanning four decades of history and seven countries, they shatter many accepted truths about the region and shed an unprecedented light on how the Saudi-Iran rivalry evolved and mutated over time, with consequences no one could have foreseen in 1979.

Although geopolitical events provide the backdrop and stage for *Black Wave*, this is not a book about terrorism or al-Qaeda or even ISIS, nor is it about the Sunni-Shia split or the dangers that violent fundamentalists pose for the West. This has been the almost obsessive focus of the headlines in the West. Instead, these pages bring the untold story of those—and they are many—who fought and continue to fight against the intellectual and cultural darkness that slowly engulfed their countries in the decades following the fateful year of 1979. Intellectuals, poets, lawyers, television anchors, young clerics, novelists; men and women; Arab, Iranian, and Pakistani; Sunni and Shia; most devout, some secular, but all progressive thinkers who represent the vibrant, pluralistic world that persists beneath the black wave. They are the silenced majority, who have suffered immensely at the hands of those who are relentlessly intolerant of others, whether wielding political power or a gun. Some paid with their life, like the Saudi journalist Jamal Khashoggi, murdered in the Saudi consulate in Istanbul in October 2018. Jamal was a colleague and a friend. I was writing a passage about his life when his brutal death provided a macabre twist to the larger tale of the Saudi-Iran rivalry.

The lives of all the characters at the heart of this book overlap in time, across generations. Some know each other; most don't. They live in different countries, but they are fighting the same battles. Their stories are contained within other stories of historical figures, famous writers, or infamous militants, a sprawling tale, a *One Thousand and One Nights* of modern Middle Eastern politics.

This tale begins just a few years before 1979, on the shores of the Mediterranean, in Lebanon, in a little-known episode that played a crucial role in setting the stage for the Iranian Revolution.

PART I

REVOLUTION

1

CASSETTE REVOLUTION

LEBANON-IRAN-IRAQ-FRANCE
1977–79

Peace died in the homeland of peace
Justice succumbed
When the City of Jerusalem fell
Love retreated and in the hearts of the world, war settled
The child in the grotto and his mother Mary are crying,
and I am praying.

—Fairuz, lyrics from "Jerusalem Flower of all the Cities" (1971)

There is an irony lodged deep in the heart of the revolution that turned
Iran from a Persian kingdom into an Islamic theocracy, a revolution
cheered and organized by secular leftists and Islamist modernists. The
irony is that the Iran of the fundamentalist ayatollahs owes its ultimate
birth pang to cities of sin and freedom: Beirut, capital of Arabic modernity,
once known as the Paris of the Middle East; and Paris, birthplace of the
Age of Enlightenment. If not for the permissive freedoms in both, Ayatollah Ruhollah Khomeini—a patient man with a cunning mind—might have
died forgotten in a two-story mudbrick house down a narrow cul-de-sac
in the holy city of Najaf, in Iraq. The Iranian cleric had agitated against
the shah of Iran for over a decade and spent time in prison in Tehran. He
was sent into exile and arrived in Najaf in 1965, where he languished in
anonymity for thirteen years, popular among his circle of disciples but
shunned by most of the Iraqi Shia clergy. In Najaf, clerics stayed out of
politics and disapproved of the firebrand ayatollah who thought he had
a special relationship with God. Outside the cities that busied themselves
with theology, there were those who saw in Khomeini a useful political
tool, someone who could rouse crowds in the battle against oppression.
Different people with different dreams, from Tehran to Jerusalem, from

Paris to Beirut, looked to Khomeini and saw a man who could serve their agenda, not realizing they were serving his.

—

On the coast of Lebanon, on the terrace of a house overlooking the glistening sea, a trio of men animated by a yearning for justice talked late into the night, remaking the world and their countries. They were an unlikely assortment: Musa Sadr, the magnetic, turbaned Iranian cleric with green eyes, known as Imam Sadr; Hussein al-Husseini, the witty, mustachioed Lebanese politician, in a suit; and Mostafa Chamran, the Iranian physicist turned leftist revolutionary in fatigues. Only one of them would survive the crush of what their dreams unleashed.

The year was 1974. The antiapartheid activist Nelson Mandela was in jail in South Africa. The Irish Republican Army was fighting the British, bombing pubs and telephone exchanges in England. In Vietnam, American firepower had come to naught. The fighting continued between the pro-American South and the Communist North, but all US troops had gone home. After nineteen years of war, the toll was devastating: two million Vietnamese civilians, a million and a half Vietnamese troops, and sixty thousand American troops were dead. President Richard Nixon had just resigned to avoid impeachment in a separate episode of infamy: the Watergate scandal. Men wore their hair long, neckties were wide, and Led Zeppelin was the biggest rock band in the world. In April 1975, Saigon would fall to the Communists. That same month, war would erupt in Lebanon and the fire of the Cold War would move from Southeast Asia to the Middle East.

But for now, in the summer of 1974, as the three men gathered in Husseini's home in the tiny coastal town of Khalde, ten minutes south of Beirut, they looked back on a year of achievements. Their dreams crossed borders, their destinations were different, but their journey against oppression was the same. War was still only a murmur around them.

That summer, Joan Baez's powerfully gentle voice had echoed from the east, farther inland, in the dry coolness of the fertile Beqaa Valley. The American folk singer and civil rights activist, a friend of Martin Luther King Jr. and onetime lover of Bob Dylan, strummed her guitar for the well-heeled crowd of music aficionados and socialites who had traveled from Beirut and around the Arab world to attend the International Baalbek Festival. She sang about freedom and answers blowing in the wind, at the site of ancient Heliopolis, the largest, best-preserved Roman city in Baalbek, a small rural town of barely ten thousand inhabitants. "How many years must some people exist, before they're allowed to be free?" asked Baez. Ella Fitzgerald, Rudolf Nureyev, and the New York Philharmonic, as well as Lebanon's own ethereal iconic singer Fairuz and Egypt's leading diva Umm Kulthum, had all performed in Baalbek under the watch of the towering columns of the temples of Bacchus and Jupiter. During the day, tourists walked around the famed ruins; in the evening, hundreds descended on the small town to attend the performances while the locals sold souvenirs and snacks at the entrance to the site.

As a town, Baalbek was an underdeveloped backwater. Some of its dwellings were less than salubrious—open sewage ran in some of the streets. There was no secondary school, but there were open fields of cannabis all around the city, which meant both money and poverty—and a lot of guns. This was a typical tale of neglect of rural areas, but here in Baalbek (as in other parts of Lebanon) there was more to the divide: religion. In this country of mind-boggling diversity for its small size, there were three groups: Christians, the minority to whom the departing colonial rulers had given the power to dominate; Sunni Muslims, the traditional bourgeois merchant class, city dwellers who also swelled the ranks of the bureaucracy; and Shia Muslims, forgotten and downtrodden, who tilled the soil for potatoes or cannabis in the Beqaa Valley or picked tobacco in the south. In the cities, Shias were the shoeshine boys, the newspaper sellers, the restaurant busboys. There were Shia landowners, but they, too, lorded it over the others. There were also Shia notables and politicians like Husseini, who had pushed through the barriers to become mayor of a small town at the age of nineteen. Baalbek had a mix of all three communities, but it was predominantly Shia.

The history of Lebanon's Shia community is said to stretch back to the early days of Islam, the oldest community outside Medina, where, after the prophet Muhammad died, some had chosen Ali, cousin of the prophet and husband of his daughter Fatima, as the rightful heir. They were known hence as the partisans of Ali, *shi'at* Ali. Others believed that the prophet had named Abu Bakr, a close companion, as his successor and first caliph of the Muslim nation. The struggle opposed two visions for the succession: one religious, through a line of the prophet's descendants known as *imams* (leaders of prayer); and the other, more earthly, centered on power, *caliphs* (literally, "successors"), chosen by consensus among wise men. The battle over who was to govern Muslims and levy taxes on the community would descend into civil war during the first decades of Islam and then settle into a theological schism. There would be Shia empires but, overall, the history

of Shiism is the history of a minority in opposition, of sacrifice and martyrdom. In Lebanon, over centuries, the Shias amassed wealth and power and
built the region of Jabal Amel in the south of the country into a center of
Shia erudition. When Shah Ismail I founded the Safavid dynasty in Persia
in the fifteenth century, he forced his Sunni subjects to convert to Shiism
almost overnight. He brought over clerics and scholars from the holy Shia
cities of Karbala and Najaf in Iraq as well as from Jabal Amel to teach and
spread the new gospel. Under Ottoman rule, the Shias of Lebanon continued to maintain a defiant autonomy, but eventually they had to submit to
their role as a minority in the Sunni empire. When modern Lebanon came
into existence, the boundaries between Shiism and Sunnism were often
fluid, from a religious and even an identity perspective. The divide was
sharpest as a rural versus urban gap. Overall, Shias lived in harmony with
their Sunni and Christian neighbors and accepted their fate.

Imam Sadr had come to wake them. He had moved to Lebanon from
Iran in 1959 to shine a light on Shia dispossession and help establish schools
and dispensaries, just like a missionary. Sadr's ancestors had come from
Lebanon, like all the al-Sadrs in Iraq, Iran, and beyond. He had now made
the reverse migration journey. He wore the black turban, which signaled
that as a cleric he was also a descendant of the prophet, a *sayyed*; the title
Imam was an additional honorific bestowed on him by devoted followers.
In the cold month of March 1974, he traveled to Baalbek to awaken Shia
political consciousness. They came from everywhere in Lebanon to listen to
the charismatic orator. They traveled from the orange orchards and tobacco
fields of the dominantly Shia southern coast, from the small Shia villages
in the Christian heartland in the north, and from the cinder-block slums of
Beirut where they had settled after escaping Israeli shelling of their southern villages. They came by bus and by car, traveling for hours, some for
more than a day, across a small country without a public transportation
network. By the time Imam Sadr had reached the outskirts of Baalbek, the
roads were jammed, forcing him to stop in towns along the way. Seventy-
five thousand men, seemingly all with AK-47s and old World War II guns,
had converged on Baalbek to hear him speak. He barely managed to reach
the podium as the crowds lunged to touch his gown; he even briefly lost his
black turban. The clatter of celebratory gunfire was deafening.

"I have words harsher than bullets, so spare your bullets," he told his
audience. Imam Sadr blasted the government in Beirut for its neglect of
Lebanon's Shias and rural areas in general, for the unpaved roads, the lack
of schools and basic rights like water and electricity. In a country with

eighteen different sects, the Shia community was one of the three largest, and yet they rarely rose through the ranks of the bureaucracy; they were passed over for promotion, shoved into lesser jobs. The speaker of the house, always a Shia according to Lebanon's unwritten constitution, had little political power—that rested mostly in the hands of the country's Christian president. Lebanon, modern and cosmopolitan, was also a country of fiefdoms and clientelism, and the Shias had never had anyone speak up for them or lead their battles. Now they had Imam Sadr.

"What does the government expect, what does it expect other than rage and revolution?" he warned, speaking to the crowd. He rattled off a list of all the ways in which the Shias were being wronged. He had made some headway during his time in Lebanon, helping to found the Higher Shia Council to lobby for the needs of the community. But progress had been too slow. It was time to raise the tone. "Arms," he told his followers, "are the adornment of men." Sadr was not calling for armed struggle but he understood the feeling of empowerment that came from merely carrying a gun. He wasn't a military leader, but then neither was he a traditional quietist cleric focused on theology and the matters of his parish. He was an activist, and though his focus was the Shia plight Sadr spoke up against dispossession and injustice across all communities. The Baalbek rally marked the launch of the Movement of the Disinherited, which Sadr had recently founded with his friend Husseini, a multi-confessional movement that was the result of more than a decade of work.

A towering six foot six, Sadr was unlike any leader that Lebanon had ever seen, a country where people stayed within the confines of their sectarian identity. Although he was Iranian-born, in the holy city of Qom, his ancestors had come from Jabal Amel. He was a modernist, a rare cleric who had studied not only in religious seminaries but also on the benches of a secular institution, obtaining a degree in political science from Tehran University. He had family ties extending across borders and ethnicities, blurring the lines between Arab, Persian, and Turk, with cousins everywhere. The holy city of Najaf in Iraq was the hub where all ties converged. Sadr crossed boundaries of the mind too, opening worlds onto one another. In Tyre, he bought ice cream from a Christian whose business was suffering because his Shia neighbors believed anything made by non-Muslims was unclean. Christian women swooned over him, and though clerics were not supposed to shake hands with women, he occasionally made an exception out of politeness. He taught at Sunni schools, gave classes in Islamic philosophy at the St. Joseph University in Beirut, and prayed in churches all over the country. The imagery was striking as he stood behind the altar, beneath Jesus on a crucifix, facing a full church with his black turban denoting lineage traced back to the prophet Muhammad. He once drew huge crowds to a small church in a tiny Christian village on the border with Israel. He arrived half an hour late, and when he finally appeared behind the pulpit the anxious crowd of Christian worshippers called out *Allahu Akbar*, God is great, a cry of relief, as though Christ himself had arrived.

Sadr understood his different audiences. He spoke with melancholy to the priests and nuns and the flock gathered in a church, paying homage to Christ as an apostle of the oppressed; he thundered in Baalbek to the men with guns, rousing them from their sorrow with imagery of Imam Hussein, son of Ali and Fatima, grandson of the prophet, killed in battle in Karbala in the year 680. The party of Ali had largely accepted that the prophet's successors would be caliphs chosen by wise counsel. Then one caliph passed the reins to his son, Yazid. There was wide discontent with this act of nepotism, and Hussein rebelled against the injustice, facing off with his followers against the army of Yazid. His death helped crystallize what was still a nascent Shia identity. He was killed on the tenth, *ashura*, day of the Muslim month of Muharram and became a tragic, exalted figure, buried near the site of the battle. For centuries to come, Shias would incant "Every day is Ashura, every land is Karbala."

But as with every historical event, there were different interpretations. Some historians dismissed Imam Hussein's endeavor as a tale of failure; some saw a battle between two fallible men each seeking power; others described Hussein as a rebel standing up for justice against tyranny. How had he gone into battle: seeking martyrdom and riding willingly to a sure death? Or clear-eyed, weighing his options, and still hoping for the best outcome? Ayatollah Khomeini would later deploy the narrative of the willing martyr. In Baalbek, Sadr gave his followers a rendition of Imam Hussein stripped of sorrow, a story not of victimhood but rebellion against injustice. And so Sadr urged his followers not to seek death, but to rebel with courage like Imam Hussein.

There was much to rebel against, especially in the south of the country. The dominantly Shia south of Lebanon, dotted with Sunni and Christian villages, was caught in the crossfire of a regional conflict. Lebanon was home to tens of thousands of Palestinian refugees, stateless since the end of the British mandate over Palestine and the creation of the state of Israel in 1948 on parts of the territory. Among the refugees, since the 1960s, were Palestinian guerrilla fighters running amok with their guns, launching attacks against Israel just across the border, in the hope of liberating land they had lost to the new state. Israel's military superiority was felt on a regular basis as its planes raided Palestinian camps in south Lebanon and shelled villages, and Israeli tanks crossed into Lebanon. The Lebanese army was no match for Israel's Defense Forces, and the weak Lebanese state had no authority over the Palestinian guerrillas. Villagers, Muslim and Christian alike, resented the Palestinian fighters for attracting Israel's wrath onto them and ruining their world and livelihood.

Sadr chided the state for leaving its citizens defenseless but said nothing about the Palestinians. Along with his friends Husseini and Chamran, he wrestled with an impossible paradox: how to protect the community from Israeli retaliation, while staying loyal to the Palestinian cause, that of lost Arab land, and to Jerusalem, a holy city now out of reach for most Arabs after Israel had gained control over the whole city during the Six-Day War in 1967.

There was an added complexity: the Palestinian camps in Lebanon were a training hub for every revolutionary of the era, from the Japanese Red Army to the German Baader-Meinhof group but also the Iranians who wanted to get rid of the shah. One of those was Sadr's friend Chamran. Training in Lebanon was a rite of passage for revolutionaries of the period, and even before the civil war weapons were readily available. You could buy them from fat men with worry beads sitting in tea shops. If they had run out, you could go to their neighbor or competitor, the barber or the grocer around the corner. Beirut was a playground for playboys, spies, and gun dealers.

Inspired by the success of the Cuban, Algerian, and Vietnamese revolutions and insurgencies, Iranian opposition groups of all political stripes, from Marxists to nationalists, religious fundamentalists to Islamist modernists, were exploring the option of an armed insurgency against the king of Iran. Shah Mohammad Reza Pahlavi had been on the throne since 1941, when his father, Reza Shah Pahlavi, had abdicated. The Persian empire was 2,500 years old, but the Pahlavi dynasty was young. In 1925, with help from the British, Reza Shah, a brigadier general in the Persian Cossack army, had put an end to two centuries of Qajar dynasty. Both father and son had faced challenges as they tried to force the rapid modernization of the country. In 1963, Shah Mohammad Reza Pahlavi had launched a wide program of reforms he described as a White Revolution. Khomeini and other clerics denounced what they saw as the Westernization of Iran by a despotic ruler. They were particularly incensed about the greater rights granted to women, including the right to run for elected office and serve as judges. Spurred by the clergy, leftists, antiroyalists, and student activists also took to the streets, each for their own reasons. The shah crushed the protests, killing dozens. Opposition leaders who were not arrested went underground or scattered abroad. Khomeini went to Turkey, then Iraq, but Lebanon provided convenient proximity for Iranian dissidents, along with religious and social affinities and even entertainment: the more secular revolutionaries could train during the day and go to the beach in the afternoon or spend their evenings in the bars of Beirut.

Chamran was a key member of Nehzat-e Azadi-e Iran, the Liberation Movement of Iran (LMI), an opposition party that had participated in the uprising of 1963 against the shah. The group's founders, Mehdi Bazergan and a liberal cleric, Ayatollah Mahmoud Taleghani, were religious modernists: devout, but also advocates of the separation of church and state. They too rejected the White Revolution and believed that modernizing Iran did not have to empty it of its soul. After 1963, the LMI leadership had to move underground and abroad. From Tehran to Cairo, then to Berkeley in the United States, Chamran eventually moved to Lebanon in 1971. While he helped Husseini and Sadr improve the life of Lebanon's Shias, he was also busy organizing LMI training in various Palestinian camps. Hundreds of young Iranians—Marxists and clerics alike—came through these camps. They would soon become the vanguard of the Iranian Revolution.

Chamran had settled in the southern Lebanese city of Tyre, an ancient Phoenician town and the birthplace of Dido or Elissar, Queen of Carthage. Pious but secular in his outlook on life, he had no religious iconography in his living space, no religious recitations about Imam Hussein or sermons among any of the cassette tapes in his car. Driving around Lebanon, the revolutionary with a PhD loved listening to the songs of Umm Kulthum, with her melancholic lyrics that seemed to never end, and her repetitive, entrancing incantations of love. Sadr had a weakness for Iran's equivalent, Marzieh, the daughter of a cleric with a rich repertoire of over one thousand songs about love, passionate but mostly unrequited. Her mezzo-soprano could bring him to tears as he pined for his country.

On the balcony of the Husseini home, it was usually the music of Lebanon's beloved Fairuz that played in the background while the three friends engaged in late-night discussions about the role of religion in life and its limitations. Both Iranian men spoke perfect Arabic, Chamran with a heavier Persian accent. Husseini experienced his Shia identity more as a culture than religious dogma, shaped by communal traditions, philosophy and poetry from the sages of Jabal Amel, and Shia treatises about social equality. Imam Sadr indulged in the occasional water pipe, an unusual practice for a cleric. He wore his turban almost casually, with an occasional tilt or strand of hair showing. He felt that the rigid minutiae of strictures were an obstacle to a spiritual embrace of religion.

There was Shiism and the community in Lebanon . . . there was Iran and the shah . . . and then there was Jerusalem. Those were the issues that brought the three men together and where their interests overlapped. Jerusalem loomed large in the Husseini home, as a constant reminder of a gaping hole at the heart of the Arab world. A two-meter-long black-and-white poster of Al-Aqsa mosque, the third-holiest site in Islam, hung on the wall. The wounds of the Arab-Israeli conflict indisputably drove some of the action at the heart of the events that led to 1979 and the years that followed.

—

After the British captured Jerusalem from the collapsing Ottoman Empire in the wake of World War I, a headline in the *New York Herald* of December 11, 1917, declared that JERUSALEM HAS BEEN RESCUED AFTER 673 YEARS OF MOSLEM RULE. That same year, the British foreign secretary, Arthur Balfour, in a declaration named after him, promised the Jewish people a national homeland in the biblical land of Palestine but stated that it was "clearly understood that nothing shall be done which may prejudice the civil and religious rights of existing non-Jewish Communities in Palestine." In 1921, the British High Commissioner reported that Jews were only 10 percent of the population of British Mandate Palestine—most of whom had arrived in the prior forty years, including from Russia where they had fled pogroms—though they were already a majority in Jerusalem. More were arriving, and Hebrew, once rarely spoken, was being revived along with the growth of settlements, agricultural colonies planting oranges and eucalyptus and producing wine.

By 1936, there were armed clashes between Jews and Arabs. Both were revolting against the British Mandate, but Arabs were also fighting against continued Jewish immigration into Palestine. The immigrants were not only Jews fleeing persecution but also those responding to a vision for statehood in the biblical land of Israel set out by Theodor Herzl, founder of the Zionist movement in the late nineteeth century. By 1947, as the colonial powers made their way out of the Middle East and the horrors of the Holocaust came to light, the call for a Jewish homeland, a safe haven, took on a new urgency. Tens of thousands of Jewish survivors from the Nazi death camps were refugees in Europe; their former communities had been destroyed, and third countries had closed the door to Jewish immigration during the Holocaust. A new iteration of a partition plan first put out in 1937 was put forward at the UN, creating two states: one Arab and one Jewish. A new UN census determined that the Jewish population of Palestine had grown to one-third, with the other two-thirds a mix of Muslim and Christian Arabs, but the plan divided the land in half between Jews and Arabs. On November 29, 1947, the UN General Assembly approved the Partition Plan. On May 14, 1948, as the last British troops departed, Jewish leaders declared the creation of the State of Israel on the land apportioned to them by the UN plan.

But Arab countries had rejected the Partition Plan, declaring they would continue to fight for an undivided Palestine. On May 15, they went to war, sending thousands of troops and tanks across the border. The new nation of Israel was already mobilized. With logistical help and arms shipments from a number of European countries, the Israelis built an army that soon surpassed Arab firepower. Within a year, Israel controlled 78 percent of former British Mandate Palestine, including West Jerusalem, while Jordan now administered the West Bank, including East Jerusalem and its walled old city, and Egypt had control of the Gaza Strip. The Arabs had lost Palestine, it was a catastrophe, a *nakba,* as it became known. Several hundred thousand Palestinians had to flee, within the country or into neighboring countries. Palestinians felt they were being made to atone for Europe's sin of the Holocaust by sacrificing their own land. They took the keys to their houses with them and never gave up on the idea of returning home one day. But in 1967, during six days of war, the Arabs lost more land: Gaza, the West Bank, East Jerusalem, including the walled old city that is home to Al-Aqsa mosque, as well as Egypt's Sinai and Syria's Golan Heights. Jerusalem was under Jewish rule again for the first time in two millennia. Across the Arab and Muslim world, there was disbelief, shock, and tears. Arabs had put their faith in nationalism and in Egypt's president, Gamal Abdel Nasser. Just a few years prior, in 1956, Nasser had emerged victorious from a war for control over Egypt's Suez Canal, staring down not only the French and the British but also Israel. The charismatic nationalist had become a hero for millions across the Arab world. How could he have lost this time? Perhaps, some people thought, God had forsaken Muslims; perhaps a return to religion was the answer.

Palestine continued to live in the collective consciousness of millions of Arabs, and Palestinian refugees now lived among them, in Lebanon, Syria, and Jordan, mostly in tented settlements and shantytowns. The Palestinians had had enough of these large Arab armies that kept losing precious land. The time had come to intensify guerrilla warfare. The man who had risen to lead them was Yasser Arafat, a Palestinian from Gaza, who had become chairman of the Palestinian Liberation Organization (PLO) in 1969. Armed Palestinian factions that had battled the Israelis alone and alongside the Arabs began to consolidate their grip on the refugee population in Jordan and Lebanon, filling their ranks with more fighters and launching attacks into Israel. The king of Jordan would have none of it—his army crushed the PLO ruthlessly in 1970. More Palestinian fighters, and more refugees, headed to Lebanon.

Israeli retaliation against Palestinian guerrilla attacks became a constant of life in southern Lebanon. In this small country of minorities, outside patrons were essential: the Christians looked to France, the old colonial power, as their protector; the Sunnis had the choice and, depending on their political leanings, some looked to Egypt or Syria; others to Saudi Arabia. The Shias felt they had no one: the shah of Iran was an ally of Israel and was mostly concerned with keeping tabs on the Iranian opposition in Lebanon.

Husseini wanted to raise awareness about this state of affairs. He wanted a voice to speak out, someone powerful enough to pressure the shah to change his stance on Israel. In 1974, the young parliamentarian traveled to Najaf to meet Ayatollah Ruhollah Khomeini. Even in exile, his voice mattered. Husseini explained to the seventy-two-year-old ayatollah that as a Lebanese Shia he felt a double burden: his community was defenseless in the face of Israeli shelling, and yet the shah, Guardian of the Shia Faith, ruler of a majority-Shia country, was an ally of Israel. Husseini pointed out to Khomeini that he was not in jail, like colleagues back in Iran, and though his name was banned from newspapers in Iran, he was relatively free, even under Iraq's dictatorship. He urged the ayatollah to speak out and talked to him about how he and others in Lebanon, like Chamran, could support a revolution in Iran. Khomeini must have been pleased by the visit; he missed being at the center of political action. There would soon be others whispering in his ears about the Palestinian cause, which he cared about more than the plight of Lebanon's Shias—it had better potential to serve his desire to be heard outside Najaf.

After a decade in Najaf, the capital of Shia Islam, a Vatican of sorts, Khomeini was still an outsider. When he had arrived in the Iraqi city, the high-ranking clerics had rejected his entreaties to launch a Shia uprising in both Iran and Iraq, where the secular nationalist Baath Party was in power. This was not the clergy's role, they had told him. In a tense meeting, the most senior cleric told the Iranian ayatollah, "there is no point in sending people to their deaths." The tension would never subside, leaving Khomeini to wonder "what sin I have committed to be confined to Najaf in the few remaining years of my life."

Khomeini was sought after by others who were attracted to his uncompromising stance. Najaf was the oldest and most prestigious *hawza* (Shia seminary), and Shias came from all over the world, not only to visit the shrine of Imam Ali, but to study. Over time, Khomeini trained hundreds of clerics and preached to thousands of students who then returned to Iran, Bahrain, or Pakistan. During those lectures, Khomeini laid out his vision for an Islamic state ruled by Islamic law, the *sharia*, which he delivered in Persian to avoid censure by the Iraqi authorities. Traditionally in Shiism, the perfect Islamic state can come into existence only with the return of the Mahdi, or Hidden Imam, a messiah-like redeemer and the twelfth imam after Ali, who had gone into hiding, or occultation, in the ninth century. Until the return of this infallible man, governance would be in the hands of the secular state. But Khomeini asserted that the Quran had in fact provided all the laws and ordinances necessary for man to establish an Islamic state and that the prophet and Imam Ali had intended for learned men to implement them: with these tools, a wise man, or *faqih*, could be the guardian and rule over such a state, or *wilayat*, with absolute power and bring about a perfect and just Islamic society. The Guardianship of the Jurist, or *wilayat al-faqih*, had been a theoretical subsection of Shia jurisprudence, and clerics believed that in current times such guardianship could apply only to widows and orphans. Khomeini had transformed it into an immediate, political goal.

When Imam Sadr read Khomeini's booklet, he was taken aback. The two men were distant relatives through marriage, but they had little in common: one was pragmatic, the other uncompromising; one was worldly and inclusive, the other insular and exclusionary. As early as 1973, Sadr had sent a warning about Khomeini's idea to the shah through a friend: "This is the juice of a sick mind." But otherwise he kept his misgivings about the ayatollah mostly to himself. Sadr seemed to want to pressure the shah just enough to make him soften his grip and engage with the opposition, but not see him toppled. For now, Khomeini was a useful thorn; his crazy Islamic government could never come about anyway. At least that's what Sadr thought. During his visit to Najaf in 1974, Husseini did not bring up the wilayat al-faqih with Khomeini, nor argue its insanity.

In Lebanon, Chamran and his colleagues from the Liberation Movement of Iran were getting ahead of Sadr and Husseini. Among them was Sadegh Ghotbzadeh, a tall, broad-shouldered, somewhat flamboyant womanizer and former student activist who had studied at Georgetown University but never graduated. Ebrahim Yazdi traveled often to Lebanon from the United States, where he lived in exile. With his black-rimmed eyeglasses, curly hair, beard, and tweed jacket, he looked like a French intellectual, but he actually held a PhD in biochemistry. Chamran, Ghotbzadeh, and Yazdi formed the backbone of the LMI, whose members were middle-class or wealthy Iranians who had lived a comfortable life. They came from traditional merchant families, those at the top of the hierarchy of the all-powerful community of the Bazaar, the market, with its artisans, guilds, and apprentices. The Bazaar had always served as a political force in Iran, agitating against Western competition on its turf, and they often made common cause with the clerics who resented Western influence on Iranian society. That alliance had produced upheaval before, during the Constitutional Revolution of 1906. The monarchy had been shaken and transformed, but it survived as a ruling system. The current generation of young revolutionaries wanted to tear the whole structure down.

Working alongside the LMI was Abolhassan Banisadr, a leftist nationalist and professor of economics living in exile in Paris. Banisadr, Chamran, Ghotbzadeh, and Yazdi were all the same generation, born in the early or mid-1930s. They had come of age during the tumultuous period of the early 1950s in Iran, when a CIA-fomented coup had brought down Mohammad Mossadegh, a popular, nationalist Iranian prime minister who had been asserting his independence from the shah. The 1953 coup had given them all a taste for activism. Soft-spoken, with a black mustache, thick hair, and a small figure, Banisadr was the son of an ayatollah who had chosen politics instead of religion. He had met Khomeini as a child and had played with the cleric's children. But he had been unimpressed by the ayatollah when he had seen him again in Najaf in 1972, finding him unfriendly and isolated. Banisadr had also read Khomeini's book about an Islamic state with disbelief. Most of his colleagues on the left found the writings so outlandish that they assumed it was a forgery by the Iranian regime seeking to discredit Khomeini as a religious fanatic.

But the Iranian opposition needed such a firebrand to ignite the revolution and access the masses in the mosques. The nationalists and leftists were good organizers, but they didn't have a popular following, they did not have a charismatic Che Guevara. Banisadr warned Khomeini not to speak about his wilayat al-faqih because it showed him to be unrealistic: How could clerics who could barely manage the daily affairs of Najaf, the holiest city of Shiism, run a whole country? Khomeini said his writings were just a starting point to provoke conversation about the best form of government. Banisadr was satisfied. The groundwork for a revolution could begin.

——

The fire was sparked in 1977. It began with the death in June of Ali Shariati, the dangerous visionary ideologue of the revolution. Tall and dapper, in his early forties, with fuzzy hair on top of his balding head, Shariati was a nationalist who had studied sociology in Paris. He was of the same generation as Chamran and the other LMI members, and he too had grown up in the era of Mossadegh. As a young man, he was caught scrawling pro-Mossadegh graffiti and was made to lick the wall clean. Shariati was full of contradictions: the son a religious leader in the holy city of Mashhad, he disliked the influence of the clerics; he was devout but admitted once that if he were not a Muslim he would be a Marxist. Leftist and Islamist, he dressed the Western way, in a suit and tie, always clean-shaven. Nonetheless, he despised the sterile modernity of Europe and railed against Iranians who rejected their own history and embraced everything Western. At the same time, he derided the commoner wedded to tradition and stuck in the past: "A futureless past is a state of inertia and stagnation, while a pastless future is alien and vacuous." And yet in his search for a future that was anchored in his country's past and Iran's distinct identity as well as in Islam, he looked to foreign authors. He was inspired by Frantz Fanon, the anticolonialist thinker from Martinique, and by the French existentialist Jean-Paul Sartre, who was close to many Iranian revolutionaries. From all these contradictions, Shariati produced a new brand of Shiism, even more militant and mobilized than what Imam Sadr had been preaching in Lebanon. There was nothing quietist or ritualistic in Shariati's deeply political and insurgent version of Shiism. He coined the term Red Shiism, one tinged with Marxism ready for sacrifice to attain social justice. It stood in opposition to Black Shiism, the quietist, ritualistic one who submitted to rulers and monarchs. By rediscovering an authentic Islam, he asserted, Iran could be a utopian society with a perfect leader, a philosopher king, as in Plato's *Republic*. The similarity to Khomeini's faqih was striking, except that Shariati did not believe clerics had any role to play in politics. Khomeini despised secular thinkers, but he let the militant fervor that Shariati had awakened serve his purposes.

In 1971, Shariati openly called for the masses to rise against the shah. Lecturing at the university of Mashhad, he smoked while he talked, sometimes holding forth for as long as six hours, his audience enthralled, their minds captivated. By 1973, he was in jail. After four years he was released and left for London. He died a month later from a heart attack—though many felt the circumstances were mysterious and attributed his death to the shah's secret service, the SAVAK. Imam Sadr praised Shariati's efforts to produce a discourse for emancipation and change that was indigenous to Muslim societies.

The next to die was Mostafa Khomeini, the ayatollah's own son, at the age of forty-seven. The eldest of his children and his most trusted aide, Mostafa suffered from health problems due to his weight, but his father allowed conspiracy theories to circulate about a mysterious death to be blamed on the SAVAK. There had been years of unrest in Iran, but the moment when the dam truly broke was in November 1977, when the shah allowed Khomeini's relatives in Iran to mark the fortieth day of mourning for Mostafa. Khomeini's father-in-law published a notice in the mass-circulation *Kayhan* newspaper referring to Mostafa as the "offspring of the Exalted Leader of All Shiites of the World." In the Jameh mosque in Tehran, prayers were said for "our one and only leader, the defender of the faith and the great combatant of Islam, Grand Ayatollah Khomeini." For fourteen years, Khomeini's name had been taboo in Iran. Now it was in print, it was in sermons, brandished and aggrandized, a foreboding signal of how Khomeini saw himself and how some perceived him.

That same month, Arab honor died too, or so it felt for millions across the region, who watched, incredulously, as Nasser's successor, president Anwar Sadat, crossed enemy lines and traveled to Jerusalem to address the Knesset, the Israeli parliament. Tears streamed down the faces of children as rage burned inside the hearts of men. How could Egypt break rank and betray the Arab and Palestinian cause? Peace talks would soon begin between Israel and Egypt—so who would wipe the shame from the forehead of Arab men now? Arafat was furious; he felt personally betrayed by Sadat. He looked for support elsewhere. He used the death of Khomeini's son as an opportunity to contact the ayatollah, offering condolences through a friend, the Lebanese Shia cleric Sayyed Hani Fahs. The connection between Iranian and Palestinian revolutionaries, including in training camps, had mostly been a leftist affair so far. Now that there was formal contact between the PLO and the fundamentalist Islamist wing of the revolution, embodied in the ayatollah, training and support for the Iran revolution would intensify. Khomeini would exploit the connection endlessly, and his appropriation of the cause would alter the political landscape of Lebanon and the Middle East.

In the fall of 1977, with the civil war in Lebanon well into its third year, Husseini bought a state-of-the-art AKAI stereo system with a double cassette tape deck and vinyl player. His four children, all in their early teens, were delighted with this addition to the living room in their home by the sea: cutting-edge technology at their fingertips. Every afternoon after school, they played their favorite records: Led Zeppelin, Pink Floyd, the Beatles. This was a revolutionary home, mobilized for change. Pictures of Shariati and Khomeini hung on their walls. They were in awe of Chamran, who often spent the night. In the evening, if there was no shooting or shelling, they could hear the waves as they fell asleep.

After the children went to bed, the stereo system had another purpose. The message of the revolution had to be spread far and wide. Before the Internet, before Twitter, there were the cassette tape and the fax machine. Husseini and Imam Sadr got to work. The politician would operate the recorder and the cleric would speak. They made tape after tape of revolutionary messages addressed to the Iranian people, encouraging them to rise up and demand change. Sadr never promoted Khomeini and never explicitly called for the downfall of the shah, but he fervently believed that unrest could force Iran's king to make real, far-reaching reforms. Copies of the tapes were given to Iranian dissidents who were still able to travel in and out of Iran. Once the tapes were smuggled into the country, more copies were made, and the messages spread like wildfire. Khomeini made tapes, too, virulent diatribes against the Pahlavis. Some were smuggled back into Iran by pilgrims who had gone to Najaf. Recordings of his speeches were also played down an international telephone line to Tehran, recorded on a deck there, and disseminated. While the shah was focused on controlling the message on television, radio, and in the newspapers, the underground business of revolutionary tapes was mobilizing the masses and chipping away at the facade of a king in control.

The Husseini and Fahs families inhabited different worlds; they were at odds politically, but their children all sang for the revolution—separately, and each with a different vision of what it meant for Iran. They knew by heart the Persian lyrics to the first revolutionary song that echoed across Iran:

> *Allah, Allah, Allah, La Ilaha Illa Allah,*
> *Iran, Iran, Iran, bullets cast from guns*
> *Iran, Iran, Iran, tight fists everywhere*
> *Iran, Iran, Iran, blood, death and uprising.*

When 1978 rolled in, it was almost time for the action to move to Paris. Far from Lebanon, in late August 1978, a unique moment sealed the fates of Khomeini and Sadr, and with them perhaps the fate and spirit of the unfolding Iranian Revolution. On August 29, the shah was in the middle of a banquet with visiting dignitaries when he received a phone call from Saddam Hussein, the vice president and de facto ruler of Iraq. The shah broke protocol by leaving the dinner table and listening to the stunning suggestion from the Iraqi leader: Ayatollah Khomeini was becoming a nuisance for everyone; it was best to get rid of him. Saddam wanted the shah to agree first. After discussing the proposal with close aides, the shah decided against it.

A few days earlier, Sadr had traveled to Tripoli in Libya with two companions to meet with Ayatollah Mohammad Beheshti, a close political and theological ally of Khomeini. Beheshti believed in a theocratic state. Sadr was resolutely opposed to the concept. The meeting, organized by the anti-Western Libyan leader Muammar al-Gaddafi, was supposed to help them settle their differences. Sadr had just published an article in the French newspaper *Le Monde* entitled "The Call of the Prophets," describing the protests in Iran as an authentic revolution against injustice that brought together students, workers, intellectuals, and men of religion—a revolution of ideas, not one of politics or violence. This was a movement with much promise for the rest of the world, Sadr insisted, and while faith was at its core, it was motivated by humanism and revolutionary ethics. Sadr praised the guiding role of Khomeini but said nothing about the ayatollah's wilayat al-faqih. Nor did he call for the overthrow of the Pahlavi dynasty. In fact, Sadr was planning to travel onward from Tripoli to a secret meeting with an envoy from the shah in West Germany.

Beheshti never showed up. Sadr and his traveling companions grew impatient. They were also hoping for a meeting with Gaddafi. In the afternoon of August 31, they bumped into fellow Lebanese in the lobby of their hotel. One of Sadr's traveling companions mentioned they were headed to meet Gaddafi. A Jordanian journalist, who happened to be standing outside the hotel, wished them good luck and waved goodbye as Sadr and his companions got into a black Peugeot 405. They were never seen again.

Days passed before the news of Sadr's disappearance reached Beirut, making headlines in all the newspapers. WHERE IS IMAM MUSA SADR? asked the local Arabic daily *Al-Nahar* on September 12; QUESTIONS ABOUT THE DISAPPEARANCE OF IMAM SADR AND IS THE MYSTERY OF HIS DISAP-PEARANCE CONNECTED TO THE EVENTS IN IRAN? asked the leftist daily *As-Safir* on the same day. The Libyan authorities insisted that the imam had left Tripoli on August 31 on the 8:15 p.m. Alitalia flight AZ 881 to Rome. His checked luggage had indeed arrived, but the imam had vanished. More time passed with no news. In Lebanon, Muslims of all persuasions—Sunni, Shia, and the minority Druze community—held protests in their mosques. Lebanon sent investigators to Rome. No one knew about the secret meeting in Germany. Rumors flew: he had been kidnapped by the SAVAK and taken to Iran; he was in a prison in Libya. No one actually knew. In Beirut, Husseini didn't know what to make of his friend's disappearance. Sadr had asked him to come along to Libya, but Husseini had refused and advised Sadr against the trip. The young Shia politician didn't trust Gaddafi or his intentions and resented the dictator's reactionary brand of Islam, one that denigrated Christians and paid people to convert. Where was Sadr? How could someone like him just vanish? He was needed more than ever. Events in Iran were unraveling fast. Khomeini's Iraqi sojourn was drawing to an end.

—

There had been more blood on the streets of Iran. The shah sent tanks onto the streets. Riots spread across the country. The turning point in the heat of a summer of unrest had been an arson attack on the Rex Cinema in the city of Abadan, killing 420 people on August 19. The date of the attack seemed highly symbolic: the twenty-fifth anniversary of the 1953 coup against Mossadegh. The doors of the theater were locked; there was nowhere to run from the flames. The government blamed religious reactionaries for the fire. Khomeini angrily denied it, accusing the SAVAK of being behind it. Khomeini's zealots had already burned down twenty-nine movie the-aters and hundreds of private businesses in the previous months; they'd even targeted the Rex before. In Tehran, the Baccara Super Night Club at the Hilton Hotel, a regular stage for international stars, had also been gutted. It was all part of a concerted plan to sow panic in Iran and assert new rules of religious conservatism. But the Rex Cinema arson stood out in its enormity, described as "a holocaust" by one newspaper. In the fervor of anti-shah sentiment, a twisted logic set in: the ruling regime would burn down a cinema to damn the opposition. Thousands of Iranians had stayed on the sidelines for various reasons: they had not suffered in jails or been exiled, they were apolitical, they disliked the clergy. But in that instant of rumormongering, many came to believe that the shah could, and would, dispose of them—even kill them—to score against the fundamentalists.

A few weeks later, in Tehran, the ranks of protesters swelled to almost half a million. September 8, 1978, Black Friday, was another dramatic turning point. Thousands converged on Jaleh Square, chanting *Marg bar shah*, Death to the shah. The crowd of mostly men was a mix of Khomeini supporters, students, and leftists. Among them, behind the first lines of women and young people, there were guerrilla fighters, many trained in Lebanon by the Palestinians. By 9:21 a.m. the first shots rang out. The result was a gun battle, a stampede, and—according to the official toll—eighty-six civilian deaths. But the revolutionaries claimed at least three thousand had died, purposely exaggerating the number to fan the flames. It worked, and headlines about three thousand deaths made it all the way into the Western papers. The shah was shocked by the violence. Even before this tragedy, he had decided to go into exile, at least temporarily. He had done it in 1953, returning after only a few days. This time, martial law was imposed. Gloom descended onto Iran as autumn arrived with an evening curfew and fear of more attacks by religious fundamentalists. Cultural festivals were canceled from Shiraz to Isfahan, as was the renowned Tehran International Film Festival. Nightlife came to a halt. The end of an empire was near. The shah was still hoping against all odds that Imam Sadr would resurface. Ties between the two men had never completely broken down, and the shah saw the cleric who had warned him about Khomeini as a possible lifeline, a popular, progressive leader who could still help him counter the radical, reactionary ayatollah.

In Iraq, Saddam had had enough of Khomeini. The Iranian cleric was beginning to stir hope in the hearts of people across the region, Sunni and Shia alike, who resented their kings or their dictators and wished for a more just rule. Some wanted more religion, more Islam, more spirituality. The ruling Baath Party in Iraq was building a secular, progressive

state with abundant repression: Sunni and Shia clerics were united in sporadic protests against what they saw as the forced secularization of society,
which (as in Iran) was eating away at their privileges and giving rights to
women. Clerics of both denominations faced harsh repercussion, torture
in jail, and execution. Shias, long discriminated against, bore the brunt of
the repression. A leftover of Ottoman and Persian competition and wars,
the policy of discrimination against Shias in Iraq continued. Worryingly
for Saddam, some Shia clerics were now beginning to use more sectarian language, and Khomeini's Iraqi adepts were agitating against the state.
Saddam put enough restrictions on Khomeini that the Iranian cleric finally
opted to leave. He tried to go to Kuwait but was refused entry. Traveling
with Khomeini were his son Ahmad, the LMI operative Yazdi, and two
other aides. In France, Ghotbzadeh, the flamboyant revolutionary, and
Banisadr, the Parisian intellectual, quickly arranged for three-month visas
after convincing Khomeini that Paris would afford two key advantages:
freedom to speak and access to the world media.

The ayatollah arrived in France on October 6. Within a few days, still
reluctant to be in a country of heathens, he settled into the small village of
Neauphle-le-Château, outside Paris and just half an hour from Versailles
and its château, the seat of power of French kings. The French president
asked the shah whether he had any objections to the cleric's presence in
France. The shah did not. What could "a frail and crazy old man" really
achieve from a perch all the way over in Europe in a small French village?

In Najaf, Khomeini had been a tired exile with no clear path home.
Before his French sojourn, Khomeini's name had barely appeared in the
international media. In Neauphle-le-Château, over the course of a four-
month stay, he would give 132 interviews and become the face of the revolution, recognized throughout the world. The seventy-six-year-old cleric
was invigorated.

The LMI got to work. It was joined by more cadres flying in from
everywhere. Mohsen Sazegara was one of the youngest of the Paris group.
Devout from a young age, though raised in a mostly secular family, Mohsen
had left Iran in 1975 to study in Chicago, where he befriended Yazdi and
joined the LMI. He managed to make trips to Iran until 1978, bringing
in pamphlets about the revolution and secret documents for fellow LMI
activists. Mohsen had helped organize strikes and demonstrations and
came up with some of the slogans for the revolution. Some of those became
more radical as they traveled through the excited crowds. The chant *Marg
barg shah*, Death to the shah, had started out as *Shah beyad beravad*, The

shah must go. Yazdi had called Mohsen from Paris to ask him to join them. Within hours, he was on a transatlantic flight with $8 in his pocket. In Neauphle-le-Château, Mohsen would help manage media interviews for the ayatollah.

For years, the savvy LMI revolutionaries had cultivated relationships with a number of American and European journalists who covered Iran, loading their coverage with details of the abuses of the regime and the excesses of the shah while feeding their sympathy for the movement. Their efforts had been mostly clandestine. In Neauphle-le-Château, they now had a central headquarters in the house's redbrick garage, with four telephones, two telex lines, and duplicating equipment to make hundreds of cassettes to spread the ayatollah's message. The strategy was twofold: radical, reactionary messages for inside Iran, carefully curated words for Western ears.

Every day around noon, Khomeini would emerge from the house with blue shutters to give a speech and lead prayers in the garden across the street. He sat on a mat under an apple tree and held court. Dozens, sometimes hundreds of journalists descended on the tiny village every day. In their blazers and neckties, in perfect English and French, Yazdi, Ghotbzadeh, and Banisadr translated (and sometimes purposely mistranslated), adding context and rounding the edges for sensitive Western reporters. In doing so they constantly molded the ayatollah's words and his image to reflect their own vision of the future of Iran. The resulting impression was that of an ascetic sage who had no interest in politics and would "spend the rest of his days in a seminary in Qom" once his goals of removing the shah and returning to Iran had been achieved. He was quoted in the *Guardian* as saying, "I don't want to have the power or the government in my hand. I am not interested in personal power." Even those who spoke Persian and had more knowledge were misled by Khomeini's statements. Khomeini had been admonished by Banisadr after his first press interview, during which he had talked at length in Persian to a French reporter about his plans to turn Iran into a Muslim theocracy. Banisadr took liberties with the translation to polish the message, and Khomeini never again discussed the wilayat al-faqih in public. Instead, he talked of an Iran where even a woman could become president.

There was a third crucial element: France's leftist intellectuals. Hugely influential in shaping public opinion, they were antiestablishment, antipower, and anti-imperial. They saw in the Iranian revolutionaries the embodiment of the values they had fought for themselves in the revolution of May 1968 on the streets of Paris. They wanted to believe in Khomeini, the sage under the apple tree. As early as 1964, Banisadr had enlisted Sartre to preside on a committee to raise awareness about Iranians in the shah's jails. Sartre had once declared: "I have no religion, but if I had to pick one it would be Shariati."

Though the opposition had indeed inflated the numbers of those in jail and those killed by the regime, for those who *had* been imprisoned by the shah the experience was very real. Reza Baraheni, one of Iran's greatest poets of that era, was tortured brutally while in prison for 102 days. His release was the result of pressure from American and European writers. His verses were irreverent and unforgiving:

> *The Shah is holding the oil in his hand like a glass*
> *   of wine drinking to the health of the West*
> *And the Queen with her thick lips milks the tits*
> *   of Motherland's doe*
> *At night under the stars*
> *In the day in the passage of sun*
> *Every month every year*
> *And a glove the color of blood remains on the snows of*
> *   St. Moritz.*

In October 1978, while Khomeini was in Neauphle-le-Château, the philosopher Michel Foucault traveled to Iran and wrote long dispatches in which he described the calls for an Islamic government as a utopian, romantic ideal, while chiding the Christian West for having abandoned what he described as political spirituality. Meanwhile, the CIA was apparently unaware of Khomeini's thesis about Islamic government and was more obsessed with a possible communist takeover of Iran. The Americans hoped that "Khomeini was a moderating influence over the leftists and radicals in his entourage." The Saudis also seemed to know little about Khomeini and were worried about a "Soviet onslaught," as some Saudi newspapers had described it. Saudi Arabia and Iran were allies and twin pillars in the US policy to counter the spread of communism and Soviet influence in the region. Iran was more powerful, and the shah had a formidable army and naval force, posing as the regional policeman. The Saudis were wary of his regional ambitions but saw him as a friendly adversary. There had been decades of mutual royal visits, and the two countries had a good working relationship. As the revolution rumbled on, Crown Prince Fahd expressed Saudi support for the shah as the legitimate ruler of the country.

In Neauphle-le-Château, hundreds of Iranian supporters came to visit Khomeini, chanting *Allahu Akbar* when he appeared, or, in French, *Longue vie, Khomeini,* long live Khomeini. Arafat came too, keeping the flames of the new relationship with Khomeini alive. No one noticed, or perhaps understood, the significance of visitors who were neither Western journalists, nor Iranian followers, nor Shia well-wishers, neither aides in neckties nor turbaned clerics. Arab visitors were making the pilgrimage to Neauphle-le-Château from Egypt, Tunisia, and other countries. Members of Sunni Islamist movements, like the Muslim Brotherhood, traveled from as far as Sudan to see for themselves the man they'd so far heard about only through his exiled aides. The Brotherhood had been banned in Egypt for over two decades, and alongside Khomeini's other visitors, the Brothers were anxious to hear his message. They went home inspired by new ideas, new tactics, even new words to confront the despots in their own countries. They learned how to deploy Islamic terminology to bring down tyranny. They rooted for Khomeini's success and promised to visit again soon. Victory felt near.

Meanwhile, Iran was in chaos. Basic services were collapsing, and people close to the regime were running for the exits, while hundreds of Iranian dissidents were returning to participate in the revolution: communists, leftists, religious extremists. In January, the shah decided it was time to leave. He had appointed a new prime minister, Shahpour Bakhtiar, and was ready to hand over the reins. He was also ailing, sick with lymphoma. Ostensibly he and his wife would be leaving for a rest, a short break. The children were already out of the country. On January 16, 1979, the shah and the queen left their residence at the Niavaran palace complex in northern Tehran and flew west on two helicopters to the nearby Mehrabad airport. Outside the Imperial Pavilion, a blue and silver plane was waiting on the tarmac to take them out of the country. Servants at the palace cried, beating their chests, petrified by fear of what would happen to them now. At the airport, two guards flung themselves at the shah's feet. With tears in his eyes, he stooped to lift them up. The empress, Farah Diba, in a fox fur coat and hat and wearing diamond earrings, had taken tranquilizers to keep her composure.

At 1:24 p.m., the wheels of the Boeing 707 lifted off. The shah himself was piloting the aircraft. They flew to a small military airport in Aswan by the Nile where their friend President Sadat gave them a royal welcome. There was a long and personal history between the two countries. In 1939, the shah had married a first time, taking for his wife Fawzieh, daughter of Fouad I, king of Egypt—a Shia monarch and a Sunni princess. The marriage did not produce an heir and did not last. But the shah was now in the land of his former in-laws.

On the streets of Tehran, there were wild scenes of joy. Jubilant Iranians danced, tooted their horns, and hung out of their car windows. Statues of the shah were toppled. SHAH RAFT, the shah is gone, was printed in huge letters across the front page of the afternoon newspaper *Ettela'at*. The time had come for a new rallying cry: *Marg bar Bakhtiar*, Death to Bakhtiar—the French literature–loving prime minister to whom the shah had entrusted the country.

—

In Lebanon, Chamran and Husseini followed the news with both disbelief and a sense of accomplishment—but the victory was incomplete without their missing friend. The older and wiser Imam Sadr would have known what was about to unfold and perhaps would have tried to stop it. Chamran's time by the Mediterranean was coming to an end. Next stop Tehran, where his comrades were gearing up for guerrilla warfare to bring down every last vestige of the shah's reign. They worried about a possible counterrevolution, a CIA coup. They expected a long battle: it was essential to lay the groundwork for Iran's new beginning ahead of Khomeini's return. But the ayatollah was in a hurry.

2

TODAY TEHRAN, TOMORROW JERUSALEM

IRAN 1979–80

When the demon goes out, within the angel's light will come.
The darkness of night is the close companion of dictators.
—Hafez, *Divan*, 159

Mohsen Sazegara did not have time to think about what it meant to be landing in Tehran on February 1, 1979, on the plane that was bringing Ayatollah Khomeini home after fifteen years in exile. The devout graduate student with an organized mind had been so busy from the moment he had arrived in Neauphle-le-Château just a few months earlier that he couldn't process information at the speed with which things were happening. A slow simmering revolution, years in the making, was suddenly hurtling forward. They had taken off from Paris around one in the morning, and he hadn't slept a single moment. He was busy making a list for the LMI welcome committee in Tehran with the names of the journalists on the plane. The departure had been rushed. Mohsen and his colleagues had initially planned to bring two hundred fifty journalists along on the Air France Boeing 747. Tickets were issued for $500 each. Prime Minister Bakhtiar had reopened the airport and indicated he would allow Khomeini's plane to land, but there were no guarantees beyond that. Air France asked to reduce the number of passengers so it could carry enough fuel to fly back to Paris if landing rights were not granted. Mohsen and the team wanted as many high-profile journalists on the plane as possible, human shields to deter the Iranian generals, still loyal to the shah, from shooting down the plane.

As the plane entered Iranian airspace, snowcapped Damavand Mountain appeared in the morning light. Khomeini had slept on the floor, in the lounge area of the first-class upper cabin. He performed his morning prayers on an Air France blanket, then went to sit by the window, stroking his beard and smiling contentedly for the first time in months, maybe years. The American reporter Peter Jennings and his ABC News crew were allowed into the first-class section to ask a question. "Ayatollah, would you be so kind as to tell us how you feel about being in Iran?" In his tie and jacket, a beaming Sadegh sat next to the ayatollah and translated. *"Hichi"*—nothing—came the answer. Sadegh paused, smiled and echoed him, somewhat incredulous: *"Hichi?"*

Khomeini repeated the sentiment. *"Hichi ehasasi nadaram."* I don't feel a thing. Sadegh did what he and others had done for weeks in France; he softened the edges. "He doesn't make any comment," said Sadegh. Jennings pressed: "Is he happy, is he excited?" Sadegh again said the ayatollah had no comment. But the real meaning of *hichi* would not stay hidden long—there were too many people watching those few seconds once ABC's tape was beamed to America and the rest of the world. The ayatollah's words were a portent, parsed and understood differently by supporters and foes, in the moment, and in hindsight.

Sitting in Texas, at Reese Air Force Base, where he was on a pilot training program, Reza Pahlavi, the exiled shah's son, was among those stunned by the lack of emotion he saw in the television footage. Khomeini had no attachment to the grandeur of the Persian empire, or the cultural and intellectual richness of its history, only to his own sense of importance. He had been that way ever since he was a young boy, when he insisted on playing the role of the shah in the games he played with friends. Confident of his relationship with God, Khomeini had seemingly no connection to the worldly concept of nation—he looked beyond countries and borders to the Muslim nation, the *ummah*.

For his most ardent supporters, this imbued him with the charismatic mysticism of a savior. Mohsen was mesmerized by such spiritual composure. Later that week, in Tehran, Mohsen's father would try to warn his son that this was a sign of danger, but the young student wouldn't hear it. Years later, on hunger strike in solitary confinement in the jails of the Islamic Republic, Mohsen would think back to that one word, *hichi*, and wonder how he had not understood the warnings, in Khomeini's response but also in his writings. At the time, there was only elation—a sense of accomplishment, yet also trepidation at what was bound to be a drawn-out insurgency. For months, Mohsen had been reading up about guerrilla tactics in Vietnam and elsewhere, but his favorite manual was the 1969 *Minimanual of the Urban Guerrilla* by the Brazilian Marxist revolutionary Carlos Marighella, which the LMI had translated to Persian. In Neauphle-le-Château's only hotel, away from the crowds swarming around Khomeini, Mohsen had rented a room where he focused on building a people's army and meeting with Iranian volunteers from around the world to teach them the art of revolution from the chapters in his books: firing groups, sabotage, guerrilla security, war of nerves. The volunteers were then sent to Lebanon for quick military training. Now that Khomeini was coming home, hundreds of Iranians were getting ready to fly back too and fight the remnants of the shah's regime.

At nine thirty in the morning, Air France flight 4271 landed at Meh-rabad airport just outside Tehran, the same airport from which the shah had departed. The ayatollah, wearing a bulletproof vest under his robe, came down the steps with the help of an Air France steward. The welcome committee set up by the secret Islamic Revolutionary Council was there to take charge of him. The clerics on the plane and on the tarmac pushed aside anyone who did not look religious enough, and Khomeini was immersed in a sea of turbans. Yazdi, Ghotbzadeh, Mohsen . . . the LMI were all left behind. Banisadr, the man who had first identified Khomeini as the conduit to the masses, would later remark, "It seemed that the duty of the intellectuals was to bring Khomeini to Tehran and hand him over to the mollahs."

Deep inside, the modernist revolutionaries knew the risks of coming back in haste to a country they had themselves left years before, without first consolidating their power. Their initial plan, formulated in Paris, had been to form a government in exile that would get international recognition and force Prime Minister Bakhtiar to resign. Another variation would have had Bakhtiar tender his resignation to Khomeini in France and be commissioned by the ayatollah to form a provisional cabinet and then hold a referendum to determine the form of a new government. But within days of the shah's departure from Iran, Khomeini decided to reverse the order, and return to Iran as a first step. The LMI tried to discourage such a hasty move. Bazergan was in talks with Bakhtiar, an old colleague, trying to negotiate a way forward. The country was ablaze, the armed forces were still loyal to the shah, the ayatollah's safety would be at risk. But Khomeini was adamant: "There's no reason to stay, let's go to Iran."

Walking back to the hotel in Neauphle-le-Château with Yazdi one evening, Mohsen had tried to sway his wiser colleague with his youthful enthusiasm. "Ayatollah Khomeini is right, Dr. Yazdi," Mohsen said. "If he goes back to Iran, the excitement of people, millions of people will sweep away the government of Bakhtiar; Bakhtiar has no power." Yazdi stopped in the middle of the street. "Mohsen, I understand, you're right, but here in Neauphle-le-Château, there are only low-ranking clerics around Ayatollah Khomeini. We can control them, we can control the ayatollah. In Iran, there are high-ranking clerics, his friends, and they will take him out of our hands. Whatever we have done so far will be ruined by them."

Khomeini understood that dynamic too, which is why he wanted to go home. He wanted to seize the moment and seize the revolution. There were others in Iran who were leaders of this movement in their own right; plastered around town were posters of their faces, like that of the more liberal and hugely popular ayatollah Taleghani, of the LMI, who had spent fifteen years in the shah's jails. They were Khomeini's allies but also his rivals. Khomeini wanted to land at the peak of the fervor, so that the people's relief at being saved would pour in his direction only.

And indeed the masses were there to welcome the ayatollah. They lined the streets, packed the roofs, hung from lampposts as the ayatollah's convoy of eight vehicles and ten motorcycles tried to inch its way along the twenty miles from the airport to the cemetery of Behesht-e Zahra where Khomeini was planning to speak and pay tribute to the martyrs of the revolution. Three million turned out, according to the BBC. Other estimates put it at six million—a sea of humanity to greet the savior, as though Khomeini were the Mahdi, the Hidden Imam returned from occultation, the Shia messiah. Khomeini's long exile, his occultation, during which Iranians had heard his voice on contraband cassette tapes and read his pamphlets passed around in secret, was over. Now he reappeared in the flesh, not in Mecca, as tradition had it, but for a triumphant return in his own land. Millions of supporters hoped he would lead Iran to justice, freedom, and a better future. But Khomeini's devotion was to the past, to re-creating an Islamic society fashioned after the one in the days of the prophet.

Sitting in the front passenger seat of an armored blue and white Chevrolet Blazer, his son Ahmad in the back, Khomeini was almost in the dark as the masses overwhelmed the car. An Imperial Guard helicopter came to the rescue and flew him to the cemetery, where he paid his respects by blasting the shah as a vile traitor. Wagging his finger, he intoned: "I will decide the government, a government for the people. I will slap this government in the face." Khomeini's tone had already started to change. Bakhtiar's days were numbered.

The LMI had arranged for Khomeini to stay at the Refah girls' primary school, transformed into a meeting place for the Revolutionary Council. But by the next day, Yazdi's worst fears had been borne out: the powerful fundamentalist clerics closest to Khomeini had whisked him away to a school that they owned and controlled. Khomeini's loyal acolyte Beheshti, the cleric who had stood up Imam Sadr in Libya, was there—he had been waiting in the wings for this moment, and was now acting as a kind of chief of staff. He was working quickly to seize the levers of power and coalesce the forces that were unconditionally loyal to Khomeini under the newly formed Islamic Republican Party. Among them was Akbar Hashemi Rafsanjani, a future president, and Ayatollah Sadeq Khalkhali, once a pupil of Khomeini, who later wrote in his memoirs that moving Khomeini out of the Refah school had indeed been a "coup d'état, which saved the Imam from the clutches of Bazargan's Freedom Movement and the National Front." Khalkhali had long been an active Islamic militant member of the Fedayeen-e Islam, the Devotees of Islam.

A clandestine group of marginal radicals, the Fedayeen was founded in 1946 by Navvab Safavi, a theology student, and is often described as one of the first Muslim fundamentalist groups in modern times. Initially, Safavi and his devotees were dismissed as dangerous eccentrics by most of the established clergy. He aspired to the purest application of his understanding of Islamic law, shari'a, including the banning of music, gambling, alcohol; the mandatory veil on women; and the chopping off of limbs as punishment for theft and other misdemeanors. According to his widow, Safavi was a frequent visitor to Khomeini's home; the two men seemed to influence each other and shared the same ire against what they saw as the corrupting influence of secularism and modernizing intellectuals and politicians. The Fedayeen assassinated a number of them in Iran, including government ministers. When the shah sent Safavi and other Fedayeen to the gallows in 1956, the devotees turned to Khomeini for guidance. In him, they found recognition from an established high-ranking cleric, an ayatollah. When Khomeini was sent into exile, the devotees awaited his return.

Mohsen, for his part, thought Khomeini had been moved against his own will, that the LMI had lost him to the clerics, but the truth was that they'd never really had him. Khomeini was right where he wanted to be, with his closest friends. He had manipulated the secular left and the Islamist modernists, as a vehicle, and he would dispose of them at the moment of his choosing. In time, he would even push back against the Fedayeen. But Khomeini's first concern was seizing power.

On February 5, Khomeini appointed a provisional civilian government, with Bazergan as his prime minister. This was the first step toward a referendum to decide what form the government would take in the new Iran. The authority to do so, asserted Khomeini, came from his guardianship of the holy law of the prophet in the wilayat, therefore based on the shari'a—therefore any opposition to the government meant opposition to the shari'a. "Revolt against God's government is a revolt against God," Khomeini said. "Revolt against God is blasphemy." Not everyone noticed Khomeini's reference to the wilayat. Few had heard of it or even understood it outside the fundamentalist circle close to Khomeini. Those among the LMI who knew what he meant were probably dismissive, certain that it wouldn't come to pass or that they would prevail. But Khomeini had set the tone and was ahead of them all. Bakhtiar laughed it off as a joke. But the dictatorship of the shah had been replaced by the autocracy of the holy law.

After a few days of insurgency and street battles, now reinforced by those who had been trained in Lebanon and in Neauphle-le-Château, with mutiny in barracks and tanks on the move in cities across the country, the army declared its neutrality on February 11, 1979. Bakhtiar had nothing left to fight with. He resigned and slipped out of the country. The Pahlavi dynasty had been defeated. The revolution was victorious.

Revenge started almost immediately. Khalkhali was appointed chief of the Revolutionary Courts, which meant he could pick up where Safavi had left off and begin executing the "corrupt." In the Refah girls' primary school where Khomeini had spent his first night, a room was converted into a makeshift courtroom. The trials were swift, the sentences were death. Yazdi tried to delay the process but Khalkhali would have none of it. The executions began just before midnight on February 15, on the roof of the school: four leading generals were shot, after a summary trial in which they were accused of treason and mass murder. Khalkhali's reign of terror had begun; it would continue for a decade, beyond his own tenure. He would become known as the "hanging judge," and would later write, "I killed over 500 criminals close to the royal family, hundreds of rebels of Kurdistan, Gonbad and Khuzestan regions, and many drug smugglers . . . I feel no regret or guilt over the executions. Yet I think I killed little. There were many more who deserved to be killed but I could not get my hands on them." His biggest regret? That the Pahlavis had gotten away.

Photographs of the four generals' bodies in a pool of blood, blind-folded, their hands tied behind their backs, were splashed on the front pages of newspapers the next day, making international headlines. There was no more pretending. Those revolutionaries whose stomachs churned tried to dismiss it as the inevitable excesses of pent-up rage let loose—it would pass, they thought. Others wanted to believe this was happening without Khomeini's direct knowledge or consent. It would take years for some of the early revolutionaries to accept the truth: they had delivered their nation to a theocrat, an irredeemable monster.

One man purely rejoiced, even before the fall of Bakhtiar, boasting he had made the right bet from the very start: PLO chairman Yasser Arafat, who was close to the Beheshti camp. He felt that this was his revolution as much as it was Khomeini's, and he was eager to claim credit. After all, Palestinians had helped train the men who had brought an end to 2,500 years of Iranian monarchy. The training had intensified under the guidance of Arafat's own Fatah party. In PLO offices in Lebanon plastered to the wall were posters titled "A List the People Will Complete." There were red check marks beside Ethiopia, Vietnam, and Spain: wars won by the people against imperialism in the days of the international left. A red mark had just been added next to Iran. Still on the list were Egypt and Palestine.

In Beirut, in the early hours of February 17, Arafat got into the passenger seat of a white Peugeot station wagon and traveled an hour and a half east, across the Lebanese mountains and the Beqaa Valley through the Masnaa border checkpoint and into Syria, to Damascus. His friend Hani Fahs, the man who first helped contact Khomeini in 1977, rode with him. There were a few others in the delegation, including Mahmoud Abbas, a member of Fatah and the future Palestinian president, and Elias Khoury, a thirty-year-old leftist activist intellectual in the style of the time, a type reminiscent of pro-revolution writers from an earlier period, à la Ernest Hemingway in the Spanish Civil War. Khoury, a Christian Lebanese, had moved to Jordan to join Fatah after the 1967 war. He studied in Paris, then edited a quarterly magazine called *Palestinian Affairs*. Born in the year Israel was created, he was also a novelist who published acclaimed works about the Lebanese civil war and the dispossession of Palestinian refugees. One day he would be described as a possible candidate for the Nobel Prize in Literature. But on this cold February afternoon, he was boarding a plane from Damascus with Arafat and Fahs, en route to Tehran. It wasn't just any plane: it was a Syrian presidential aircraft, courtesy of the dictator Hafez al-Assad. The two-hour flight was uneventful, though the atmosphere was palpably jubilant. There was no guarantee they would be allowed to land, as the airport was still officially closed and other planes had been turned away. Arafat was confident. He had friends in Tehran, and they were waiting for him.

Fifteen minutes from Tehran, air traffic control requested the identity of the passengers. Arafat, fearful of remnants of the shah's SAVAK and its ties with Israel, insisted that the pilot state only that he "had an important Palestinian delegation" on board. Traffic control insisted on more details, but none were given. Suddenly, six Phantom jet planes surrounded the Syrian plane. The mood turned tense. There were new instructions from traffic control: "We will let you know in ten minutes if you are cleared to land." A few minutes later, the pilot of one of the fighter jets waved to Arafat, who was sitting by the window. Arafat's face had become widely recognizable over the years—he had distinct features, with thick lips, always sporting a stubble and a black-and-white-checkered scarf headdress, the Palestinian *keffiyeh*. The fighter jet's nose lifted up in salute. Traffic control cleared the plane for landing.

Mehrabad airport was besieged. Thousands of foreigners and Iranians were trying to leave the country, while the Americans were evacuating their nationals on Hercules C130 military planes. But Arafat was delighted to land in Tehran at six in the evening on that Saturday, the first foreign leader to visit Iran after the revolution. Wearing his trademark revolutionary outfit—a khaki field jacket and the keffiyeh—he walked out of the plane, wiped a tear, and flashed the victory sign to the crowd on the tarmac. There to welcome him was Yazdi, now a deputy prime minister and foreign minister, in a suit and a necktie. (Neckties would soon be banned in Iran as a symbol of Western culture.) Inside the terminal, a raucous welcome greeted Arafat. "Landing in Tehran felt like I was approaching Jerusalem," said the Palestinian leader. "Iran's revolution doesn't belong only to Iranians, it belongs to us too. What you have achieved is an earthquake and your heroism has shaken the world, Israel, and America . . . Your honorable revolution has lifted the siege on the Palestinian revolution." What ensued was a five-day lovefest that made headlines around the Arab world. In Beirut, there was celebratory gunfire in parts of the city, and thousands rallied to cheer the achievement. Socialist leftists, pro-Syrian and Palestinian leaders, all said the same: this was a triumph for their cause and for Arab unity over Israel and the United States. THE SHAH IS GONE. TOMORROW SADAT, read one banner.

While Arafat took a victory lap in Tehran, the Egyptians were making headlines with their negotiations with the Israelis at Camp David. The juxtaposition of those news stories on front pages made Arafat look like the hero and the Egyptians like sellouts. The Palestinian leader went straight to meet Khomeini. They sat on the floor and held hands and talked for an hour and a half. Khomeini declared he had carried the Palestinian cause in his heart for fifteen years. Arafat leaned over and kissed the ayatollah on his left cheek. Khomeini smiled broadly. "Can you believe that the Palestinian revolution is in Iran?" asked Arafat. "Who can believe it! But a new era has begun."

The Iranian Revolution had changed the balance of forces in favor of the Palestinians, according to Arafat. At a press conference, Arafat was joined by the ayatollah, and the two men held hands and raised them together as the crowd chanted "Today Iran, tomorrow Palestine." Khomeini's son Ahmad went everywhere with the guest of honor and declared: "The victory of the people of Iran did not end with the defeat of the shah. Our hope is to raise the flags of Iran and of Palestine on the hills of Jerusalem."

Before they could do that, they had a closer target over which they could raise the Palestinian flag: the Israeli embassy. Ties between Iran and Israel had been severed right after Arafat's arrival in Tehran, and the few Israeli diplomats who had remained in the country were expelled. They had already burned all sensitive documents. The fifteen hundred Israeli citizens working in the country had been evacuated before the shah had even left the country. Thousands of Iranian Jews had been airlifted out. Yazdi now took his guests to a three-story building with a Persian blue fountain in the courtyard, where the Israeli diplomatic mission had been based. Inside the ransacked building, broken desks, shattered glass, and mangled lamps covered the floors. Office drawers had been thrown out of the windows. A notice in Hebrew was still posted on an office door. The close cooperation between Israel's intelligence services and the shah's SAVAK was a source of anger in Iran and fueled the destructive fury against the building. Arafat, Yazdi, Fahs, and Ahmad Khomeini went out to the balcony on the second floor, with a ragtag group of gunmen. Above their heads, spray-painted in red, were the words: "VIVA PLO." Arafat gave a rambling speech, and then he, Yazdi, and Ahmad held hands and raised them above their heads, flashing the victory sign. A Palestinian flag on a stick was attached to the railing, above an improvised placard with the words "PLO Embassy." On the street outside the gates of the embassy, hundreds had gathered. They climbed on the walls and hung from the fence to get a glimpse of Arafat. They raised their fists and chanted: "Khomeini; Arafat! Khomeini; Arafat!" Standing on the balcony, wearing his clerical robe and his black sayyed turban, Fahs marveled at the sight of these revolutions joining together, erasing borders, sects, and ethnicities. He felt at one with Iran and with Palestine, with an Islam that transcended it all. He felt part of something bigger than any one nation. He believed in the revolution more than he believed in God, and for it Fahs would leave everything: his country, the Arab nation, his home. Soon he would bring his family to Tehran, and his daughter Badia would later study in the religious seminaries of Qom.

Beneath the unifying smiles of Arafat's visit were tensions and divergent agendas. Yazdi and most of the LMI had been slow to embrace the Palestinian cause: beyond getting the military training they needed from the Palestinians, they thought it was a distraction from the main goal of bringing down the shah. In Lebanon, Chamran had had sharp differences with the Palestinian guerrillas running amok in the south of Lebanon, bringing Israel's wrath upon Shia villages. But standing on the balcony of the Israeli embassy, embraced by huge crowds everywhere he went with Arafat, Yazdi could see the utility of championing a cause that went beyond his country's borders. It gave Iran's revolutionaries an even bigger aura, one that could inspire the region, maybe the world—every revolutionary's dream. He didn't understand the extent to which Khomeini was hoping to utilize this aspiration for his own purposes.

Yazdi had come up with the idea of holding al-Quds Day, Jerusalem Day, every year on the last Friday of the fasting month of Ramadan. The first would be in a few months, during the long hot days of August. Khomeini would take credit for what served him, including the idea of this new ritual marking Iran's calendar. It would bring hundreds of thousands of Iranians out on the street, in support of Palestine, renewing Khomeini's credentials as their most vocal supporter. The vision was for a worldwide day of protests, to counter Israel's own Jerusalem Day, which marked the reunification of Jerusalem under Israeli control. The ritual of protest, which would include burning of flags and chants of "Death to Israel," would never really take root outside Iran. Khomeini wanted to control the Palestinian narrative and pressed Arafat to label his own movement an Islamic resistance. Although one man was Shia and the other Sunni, this was not an obstacle, as those words rarely featured in the politics of that era. The tension that was setting in was between nationalism and religion, between secular activism and religious fundamentalism. And Arafat, just as cunning and unscrupulous as the ayatollah, didn't want to be owned; he wanted to lead. He would never adopt the name of Islamic resistance.

That inherent tension would never be resolved. By the end of 1979, the Palestinians would become disillusioned, with some describing the Iranians as "real nut cases." The "nut cases" were in turn disappointed with the Palestinians: most didn't pray, they drank, they wore ties, and had dalliances with women. By that stage, Khomeini didn't care; he had what he needed. During Arafat's visit he said he had carried the Palestinian cause in his heart for fifteen years. Although Khomeini was an ideologue when it came to Israel and Jerusalem, he had also made a calculated political move latching on to an issue that would help make up for his Persian and Shia identity by taking up the Sunni Arab cause par excellence. And even if Arafat didn't want to be a part of the "Islamic Resistance," Iran now had the means to create its own, by rallying those Lebanese and Palestinians who were drawn to Khomeini's fundamentalist agenda. Some of those who would come to oppose Arafat's leadership would be Palestinian Islamists, like the Hamas movement, and they would look to Iran for support.

—

The Palestinian cause had not stirred many passions in Iran after the creation of Israel, except among a small minority, which included Safavi. The shah had initially warned that the partition of Palestine would lead to conflicts for generations, but in 1950 he recognized the new state and maintained ties with Israel throughout his reign. Iranian Jews were the oldest Jewish community in the region, dating back to the days of Esther, the Jewish queen married to a Persian king, who had thwarted the massacre of her people, a story at the heart of the festival of Purim. Since the late 1800s, hundreds of Jews had migrated from Iran to historical Palestine but the community was also deeply attached to its Persian identity and had prospered under the shah. Many Iranian intellectuals visited Israel before 1979, including a prominent secular essayist, Jalal Al-e Ahmad, who traveled there with his wife in 1964. He was mesmerized by the young, energetic state and wrote deeply admiring articles about the country, which he referred to as Vilayet-e Izrael: a state guided by clerical guardians, a Jewish wilayat, a model for Muslim governance. In the 1960s, Al-e Ahmad was the key intellectual of the revolution, the most important thinker in the secular opposition to the shah. After his articles about Israel appeared, Al-e Ahmad received an angry phone call from Ayatollah Ali Khamenei, a close acolyte of Khomeini and the future leader of Iran. His writings had rattled both men—how could someone they saw as one of *theirs* write about Israel, not only in such a positive way, but using terms that echoed Shia religious traditions and their own theological arguments?

Khomeini and Khamenei knew of Al-e Ahmad because in 1962, before his trip to Israel, Al-e Ahmad had written what would become the seminal, foundational text of the Iranian Revolution: *Gharbzadeghi*, commonly translated as *Westoxication* or *Occidentosis*. In it, he critiqued a society that was being flattened by rapid modernization and desperation to emulate the West, a country losing its distinct Persian identity to capitalism. That's why he had been so taken by the model Israel could offer to Iran. He had visited the Holocaust memorial at Yad Vashem and expressed his admiration for the revival of the Jewish people after World War II. He had stayed in a kibbutz and marveled at the organic adaptation of Soviet socialist ideals: here was a country that was neither East nor West; it had not simply adopted outside models, it had created its own authentic one. *Gharbzadeghi* made the case for a return to Iran's cultural roots, including Islam. The point was not to reject everything from the West, but to find Iranian answers to the Western machine rather than simply submitting to it in an exercise of self-loathing. Persian and Shia culture were deeply intertwined with Western culture; religious seminaries taught ancient Greek and philosophy, Iranians abroad influenced as much as they were influenced by the culture they encountered. Al-e Ahmad also referred to the work of the Western greats, like Albert Camus or Eugene Ionesco. But at its most basic level, *Gharbzadeghi* was a concept that appealed to Khomeini—here was yet again an idea he could manipulate. He adopted the term to feed anti-Western sentiments. Al-e Ahmad died in 1969; his intellectual heir was Shariati who kept the fire burning strong. By 1979, they were both conveniently gone, leaving Khomeini in charge of translating and twisting their thoughts. He would eventually erase these secular men from the narrative of the revolution.

Khomeini had in part been introduced to the cause of Palestine through his contacts with the young radical cleric Safavi, who had attended the Islamic Conference in Jerusalem in 1953. One of the participants was Sayyid Qutb, an Islamic thinker who was fast becoming a key ideologue of the more radical members of the Muslim Brotherhood and whose writings would inspire generations of violent fundamentalists. (His first name was Sayyid but did not denote lineage to the prophet.)

At its core, the Brotherhood was a missionary, revivalist movement, similar to the Fedayeen. One was Sunni, the other Shia, but they had much in common ideologically. The meeting in Jerusalem recommended declaring the cause of Palestine as a Muslim cause, transcending the Arab nation, while cooperating or making peace with Israel was deemed treason. Afterward, Safavi traveled to Cairo, where Qutb hosted him for a week. The Iranian was disappointed by the reception. No one in official circles would meet him. He thought he had come to a country that was ruled by Islam, where the Muslim Brotherhood was the dominant force. Instead, he had found a conservative but secular country with music and theater, where women spoke back and even a sheikh had ridiculed him for turning his face away when speaking with a woman. Still, the young zealot remained inspired by what he had heard in Jerusalem and brought his observations to Khomeini and Khamenei. Two years later, Safavi was executed by the shah and mourned as a martyr of Islam by Sunnis and Shias alike.

The connection between the Brotherhood and the Fedayeen outlived Safavi. To develop his theory and plans for an Islamic state, Khomeini borrowed heavily from Qutb (and both had leaned heavily on concepts first elaborated well before them by Abu A'la al-Mawdudi, a Pakistani ideologue and founder of the Sunni fundamentalist group the Jamaat-e Islami). Khamenei translated a couple of Qutb's books into Persian and wrote admiring introductions. Khomeini's *Islamic Government* was translated and widely read in Egypt. In revolutionary Iran, Qutb's books would be taught in schools. He spent more than a decade in jail in Egypt and was executed by hanging in 1966. Revolutionary Iran would honor him with a postage stamp. When Khomeini was in Neauphle-le-Château, members of the Brotherhood had gone to visit him. Now it was time to congratulate him for his success in Tehran.

—

On February 22, just a day after Arafat left, Yazdi arranged for another plane to land at Tehran airport. This one was a private charter coming from Islamabad, and it carried several members of the Syrian and Egyptian Muslim Brotherhood, the current leader of Pakistan's Jamaat-e Islami, and others from Kuwait, Indonesia, and (according to some reports) even from Saudi Arabia. The man who paid for the plane was Youssef Nada, the Egyptian Brotherhood's key financier. Yazdi took care of the delegation, hosting them in his house. The group was meant to visit for five hours, but they stayed for three days, meeting Khomeini and Prime Minister Bazergan and visiting the cemetery of martyrs. Mian Tufayl, from the Pakistani Jamaat, later wrote that "we felt like members of the same family, travelers in the same caravan, wayfarers to the same destination who were transporting their provisions to the same place." Though full of praise for Khomeini's success, they all had a slightly different agenda. The Pakistanis seemed content to bask in the glow of the ayatollah and a universal, ecumenical Islam. Khomeini had met Mawdudi, the founder of the Jamaat, during a pilgrimage to Mecca in 1963. They had talked about their visions of an Islamic state.

The Brotherhood had more specific goals. According to some accounts, the Brothers offered to pledge allegiance to Khomeini and elevate him as the leader of the Muslim nation. They saw his victory as the victory of every Muslim fighting against oppression, imperialism, and colonialism. Short of anointing him a caliph, men like Youssef Nada indicated they at least hoped Khomeini could be the spiritual leader of millions across the world. But it required that Iran shed Shiism as the official state religion and become simply a Muslim nation. When the Persian shah Ismail I had founded the Safavid empire and forced his subjects to convert to Shiism in the fifteenth century, the decision had been mostly tactical. The shah belonged to a small messianic Sufi Shia order, which had started out as Sunni. As he conquered Ottoman territory and solidified his empire, the Safavid ruler sought to rally his subjects around a distinct identity, sharpening the front line with the enemy. Battles between the two empires meant that Sunnis and Shias, albeit very recent converts, were killing each other for the first time in centuries. Every king of Iran since Shah Ismail I was now the Guardian of the Shia Faith, all the way up to Shah Reza Pahlavi.

While the Brotherhood's request to break with this tradition and become an ecumenical political leader for millions was extraordinary, it was emblematic of the fluidity of sectarian identity in politics. It also showed the enthusiasm that the Iranian Revolution had generated across borders and sects. Khomeini listened, but did not answer. The Brotherhood visited Iran again in May. One of the men in the delegation was a radical ideologue of the Syrian Brotherhood, Sa'id Hawwa. He had yet another request: the group was engaged in a low-level insurgency against their own dictator, Assad, and they sought Khomeini's support. Assad was not a friend of the West, like the shah, but he was a secular nationalist. The Syrian Brothers had great hopes that the Islamic fervor that Khomeini had brought to Iran's revolution could spread to their country.

Assad had offered Khomeini sanctuary in Damascus when the ayatollah had to leave Iraq. Shariati had been buried in Damascus when his
body couldn't be taken to Tehran. Syria was the first country to recognize Khomeini's victory and sent congratulations two days after the fall of
the Bakhtiar government. The Syrian leader had even provided the plane
that took Arafat to Tehran. Now that Egypt was friends with Israel and
America, Assad rejoiced at this new hardline addition to the anti-Western,
anti-Israel camp. Khomeini likely saw the benefits of a continued relationship with Assad. Again, the ayatollah listened to Hawwa's plea, but did not
answer.

—

On February 24, Husseini and Chamran traveled together to Tehran.
However much they knew of Imam Sadr's misgivings about Khomeini,
they were confident that his militant, radical ardors would be curbed by
the LMI and other moderate clerics. There were still pictures of Ayatollah
Taleghani on the walls across Tehran. Taleghani was ten years younger
than Khomeini, with deep-set, melancholic eyes and a somewhat gaunt
face. He had been released from his latest stint in jail only in October
1978, so had missed some of the building momentum that Khomeini was
harnessing, but he was hugely popular in his own right and one of the
most powerful clerics in the country. There were other, more senior and
wiser clerics as well, like Kazem Shariatmadari, the gentle ayatollah with a
kind face and round eyeglasses, who had a huge following and had favored
gradual change in cooperation with the shah. Khomeini owed him his life:
when he was arrested for his role in the 1963 uprising against the shah's
White Revolution and faced possible execution, Shariatmadari had inter-
vened.

Husseini stayed at the Intercontinental Hotel, where just three years
prior Andy Warhol had been a guest invited by the queen to make a portrait of her. North Tehran looked like Beverly Hills, the queen was known
as the Jackie Kennedy of the Middle East, and Warhol was ordering caviar
from room service. Now there were snipers on the streets and the portraits were stacked in the vault of the Tehran Museum of Contemporary
Art, along with another three hundred masterpieces from the world's great
painters, a collection valued at $3 billion. There would be no more Western
art. The only consolation was that the works had not been destroyed.

Husseini had joked with Bazergan that Chamran was only on temporary loan to Iran, that Lebanon wanted him back. Bazergan joked back:

"Persians don't return loans, we're keeping him." Chamran was delighted to be home. The guerrilla fighter was appointed minister of defense. He would never go back to Lebanon. He may have wanted to return to visit his friends, or look out to the sea, or walk the streets of Tyre. But Khomeini's folly was going to get him killed soon.

—

Events in Iran were hurtling forward at breathtaking speed. Mohsen was at the heart of it, still thrilled and exhilarated by this opportunity to build the new Iran. Victory had come much quicker than he had expected. He had been right: the fervor of the people was enough to sweep away the last vestiges of the shah's power, after just a few key battles. The long drawn-out insurgency that he had envisioned, with a people's army fighting for years like the Vietcong in Vietnam or the National Liberation Front in Algeria, had not materialized. But with the shah still alive and not far away, and the CIA's intentions always the eternal unknown, everyone was fearful of a possible coup. Amid the chaos of revolution, the breakdown in law and order, and the paralysis of the armed forces, there were militias springing up everywhere and guns galore. Within weeks, Mohsen helped to set up an organization that would guard the revolution from these excesses and from any possible counterrevolution. The Sepah-e Pasdaran-e Enghelab-e Islami, the Army of the Guardians of the Islamic Revolution, was born: armed vigilantes operating across the country to beat down any dissent, any counterrevolutionary groups, any non-Islamic militias. The communists and Marxists were still armed, so they were targeted, too. Mohsen and some of his comrades set out to write the founding charter of the Guardians, a document to spell out duties and limits and bring all the disparate groups under one umbrella. Mohsen, one of the provisional commanders, went to the headquarters of the SAVAK. The physics student, a revolutionary at heart but a technocrat in practice, got a bit queasy about what intelligence work would entail. He talked to others around him and with colleagues like Yousef Kolahdouz, a former officer in the shah's army. They rewrote the charter and named new commanders at the top. The far-reaching consequences of what Mohsen was helping to found were not clear to him—or, if they were in that moment, he would never admit it. The informal resistance movement became an organ of the state, a feared, all-powerful paramilitary organization that struck at anyone who opposed the revolution. Its emblem was a raised fist holding a Kalashnikov rifle.

Over time they became known as the Islamic Revolutionary Guards Corps (IRGC), their power extending well beyond the borders of Iran.

Mohsen moved to the radio and television authority and later to the industrial development authority. As he tried to preserve his belief in the core ideals of the revolution and in Khomeini, he would go from disappointment to disappointment. The utopia he had once envisioned never materialized. Instead, there was now an Islamic republic.

The Islamic Republic of Iran was now the official name of the country, after a referendum at the end of March 1979, when Iranians went to the polls to vote on a simple question: Should the monarchy be replaced by an Islamic republic? There were no voting booths, so everyone could see what people were choosing on their ballot papers. "Yes" was colored in green. The turnout was massive, and 98 percent picked green, even though there was no definition of what an Islamic republic entailed. Bazergan and his allies had been working on drafting a constitution since their days in France, inspired by the text drawn up after the revolution of 1906, which had been implemented for only a few years then. The new text, published on June 14, envisaged an executive presidency whose power was vested in the people, not in a monarch. A committee of religious leaders would have limited veto power over laws. Men and women would be equal under the law. In Bazergan's document, there was no reference to the wilayat al-faqih.

Tensions began to surface between Khomeini and the more progressive and highly regarded ayatollahs like Taleghani and Shariatmadari. Taleghani's children were briefly arrested in April by militiamen from revolutionary committees, komitehs, that had sprung up everywhere. Taleghani, the country's second-highest-ranking cleric, retreated home in protest, closed his offices in Qom, and warned that the nation could "once more fall back into the hands of dictatorship and despotism." After meeting Taleghani in Qom, Khomeini chided him rather than the komitehs, making clear who was staying. He pointedly avoided addressing Taleghani as Ayatollah, instead calling him Mr. Taleghani. Protests erupted. "Disrespect to Taleghani is disrespect to the nation," the demonstrators chanted. A few months later, in September, Ayatollah Taleghani died in his sleep at the age of sixty-eight. He was a healthy man and the timing of this death was convenient, leading some to believe there had been foul play.

Meanwhile, Shariatmadari, who himself wanted a return to the 1906 constitution, had launched his own political party. Within days, more than a million people signed up. He was one of Khomeini's most prominent challengers, and all year he campaigned against Khomeini's brand of Islam. But the radical clerics were better organized, well ahead, and far more ruthless. Even before Khomeini's return they had formed a kind of shadow government under the banner of the Islamic Republican Party (IRP), which Beheshti, Khomeini's closest ally, was leading. Tightly organized, authoritarian, it gathered all those who accepted Khomeini's leadership unconditionally. Beheshti was using the party to consolidate control over the revolution and marshaled support from the komitehs, as well as the clerics, Islamic militias, and the Revolutionary Guards. The IRP had worked hard to make sure that the April referendum would result in an Islamic republic. It had its own thugs: Hezbollah, or the Party of God, and attacked demonstrators who opposed Khomeini, terrorized students on university campuses, shut down critical newspapers, and rode in the streets in convoys of motorbikes, waving black flags and banners.

If the IRP was slowly seizing the levers of power, the secular leftists still dominated the streets and could bring out hundreds of thousands of Marxists, socialists, and communists. They had been working underground for decades, they were the oldest opposition groups in the country, and they had in effect laid much of the groundwork for the revolution inside the country, alongside nationalist secular forces. Their formerly underground guerrillas were now out in the open, having picked up weapons from abandoned army bases. Within days, they were distributing pamphlets and newspapers on the street. They could mobilize huge demonstrations: between five hundred thousand and a million people took to the streets on Labor Day. Leftist student organizations still wielded huge power across the country on university campuses. They held debates with Hezbollahis and won, because theirs was still the ideology of the day, and anti-imperialism the most popular rallying cry.

Khomeini had not expressed openly anti-American sentiments while in exile and had barely done so since his return. He bemoaned the United States' backing of the shah and ranted against Israel, but he did not seem to be gearing up for a confrontation with America. Khomeini, the provisional government, and even Beheshti had maintained ties with the United States. They had negotiated the release of US diplomats when a Marxist-Leninist group had briefly seized the American embassy earlier in the year. But leftist groups were now brandishing the anti-imperialist banner higher and higher, demanding that Khomeini break ties with the American government and cancel contracts with American companies. Toward the end of October, the shah arrived in the United States for medical treatment. Few outside the shah's close circle knew of his illness and, in Iran, many imagined this visit was the prelude to another CIA coup. The left jumped on the occasion, mobilizing on university campuses that had just reopened for the start of the academic year, and launched the slogan "Death to America," *Marg bar Amreeka.*

Khomeini's most radical followers did not want to be left out—it was time to show who were the true revolutionaries. On November 4, some four hundred students climbed the walls of the American embassy compound in central Tehran. Led by a group calling itself Students Following the Imam's Line, they took sixty-six American hostages. Khomeini did not order the seizure but quickly recognized its benefits. He could outbid the secular left, undermine the nationalists, and appropriate the popular anti-imperial slogan. He would have a whole new arsenal at his disposal to solidify his grip on the country. Khomeini began to pitch in with more anti-American rhetoric, and he gave his blessing to the seizure of what the students called "the nest of spies." Two days later, Prime Minister Bazergan resigned in protest. As did Yazdi. There had been months of tussles with the ayatollah over governing style and vision for the country but the hostage crisis was the final fissure. The radicals now had free rein. Within a month, a new constitution was put to a referendum. This latest version was unrecognizable from the version Bazergan had drafted in France and finalized in Iran in June—it was almost wholly the work of Beheshti and his allies, who had spent the summer reworking the text. The wilayat al-faqih had been enshrined and tailored to fit Khomeini. The faqih had very broad powers: it enabled him to name top military leaders and judges, dismiss the president, and disqualify political candidates, with or without cause. He could declare war and peace. A national referendum was called to vote on the constitution. Turnout was slightly lower than in April, but on December 3, the result was an overwhelming yes.

Khomeini was now the Supreme Leader, the delegate of the Mahdi on earth.

In Qom, the gentle Ayatollah Shariatmadari did not vote in the referendum, and he made his views known. He vehemently opposed the constitution and the role of the faqih. He warned of civil war. His supporters began an insurrection in his home province, and he became a rallying point for all dissenters. It wouldn't last because, unlike Khomeini, Shariatmadari did not want to spill blood. He dismantled his party. Soon after, he was put under house arrest and stripped of his religious rank.

Several articles in the constitution were of particular interest to supporters of the revolution outside Iran. The Muslim Brotherhood had been waiting for Khomeini's answer to its proposal that he be the ultimate leader of an Islamic awakening. But article 12 of the new constitution declared that Iran's state religion was still Shia Islam. The Brothers who had visited Khomeini in Iran were deeply disappointed. Khomeini wanted to be a leader on his own terms; he wanted to be separate from the rest. He didn't want to dissolve himself into a Muslim world that was 80 percent Sunni; he wanted to lead the opposition forever. When it suited him, he would reach out to those Sunni groups that could serve his agenda. Article 154 of the constitution was designed exactly for that, implicitly expanding the jurisdiction of the faqih beyond the borders of Iran. Indeed, the constitution declared that the Islamic Republic of Iran supported "the just struggles of the oppressed against the oppressors in every corner of the globe." Khomeini's revolution was just beginning.

In America, millions were tuning in for a nightly update from ABC on the hostage crisis at the embassy in Tehran. Every evening, Ted Koppel delivered the latest in a special program: *The Iran Crisis—America Held Hostage: Day 5.* Then there was day 10, and day 12. On days 14 and 15, a total of thirteen Americans were released. Except for one hostage released in 1980 for health reasons, the other fifty-two remained hostages until January 1981, a total of 444 days, throughout which Khomeini continued to eliminate the left and solidify his grip on the country with his radical posse. At exactly the same time in Saudi Arabia, a similar crisis was unfolding. The Mahdi had seemingly returned from occultation and appeared in Mecca. And he, too, had taken hostages.

3

BLEEDING HEART

SAUDI ARABIA

1979

Yet I wondered fancifully if he had seen more clearly than they did,
had sensed the threat, which my presence implied—
the approaching disintegration of his society
and the destruction of his beliefs.
Here especially it seemed that the evil that comes
with sudden change would far outweigh the good.
—Wilfried Thesiger, *Arabian Sands*

Sami Angawi overslept on November 20, 1979, and missed the dawn prayers. He prayed five times a day, every day, as dictated by Islam. He found peace in every word, every movement, as he bowed and knelt in rhythmic, meditative motion, trying to reach a mystical state of communion with the Almighty. He loved dawn prayers in the silence of a world still asleep; he could almost feel the vibrations of the thousands, even millions of those who were praying across the country at the exact same time, uttering the same words, facing in the same direction: the Ka'aba in the Holy Mosque in Mecca, the holiest site in Islam. He would have to make up for this missed prayer when he reached Mecca. He and his Quran teacher had chosen to make a pilgrimage to the Holy Mosque on what they thought was an auspicious day: the beginning of a new century in the Islamic calendar, the first of the month of Muharram of the year 1400. While many conservative Muslims memorize the Quran's 6,236 verses, Sami had not learned them by heart as a child. Then, as a teenager, he had gone to school in the UK and then off to university in Texas. Back in Saudi Arabia, he was learning to reconnect with his faith. The architecture graduate was only thirty years old, but he was an old soul. He was a towering figure, physically, and already considered a thought leader in Saudi Arabia,

an absolute monarchy sitting on the world's second-largest oil reserve, at a
time when the only trend—the only thought that seemed to dominate and
drive the country—was money.

The discovery of oil in 1938 launched the transformation of a mostly
desert kingdom into a modern country. The country was barely six years
old and its founder, King Abdelaziz ibn Saud, was already courted by world
powers. In 1945, Franklin D. Roosevelt struck a deal with the Saudi monarch, sitting aboard the USS *Quincy* on the Great Bitter Lake. The two
men agreed that Saudi Arabia would provide America with unimpeded
access to exploit the oil, in exchange for military protection and support.
The price of a barrel was low for years, the revenues limited, but it was
more than enough to build a country from scratch, and by the late 1960s
a wave of construction was under way across the kingdom. There was no
local expertise, but plenty of money to hire help. Then, in the fall of 1973,
the price of oil quadrupled almost overnight from $3 to $12—roughly the
equivalent of $50 in 2019. That October, Egypt and Syria had gone to war
against Israel, hoping to regain land lost in the Six-Day War of 1967. Oil-
producing Arab countries declared an embargo on exports to the United
States and other countries that supported Israel in the conflict. Saudi Arabia was reluctant to undermine its alliance with the US but ultimately led
the charge and reaped the benefits: Arab hearts filled with pride, briefly
grateful to the kingdom for standing up to the West and Israel—a small
consolation for past humiliations. Most important, the young country was
now awash with cash as billions of dollars flooded the kingdom. Between
1970 and 1974, Saudi Arabia's oil revenues ballooned from $1.2 billion to
$22.5 billion.

Construction became frenetic, and cranes appeared everywhere.
Neighborhoods were being transformed or built almost overnight. Every
major American hotel chain was setting up in town: Intercontinental, Sher-
aton, Holiday Inn, Hyatt, Hilton, Marriott. Thirty thousand Americans had
moved to the kingdom to offer their expertise, from oil engineers to hotel
managers to accountants, building everything from roads and airports
to hospitals and schools. The Americans used the model they knew best.
Small urban settlements in the middle of the desert, like Riyadh, began to
grow into cities that looked like Arabia's answer to Houston: urban grids of
wide streets with massive shopping centers and no public transportation.
Big American cars, Cadillacs and Chryslers, cruised the streets, adding to
the American illusion, broken only by the minarets of mosques. Everyone
was dazzled by the unimaginable wealth that had descended on them. Two

hundred foreign companies opened offices in the kingdom in the span of just a few years. World-renowned architects were flown in. The American architect Minoru Yamasaki, who was designing the World Trade Center in New York City, was also working on the Dhahran airport in the east of Saudi Arabia, and the Riyadh headquarters of the newly established Saudi Arabian Monetary Authority. Even the country's currency was brand-new.

The royal family handed out generous subsidies to most of its subjects. On the fringes in the desert, in distant areas of what was barely a country, many were left out of the frenzy, still in poverty, in thatch-roofed huts with no running water. Princes sank fortunes into every imaginable luxury: yachts, jewelry, opulent new palaces, and high-stakes gambling in Monte Carlo. The state budget was the royal family's private coffers, just as the country was, in essence, their private property. People had more money than they knew what to spend it on, and many were losing all sense of bearing or balance. Sami remained unperturbed. He was different, indifferent—not that he was completely uninterested in the material things of this world, but he hailed from a well-established Meccan family, descendants of the prophet. His father had served as both the chief of police in Jeddah and a *mutawwif*, the guide who leads pilgrims through the rigidly codified rituals of the *hajj* in Mecca, the yearly pilgrimage and one of the five pillars of Islam. He was a servant of the state, but mostly he was a servant to the pilgrims, whether peasants or ministers. It was a privileged position, held by only a few thousand families, handed down through generations, a position that preceded the creation of the kingdom of Saudi Arabia by centuries. With the honored status also came wealth and, above all, a deep connection to Mecca, the birthplace of the prophet and of Islam.

Sami was deeply unsettled by how the new oil wealth was leveling the country's heritage. Sami's childhood home in Mecca had already disappeared. The old Souq el Layl, the night market with its busy stalls and magic mix of smells and noises, had been torn down in the 1950s to make way for the expansion of the Holy Mosque, ordered by the king. The last expansion before that had taken place in the tenth century. Since then, for over a thousand years, the Holy Mosque had been preserved and renovated with utter devotion; its shape and size, but mostly the history imprinted in its walls and floors, had been left unperturbed—until the arrival of its new moneyed custodians. Unlike the barren, desert interior province of Najd, from which the new rulers of the kingdom hailed, Mecca was in the richer, more vibrant, and cosmopolitan Hejaz province along the Red Sea. The Hejaz, home to both Mecca and Medina, the two holiest sites in Islam, and the nearby port city of Jeddah, had been part of every great Islamic empire, its people open to the world, its architecture delicate and intricate, its practice of Islam rich and diverse. Najd wasn't poor, but it was sterile and xenophobic, and remained on the periphery of a culturally diverse and rich world religion.

Since returning from the United States, Sami was living in Jeddah, a city that had stood at the crossroads of trade and religion for centuries. In the seventh century, the third caliph after the prophet, Othman ibn Affan, declared the seaport to be the official gate to Mecca for all pilgrims arriving by sea. Others came overland in caravans through Damascus or Baghdad. Since then, Jeddah was flooded every year by thousands of Muslims from all corners of the world. Many would settle in the city, whose connection to the spiritual realm went even further. According to one interpretation of the Quran, after being exiled from paradise, Eve and Adam were reunited on Mount Arafat near Mecca. Legend had it that Eve, the mother of mankind, was later buried in Jeddah, the city whose name means "grandmother" in Arabic. There had even been a tomb in the city that was said to be Eve's. For centuries, pilgrims would visit the site, especially barren women, with supplications to the divine. Famed travelers wrote about and sketched the tomb, which was approximately five hundred feet long with a carved square stone representing the navel. It had survived the passage of time and the weight of countless pleas, only to be destroyed during the 1926 conquest of the Hejaz by Abdelaziz ibn Saud, who was working to unify the provinces of the Arabian Peninsula under his rule. His son Faisal, the future king, had led the assault on Jeddah after the city had been besieged and starved for over a year. Barely nineteen, Faisal was named viceroy of the province, and he ordered the destruction of the tomb. An ancient cemetery in Medina dating back to the days of the prophet was also razed. The new rulers of Arabia saw the dangers of *shirk* (idolatry) everywhere. From sultan of Najd to king of Najd and the Hejaz and then king of the whole peninsula, Abdelaziz gave his name to the new kingdom and his new subjects.

Abdelaziz was the descendant of Muhammad *ibn* (son of) Saud, founder of the Al-Saud dynasty. From the deep interior of Najd, Abdelaziz brought with him two centuries of a particular brand of Islam that his ancestors had espoused in a political and familial alliance with one man: Muhammad ibn Abdelwahhab. Ultra-orthodox and fundamentalist, the eighteenth-century religious preacher led an exclusionary revivalist movement, following in the footsteps of others who had called for a return to the ways of the *salaf*, the ancestors, the first generation of Muslims. There were those Salafists who believed that following the righteous salaf, *al-salaf al-saleh*, dictated a return to the exact way of life of the prophet. In the early twentieth century, there would be modernist Salafists, such as the Egyptian Muhammad Abduh, who believed it was important to rid Islam of centuries of acquired traditions and accretions and return to the purity of prophet's teachings, which actually provided the answers needed to adapt religion to modernity. Only after 9/11 did the term *Salafist* become known worldwide, used exclusively to denote the stricter outlook with Salafist jihadists resorting to violence to impose their views. In his days, Ibn Abdelwahhab was so extreme in his interpretations that he was regarded as an outcast by his contemporaries. The Ottomans were the first to describe it as Wahhabism, to denote a movement outside the mainstream of Islam, one that seemed intently focused on one man as though he were a kind of prophet. The Wahhabis, with the Al-Sauds as their standard-bearers, tolerated nothing that could come between man and his God: not the intercession of saints, not tombstones in cemeteries or visitation of the graves of loved ones, not even worship of the prophet—all of it was shirk. The dynasty had suffered serious reversals, including almost total annihilation and exile over two centuries, but the alliance between the House of Saud or Al-Sauds and the preacher, sealed in the desert in 1744, had persisted. The tomb of Eve became one of its victims. In 1975, what was left of the tomb was covered with concrete and lost in a large cemetery among hundreds of graves that looked like rows of empty, white concrete planters with paved pathways in between.

This fanatical, uncompromising attitude was at the source of events unfolding that November morning in Mecca as Sami overslept, unaware of the momentous turmoil occurring inside the Holy Mosque itself. As he started his morning, Sami reviewed the verses he had memorized the day before. Only later would he understand how ominous his recitations were.

"And fight not with them at the Sacred Mosque, until they fight you in it: so if they fight you in it, slay them. Such is the recompense of the disbelievers."

Sami wasn't the only one who had thought that the first day of the new century was auspicious for religious initiatives, small or big.

—

Before the break of dawn, Sheikh Muhammad al-Subail, the grand imam, leader of prayers, of the Holy Mosque, performed his ablutions. The bearded fifty-nine-year-old draped his gold-trimmed black cloak around his shoulders. *Fajr* (dawn) prayers were minutes away. The cool darkness of the November night still enveloped the city, hugging the craggy hills overlooking Mecca with their evocative names—*noor*, light; *rahmah*, mercy. But the very heart of the city, the beating heart of Islam, was never dark (certainly not since the arrival of electric power at the turn of the century, followed by the installation of floodlights). The Holy Mosque and its large square courtyard remained dimly lit throughout the night. In the center stood the House of God, the Muslim tabernacle: the Ka'aba, a forty-foot-high granite cube structure covered in black silk cloth embroidered in gold with Quranic verses. Purportedly, it had first been built by the prophet Abraham (Ibrahim in Arabic).

The call to prayer echoed through the loudspeakers at 5:18 a.m.

> *Allahu Akbar*—God is the Greatest.

Among the worshippers from Mecca, from around Saudi Arabia and from the four corners of the Muslim world, were three hundred Sunni men on a divine mission—or so they believed. Some had been there for days, reconnoitering the labyrinthine interior and underground of the mosque. Others had arrived overnight, some with their wives and children, to allay the suspicions of guards. Most were Saudis but others were Egyptian, Pakistani, and there were even two African American converts to Islam. The call to prayer continued.

> *Ashhadu anna la ilaha illa Allah*—I bear witness that there is
> no god except God.

The worshippers had all been roused from their sleep; people living nearby had already filed into the Holy Mosque. They performed their ablutions and started gathering for prayers in concentric circles around the Ka'aba. They knelt in prostration on the white marble floor. Many were wearing the simple unhemmed white *ihram* cloth that male pilgrims wrap around themselves for the hajj or the *umra*, the small pilgrimage. The men on a mission were dressed in a traditional white or beige *thobe*, the customary Saudi garment. Some stood out because of their unkempt appearance, the result of days of preparations and weeks in the desert.

> *Ashhadu anna Muhammad rasool Allah*—I bear witness that
> Muhammad is the messenger of God.

The group of three hundred believed another messenger had come—the Mahdi. Sunni beliefs also allowed for an apocalyptic redeemer whose arrival by the Ka'aba, alongside Jesus, signaled the end of times before the age of righteousness. But unlike Shias, Sunnis did not hold this as a central tenet, nor did they believe the Mahdi been born centuries ago and gone into occultation. He would instead reveal himself as a man from the people with particular attributes spelled out in the *hadith*s, the records of prophet Muhammad's sayings and actions, written after his death. The truth of this Mahdi's presence had been revealed to the leader of the group in a dream, while he had been out in the desert: the Mahdi was one of his own companions, soon to be his brother-in-law, Mohammad ibn Abdallah al-Qahtani. His name and physical appearance matched what the hadiths had predicted. The Mahdi was meant to be a descendant of the prophet through his daughter Fatima, and a story was concocted to explain how al-Qahtani, who came from a different tribe and area, did in fact have the right ancestry. Soon, many in the group were having dreams confirming that Qahtani was the Mahdi.

> *Hayya 'ala as-salah . . . Hayya 'ala al falah*—Rise up in prayer,
> rise up for salvation.

The group began to congregate, preparing for their moment. They believed salvation was now, on this new day of the new dawn. Those who were not true believers of the idea of the Mahdi and the impending apocalypse were still devoted to the leader of the group and his message of religious purity, his criticism of the spendthrift royal family bringing the corrupt, immoral ways of the infidel West to the birthplace of Islam. The Al-Sauds may have been puritans in their beliefs but they also bowed to the god of money. The voice of the *muezzin*, the reciter, echoed.

> *As-salatu khayrun min al-nawm*—Prayer is better than sleep.

For weeks, they had been training. And for days, they had been hoarding weapons in the cellars of the mosque. They had bribed guards and driven three pickup trucks through the access point used by the construction company that was expanding the mosque. The Toyota, Datsun, and GMC were packed with weaponry, ammunitions, and food. The men were preparing for a siege. They had brought in even more weaponry before dawn that morning, wrapped in shrouds and concealed in coffins, pretending they were bringing deceased relatives for the ultimate benediction by the grand imam of the Holy Mosque.

Allahu Akbar, la ilaha illa Allah. God is the greatest, there is
no god but God.

Suddenly, gunshots. The sound shattered the peace, echoing across
the courtyard. Another shot. Scared pigeons flew away. A man with a
rifle was walking toward the Ka'aba. Worshippers were stunned. Why a
gun in such a sacred place? Even the guards carried only sticks. Violence
was *haram*, forbidden, in the holy sanctuary. The leader of the group then
appeared, flanked by militants armed with rifles, pistols, and daggers. He
was tall and slender, with full lips and long black hair that blended with
his full black beard. He looked like a messiah himself; there was something magnetic in his eyes. But his name in Arabic signified "angry face,"
or "the scowler." Juhayman al-Otaibi was a forty-three-year-old Bedouin
who had served in the Saudi National Guard for some twenty years. He
had no formal education, spoke mostly Bedouin dialect, and had little
religious training, but he was a pure product of the system—or rather, the
extreme expression of its in-built contradictions and ideological excesses.
Juhayman shoved Sheikh al-Subail aside and grabbed his microphone.
The imam was horrified, not only by the surreal events but because he'd
had a sudden flash of recognition: these men had attended his lectures,
they had studied at his feet, right here in Mecca. The sun had now risen
and all fifty-one gates of the Holy Mosque were chained shut. Juhayman
and his men began broadcasting their message to the thousands who were
now trapped inside. In simple tribal dialect, Juhayman shouted short military commands to his men: seize the high ground, the rooftops and minarets. "*Ahmad al-Luhaybi!* Up to the roofs, and if you see anyone rebelling,
shoot them." "*Abdallah al-Harbi!* To the northern side, the northern side!"
Machine guns were set up in the seven minarets. At nearly 300 feet
high, they provided snipers with a perfect vantage point, overlooking the
whole city. The takeover had been swift and complete; the men were ready
for a siege. Mostly they were preparing the moment when the pilgrims
would vow their allegiance to the redeemer. Juhayman handed the microphone to one of his aides who spoke better classical Arabic. He began
to explain the mission to the thousands of worshippers who were now
hostages. The message was blasted to thousands of others across the city
through the loudspeakers, and it would be a message that would soon
make waves across the kingdom and the world. An ancient prophecy had
been fulfilled, said the speaker, the Mahdi was among them. For the next

hour, the spokesperson of the armed men read out selections of ancient hadiths that had predicted the arrival of the Mahdi, describing him and the day of his appearance. The moment to consecrate the Mahdi and declare loyalty to him was approaching, said the speaker. There were many holes in their story—including the dubious ancestry of Qahtani—but for those not versed in the details of theology and ancient texts, the whole event was too confusing to even pick at details. Even more perplexing was the fact that Sunnis gave little thought to the concept of a Mahdi, even though there had been a few Sunnis with messiah complexes. Most of them were fighting a political battle, usually against a colonizer like the British, the French, or even the Ottomans. But Juhayman and Qahtani had their sights set on the House of Saud.

The rebels spelled out their demands: they wanted the country to cut ties with the West, stop all oil exports to the West, expel all foreigners, and remove the House of Saud and their clerics who had failed to uphold the purity of Islam. (Some of these demands were similar to ones that Osama bin Laden would make in a few years.) But crucially, Juhayman also demanded the redistribution of oil wealth among the people. This was the first time that the conduct of the Saudi royal family had been challenged since the official founding of the kingdom. The rebels may have been religious zealots, but theirs was also a rare political, popular protest in this absolute monarchy. The country had seen power struggles between royals, a challenge by one liberal prince demanding a constitutional monarchy, and even the assassination of a king. There had been labor strikes in the 1950s. But this was the first time that people were using violence to protest. They were expressing real grievances shared by many poor and disenfranchised Saudis who had been left behind by rapid, badly planned modernization and rising social tensions and inequalities. Many Saudis were horrified by the corrupt ways of the Al-Sauds, their ostentatious spending, their palaces dripping with gold. The economic aspects of Juhayman's protest would be conveniently written out in the official Saudi version, and would barely register in the retelling of the events even outside the kingdom. The Saudis would use the more outlandish religious claims of Juhayman and his men to reduce the movement to the work of religious deviants who had lost their way. But the leaders of the "deviants" had been groomed by the top stars of the Saudi clerical establishment. That too would be obscured by the Saudis. In fact, when the siege began, they tried to hide the news from their own citizens and from the rest of the world.

"Mecca, Medina, and Jeddah are now in our hands," the spokesperson proclaimed through the loudspeakers. The hostages in the courtyard had no way of knowing it wasn't true. Meanwhile, Sheikh al-Subail had managed to escape to his nearby office and telephone colleagues to alert them to what their former students had wrought in the holiest of sites.

Details of what was unfolding had trickled down to Jeddah before Sami had even set off on the two-hour drive to Mecca. The architect had a meeting with a government official to discuss the maintenance of the Zamzam holy water well in the Holy Mosque. When he walked in, the official exclaimed: "The Mahdi has arrived!" which Sami first took as a joke about his attire. Sami stood out in more ways than one in 1979 Saudi Arabia, and not only because of his height or ponytail. As a proud Meccan and Hejazi, he had stayed loyal to the province's culture and Mecca's diverse practice of Islam, which the Al-Sauds had tried their best to eradicate after their conquest. He wore a traditional Hejazi turban—an off-white cloth embroidered in orange hues, double-wrapped around the head. With this simple gesture, he was defying the state. Turbans were considered haram by the most conservative Muslims and had been hotly debated when the kingdom was founded. The Al-Sauds had also set out to homogenize the patchwork country by erasing local differences and declaring the Najdi headdress obligatory for government officials: the *ghutra*, a checkered or white square of cloth, folded in half and held in place on the head by the *'igal*, a thick double black cord. Later, the flowing white thobe would also become the unofficial unifier, replacing the more interesting costumes worn in the Hejaz. The Hejazis chafed under this new puritanism; they had enjoyed centuries of semiautonomous rule and both resented and feared their new lords.

Deep in Sami's DNA and heart was the mysticism of Sufism, a deeply spiritual practice of Islam combining intense, almost transcendental devotion and asceticism, a practice as old as Islam itself, common to Sunnis and Shias and ingrained in the history of Mecca. For Wahhabis, Sufi practices, including melodious incantations and especially prayers to the shrines of saints, were heresy. As an architect and lover of history, Sami was also intent on preserving the country's past. In 1975, he had set up the Hajj Research Center in an effort to save Mecca from the modernizing rampage of the Al-Sauds. By helping to study the rapidly growing flow of pilgrims to the holy city, he hoped to devise a way to expand and modernize the city while still maintaining Mecca's Islamic heritage.

The House of Saud had used its custodianship of Mecca and Medina to claim leadership of Muslims everywhere, using the pilgrimage as a conduit for its influence around the Muslim world. Wanting to welcome an ever-increasing number of pilgrims all year long to the hajj, it had embarked on huge expansion projects, bulldozing and paving over ancient, religiously significant sites. Medina—where Islam was born—was already lost to savage modernization. The old roads, once lined with stucco houses, their facades ornamented with delicate wooden latticework, had been replaced with multi-lane streets and modern, soulless buildings. The Prophet's Mosque, al-Masjid al-Nabawi, Islam's second-holiest site and the second mosque to be built after the one in Mecca, had also been transformed, with gray stone replacing the delicate rose-red stone and graceful Ottoman style, making way for more grandeur. On that November morning, Sami wondered what new catastrophes Mecca had to be saved from now.

By midmorning, at least six police officers had been shot and thirty-six wounded as they tried to approach the mosque in a convoy of cars. Reinforcements were on their way, checkpoints went up, and the streets around the mosque were blocked to traffic. Sami finally arrived in the city of his childhood to see what was happening and found the streets empty. Sami was doubtful that the true Mahdi had arrived: he knew the real Mahdi would not need guns or hostages. Sami conferred with some Islamic luminaries and fellow Sufis, like Sheikh Mohammad Alawi al-Maliki, who had held on to his green turban and managed to continue practicing and teaching a more moderate Islam in the holy city. For the sages of Mecca, there was no doubt that there was no Mahdi here. While there was still resentment toward the Al-Sauds and Najdis for bulldozing the Hejazi way of life, Meccans were ready to sacrifice anything to save the holy site that their families and ancestors had embraced with faith and devotion. Everyone pitched in to help the Saudi troops and officials who had begun to converge on the city: they offered food, helped transport supplies in wheelbarrows, and provided shelter.

Sami prayed, asking God for guidance, and concluded he should help, too. He had something very valuable: floor plans and aerial photographs from his research on the hajj. Sami called the office of Prince Ahmad, the younger, half-brother of the king and deputy interior minister, offering his help. The authorities had nothing to work with so far—the troops didn't know much about the inside of the mosque, the inner labyrinthine rooms, the underground cellars. The construction company that was working on the expansion had the blueprints but was slow to provide them.

Sami was summoned to the Shoubra hotel, a kind of temporary command post, where the ministers of interior and defense, Princes Nayef and Sultan, were also gathered. Sami wanted to participate in the operation to liberate the Holy Mosque. He suggested using sledgehammers to create openings around the gates and bulldozers to knock them down, providing protection to soldiers who could then storm the courtyard. But he quickly understood that the royals, eager to put an end to this humiliating challenge to their authority as quickly as possible, were already contemplating tanks and artillery. Sami could not abide that. The only man who had used violence in the sanctuary was the prophet himself, during his conquest of Mecca, after returning from exile in Medina. But according to the most trusted hadith, the prophet's instructions had been clear: "Beware! (Mecca is a sanctuary!) Verily! Fighting in Mecca was not permitted for anybody before me, nor will it be permitted for anybody after me." All life and all things in the sanctuary should be respected: "It is at this moment a sanctuary; its thorny shrubs should not be uprooted; its trees should not be cut down." After providing the officials with the floor plans, Sami went home with a heavy heart.

By noon of that day, November 20, the country was already cut off from the outside world. All international lines were shut, no calls could be made, no telex or telegrams sent. Land borders were closed to non-Saudis. A total news blackout was imposed. Uncertain about the exact nature of what was unfolding and of the threat to the House of Saud, all royals outside the country were called back, from the most inconsequential prince vacationing on a beach in California to the deputy head of intelligence, Turki bin Faisal, son of the previous king, who was in Tunis for the Arab League summit. Crown Prince Fahd, also in Tunis, stayed put. His aides dismissed the reports from Mecca as a mere "domestic incident." King Khaled was in Riyadh so there would be no panicked departure for Fahd. The key was to give the impression that everything was under control.

Night fell over Mecca, and with it came an eerie calm, shattered by occasional bursts of sniper fire. Prince Turki arrived that night and narrowly escaped death: as he entered the Shoubra hotel, the glass door was hit by a bullet and shattered in his hands. The power lines to the Holy Mosque had been cut, and the structure, the size of a stadium, was a gaping black hole at the heart of the city.

News of the disturbances made its way across the Atlantic, where the day was starting at the White House and everyone's mind was occupied by the hostage crisis in Tehran, now in its third week. The American ambassador in Jeddah, where the foreign embassies were based at the time, had managed to send out a diplomatic cable, thanks to a hotline to the State Department that remained unaffected by the Saudi efforts to cut all communications to the outside world. In his first dispatch, the ambassador emphasized how much still remained unclear about the events unfolding inside the mosque. The armed attackers were likely Saudi but possibly Iranian, or maybe Yemeni. The only certainty was that the well-armed men posed a huge challenge to the House of Saud. With Khomeini looming large over everyone's mind at the White House, the only word that everyone seemed to retain from the information coming out of Saudi Arabia was: "Iran."

On Wednesday, November 21, two-thirds of the front page of the *New York Times* was devoted to the Tehran hostage crisis and the Mecca events, and the two had been linked: U.S. WARNS IT HAS "OTHER REMEDIES" IF DIPLOMACY FAILS; CARRIER FORCE HEADS TOWARD IRAN, read one headline. Another article, titled NEW KHOMEINI ATTACK, focused on the ayatollah's call for the shah to be sent back to Iran for trial, and his threat to put the American hostages on trial as spies. In the bottom half of the front page, a wide picture of the Ka'aba in the courtyard of the sacred mosque was accompanied by an article about the unfolding crisis in Saudi Arabia, reporting "Mecca Mosque Seized by Gunmen Believed to Be Militants from Iran." In the piece, American officials speculated that the takeover was a response to Khomeini's call for a "general uprising by fundamentalist Moslems in the Middle East." The Mahdi element of the shocking events only added to the impression that this must have been an Iranian takeover. Even in the Arab world, where Khomeini had fired everyone's imagination, many believed it was possible that, whether Iranian or Saudi, whether Sunni or Shia, the rebels in Mecca could well have been inspired by the ayatollah. Iran was in fact helping to agitate against the House of Saud at that exact same time, but in the eastern part of the country, where an uprising was about to start.

For now, the focus was still on the events in Mecca, and there was wild speculation about what was really going on. The most dangerous rumor was one promoted by Khomeini himself in a statement read out on Radio Tehran on Wednesday morning. "It is not farfetched to assume that this act has been perpetrated by the criminal American imperialism so that it can infiltrate the solid ranks of Muslims with such intrigue . . . It would not be farfetched to assume that, as it has often indicated, Zionism intends to make the House of God vulnerable and create riots." With communications restored, details of the shocking events were trickling out of the country. That morning, the news was on the radio from Egypt to Pakistan where, in some circles, anti-imperialist sentiments needed little stoking. An angry mob of students converged on the US embassy in Pakistan, a sprawling compound with housing and a swimming pool, on the edge of Islamabad. "Death to the American dogs," they chanted. "Avenge the sacrilege of Mecca!" The mob forced its way into the enclave, setting cars and buildings on fire. The attack lasted six and a half hours, during which time the Pakistani police and army were nowhere to be seen. Two American servicemen died, as did two embassy employees and two protesters. The embassy building was destroyed. The anti-American violence continued to rage across the country, and by Friday more than three hundred Americans had been evacuated from Pakistan.

On Wednesday evening in the kingdom, more than thirty-six hours after wild rumors had circled the globe, the Saudi interior ministry issued a statement maintaining that "there are no indications that lead us to believe that foreign nationalities were involved in the incident . . . It has been confirmed that the attack has been carried out by a gang that deviated from the path of Islam." This was not enough for the American ambassador in Jeddah, John West, who was worried that his embassy could still come under attack and wanted a clear, unequivocal Saudi statement that the United States had not been involved. Foreign embassies were still located in Jeddah in those days, because the Saudis didn't want too many non-Muslims living in Najd. Writing in his diary, West reflected on a difficult, draining day and the seriousness of what was happening in Mecca. But he felt he had ascertained at least one thing by then: there was no Iranian involvement. It would take another two days for the Saudis to unequivocally state that neither Americans nor Iranians were involved. The initial tepid Saudi denials of foreign involvement were a cowardly effort to deflect attention for as long as possible from the kingdom's own responsibility in creating the monster that had hijacked Islam's holiest site. Obfuscation and the feigning of ignorance would become favorite forms of Saudi subterfuge to evade responsibility for any violence or intolerance connected to the kingdom.

The country remained on full military alert, with troops guarding "key industrial plants, airports and palaces." Whoever was responsible for the attack, whether Iranian militants or Saudi gunmen, this looked very much like a Saudi failure. A missive from Egypt was particularly alarming for the Saudis. The grand sheikh of Al-Azhar, one of the highest religious authority in Sunni Islam and one of the world's oldest universities, urged "quick, decisive action" and called for a joint meeting near Mecca of Muslim scholars in response to this "brutal aggression." This was not the unqualified message of support that the Saudis would have wanted to hear; rather it was an implicit challenge to their role as custodians of Islam's holiest sites, a call for others in the Muslim world to help protect the mosques. Unlike previous custodians of Mecca and Medina, the Al-Sauds had neither lineage to the prophet nor ancestry in the holy cities. When they had conquered the Hejaz in 1926 and destroyed ancient sites in Medina, Wahhabism was still considered heretical by much of the Muslim world. There had been calls for a committee of Muslim nations to look after the holy sites. This would always be a source of insecurity and angst for the new monarchy. The kingdom worked hard to prove it could rise to the challenge, as the young dynasty derived prestige, power, and legitimacy from the role. Now the House of Saud seemed to have failed in the most spectacular way.

That night in Mecca, the mosque remained dark and the city mostly deserted. But the sky was lit up with flashes of light from artillery shelling. The king and the country's top clerics had reached a deal during the day that allowed the use of lethal force in the Holy Mosque. They had found a way around the verse that still echoed in Sami's head:

"And fight not with them at the Sacred Mosque, until they fight you in it: so if they fight you in it, slay them. Such is the recompense of the disbelievers."

Although Juhayman and his gang were Muslims, an argument could be made they were acting like disbelievers. The clerics were now working on the text to make their case. More and more pilgrims were managing to escape. One Iranian pilgrim had fled and managed to make it all the way back to Tehran, where he spoke to journalists. He added credence to theories of a Shia takeover by saying the rebels had described the Mahdi in line with Shia beliefs, as the Twelfth Imam, hidden for eleven centuries and now returned to establish God's kingdom on earth. The Iranian pilgrim said he didn't buy any of it. Speaking either of Juhayman or Qahtani he said: "The moment I met this guy, I knew he was fishy."

On the third day, the wannabe Mahdi died. He had survived a dangerous game of capturing grenades thrown at him by Saudi soldiers and throwing them back at the troops—until one of them exploded in his hands, shredding his body. Those among the rebels who had believed in the messianic mission they were carrying out were as perplexed as they were disturbed. How could the Mahdi die if he was to lead the world to redemption? And still, the fighting went on, as the Saudi government continued lying and claiming victory. On the morning of Friday, November 23, in Pakistan, the headlines stated that the Holy Mosque was UNDER FULL CONTROL OF SAUDI FORCES. The Saudi minister of information echoed that the situation was "in control and is reassuring." But the advent of live broadcasts on radio and television also meant that around the Muslim world people waited for the Friday sermon to be broadcast from Mecca.

When Friday arrived, the sermon came instead from the imam of the Prophet's Mosque in Medina. There was no more hiding that the House of Saud was not in control of the House of God. By the end of the day, a *fatwa*, a religious opinion written by the kingdom's clerics, was ready, giving the Saudi authorities full religious cover for the onslaught they were about to unleash. The clerics had worked around the hadiths, the Quran, and their own beliefs to come to the aid of the royal family. Everyone's survival was at stake, including the clerics.

The power of the Al-Sauds still rested on their alliance with clerics upholding the legacy of the holier-than-thou preacher Ibn Abdelwahhab. Born in 1703, Ibn Abdelwahhab had been inspired by the dogmatic teachings of a literalist, medieval theologian, Ahmad ibn Taymiyya, who belonged to the Hanbali school of jurisprudence, the strictest of the four Islamic schools. A complex character with a rich legacy who had lived at the time of the Crusades and sanctified war against the Christian invaders, Ibn Taymiyya would be quoted mostly for his edicts allowing war against a Muslim ruler in certain cases. He would inspire generations of activist and jihadist Salafists who ignored the nuances of his teachings. Ibn Abdelwahhab had taken Ibn Taymiyya's pronouncements stripping Islam down to absolute monotheism and began to enforce them in Najd. He went further still by declaring war against anyone who didn't follow his teachings—non-Muslims but also Muslims. The Najdi preacher had taken theology and turned it into a political and military mission. Ibn Abdelwahhab was so extreme that his own father and brother denounced him. He sent missives around the Arabian Peninsula and beyond to scholars and notables of the Muslim world, appealing to them to follow him and what he claimed was the true version of Islam. He was rejected and mocked in scathing responses coming from as far away as Tunisia, where the scholars of Al-Zaytuna, one of the oldest, most important centers of Islamic learning, undid his arguments one by one. The locals in his desert settlement accused him of heresy and tried to kill him.

Ibn Abdelwahhab sought refuge in the settlement of Dir'iya, ruled by Muhammad ibn Saud, founder of the dynasty, and suggested they combine forces. Under the banner of religion and war against anyone who did not abide by Ibn Abdelwahhab's version of Islam, the two men could expand both territory and wealth. Preaching and military raids would go hand in hand, bringing in land, loot, and *zakat*, the mandatory alms. The marriage of convenience led to intermarriage between the two families, starting with Ibn Abdelwahhab's daughter and Ibn Saud's son. Through all the upheavals the Al-Sauds faced—annihilation, exile, revival—the alliance remained a key source of strength for both sides of what was essentially an extended family of royals and clerics: the House of Saud, the Al-Sauds, and the House of the Sheikh, Al-ash-Sheikh. They could not be separated. The agreement had been that Ibn Saud would handle politics and governing while Ibn Abdelwahhab would be in charge of religion and preaching. When the clerics or their heirs, spiritual or familial, stepped out of bounds, undermining the pragmatism essential to governing, the Al-Sauds brought them back into line. This worked most of the time. But the interaction with the West and the arrival of thousands of Westerners to help build up the country and extract oil was proving to be a great source of friction in the modern kingdom of Saudi Arabia.

One virulent critic of Western influence, and a rising star, was a young blind cleric named Abdelaziz bin Baz. His influence would shape the minds of those who would transform the region in the decades to come. In 1940, Bin Baz, neither an Al-Saud nor an Al-ash-Sheikh, had the audacity to call for a ban on all non-Muslims on the Arabian Peninsula. He landed in jail. After his release, he would continue to issue anachronistic religious opinions; among them were refusing to believe the Americans had landed on the moon, insisting the sun orbited the earth, complaining about the introduction of radio and television, of girls' education, of anything that was modern and novel. But he had understood the lesson of his time in prison: never undermine the House of Saud and the pillars of its power.

No matter the failings of the Al-Sauds, the clerics saw them as a bulwark against worse dangers, like communism and secularism. So the clerics provided the royal family with the fatwa that would save their rule and permit the use of force in the Holy Mosque. The royal family used the word "deviant" to describe the rebels, but the clerics were more careful: they described Juhayman's men only as "an armed group." How could they describe them as deviants when some of the men had been groomed and taught by the clerics themselves? Juhayman was decrying the Western infiltration of the kingdom, the decaying morals, the corruption . . . all grievances the clerics themselves had voiced.

Decades earlier, Bin Baz had also been trying to guard against such decay. As vice rector of the Islamic University of Medina in the 1960s, he had used his influence to help launch a new missionary movement to enforce Wahhabism in the Hejaz. Though now part of the kingdom, the province had, so far, managed to maintain a more relaxed application of religion and preserve its more diverse culture. Small groups of religious students in Medina began acting as vigilantes: ripping pictures and posters, vandalizing shops with mannequins, with Bin Baz as their spiritual guide and mentor. Juhayman, having retired from the National Guard after an eighteen-year career in which he did not shine, was one eager member of the movement. By 1976, the group had spread across all major cities. There was nothing secret about them, or their proselytizing, or the camps they organized in the desert for young men. In 1977, Juhayman, then in his forties with a wife and children, broke away from the main group and began attracting a band of hardcore followers in a new, cult-like movement. Even Bin Baz was too soft in their eyes, too accommodating of the royals.

Juhayman's next step was to write and dictate a series of pamphlets explaining his religious views and denouncing the Saudi state. One of the pamphlets was signed by Qahtani himself. Abdellatif al-Derbas, a Kuwaiti companion of Juhayman, found a leftist publisher in Kuwait willing to print the pamphlets at cost, barely one Saudi riyal. With protests engulfing Iran at the time, the publishers believed they were aiding another working-class uprising against a monarch. Although Juhayman's group had broken away from the establishment clerics, Bin Baz added approving remarks to the pamphlets.

This aggressive rhetoric and ensuing agitation began to attract the attention of the state, resulting in the arrest of some of the zealots, in the spring of 1978. Yet again, Bin Baz stepped in to support his former protégés—hotheads perhaps, but disciples of a sort, whose fervor he had played a role in feeding. Maybe Bin Baz wished he still had their youth and eyesight, or perhaps he felt they were taking action where he could only theorize. He called the minister of the interior, Prince Nayef bin Abdelaziz, and demanded the men be released. And so they were. To avoid arrest himself, Juhayman had fled into the desert, where he spent his time preparing for his takeover of the Holy Mosque and the appearance of the Mahdi.

Bin Baz would never apologize for, nor even acknowledge, his role in the growth of Juhayman's movement. Instead, he would use the moment to force the royal family to live up to the Islamic ideals that he felt they had let slip. With other clerics, he drove a hard bargain that would haunt the kingdom and the whole region for decades, a bargain that would make Saudis feel that time had stopped in its tracks. To get what they wanted, the clerics even agreed to the arrival of a team of infidels, French commandos, to help put an end to the ongoing siege—a detail that would surface only years later. They came with three hundred kilograms of a concentrated tear gas to snuff out the rebels, who had by now mostly retreated into the cellars of the mosque. Unable to go to Mecca as non-Muslims, the French stayed in a nearby city to train and equip Saudi teams to launch the assault to retake the mosque.

Just before dawn on Tuesday, December 4, 1979, exactly two weeks after Juhayman and his men had hijacked the Holy Mosque, the Saudis could finally declare the siege truly over. The victory had been costly and bloody: 270 people had died, according to their official numbers. The Saudi government admitted to 127 troops killed and 450 injured, with 117 rebels dead, in addition to 26 pilgrims. Western diplomats were skeptical, putting the numbers much higher. The Holy Mosque looked like a battlefield: gates blown out, a military jeep burned and riddled with bullets, staircases collapsed, minarets bombed. Crushed marble, twisted metal, and bloodstains were everywhere. The Ka'aba itself was intact. But the stench from decomposing bodies and the gas used to force the surrender of the rebels hung over the mosque and the surrounding area. The desecration of the holiest site was an excruciating sight, but one that the authorities were able to mostly keep out of the wider public's view: no foreign journalists were allowed into the country; no non-Muslims were allowed in Mecca; and Saudi journalists in the tightly controlled state media knew better than to report on the literal stains on the kingdom's reputation. The repairs took months. But by the afternoon of December 6, the mosque had been scrubbed clean enough to welcome back King Khaled himself. Prayers, in the presence of the monarch, were broadcast live on television. For the first time in over two weeks the world could see proof that the House of God was still standing. The king circled the Ka'aba seven times, prostrated himself twice, and took a sip from the holy Zamzam spring.

Before the siege, there had been underground construction work to expand the well of the spring, with pumps emptying the water. The power cut during the fighting meant the water levels had risen, and Sami was called to Mecca to enter the well and check whether the water had been contaminated by the toxic mix of gases, liquids, and bodily fluids that had soiled the underground of the mosque. Miraculously, the water was clear and clean. But as Sami surveyed the site and tested the water, he was beset with anguish. The violence was a warning. Something had gone terribly wrong. Whatever happens in Mecca, he thought, reverberates around the world, and whatever happens around the world comes back here, in an infinite spiritual loop. Mecca, the beating heart of the Muslim world, was deeply wounded. In fact, harmony had long been disrupted, ever since the Al-Sauds and their Wahhabi clerics had imposed their singular vision of religion on the Holy Mosque.

For centuries, scholars from the four different schools of Islam had taught in the Holy Mosque and crowds of students had traveled from near and far to gather in *halaqa*s, circles of study, around their preferred teachers. The faithful prayed, at slightly different times, behind their imams; there was a prayer station for each school: Shafi'i, Maliki, Hanafi, and Hanbali. When King Abdelaziz took control of Mecca in 1924, the Wahhabi clerics objected to the arrangement that had prevailed so far in the Holy Mosque. If the community of Muslims was one, and the call to prayer was one, why not pray behind one imam? The Wahhabi clerics won the debate, thereby dealing themselves all the power. But there was no rotation or compromise: the sole imam who would lead all five daily prayers in the Holy Mosque came from Wahhabi circles, with all that that entailed in puritanical intolerance. The number of halaqas dwindled rapidly, from several hundred to around thirty-five in the late 1970s. The Sufi sheikh that Sami had consulted that first day of the Mecca attack, Mohammad Alawi al-Maliki, was still drawing crowds, lecturing in his corner of the courtyard of the Holy Mosque, on the chair he had inherited from his father in 1971, the chair that been passed through generations. But few others were able to resist the onslaught of Wahhabi zeal. Harmony could be brought back, Sami thought, only if diversity was allowed to thrive again in the House of God. But this was not how the Al-Sauds would proceed. That was not the deal they had cut with Bin Baz to save their throne.

4

DARKNESS

SAUDI ARABIA, IRAN, IRAQ, SYRIA, AFGHANISTAN
1979–80

Like Saturn, the revolution devours its children.
—Jacques Mallet du Pan,
Considérations sur la Nature de la Révolution en France (1793)

There were two Islamic revolutions in 1979—one that made world headlines and was scrutinized down to its smallest details, and one that unfurled almost unnoticed. Both were misunderstood. One was a sudden, dramatic reversal of progress and rejection of centuries of history, the other was a slow but forceful expansion of Salafist puritanism. Both of them would transform their country of origin and then ripple across the Arab and Muslim world for decades to come, bringing with them darkness and oppression.

On the morning of January 9, 1980, Saudi Arabia carried out the largest execution in its history. Sixty-three captives were brought out to face the steel swords of Saudi justice in public, as was the custom in the kingdom. Sixty-three heads rolled in the sand. There would be no pardon for Juhayman and his acolytes. The women who had helped with food and supplies were jailed for two years. The underage boys among them were sent to orphanages. The beheadings took place in eight cities across the country, simultaneously. The Al-Sauds wanted to demonstrate they were in control of the whole country, for they had faced another serious challenge at the same time as they were trying to quell the rebellion in the Holy Mosque: this one coming from the oil-rich Eastern Province.

Beginning on November 25, five days into the siege of Mecca, hundreds of men had taken to the streets in the coastal areas of Qatif, Saihat, and Safwa. They chanted "Death to Al-Saud"; they ransacked a foreign bank and blocked the highway to a key oil installation. Oil and religion were the Al-Sauds' two levers of power and sources of legitimacy, and they seemed on the verge of losing both. The province was sealed off and telephone lines were cut. The government pulled away some of the National Guard from the Mecca area and sent them to the East. Reports talked of twenty thousand troops moving into the region to quell the protests. There were clashes, then battles. Military vehicles were set on fire and live ammunition used against the crowds. By November 30, the disturbances had been mostly quelled, but twenty protesters were dead.

There was a little-known history of protest in the Eastern Province, going back to the early days of the Arabian-American Oil Company (ARAMCO), when hundreds of workers started rioting over poor working conditions. The 1950s and 1960s were the era of left-wing nationalist politics across the Arab world, and even the kingdom of Saudi Arabia was not immune. In 1953, thirteen thousand of ARAMCO's fifteen thousand Saudi laborers went on strike for two weeks, protesting the arrest of colleagues who had been trying to organize a union. The library in Qatif stocked the classics of the global left, including Karl Marx. Communist pamphlets with the hammer and sickle insignia circulated, denouncing the royals. With help from ARAMCO, the Saudi government crushed the movement, imprisoning the agitators and sending its leaders into exile. One of them was Nasser al-Sa'id, the leader of the Arabian Peninsula People's Union, who fled to Beirut after 1956. When Juhayman and his men took over the mosque, al-Sa'id described it as a people's revolt. A few weeks later, he disappeared mysteriously in Beirut, reportedly abducted and killed by the Saudi authorities.

When the towns of the Eastern Province rose up in 1979, it was still to protest exploitation and discrimination, but while the tiny Saudi Communist Party and remnants of leftist groups participated, this was no longer a mere labor movement: in tune with the mood sweeping the whole region, this uprising now had clear religious overtones. The province was dominantly Shia, and though the community sat on top of the country's black gold and provided the majority of the workforce for the oil extraction, they had been mostly left out of the rapid modernization of the kingdom, toiling in poverty. If Juhayman and the Shias had one thing in common, it was their anger about corrupt royals. But as hardcore Wahhabis, Juhayman and his men also hated their Shia countrymen. In the absolute monotheism of

Ibn Abdelwahhab, the Shias were considered heretics who had rejected the leadership of the caliphs, the companions of the prophet. With their veneration of imams and visitation of graves, they were also seen as idolaters. Wahhabism remained deeply anti-Shia; the clerics of the kingdom continued to issue religious edicts condemning them as heretics, some even calling to kill Shias who did not embrace Sunni Islam. The community faced multiple levels of discrimination: their towns were the least developed in the kingdom; they were excluded from the royal court, sensitive ministries, and the diplomatic corps; they did not rise in the ranks of government bureaucracy or even ARAMCO; they could not build new mosques and were banned from holding any public rituals. But the Shias of Saudi Arabia had seen what people's power had achieved in Iran and, with both inspiration and some instigation from Tehran, had taken to the streets to demand more rights. After quashing the protests, the Saudi government tried to address the grievances and announced electricity projects, plans for new streets and schools, a better sewage system. But Saudi Shias would continue to be seen as "the other," the unbelievers.

—

The House of Saud had barely survived this double challenge to its legitimacy. To maintain their grip on power, they knew it was time to deliver on the deal they had struck with the clerics during the Juhayman crisis. When the minister of interior Prince Nayef was asked during a press conference in January 1980 whether the kingdom would now clamp down on men who appeared zealous because they sported a beard, for example, he scoffed. "If we did this most Saudis would be in prison by now," he said. Even before the attack in Mecca, Prince Nayef had been amenable to the blind sheikh's implorations on trivial matters. Bin Baz had complained about "violations of Islamic morality" in Riyadh, like foreign women eating in public, Christians wearing visible crosses, Western music being played in stores, and the apparently corrupting game of foosball, idolatrous because of the little statuettes. Directives were promptly sent to address Bin Baz's complaints—but only in Riyadh and the province of Najd.

Despite the religious strictures the House of Saud had imposed on the country since the kingdom was founded, many of their subjects still felt that every year brought more modernity, more freedoms, however small. The push and pull between the royals and the clerics had been a constant in the relationship, determined by the personality of each king and his standing with the clerics. The king who had succeeded most in plying the religious establishment to his will was King Faisal, who ruled from 1964 until he was assassinated in 1975. He introduced television and education for girls despite the clerics' protestations, and he sent emissaries well versed in matters of religion to reason with them. These were often members of the Muslim Brotherhood from Syria or Egypt who had fled repression in their countries and been embraced in the kingdom for their skills at building a modern state—they were often engineers but also educators, and they fanned across schools and universities in the kingdom.

Austere and devout, a direct descendant of Ibn Abdelwahhab through his mother, King Faisal spent time in his maternal grandfather's house participating in theological debates, and he "embraced the fundamentals of religion and norms of the shari'a according to the formulations of Ibn Abdel Wahhab." His own father, King Abdelaziz, referred to Faisal as "the boy from the Al-ash-Sheikh family." Above moral reproach, King Faisal could afford to push for those aspects of modernization he felt would benefit his country. The events of 1979 had frozen that courage in his successors, and the kings now kowtowed to religious forces. Juhayman had died, but his mission lived on. The impact was immediate and deeply felt in the provinces outside Najd, which Bin Baz had been trying so hard to discipline in the proper Wahhabi ways.

Women presenters were yanked off television. Newspapers had to blot out the faces of women in any pictures they published. The authorities also cracked down on the employment of women, which had always been theoretically forbidden but tacitly approved. Even Saudi branches of foreign companies had to lay off female employees. The handful of small makeshift cinemas in Jeddah were closed. Beach clubs patronized by Saudis and foreigners alike on the coast outside Jeddah were mostly shut down. Gone were the television and radio broadcasts of Fairuz concerts. The religious police started to strictly enforce prayer times, wielding their whips and righteousness. Known as the Committee for the Promotion of Virtue and the Prevention of Vice, they were now receiving massive sums of money, payment to feed the egos of small men who were otherwise failures but could now lord their supposed moral superiority over others. They drove their brand-new big GMC cars around, laying down their law and terrorizing people wherever they went. They felt so empowered they would force their way into people's homes, climbing over high garden fences, if they heard music coming from a house.

In Mecca, men from the religious police almost came to blows with the students of Sami's friend the Sufi Sheikh al-Maliki. He was still leading one of the only halaqas teaching something other than the Hanbali school of thought. The zealots from the committee wanted him gone, so the king quietly asked him to retreat home with his students.

When Jamal Khashoggi returned to Jeddah in 1982, after six years in the United States studying at Indiana State University, he noticed his country had changed. The tall young man with a jovial round face was originally from Medina. He had become devout in high school, reading magazines printed in Egypt about Islam. While Iranians were smuggling cassette tapes of Khomeini into their country, Jamal was buying cassette tapes of fiery Egyptian preachers in the shops in Jeddah for two or three Saudi riyals. He was an idealist in a country with no civil society and no politics, and he felt like a minority. Going to the mosque regularly was still considered uncool for young men, especially in cities like Jeddah. Friday prayers at the mosque were something your father dragged you to. But when he returned, married and with a child, Jamal noticed there were more mosques, and all of them were fuller. Segregation, already strictly enforced in public life, had made its way into private homes, within families. Before he had left for the United States, no one thought twice about sitting together with female cousins and aunts around the dinner table, the women unveiled. By the time he returned, extended family gatherings were segregated. Within each home, there was at least one person spreading the gospel about the *sahwa*, the Islamic awakening. In 1981, King Khaled would praise the sahwa as the reaction to the cultural, economic, and military invasions that had befallen the Muslim nation. The "blessed sahwa," in the words of the royals, was the path forward, and the Muslim nation's problems could be resolved only with Islamic solutions. Jamal started hanging out with members of the Muslim Brotherhood. He stopped listening to music. But he didn't have the heart to break his old LPs, so he gave them away.

If the cultural changes in Saudi Arabia were a case of arrested progress, in Iran it felt like whiplash, the violent and dramatic undoing of decades of social, political, and cultural advancement. Throughout 1979, the edicts fell, one after the other. Khomeini banned music from radio and television, declaring it "no different from opium." Googoosh, Iran's beloved pop diva, retreated home. Those selling music cassettes in their shop were told to change trades altogether. Alcohol was banned. Revolutionary Guards hauled crates of vintage champagne and fine European wines and 250,000 cans of imported beer from the cellar of the Intercontinental Hotel and poured more than a million dollars' worth of forbidden liquid down the gutter by the hotel's rear staff entrance. Mixed bathing in swimming pools was banned. In the summer of 1980, Iran witnessed its first executions by stoning in modern memory: two women accused of prostitution and two men accused of homosexuality and adultery. Other offenders were lashed or sent to the firing squad. There were no beheadings, as there had been in Saudi Arabia. But Iran now had its own religious police, just like Saudi Arabia: the Gasht-e Ershad, or Guidance Patrol. They harassed women who weren't covering their hair properly, because in the new Iran of Khomeini women who were not veiled were sinners.

On March 6, 1979, Khomeini declared that women working in government offices must wear the veil; "naked women" could not work in Islamic ministries. Two days later, for International Women's Day, tens of thousands of women spontaneously came out and marched on the streets of Tehran chanting "In the dawn of freedom, there is an absence of freedom." Some women were bareheaded, others veiled, including some in full *chador*, the all-enveloping black cloak that was worn only by the most pious and conservative. There were men, too, including some who formed a protective cordon around the women as they came under attack. Feminists from around the world flocked to the protests, including the American activist Kate Millett, the author of *Sexual Politics*. Soon as many as a hundred thousand women were on the streets. For six days, they protested the assault on their personal freedom. Rarely—if ever—had women organized so quickly and spontaneously after a revolution. But Iranian women in Iran had gained many rights under the shah, including the right to vote, to run for office (in 1963), and to wear whatever they wanted. In an effort at modernization, the shah's father (the first Pahlavi to rule) had briefly tried to ban the veil altogether in 1935, but that forced conservative families to keep their daughters at home for modesty. The move was quickly reversed. What Iranian women wanted was the choice: to veil or not to veil.

The flamboyant revolutionary Ghotbzadeh had been put in charge of the Islamic Revolution National and Radio authority, and he oversaw state media. The Westernized womanizer, who had fought so long for this revolution, could not abide the idea that there was any opposition to its victory. And anyway, he thought, the *hijab* (veil) would never become mandatory. The key was to portray unity and undermine the protests: in the media they were depicted as the work of monarchists. Some women were so angry about this misrepresentation that they attacked Ghotbzadeh in his car one evening as he was on his way to work. Meanwhile, the wider movement was racked with doubt as to whether they were indeed being used as a vehicle by supporters of the shah to undermine the revolution. They simply wanted this moment to live up to its promise of freedom and justice. Instead, they were finding themselves handed a black shroud. With their intentions misunderstood and put into question, and faced with increasing violence on the streets, the protests petered out. The women retreated home.

The French philosopher Michel Foucault was still writing in praise of the revolution, while others, like Simone de Beauvoir, recoiled—aghast—and sent messages of support to Iranian women. Though Foucault recognized Islam as a "powder keg" that could transform the region and the global equilibrium, he still found in the revolution the spirituality that he missed in the West. For him, the veil was just a detail, an inconvenience. The allure of anti-imperialism can be blinding to those who don't have to make any of the tough choices required of life under a repressive rule. Foucault would never recant his support for Khomeini, nor acknowledge the damage done to personal and intellectual freedom.

In the summer of 1980, all universities in the country were shut down. Iran's Cultural Revolution was now in full swing, complete with an eponymous institute that had just been charged with overhauling the curriculum in line with Islam and the new state ideology. For three years, there were no classes, while the student and professor corps were also purged. University campuses had been hotbeds of activism against the shah, but the ideologies then came in all colors and every possible combination: secular leftists, modernist Islamists, nationalists, leftist Islamists. Now there was only one stance, one narrative allowed. Seven hundred qualified scholars lost their jobs, while the country cut off the funds of a hundred thousand students who were on state scholarships overseas. Sciences were left alone, but the humanities were overhauled, producing textbooks titled *Islamic Psychology* and *Islamic Sociology*. Foreign influence had to be ripped out of books and minds.

The purge was everywhere, a reign of terror that would last ten years. The first victims were the royalists, former officials, military and intelligence officers; then came the communists, the leftists . . . Everything became a crime, yielding an entrenched paranoia and darkness that rolled over the country. The brutality of the former SAVAK paled in comparison to what was meted out in the new Islamic Republic dreamed up by Khomeini. Evin Prison in Tehran, built by the shah to house three hundred prisoners, was home to fifteen thousand by 1983. "More than 7,900 Iranian political prisoners would be executed between 1981 and 1985, at least seventy-nine times the number killed between 1971 and 1979" under the shah. In 1988, in a paroxysm of state depravity, at least three thousand political prisoners would be executed over the course of five months. Some reports put the number much higher, up to thirty thousand. The mass executions required forklifts to transport the prisoners and cranes to hang them at half-hour intervals.

———

In a poor village near the Caspian Sea, they were not marching against the veil. There was no foreign influence to purge. There wasn't even a high school. The women already covered their heads. But theirs were colored scarves, tied with a knot under their chin, Grace Kelly fashion, with strands of hair showing. They wore long tunics over their baggy trousers. They toiled in poverty and believed the revolution would bring better, more prosperous days. In the Alinejad family, the men joined the Basij, the new volunteer paramilitary force enforcing security and morality in the village: they destroyed music records and bottles of alcohol. Masih, the youngest of the family, would grow up with a veil tightly wrapped around her head, not a strand of hair showing. She even slept in it. Again and again in school, she was told she would go to hell if she took it off. One day, she would choose hell—but for now, in her village, she rebelled in smaller ways, asking why her brother could swim in the river and she couldn't, why he could ride a bike and she couldn't. It was all for a higher purpose, one that her parents believed in: the revolution.

But the revolution was devouring its own children. Taleghani had already died under mysterious circumstances after denouncing the inclusion of the wilayat concept in the constitution. Shariatmadari would die under house arrest in 1986. Ghotbzadeh was accused of plotting the overthrow of the Islamic Republic and executed by firing squad in September 1982. President for a year and a half, Banisadr was never able to rule or match the ruthlessness of the clerics. He fell out of favor fast with the man he had once considered a father figure. Khomeini pushed for his impeachment, and Banisadr went underground to escape jail in June 1981, before slipping out of the country. Bazergan, the founder of the LMI who had resigned during the hostage crisis, and Yazdi, the PhD graduate who had become close to Khomeini in Najaf, became harsh critics, but both survived, staying in Iran. Baraheni, the poet who had written searing verses against the shah, had flown back to Iran the minute Khomeini returned. In the first few months of the revolution, he was on the streets fighting against those who were resisting the birth of a new Iran—not with a pen, but with a gun. He, too, would end up in jail, tortured, and then forced into exile. Mohsen, the believer who had helped found the Revolutionary Guards, would also fall afoul of the clerics and end up in jail, tortured brutally. He would one day return to the United States and reflect, aghast, at what he had helped bring about.

But it was Musa Sadr who had first paid the price for what had been unleashed by men with hopes of freedom. His disappearance was not a mystery for those closest to Khomeini, perhaps even for Khomeini himself (though there is no record of that). After his stop in Tripoli in that fateful month of August 1978, Imam Sadr had been due to travel onward to West Germany for the secret meeting with an envoy of the shah. There were reportedly plans to bring Sadr back to Tehran to lead a moderate religious bloc against Khomeini, perhaps even serve as prime minister in a government under the shah and help save the monarchy. The shah was deeply distressed when news emerged that the imam had disappeared. We don't know if news of the planned secret meeting had reached Khomeini's entourage. Either way, it was clear that Sadr was a threat to the ayatollah's plans. Sadr was the only cleric with the stature and charisma to rival the exiled ayatollah. He was beloved and well known in Qom, with close ties to other key clerics who feared Khomeini, including Taleghani and Shariatmadari. Most of all, Sadr had political experience: he had lived and functioned in the real world, outside the rarefied environment of religious seminaries. The hardline ayatollah Beheshti, Khomeini's close ally, who was supposed to meet Sadr in Tripoli, had instead called Gaddafi and asked him to detain Sadr—victory against the shah felt within grasp and there was no way that Khomeini's acolytes were going to allow anybody to disrupt their path to Tehran. Sadr and his two companions were reportedly detained for a few months in Libya, and by the time Khomeini and Beheshti were busy writing Iran's new Islamic constitution, in the summer of 1979, they did not want him to ever reappear. Years would go by before this information surfaced, from Palestinian sources and US intelligence files; reports implicated Beheshti, but also Arafat, who was said to have had a hand in the disappearance, keen to help eliminate the man who had dared put Lebanon's Shias ahead of the Palestinians.

Who knows how the Iranian Revolution would have unfolded if Imam Sadr had returned to Iran and joined forces with other moderate clerics?

Would the shah have stayed? If Sadr had returned to Iran after the departure of the shah, would he have survived Khomeini's ruthless campaign?
There was nothing preordained about Khomeini's becoming Supreme
Leader in the wilayat al-faqih he had created. That journey required vigi-
lant cunning, constant maneuvering, and the weakness or naive loyalty of
others. The Islamic Republic of Iran was born in a bath of blood, cruelty,
and darkness.

—

Within their borders, Saudi Arabia and Iran seemed to echo each other
with the kind of cultural and social changes they were introducing into
their societies—though the comparison may seem unfair or unbalanced.
Iran had centuries of civilization and culture, including pre-Islamic, that
would continue to resist the Khomeinization of the country. Iran was
ancient Persia; its kings Cyrus and Darius had ruled over the world's first
superpower, centuries before Jesus and Muhammad. The power and size
of the Persian empire naturally changed over time, but much endured.
Though ethnically diverse, a common Persian identity dominated. In contemporary Iran, art, literature, and cinema produced their own distinct
movements, influencing others as much as it was influenced.

The Saudi kingdom prided itself on being the birthplace of Islam but
obscured the rich pre-Islamic past of the Arabian Peninsula dating back
to the Nabataeans. Ancient cities lay forgotten, hidden from the world to
avoid veneration of buildings, especially ones belonging to the age of ignorance, *al-jahiliyya*, that preceded Islam. The ancient, intricate art of fres-
coes and the tradition of men wearing crowns of flowers survived in the
distant villages of southern Asir province, away from the religious police.
Even in the era of the Al-Sauds, before 1979, a daring, avant-garde mayor
of Jeddah had transformed the seaside corniche into the largest open-air
sculpture gallery in the world, commissioning works from the greats of the
era like Joan Miró and Henry Moore. (There were no human representations.) But poetry, literature, and art did not flourish beyond limited circles
in a country shaped by the desert and religion. There were no wild disco
nights in Jeddah, as there had been in Tehran.

In Iran, there was more to stifle and shut down. The onslaught had
to be, and was, systematic, rapid, and widespread; it was a highly organized state-led effort. The country changed in front of people's eyes, as
life retreated indoors. And so there were two revolutions in 1979, one
that made headlines and one that unfurled quietly, a black wave with far-

reaching consequences for millions. These revolutions were amplified by the bitter rivalry that emerged that same year between two countries that had once been allies, a rivalry born out of Khomeini's desire to upstage the Saudis as leaders of the Muslim world.

—

The shah had once courteously referred to King Faisal as *Amir al-Mu'meneen*, the Commander of the Faithful. The portrait of another Saudi king hung in a hotel in Isfahan. When the shah had visited Saudi Arabia on several occasions, he had been greeted by excited crowds along the roads. In Jeddah, little girls and boys draped in the Saudi and Iranian flags had recited poetry about the love between the two Muslim nations. The two countries were both part of the Safari Club, an alliance of intelligence services started in 1976 along with Morocco, Egypt, and France, which fomented anti-Soviet operations and coups from Angola to Afghanistan. The two dynasties—the Pahlavis and the Al-Sauds—had come to power around the same time, and both had to contend with the disruptive effect of the rapid modernization driven by the riches of oil. Until 1979, the secular ambitions of the shah as a regional power and the aspiration of Saudi kings to lead the Muslim world did not clash on the same terrain. And though Sunni Wahhabism was inherently anathema to Shia Islam, the antagonism was contained within the kingdom's border; it did not get in the way of relations between the two states.

When Khomeini returned to Iran, officialdom in Saudi Arabia stayed mum for a few days. They were still worried about Iran turning communist and appalled by how quickly Washington seemed to have abandoned its stalwart ally in Tehran. On February 14, a few days after Khomeini declared victory, Crown Prince Fahd sent Prime Minister Bazergan a congratulatory message, wishing him success and looking forward to cooperation between "our brotherly nations." On February 19, the day of Arafat's visit to Tehran, a big headline on the front page of the Kuwait newspaper *Al Ra'i al Am* declared SAUDI ARABIA PRAISES THE IRANIAN REVOLUTION. The Saudis, reported the paper, were also "warning against anyone undermining the revolution's support for the Arab struggle against the Zionist enemy." The shah's support for Israel had been a sore point in the Saudi relationship with Iran, but now Khomeini was promising to uphold the Palestinian cause. A few months later, Prince Abdallah, the future king of Saudi Arabia, would declare he was very relieved that the new Iran was "making Islam, not heavy armament, the organizer of cooperation" between the two countries. "The Holy Koran is the constitution of both countries," he added. The Saudis saw no reason to worry about Khomeini, a man who was just as puritanical as they were, and promising an Islamic state, albeit a Shia one. The Saudis were likely not aware of Khomeini's lesser-known book published in 1945, *Kashf al-Asrar* (*The Unveiling of Secrets*), in which he had shown nothing but contempt for "the camel grazers of Riyadh and the barbarians of [the Saudi desert of] Najd, the most infamous and the wildest members of the human family." Khomeini felt so strongly about the Saudis that his diatribe against them and Wahhabism was the first section of the book. Soon he would challenge the House of Saud's custodianship of Mecca and Medina.

Throughout 1979, the Saudis were slow to grasp the extent of Khomeini's enmity. The overtures of all the Gulf countries were rebuffed by the Iranians, who lectured them about the rights of Shia minorities in their countries or even the availability of alcohol in places like Bahrain. Khomeini responded by repeatedly labeling the Gulf countries as purveyors of the "American Islam." The Shia uprising in the Eastern Province had been a shock for the Saudis. Some Shias did begin to look to Iran for support. By the end of 1979, the new Saudi policy was to "demote the Iranian Revolution from the status of an all-Muslim one to a purely Shiite one, then to downgrade it to a purely Iranian Shiite one and finally to a revolution of only one party of the Iranian Shias," the ones who followed Khomeini. They were hoping to reduce the revolution to the smallest group possible, but Khomeini now spoke in the name of the whole country.

The Saudis became determined to position themselves as the sole defenders of the Muslim faith, at all cost, and on every front, from education to politics, from culture to the battlefields. In the 1960s and 1970s, King Faisal had deployed his oil dollars to promote religion as a counter to communism and pan-Arab nationalism. Several organizations had been founded, like the World Muslim League, the World Assembly of Muslim Youth (WAMY), and the Organization of Islamic Cooperation. They were all based in Jeddah, and while they were not state organizations, they were mostly Saudi-funded, and they became channels for Saudi influence. A reflection of the king's largesse, the money's impact was limited, neither disruptive nor transformative. Now the same tools were going to be deployed in a much more systematic and focused campaign. In 1962, Saudi funding for WAMY was $250,000 a year. By 1980, the spigot had opened: funding jumped to $13 million. By 1999, WAMY would have spent $22 billion on "services to Islam and Muslims" worldwide, including education and culture. With that money came the expectation of how Islam should be understood or taught, a homogenizing current reverberating from the kingdom to the rest of the Muslim world. The Saudi official discourse became more religious than ever. The more the Saudis lurched to the right, reviving Wahhabism at home and expanding it abroad, the more they provoked the Iranians. Saudi Arabia and Iran would develop their revised identities, their state narratives, in opposition to each other. There would be many front lines.

—

On Christmas Eve 1979, columns of Soviet tanks crossed the border from the Uzbek Soviet Socialist Republic, across the Amu Darya River, and rolled into Afghanistan. At five o'clock on the morning of December 25, the Soviets began a massive airlift of combat troops into Kabul. More than two hundred flights were reported to have landed and departed by two o'clock that afternoon, multiplying the number of Soviet troops in the country from fifteen hundred to six thousand almost overnight.

In the years and decades that followed, that invasion would be remembered as the starting point, a provocation. But it was also a reaction, part of the competition of the Cold War. The score was ever changing: America had lost Vietnam; the proxy war was still raging in Lebanon; but Egypt, as part of its peace dance with Israel, had turned its back to Moscow and joined the US camp. The Soviets could not afford to lose more territory. They had to preserve their hold on Afghanistan, where the Communist Party had seized power in April 1978 but was facing an ongoing insurgency. Some rebel leaders, mostly Islamist, had sheltered in Pakistan, where, by early February 1979, some two thousand were already getting military training. The Saudis had also been pushing the United States to help the insurgents, and even offered to fund the effort. In July 1979, President Carter approved a small program of covert assistance: radio transmitters and propaganda support, no weapons. The small but mounting support for the insurgency was enough to provoke Moscow.

A month after the Soviet invasion, the Saudi intelligence chief Turki al-Faisal, who had just overseen the operation to take down Juhayman in Mecca, traveled to Peshawar. He was briefed on the Afghan resistance by his Pakistani counterparts and visited Afghan refugee camps. The Saudis were worried that the Soviets would push further and invade Pakistan. But they also saw an opportunity: a playground where they could export the countless Juhaymans their system had created, and a noble cause around which these zealots could rally, shifting focus away from the sins of the royal family. Most important, with the House of Saud's credentials as custodians of the two Holy Mosques lying in tatters after the siege, the Saudis could now rebuild their reputation by being the champions of Islam against the godless communists. They could impress the Muslim world with more than just oil money. They could lead the faithful into a holy war. Or at least pay for it.

—

In 1979, Yassin al-Haj Saleh was a third-year medical student at Aleppo University, both hopeful and fearful about the future. His eyes sparkled but drooped slightly; even his smile had an edge of seriousness to it. He was hopeful, because these were heady days of change across the region, and change always carried hope within it, the possibility of a positive outcome. But he was worried because there was violence. The atmosphere at the university was tense, with secret police everywhere and the cult of Syrian president Hafez al-Assad silencing people's minds. Yassin was an active member of the Syrian Communist Party, independent of the Soviets and closer to European communism. The party was fiercely opposed to Assad's dictatorship.

Assad had come to power in a bloodless palace coup in November 1970, building on previous coups by his own party, the nationalist, socialist, and ostensibly secular Baath Party. A former commander of the air force and former defense minister, he came from Syria's tiny Alawite minority, a tenth-century offshoot of Shia Islam deemed heretical by some Muslims. Assad now ruled over a Sunni majority. The Alawites, long Syria's rural downtrodden, were climbing the social and military ladders. Assad had brought relative stability after years of repeated coups; he built schools and brought electricity to poor villages. But this was still an impoverished country, in the Soviet camp with a socialist economy. The Baath Party had been ruthless from the start in quelling all opposition, and Assad was no different. The struggle against Israel was used to justify everything: it was why military expenditures were so high, draining the state coffers. In the face of the enemy, the nation had to close ranks, and no one was allowed to speak out and demand freedom. Prisons were filling up. Resentment was building, and simmering social unrest also pushed young Sunnis into the arms of the Islamists.

In 1973, Assad announced a new constitution, which for the first time in Syria's history did not require the president of Syria to be a Muslim. The Muslim Brotherhood organized protests in Hama against the secular

Baathists. The riots spread to large cities like Homs and Aleppo. Assad backed down and amended the constitution, though he rejected demands that Islam become the religion of the state. Unrest continued for years, building up with hit-and-run acts of violence against Alawite officers, doctors, sheikhs, and intellectuals. The violence was not all Islamist. Local gangs of young men, disenfranchised losers, school dropouts, all those alienated by the oppression of Assad, were also engaged in the popular insurgency. The opposition to Assad was political and peaceful, with protests, union strikes, and student marches in cities across the country. But the dictator was ruthless.

"The good are silent, and violence has spiraled as the government's secret police have viciously repressed dissent or potential dissent," wrote an American professor, Samuel Pickering Jr., who was in Syria in 1979 with his wife, on a Fulbright grant, teaching English in the coastal town of Lattakiah. "At times during the year, Aleppo and Hama seemed foreign countries brought back under Damascus's rule only by tank law. 'You don't know,' a student told me with tears in her eyes. 'The people die like rain.'"

Then came a declaration of war against Assad. One June 16, 1979, possibly inspired by events in Iran, a Sunni captain at the Aleppo artillery academy and a squad of gunmen fired on uniformed cadets, most of them Alawites. Government-run newspapers didn't report it until a week later, putting the death toll at thirty-two, with no mention of the sectarian targeting. Even before the news was printed, Yassin had felt fear in the air. There were even more security forces on the street, more checkpoints. Unofficial sources had put the toll of the artillery school massacre at eighty-three. The Brotherhood would always deny any involvement, but the Assad regime still blamed them and launched a widespread clampdown on the group, netting hundreds and executing dozens. Assad would furthermore claim that all of the opposition to his rule was nothing more than an Islamist insurgency, using that as an excuse to silence all his critics.

Sa'id Hawwa, the Brotherhood ideologue who had gone to Tehran in May 1979 to meet Khomeini, was in exile in Jordan, still waiting for the ayatollah's help. There would be no answer. In 1982, the Assad regime would crush the Muslim Brotherhood by leveling whole parts of the city of Hama and killing more than fifteen thousand people. Hawwa and the Syrian Brotherhood would never forget, nor forgive, Khomeini and Iran for abandoning them. After praising Khomeini and his revolution, Hawwa would soon begin to lambast the ayatollah as a danger to the Sunni Muslim world.

Khomeini may have been an Islamic revolutionary, but he was pragmatic, as politically shrewd as he was ruthless. He supported Islamists,
Sunni or Shia, who could serve in his anti-Western, anti-Israeli front—and
always on his terms. He would even help revolutionaries with dubious
Islamic credentials (like Arafat), so long as they served his purposes. He
had no use for pro-American leaders like Sadat, but Assad was already in
his camp. Together they would form what would be known as the axis of
resistance for decades ahead. Assad, in turn, had learned a lesson from
watching the shah diddle: crush your opponents ruthlessly. And with a
new ally in Iran, the Syrian president saw the potential of a Shia-Alawite
geographical axis, with which to scare and blackmail countries like Saudi
Arabia.

Before even graduating, Yassin was arrested. He had been in hiding
for two months but the security forces found him on December 7, 1980,
at one in the morning. He was clearly not an Islamist—he was as secular
as they came—but everyone who opposed Assad was a target, including
the left. Hundreds were arrested. Across the region, leaders differed about
how to handle the rise of Islamic fervor, but they all agreed on one thing:
leftists and communists were a threat to their grip on power and therefore had to be crushed. The intellectuals, the writers, the student activists
were still an alternative to the authoritarian rulers, with ideas and ideals.
Yassin would spend sixteen years in Assad's darkest dungeons. Once out
of prison, he would rise as one of Syria's foremost intellectuals, advocating
relentlessly and fearlessly for inclusive democracy. But he would find that,
as the decades went on, the enemies of freedom multiplied within his own
country, as did the battlefronts. By 2013, his struggle, and that of millions
of Syrians, against dictatorship would be submerged by the Saudi-Iran
rivalry. He would witness how Iran would again stand in the Assad camp,
knees deep in blood.

———

In the summer of 1979, Saddam Hussein decided it was time to consolidate his rule. He knew the ayatollah and the pull this man could have on
Iraq's Shia community. He forced his cousin, the aging and ailing president
Ahmad Hassan al-Bakr, to resign, and on July 16, 1979, Saddam became
the fifth president of Iraq. He went on to crush anyone who represented
an alternative. He squeezed the Shias tighter, expelling hundreds to Iran,
putting clerics under house arrest. They had no recourse anymore against

the brutality of the Baath regime. They were now stuck between two crazy men: Saddam and Khomeini. The Iraqi president also dismantled the backbone of a progressive Iraqi society, the left, by harassing and jailing people in droves: intellectuals, professors, journalists, artists, women's activists—all went into exile. Finally, he went after Kurds, pursuing guerrilla fighters even across the border into Iran, with air raids. Saddam was hollowing out his own society.

There was one group that had been forming that Saddam couldn't quite figure out. They dabbled in religion, they organized around prayer, they preached. Though they declared the secularism of the Baath Party to be heresy, there were no calls to overthrow him. He rounded some of them up and charged them with illegally organizing a charity. They would be released after a few years, then jailed again. In prison, they'd recruit others, form cells, and expand their network through the country's mosques. They called themselves al-Muwahidoun, those who enforce absolute monotheism, just as Ibn Abdelwahhab had preached. They revered one man: Sheikh Abdelaziz bin Baz. They called him *al-sheikh al-waled*, the father sheikh. Saddam's oppression was not sectarian per se at the outset; he focused his ire on the Shias because as the oppressed majority they were the greatest threat to his grip on power. Meanwhile, the Muwahidoun would continue to grow, organize, preach, and lay low. Their time would come.

On April 1, 1980, Saddam's vice president, Tariq Aziz, escaped an assassination attempt in Baghdad. Iraq blamed Shia activists backed by Iran. Saddam chose the targets of his retribution carefully. On April 8, 1980, Ayatollah Mohammad Baqer al-Sadr and his sister Amina bint al-Huda al-Sadr were executed. Sadr had founded the Islamic party Da'wa (Islamic Call), modeled after the Egyptian Muslim Brotherhood. He was the only leading cleric in Najaf who had openly supported Khomeini's wilayat al-faqih, and he had been agitating against the Iraqi government, issuing religious edicts against joining the Baath Party. His supporters described him as the future Khomeini of Iraq. Now he was a martyr. Khomeini called for the overthrow of Saddam.

On August 6, 1980, Saddam went on a surprise twenty-four-hour visit to Saudi Arabia to meet King Khaled at his summer retreat in Taef, in the cool six-thousand-foot-high mountains outside Mecca. Saddam rarely traveled; this was his first foreign trip as president and the first visit of an Iraqi president to Saudi Arabia since the overthrow of the Iraqi monarchy in 1958. Iraq was in the Soviet camp, and Moscow was the country's chief supplier of arms. Iraq didn't even have formal diplomatic ties with America. The state-run newspapers in Saudi Arabia and Iraq gave the usual bland reports: the leaders had discussed affairs in the Gulf and Arab unity in the face of the Zionist enemy. Israel had just unilaterally annexed East Jerusalem and declared Jerusalem the undivided eternal capital of the Jewish state. This was in contravention of international law and UN resolutions. Mostly, it rubbed salt in the Arab wound. Crown Prince Fahd called for a holy war against Israel.

Instead, at noon on September 22, Saddam declared war on Iran. Two hundred Soviet-made Iraqi jets bombed dozens of targets inside Iran. Iraqi tanks and ten thousand infantry soldiers crossed into Iranian territory at nine points along the border. The Saudis always denied they had given Saddam a green light, but the timing of his visit to Taef remains a mystery. Perhaps it involved nothing more than a silent nod of acquiescence to finding ways to contain Khomeini. Either way, within a year, Gulf countries had given oil-rich, prosperous Iraq a $14 billion loan to help war efforts. The battle lines were drawn: Jordan sent volunteers to fight with Saddam. Kuwait and Saudi Arabia continued to give him billions. The ranks of Iraq's army were filled with Shias who fought for their country—this was a war between nations. Syria sided with Iran. Chamran was Iran's defense minister, and several hundred of his former comrades from Amal in Lebanon flew to Iran to fight by his side. They left when he was killed in 1981 on the battlefront. They had idolized him but could not relate to Khomeini's Iran. There were rumors that Chamran had in fact been shot in the back, another treacherous act in the campaign to eliminate Khomeini's rivals.

An Iraqi military assessment had declared Iran weak and isolated, unable to defend itself or conduct offensive operations. Most of all, it did not have powerful friends. Saddam thought he could win the war quickly and easily, emerge even more powerful while cutting Khomeini's ambitions down to size. But the war was a gift for the ayatollah, who could now use it to solidify his grip on the country in the face of an external enemy, sending thousands of young Iranians, boys even, to their deaths. Old wounds, long buried and forgotten, were reopened by Saddam and Khomeini, two men with delusions of grandeur reaching into ancient Persian and Arab history to justify their modern murderous campaigns. The mighty Persian Sassanid Empire had succumbed to Arab conquest in 636 during the Battle of al-Qadisiyya. Now, over a millennium later, Khomeini and Saddam wanted a redo. Or revenge. Iraq would begin to refer to the war as Saddam's Qadisiyya. And so began an eight-year conflict, one that would devastate Iran and provoke and solidify deep fissures in the region. If 1979 was a turning point, 1980 was the point of no return.

—

In 1980, the shah was still roaming the earth, a monarch without a country. After his quick stop in Aswan in 1979, he had traveled onward to Morocco, the Bahamas, Mexico, and New York, seeking refuge and medical attention. His admission to the United States for medical care had triggered the hostage crisis in Tehran. Fearing extradition, the shah had flown to Panama and finally landed back in Egypt, in March 1980. Sadat thought Cairo would provide his friend a good base to mount a counterrevolution, or at least wait for the demise of a man Sadat had dismissed as a crazy cleric who was bound to fall soon. But in Egypt, too, there were those who looked to Iran and felt inspired by the ayatollah.

PART II

COMPETITION

5

I KILLED THE PHARAOH

EGYPT

1977–81

Do not reconcile
Even if it is written in the stars
And the astrologers break the news to you
I would have forgiven if I had died inadvertently
Do not reconcile
Until existence returns to orbit . . .
And the martyr to his waiting daughter.

—Amal Dunqul, "Do Not Reconcile" (1976)

Nageh Ibrahim was in awe of the Iranian Revolution, mesmerized by the masses on the street and the sight of people power at work, bringing down a tyrant, a traitor to his people and to Palestine. The medical student with the bushy black beard and intelligent eyes was in his final year at the Asyut University in Upper Egypt. He watched the news reports of the crowds thronging the streets for weeks, the departure of the shah, the triumphant return of Ayatollah Khomeini, and the exhilarating victory of Islam. He liked what he saw—it gave him and his friends ideas. The year of the revolution was also the year of *Migrant Birds*, a blockbuster starring the actress Shams al-Baroudi that was showing in all the cinemas. Nageh didn't watch that.

No one had banned the film, no one had stopped Nageh from going to the movies or burned down the theater. This was neither revolutionary Iran nor puritanical Saudi Arabia. As a child, Nageh had read Shakespeare and Agatha Christie; he had listened to the concerts of Umm Kulthum on the radio every first Thursday of the month, like millions of Egyptians in the country. Daughter of a cleric, named after a daughter of the prophet, Umm Kulthum had developed her singing skills reciting the Quran as a child. From the 1930s until her death in 1975, the woman known as Kawkab al

Sharq, the Star of the Orient, sang about undying and unrequited love. She also sang about war and nationhood. She ruled the Arab world with her voice; her concerts brought millions to tears and her country to a standstill.

In the years since the Six-Day War, there had been much upheaval in Egypt. Nasser had died in 1970, and Sadat had taken over and moved Egypt from the Soviet camp to the American camp. He had gone to Jerusalem and made peace with Israel. His aggressive reforms, copying the West, and economic programs, which led to solid growth but also deep inequalities, were causing much angst and poverty, a sense of dislocation, similar to what Iran had experienced. The country's pride was still mortally wounded from the loss of territory to Israel. This had led Nageh, and many others, in search of answers down a more militant path where there was no lei-sure reading and no music. Nageh had always been devout; by 1979 he was a fundamentalist, a founding member of the recently formed Gama'a Islamiyya, or Islamic Group, that sought the strict application of Islamic laws in society. He disapproved of cinema and all this acting nonsense. He was restless.

Shams al-Baroudi, the actress, came from a different world. She was one of Egypt's biggest movie stars. A brunette with long hair, she was glamorous and made heads spin. In *Migrant Birds*, she played the role of a young working woman who follows a co-worker to Australia for love. Even the movie poster was offensive in the eyes of Islamists: Baroudi in a low-cut pink dress, leaning against a man kissing her on the cheek. It didn't matter that the man in question was her husband in real life. Egypt's actresses were among the best in the Middle East, beloved across the region and in their own country. Frank Sinatra concerts by the pyramids were for the elite, but everyone went to the movies in Egypt, for slapstick comedies or social dramas. Once frowned upon as a profession, an acting career was what little girls now dreamed of. In a region with different Arabic dialects, Egyptian crossed all borders as the lingua franca during the golden age of Egyptian cinema, from the 1940s to the early 1970s. By the 1950s, Egypt's movie industry was the world's third largest—the Arab world's Hollywood.

Everyone had their favorite actress. There were the adoring fans of Baroudi, prolific with a vast repertoire; there was Egypt's Cinderella, Soad Hosny, with her lustrous auburn hair and disco dance moves; others pre-ferred the daring Madiha Kamel, who could undulate à la Marilyn Mon-roe. She played the role of a spy in France in a 1978 movie that included a scene showing her in a demure but clearly amorous embrace in bed with another woman. Then there was Faten Hamama, the classy doyenne who had started acting in 1939, at the age of seven, encouraged by her math-ematician father. She was elegant and soft-spoken and gave interviews in perfect French. She was something of an ingénue, but she had political opinions and she believed in her role as an agent of social change and in movies as social critique. She was always pushing the boundaries in a tra-ditional society that was slowly opening up.

In 1975, Hamama had played the role of Doria, a woman seeking a divorce from her abusive husband—a difficult proposition in Egypt, which at the time afforded only men the right to ask for a divorce. *I Want a Solu-tion*, one of the gems of Egyptian cinema, was selected as the country's entry for an Academy Award, provoking a discussion about the status of women in Egypt. By early 1979, with much prodding from First Lady Jehane Sadat, the president issued a decree amending the personal status law: women could now demand and be granted a divorce in certain cases. The period was not free of censorship, and a lot of the progressive, secular art was also the result of state support and funding. Nasser even cultivated Umm Kulthum as an asset to the state, and some of her songs lauded the nation.

Egypt's women were pioneers, the leading lights of Arab feminism, which carved a space for itself within a conservative society, not outside of it. They founded the region's first feminist union in 1923 and started national newspapers, like the actress and journalist Rose al-Youssef and her eponymous publication in 1925; they were filmmakers like Aziza Amir, who produced *Leila* in 1927, the first long feature film in Egypt. In the late 1970s, women were rising in the workforce and held senior positions in ministries.

Amir, Hamama, Baroudi, filmmakers, feminism, the right to divorce, working women—it was all a parallel universe, almost a different coun-try from the one Nageh inhabited. University campuses had always been hotbeds of activism in Egypt, keeping up with the movements of their time: liberalism, anticolonialism, nationalism, or socialism. Now it was Islamism. Nageh and his friends pursued their goal of an Islamic soci-ety on campus relentlessly. They began to demand segregation wherever they could, imposed prayer time before classes, stopped music classes, organized public prayers on Friday on university campuses. They were a slowly growing force, filling a void left by the shrinking left and the Muslim Brotherhood, which Nasser had banned in 1954. The Brothers had been rounded up or exiled; most had gone to Saudi Arabia. But in the 1970s, students from the Islamic Group and other Islamists had found an unexpected ally in President Sadat, who gave them almost free rein.

After Nasser had died of a heart attack in 1970, Sadat, his vice president, stepped in as acting president. He was supposed to hold the position for only sixty days but lasted longer than anyone expected. As he solidified his power, his every move seemed driven by the obsession to step out of Nasser's gigantic shadow. Sadat was the focus of many jokes at the beginning of his time in power.

> Sadat's presidential limousine stops at a traffic light.
>
> Sadat asks the driver: And here, which way did Nasser turn?
>
> The driver answers: To the left, Mr. President.
>
> Sadat instructs his driver to signal left and then turn right.

Others described Sadat as walking in Nasser's footsteps, but with an eraser. Nasser had rid the country of the monarchy and the colonial powers. He nationalized the economy. Sadat would usher in what he called *infitah*, economic openness. He loosened the rules, liberalized the economy, and encouraged private and foreign investment. Where Nasser exhorted his countrymen to join together to build up the country, Sadat encouraged the migration of Egyptians to neighboring countries, especially the oil-rich Gulf, to send home remittances. Nasser was a reluctant warrior. Sadat took the Israelis by surprise and launched a war to snatch the Sinai back in October 1973. He didn't win, but the initial success of the attack restored some national pride.

But the titanic shift that truly altered the geopolitics of the Middle East at the height of the Cold War was Sadat's decision to make friends with America. Sadat believed that Nasser had bankrupted Egypt by being a Soviet ally and turning his back on the West. Even worse, Soviet backing had not helped deliver victory against Israel. Sadat was convinced that only America could help regain lost Arab land. Ties with the United States, broken off after the Six-Day War, were restored on November 7, 1973, barely two weeks after the cease-fire with the Israelis. Sadat hosted the American secretary of state, Henry Kissinger, in Cairo and began calling him "my friend Kissinger." There were rumblings in the pro-Soviet, anti-imperial camp that included Syria, Iraq, and Libya.

Sadat was making smaller adjustments that were just as significant as his rapprochement with America. He was surrounded by a staunchly Nasserist bureaucracy. He was not the orator that his predecessor had been, but he was ruling at a time when the country needed direction and a sense of purpose. He believed religion would provide an answer to both of those problems. Sadat conducted a purge of Nasserists not only by removing some of them but also by unleashing against them what he believed was the benign force of Islamism, including Salafists. And he molded himself into the "Believer President," encouraging public displays of piety and making sure pictures were taken of him at Friday prayers. Nasser's speeches had started with a grandiose *Ayyuha al muwatinun*, O my fellow citizens; Sadat now began his addresses with *Bismillah al Rahman al Raheem*, In the name of God the most Beneficent the most Merciful. In a nation that felt adrift amid economic upheaval and geopolitical shifts, religion was a tool to help shore up Sadat's own legitimacy.

He was not putting on an act. The president was in fact pious, as was his wife, Jehane. Sadat prayed and fasted; he had a Swiss watch with a compass pointing in the direction of Mecca. He was a village boy who had studied with a *kuttab*, a tutor in traditional village schools focused on teaching the Quran, and he knew all the verses of the Muslim holy book. He recited them in a recording to be left for his children and grandchildren—the word of God, spoken by Sadat.

But he was inadvertently planting the seeds for a trend that would long outlast him. Egypt's transformation was a prime example of how local dynamics would become exacerbated and magnified by the Iranian Revolution. Sadat was altering the fine balance between private piety and public policy, injecting religion into politics. In September 1971, he had already amended the constitution by making the shari'a a source of legislation. In 1980, a year after the Iranian Revolution, he would make it "the principal" source of legislation—a change no future leader would ever dare undo, for fear of being branded an enemy of Islam. And during the decade in between, Sadat unthinkingly assisted and enabled a new generation of activist Islamists, some of whom would later embrace violence.

Although Sadat had not allowed the Muslim Brotherhood to reconstitute as a group legally, he had relaxed restrictions, allowing their publication *Al-Da'wa* to circulate again, and going as far as releasing some of them from prison. But the Brothers were not the power they once were, and a younger, more impatient, and more militant generation of Islamists was spinning off from their legacy. This was the terrain that Nageh's group, the

Gama'a, was reclaiming. The president wanted to rid university campuses, hotbeds of activism, of all traces of Nasser and all possible challenges to his rule. In the name of democracy, he allowed Islamist groupings to run in student elections—with heavy support from the security services.

By the end of 1979, just as Khomeini was imposing his wilayat al-faqih on Iran, the Gama'a had won control of student unions in most of the big universities across the country, from Alexandria to Asyut. The Islamists had been proselytizing heavily on campuses, keen to eradicate the sinful secularism of socialists and communists. They were well organized and provided services for newcomers to the big city. At a time of great migration and urbanization in Egypt and across the Arab world, the rural-urban tension provided a soft spot that Islamists everywhere were able to exploit. In Egypt, they targeted lower-class and lower-middle-class students, children of middle- or low-ranking bureaucrats who had moved from villages and small towns to big cities where they had no family or relatives. The Gama'a offered a new tribe and a sense of belonging in the city, a soft landing. Many of the Gama'a cadres, like Nageh's, were high-achieving students in the medical and engineering departments. Many of those who were joining and would become leading names of the Islamist movement had started out as young socialists and Nasserists. They were young, disillusioned, and looking for direction. The Gama'a provided similar ideals—patriotism, loyalty to Palestine, belief in the armed struggle against Israel—in a new, appealing packaging that included discipline, prayer, and the promise of salvation thrown in. Seemingly overnight, socialist summer camps were renamed after Abu Bakr al-Siddiq, the first caliph after the prophet. Across the Middle East, the left in its various shades—progressive, secular, socialist, nationalist—was being beaten into oblivion. In Egypt, it dissolved into thin air. New generations of Arabs would grow up without the chaotic but fertile plethora of political parties and ideologies that had enriched the minds of their parents. The choice was now dictatorship or Islam, or worse: the dictatorship *of* Islam. Sadat thought he was using the Islamists, but in fact they were using him, and he was accumulating the mistakes, feeding their rage.

He was obsessed with getting back the Sinai. He had tried war; it didn't work. He would then try peace. The man everyone had underestimated as Nasser's shadow was proving himself a daring leader who could make brash decisions and theatrical moves. No one knows for sure when and how the idea of traveling to Israel first came to him. There had been secret diplomatic contacts with the Israelis in September 1977, but such an approach to peace would be slow. Sadat opted to take the enemy by surprise. On November 9, 1977, during an address to the Egyptian parliament, he launched a trial balloon: "I will go the ends of the earth for peace, even to the Knesset itself." He found a willing partner on the other side: Menachim Begin, the country's first-ever prime minister from the right-wing Likud party. The hawk felt he could risk peace overtures. On November 18, 1977, Sadat flew to Tel Aviv. More than two thousand journalists were covering the visit, and the world was transfixed. On the tarmac, an Israeli army officer saluted the Egyptian leader. Sadat then inspected the guard of honor of the Israeli Defense Forces. In Jerusalem, he spoke at the Knesset. Israeli army radio played Umm Kulthum. Arafat was furious.

Egyptians were initially euphoric. The welcome reception Sadat got in Cairo after his two-day visit to enemy territory was rapturous—much of it perhaps organized by the state, but it didn't matter. There was deep relief that true peace might be in sight, for a country exhausted by repeated wars. "Sadat, Sadat! The man of peace!" chanted Cairenes, as Sadat drove through the city in an open-top limousine.

But across the Arab world and beyond, rage had quickly replaced the initial incredulity. There were protests on the streets of Beirut; the Egyptian embassies came under attack in Tripoli and in Athens. Newspapers in Iraq and Syria declared it the "trip of treachery and shame," denouncing Sadat for destroying Arab unity and unilaterally recognizing the "Zionist entity." Lebanon's leftist *As-Safir* newspaper highlighted Sadat's isolation in the Arab world and called on Syria, Libya, and the PLO to close ranks against Israel and Sadat. This was the moment when Arafat had first connected with Khomeini, thanks to his cleric friend Hani Fahs. The Saudis were irritated but kept their distance—they neither denounced nor applauded, but secretly King Khaled had prayed that Sadat's plane would crash on the way to Tel Aviv.

When Sadat launched peace talks with Israel in 1978, Syria and the PLO began to clamor to eject Egypt from the Arab League, even pushing for sanctions. The Saudis were privately supportive of Sadat's efforts but publicly silent, waiting to see whether the Egyptian negotiations would also deliver for the Palestinians and the rest of the region. They shielded Sadat from diplomatic retribution and took out their checkbooks to provide billions of dollars to silence the dissenters: Jordan, Syria, and the PLO, the Arabs with land occupied by Israel. When Sadat signed his bilateral peace treaty with the Israelis on the White House lawn, on March 26, 1979, he had recovered the Sinai, but he had also made concessions, including acquiescing to full diplomatic relations with Israel. The peace treaty with Israel made no mention of the Palestinians: it was a purely bilateral, and a very final, accord. And although there was a side letter about Palestinian autonomy in the West Bank and the Gaza Strip, with no discussion of Jerusalem, the Palestinians, and especially Arafat, felt betrayed. These discussions had taken place without them, and they didn't want to settle for autonomy, they wanted statehood. Sadat had irrevocably shattered the united Arab front in the face of Israel, and had chosen a bad time to do so. Immersed in his pursuit of peace, Sadat had failed to recognize how the region around him had changed since his trip to Jerusalem. Khomeini was now in Tehran, and Arafat had a new best friend.

On March 31, a few days after Sadat had signed the peace treaty, Arafat arrived in Baghdad to attend the Arab League summit, fresh off his victory lap in Tehran and ready to lead the charge against Sadat with other hardliners, like Syria's Assad. He publicly predicted Sadat would be assassinated. He demanded that Arab countries cut all diplomatic and economic ties with Cairo. Saudi Arabia's foreign minister Saud al-Faisal rejected it as "empty out-bidding, slogans and rhetoric." The talks went on for three tense days. The dispute between the PLO and the Saudis flared into the open, until one evening Arafat walked out of the session. Saudi Arabia was being shown up as weak and too compromising. Unable to sway the hardliners, Saudi Arabia had to join them: Arab countries cut ties with Egypt, ejecting it from the Arab League and moving the league's headquarters from Cairo to Tunis. Not to be outdone, a month later, Khomeini also cut diplomatic ties with Egypt. Sadat found himself isolated in the region but seemed to care little. He dismissed the leaders of Gulf monarchies as a small clique with no cultural, economic, or political relevance. And he mocked Khomeini as a lunatic madman who had "turned Islam into a mockery," an impostor who he predicted would soon be overthrown in a coup.

When Saudi Arabia looked to Egypt, it saw a regional rival with whom it sparred and had fought in the past but that was essentially in its camp of moderates. But when Khomeini looked at Egypt, he saw a country ripe for an Islamic revolution. On the streets of Tehran came calls for the death of Sadat. Parallels were drawn between the shah and Sadat, as well as between the two countries, economically and politically. And in the early days of the revolution, before the American hostage crisis, Yazdi had described the Iranian Revolution as an inspiration for other countries, including Pakistan or even Saudi Arabia. "The success of the Islamic revolution has shown our Arab neighbors that Islam provides the ideological basis for change . . .

All Islamic movements that were dormant or apologetic in their approach will come out in the open in the Arab and Muslim world." Khomeini went further in an interview with the US media: "I demand that the Egyptian people try to overthrow [Sadat] just as we did the shah."

The parallels between Sadat and the shah were indeed many: Westernized, with progressive first ladies, cornerstones of American strategy in the region, friends of Israel, imperial, and authoritarian. The more Sadat Westernized his country, as the shah had done with his, the more fundamentalism spread, as it had in Iran. However, unlike the shah, Sadat never turned his back on the clerical establishment or religion itself. Sadat kept insisting, in public and in private, that his country was not Iran, that there would be no Khomeini in Egypt. All the while, he was starting to believe there was a conspiracy against him. The comparison became even harder to deny when the shah arrived in Egypt on March 25, 1980, seeking haven and medical attention, and the two men stood side by side at the airport. Sadat, invoking Arab hospitality and loyalty to the man who had been a good friend, offered him permanent asylum. There were protests everywhere, from Cairo to Asyut. At Asyut University, Nageh helped organize the largest protest Egypt had seen in recent memory—certainly the largest by Islamist forces. More than twelve thousand people descended onto the streets, protesting the arrival of the Iranian monarch. There were clashes and one protester died. In Nageh's mind, it felt like a turning point, like the first spark of a bigger confrontation to come. The shah's stay was short—he died a few months later and was buried in Cairo with great pomp. But the damage to Sadat was done.

For many Egyptians, removed from the gruesome details marring the birth of the Islamic Republic, the Iranian Revolution had been the stuff of dreams. Leftists saw only the power of the masses bringing down a tyrant—like the one oppressing them—as well as a new era of social justice. Inspired by what they saw unfold in Iran, some Egyptian women put on the veil to signal rejection of their own Westernizing ruler. Nageh and his friends saw the ultimate victory of Islam and a country that was now on the righteous path, a model Islamic society. Khomeini had shown that the future did not have to be a secular, Westernized society; it did not have to include friends of America like the shah. Or Sadat.

> *Good morning dear Tehran . . . Good morning of victory . . .*
> *of reaching the goal. We sang our joy, we told poems, we rode*
> *our dreams . . .*

Thus went the ode to revolutionary Iran in the words of Egypt's poet of the people Ahmad Fouad Negm. Sung in irreverent verses by his partner, the hugely popular blind singer Sheikh Imam, "Good Morning Tehran" was hummed across the Arab world.

Iran's revolution raised many questions for Islamists in Egypt: Why can't we replicate this here? Why is the opposition in Egypt unable to channel revulsion at the establishment into a similar uprising that will overthrow the government? Islamist students concluded it was a structural problem. The religious establishment in Iran was independent of the government; it was much more organized, with a long history of activism against the ruler. In Egypt, the religious establishment was subservient to the government. The country's highest Islamic institution, Al-Azhar, had never played much of an opposition role, even against British colonialism. Every government since the 1800s had tried to control Al-Azhar, but Nasser had understood the challenge such an institution could pose to his rule as he struggled against the Muslim Brotherhood. He practically turned it into an arm of the state, putting the government in control of its finances and the president in charge of appointing its leadership. Outside Al-Azhar, there were rabble-rousing preachers, like Abd al-Hamid Kishk, whose sermons were copied onto cassette tapes that sold tens of thousands—the ones that Jamal Khashoggi was listening to in Jeddah. But Kishk was no Khomeini. And yet the maelstrom of forces at play in 1979 was about to produce another small but key event: a meeting between two young university graduates. This pair of Islamists would introduce violence to the national stage, changing the course of Egypt's history and of political Islam.

—

Karam Zuhdi was a twenty-seven-year-old agricultural studies graduate who came from a poor, conservative family and was now focused on studying Islamic law. He was one of the founding members of the Gama'a, but he was an impatient man—proselytizing was slow work. Mohammad Abd al-Salam Farag was the same age, an electrical engineer working as an administrator at Cairo University. Thin and wiry, with a short, neatly trimmed beard, Farag was a restless reactionary; in his sermons in mosques, he preached revolution. He was inspired by the great ideologues of his youth: Sayyid Qutb of the Egyptian Muslim Brotherhood, who had been executed in 1966, and Abu A'la al-Mawdudi, the founder of Pakistan's Jamaat-e Islami. Qutb had been introduced to Mawdudi's ideas through one of the Pakistani thinker's disciples, and while in prison Qutb had read a copy of Mawdudi's book *The Four Expressions*. He had been deeply affected by it, and he expanded in his own writings on key concepts elaborated by Mawdudi, such as the idea that the *jahiliyya*, the pagan era of ignorance before Islam, had not in fact ended with the prophet Muhammad, because no ruler was truly governing according to the tenets of Islam. The answer, in Mawdudi's eyes, had to be the *hakimiyya*, the rule of God, or God's sovereignty, through the full application of God's word: the Quran. Khomeini had opted for revolution, but Mawdudi believed a true state of Islam would be born when society, through slow methodical proselytizing and education, embraced the shari'a by itself. Even Qutb—though he asked urgently in his writings "What is to be done?"—counseled patience.

Farag had no patience: the answer was action now. In his eyes, Egyptian society had already embraced religion and was basically sound. The problem was with the rulers: remove them and a true Islamic society would be revealed. He published a badly, quickly written book compiling the wisdom of past radical theologians and called it *Neglected Duty*. That duty, the obligation of every Muslim, was jihad, a pressing call to action to remove leaders who were not ruling through shari'a. In Arabic, *jihad* means "to strive or struggle," and in a religious context the greater jihad is the constant struggle against evil to conform to God's ideals, while the lesser jihad in Islam is the military struggle to defend the religion or the community. Taken further by Salafist jihadists it becomes a war to impose a single interpretation of God's ideals and an Islamic society. Farag had Sadat in his sights, and he'd persuaded Zuhdi and the Gama'a to join him on this mission. Qutb would forever be known as the learned ideologue whose erudite writing inspired generations of Salafists and jihadists. But it was Farag who had written the pamphlet to action and founded the Islamic Jihad, the same organization that Ayman Zawahiri, of future al-Qaeda infamy, would take over in the 1980s.

Inspired by Iran, angry at their own country, Islamists started hoarding weapons. Violence was in the air. The dividends of peace with Israel and friendship with America were nowhere to be seen other than in television ads for fancy products most Egyptians could not afford to buy. Corruption was endemic, the gap between rich and poor growing rapidly, and mismanagement of the economy was a disaster: Egypt, a country that had been an exporter of agriculture goods, was now reliant on imports for half its foodstuffs. Opposition to the peace treaty was building.

"Shaking with fear, shaking with fear," went Negm's poem. "Those who danced in Carter's lap, those who traveled to Golda Meir, they are shaking with fear."

In early September 1981, sensing danger, Sadat launched a purge. He ordered a wave of arrests, netting some three thousand people, not only Islamists but also leading leftists and socialists as well, including the feminist activist Nawal al-Saadawi and the renowned journalist and author Mohammad Heikal. Sadat had managed to unite a very disparate group of people who had one thing in common: opposition to his peace treaty with Israel.

Sadat, the imperial president, stood his ground, giving speeches and interviews to defend his actions. He only made things worse. After having harassed and hounded the left all this time, he was mocking the Islamists he had enabled. He derided the women who wore the full Islamic cloak, "going about like black tents," and banned the *niqab*, the face veil with a slit for the eyes; he dissolved all religious student organizations and shut down the summer camps of Islamist groups. And finally he declared there would be "no politics in religion and no religion in politics." Sadat stooped even lower: he attacked a popular preacher, Sheikh Ahmad al-Mahallawi, the voice of the poor, whose sermons on cassette tapes sold like hotcakes and who had criticized the First Lady. "Now this lousy sheikh finds himself thrown into a prison cell, like a dog."

Nageh and his friends in the Gama'a Farag and Zuhdi, as well as the Jihad, were choking with rage. Years later, Nageh would wonder what would have happened if the Islamists had somehow found a way to accept Sadat's peace treaty. The president would likely have acquiesced to many of their other demands, which would have paved the way to their ultimate goal: an Islamic republic to rival Iran. The Gama'a would not have needed to resort to violence; so much would have been different. But in those fall weeks of 1981, the autumn of fury, in those weeks, Nageh and his comrades in the Gama'a were about to sanction the ultimate violent act: the assassination of a leader. Sadat had committed so many mistakes, he had signed his own death warrant.

Farag and Zuhdi had evaded capture when Sadat launched his wave of arrests. They were both on the run, as were Nageh and Abboud Zomor, a decorated army officer who was also a founding member of the Jihad. Farag had broken his leg escaping the police. They all felt hunted by their enemy. It didn't matter that leftists and Nasserists had also been arrested. Islamists felt that they were the ultimate target and they feared a repeat of the 1954 clampdown by Nasser that had decimated the ranks of the Brotherhood and fed their feverish anger with tales of torture in prison—this was a question of survival; they had to strike first, and strike hard.

The heightened sense of danger accelerated the process; the opportunity was around the corner: a military parade on October 6, in which a young officer who had befriended Farag a year prior would be participating. Khaled Islambouli came from a nationalist and conservative family, in a very Egyptian way: he had gone to a missionary school; his sisters were all university graduates. But the twenty-four-year-old was also a typical recruit of Islamists: the son of a lawyer in a small town, recently arrived in Cairo and looking for a new tribe. Farag had taken Islambouli under his wing and given him a copy of *Neglected Duty*. Islambouli was devout but raised no suspicion among his superiors—though his brother had been picked up in the wave of arrests. He didn't need to do any secret scouting: he had participated in previous military parades and there would soon be a rehearsal before this year's event. He reported back to Farag the evening of the rehearsal: he could pull it off. Zomor, the army officer, wanted to wait. He didn't think Islambouli could carry out the attack. But more important, he envisioned a much broader plan to take over the country, killing its key leaders and seizing army headquarters as well as state radio and television. This required at least two years of preparation, just as it had in Iran, with the building of determined revolutionary committees that would organize protests so large that the army and police would be overwhelmed. But Farag was confident that the assassination of Sadat would create a whole new set of circumstances: it would free the people from their fear, they would "rise as the Iranian masses had risen," and other pillars of the state would consequently fall. Farag overturned Zomor's objection and Islambouli convinced the others he could do it.

On September 26, the decision to kill Sadat was put to a vote. The leadership council of the Gama'a approved it. Nageh would often marvel in the years to come about how everything seemed to have aligned perfectly to make the assassination possible: fateful meetings of the mind, serendipitous friendships, access . . . but mostly opportunity. Theirs was a daring yet simple plot. In the end, Zomor was right. Although the assassination went according to plan, the uprising failed.

—

Sadat loved the pageantry of military parades, and the one commemorating the October War, his war, was his favorite. He was wearing a new blue-gray uniform, bedecked with military decorations. He refused, as always, to wear a bulletproof vest. He was relaxed and smiling during the show, puffing on his pipe every now and then as he sat in the front row behind a low five-foot-long concrete wall decorated with Pharaonic motifs in relief. The tension surrounding the purge, the reports of foiled coups were all seemingly forgotten. Two hours into the military parade, at 12:40 p.m., the audience was looking up at the sky, marveling at the Mirage jets swooping above leaving behind a trail of white, red, and blue smoke. No one was paying attention to the slow-moving Soviet military truck that veered to the right, out of the line, and stopped in front of the reviewing stand. Sadat, flanked by his vice president, Hosni Mubarak, and his defense minister, got up, probably expecting the men in the vehicles to salute him. Instead, Islambouli and his crew climbed out of the truck, lobbed a couple of grenades against the concrete wall of the reviewing stand, and started shooting with AK-47s. The attack was so stunning that there was no reaction for a full thirty seconds. Some people thought the grenades were part of the show. The shooting went on for two minutes. Pandemonium broke out among the two thousand guests, as Islambouli cried out: "I killed the Pharaoh." Sadat had been shot in the neck. Ten others were dead. State television and radio had interrupted its live broadcast as soon as the explosions had rung out and started broadcasting patriotic songs. Only at 6:25 that evening did they start broadcasting Quran recitations, acknowledging what had been true for several hours: Sadat was dead. Within hours, Tehran radio was lauding the "death of the traitor mercenary" who had "joined his old friend Mohammad Reza Shah."

In the hours that followed the shooting on the reviewing stand, officialdom was gripped by panic. No one knew for sure the extent of the plot beyond the assassination. Zomor headed to Asyut, home of Nageh's alma mater, and a stronghold of the Gama'a. From there, he hoped he could launch the uprising, making Asyut the nucleus of the new order until Cairo and the rest of the country swung into line. The plotters had managed to recruit an official of the state broadcasting service and provided him with a statement written and recorded by Farag himself calling on Egyptians to rise in the name of religion. The statement asked the armed forces to stay neutral if they could not support the Islamic Revolution. But the statement never aired. For three days, the radio broadcast Quran recitations. The insurrection lasted only for about as long. The masses never rose.

On some level, the Gama'a had misjudged the whole of Egyptian society. Nageh and his friends were buoyed by their successes on campus, heartened by the responses to their preaching of the rightful *da'wa*, the call to Islam; by the growing readership of their publications; and by the multitude of women around them who were putting on the veil. They were young, brash, and confident in the reach of their messages. They didn't mix much with those who had differing opinions or worldviews, so they had come to believe they represented a silent majority that had been awaiting this moment to be liberated from oppression. But the Gama'a was still a marginal group in a country of over 45 million people. There was no love for Sadat—but there was also no appetite for an Islamic uprising that would upend the system overnight. The Iranians renamed a street in Tehran to honor Islambouli, but they, too, had misjudged Egypt. The parallels between the two countries, like the parallels between the shah and Sadat, were many but, crucially, Egypt did not have a Khomeini to lead a revolution following the assassination of Sadat. And while Egyptian society was indeed conservative and pious, it had never gone through a forced secularization as the Iranians had, so it never had to yearn for the forbidden, like the veil, banned by the first Pahlavi shah. They did not have to rise to demand more religion in their life; those who wanted it could have it. Sadat's vice president, Hosni Mubarak, stepped in as president and quickly asserted his control.

A few weeks after the assassination, Nageh's luck ran out. He'd been on the run for almost a month, hiding in fields, surviving on the generosity of villagers and the network of fellow Islamists, but someone had ratted him out. He was arrested in a small village in the governorate of Asyut. He had heard the news of Sadat's death on the radio and felt a calm sense of achievement, a matter-of-fact assessment of a job concluded. Thousands of Islamists had already been picked up, and the key leaders and members of the plot from Gama'a and Jihad were already in custody by the time Nageh landed in a cell. Most of the details of the plot had been tortured out of the detainees, sparing Nageh the worst of the investigators' wrath. Or at least that's the version of events he would maintain in the years to come. Whatever torture he endured, Nageh would never speak of it. He remembered the anger that had built in young men's hearts hearing the stories of the Brothers suffering in jail under Nasser. It swelled and it swelled for years, until it exploded in Sadat's face, even though he had in fact legally banned torture in prison. Now, under Mubarak, torture was officially back, and the methods used by the security forces were more sadistic and humiliating than ever before. Nageh would spend twenty-four years in jail; he would mellow and renounce violence. One day, he would apologize to the Egyptian people and even in person to Sadat's daughter for the assassination of the Believer President.

But long before that, others would be released, still young and hardened with rage, their bodies scarred by indescribable abuse. One of them was a young doctor from the wealthy Cairo neighborhood of Ma'adi,

Ayman al-Zawahiri. He had been convicted of participating in the planning of the assassination and dealing in weapons. He was sentenced to three years in jail. He was a leading member of the Islamic Jihad and would take over the organization from Zomor. Zawahiri had traveled to Peshawar in 1980 for relief work with the Red Crescent and even crossed into Afghanistan a few times. After he was released in 1984, he returned to his medical practice. By 1985, he was in Jeddah. Osama bin Laden was there too, already running a pipeline of money and *mujahedeen* (Islamic guerrilla fighters) to Afghanistan.

On October 10, 1981, Ebtehal Younes, a thirty-year-old French literature professor with dark brown almond eyes and shoulder-length brown hair, sat at home, in silence, watching Sadat's funeral procession. Outside, Cairo was quiet (so quiet it became the title of a BBC documentary about the assassination and funeral: *Why Was Cairo Calm?*). The streets were not thronged by millions as they had been for the funeral of the Arab hero Nasser, when time stopped and mourners poured into the streets five hours before the start of the funeral procession, hanging from lampposts and balconies to get a view. That day, a delirious crowd of men and women cried as they walked through the streets and radio stations across the Arab world broadcast the event or Quran recitations. On the day of Sadat's funeral, the silence was eerie. The Believer President had shocked his nation and the Arab world with his peace treaty with Israel and his love affair with America. And he had died like an American president, on television.

Three former American presidents attended, but Ronald Reagan—who had survived an assassination attempt earlier in the year—stayed away for security reasons. Sitting presidents and prime ministers from Germany, Italy, France, and of course Israel all attended. Admittedly, it was a Muslim holiday, Eid al-Adha, and unrest was still gripping parts of the country, but had Egyptians carried their president in their heart, they would have braved the fear and the security restrictions. Only two Arab leaders, from Sudan and Somalia, traveled to Cairo to join the procession. On the front page of Syria's official newspaper, *Tishreen*, a brutal headline: EGYPT TODAY BIDS FAREWELL FOREVER TO THE ULTIMATE TRAITOR.

Ebtehal wasn't exactly celebrating, but she wasn't shedding any tears. She too saw Sadat as a traitor to the nation and to Palestine. But in that instant, she overlooked a crucial detail: that his assassins were radical Islamists with a different vision of the future of Egypt and her role in it. She had nothing in common with Nageh or Farag. She didn't sense the danger. Few people did. Political Islam and violent Islamists were still a marginal force, undetected and unacknowledged, and the assassination looked like a fluke; there was no threat to anyone but those who made peace with the enemy. She should have remembered the sight of young women clad in black from head to toe, distributing veils on campus, or the women-only buses that had started offering their services to female students. Mostly, she should have taken notice of the fundamentalist zealot who had barged into her classroom at Cairo University in the fall of 1979 and beaten her French literature professor with a chain. French was the language of the infidels; it had no place in Egypt. The man looked like a lunatic to her, an exception. In just over a decade, this new generation of zealots and Zawahiri himself would come after Ebtehal and upend her life.

Miles away, in Pakistan, the rise of religious fervor fed by another dictator was also transforming the lives of millions, especially the women.

6

NO DUPATTA

There is no doubt in the sanctity of Mecca,
but a donkey won't become a Hajj pilgrim
by just going through the motions.
—Rahman Baba, sixteenth-century Pashtun Sufi poet, Peshawar

When Mehtab Channa flew to the United States in 1976 to complete her master's degree at Amherst College, the Pakistan she left behind was a young, imperfect democracy. When she returned home two years later, in the summer of 1978, it was a dictatorship. She noticed the changes around her, in the way people dressed or how news anchors started their evening broadcast—small, strange details that could not be explained by the simple fact that the country was under martial law.

The twenty-nine-year-old Mehtab had heard the news about the military coup while she was in the United States. In the early hours of July 5, 1977, Prime Minister Zulfiqar Ali Bhutto, popular and charismatic, was arrested and thrown in jail. The man who had ousted Bhutto was his own army chief, General Zia ul-Haq. Zia, as he would come to be known, promised this was temporary. "My sole aim is to organize free and fair elections which would be held in October this year," he had declared on television. "Soon after the polls, power will be transferred to the elected representatives of the people. I give a solemn assurance that I will not deviate from this schedule." There would be no elections. In September 1978, Zia declared himself president. Bhutto was still in jail.

Before her studies of International Relations in the United States,

Mehtab had been a radio and television presenter and had taught at Sindh University, her alma mater. Petite and pretty with a determined look, she was the youngest child in a lower-middle-class family. Her father was a teacher and wanted all his children, his son and five daughters, to get an education. There was no high school for girls in their small village of Naudero, near Larkana, in the southern Sindh province, so he moved the family to the city of Hyderabad and then pushed all his children to go to university. And Mehtab had somehow made it all the way to America: big, fabulous, full-of-promise America. Single, practically a spinster at that age in a conservative society, and living alone in a faraway country, she had the support of her family. She had felt free growing up, empowered by her progressive father. She didn't feel she stood out; she felt she was swimming with the times. In the mid-1970s, more than 50 percent of university students in this developing nation were women. *Purdah*, the traditional separation of women from the world of men, was never really an option for working-class women, too busy in the fields or in servitude in urban homes. But it was now also receding in the cities. Mehtab's grandmother had never worn a veil or a *burqa,* the all-in-one face veil and body cloak with a mesh in front of the eyes. Her mother put on the burqa only to visit the village. Her eldest sister wore and then discarded it as she rose to become a teacher and eventually a school principal. The sisters rode bikes, their colorful traditional *dupatta* scarves draped around their necks blowing behind them. Their father let them be, proud of the places they were going.

When Zia took over, he described himself as a "soldier of Islam." Few paused to think about what this meant in a Muslim country. Mehtab began to wonder about it when she went to visit the beloved vice chancellor of Sindh University, Shaikh Ayaz. She knew instantly that something was wrong. Shaikh Ayaz was a renowned poet, both a revolutionary and a romantic whose verses spoke to the soul of Sindh, a province with a long tradition of Sufism and home to Pakistan's first capital and seaport city, Karachi. That day, Ayaz looked sheepish, almost embarrassed. He was not wearing pants and a shirt, but the traditional *kurta* and *salwar,* a long tunic over baggy trousers. Ayaz had written fiery verses against the colonial powers of his youth in British India and infused his poetry with Sindhi nationalism under the rulers of newborn Pakistan, but he had never worn the salwar at university, nor had it ever been brandished as an act of cultural resistance or a symbol of Islam. But Zia had imposed the salwar as national dress for government officials, students, and schoolchildren. Kids across Pakistan threw fits every morning before putting on their new uncool, baggy uniform. And here was Ayaz, the rebel, trying to adapt to the new fashion constraints while his poetry spoke of freedom.

> *Who can say there is no freedom here?*
> *Jackals are free; flies are free;*
> *Here the intellectuals are free; poets are free to hold devotional*
>   *recitations on TV.*
> *The farmer is free; he can pick out lice from his head or not.*
> *Everybody is free on this land cracking up*
> *Where snakes hide in the crevices and wolves dig out dens for*
>   *their cubs.*

Prayer time was now being enforced in government offices and public institutions (including Sindh University) during working hours. So Ayaz, the secular, liberal poet who wrote about Sufi saints and women's breasts, had to lead the daytime prayers for his department staff. Piety had become exhibitionism, a competition. Mehtab felt her heart tighten in her chest. She couldn't believe what she was witnessing.

—

The changes had been small and slow at first. After he seized power, the general had promised to implement Islamic law, but few people paid him much mind. And even though he had not held elections when he said he would, no one believed Zia would last. The Islamist lobby in Pakistan had been busy for decades, but the country was too boisterous, too diverse, conservative but progressive, with a long tradition of secular politicians. People liked their liquor, their poetry, their colorful, unorthodox celebrations of religious festivals. A huge casino was being built in Karachi to lure some of the Middle East revelers who had lost their playground in war-torn Lebanon. But in the heat of August 1978, a year into Zia's rule, and for the first time in the country's history, the holy month of Muslim fasting was strictly enforced, and all eating and drinking places were shut between sunrise and sunset. Government letters, news broadcasts, and Zia's speeches now all began with *Bismillah al-Rahman al-Raheem*—in the name of God the Beneficent the Merciful the Compassionate.

Pakistan was founded in 1947 as a homeland for Muslims on the Indian subcontinent, born out of the partition of India, but it was also a home for many minorities. Muhammad Ali Jinnah, the father of the nation, was a secular Shia who nominated other Shias and an Ahmadi Muslim to his cabinet. His first law minister was a Hindu, to make clear that laws were to be written by secular jurists, not clerics and theologians. In his first presidential address marking the birth of the nation, at midnight on August 11, 1947, Jinnah told his new compatriots "you are free to go to your temples, free to go to your mosques, or to any other place of worship in this State of Pakistan. You may belong to any religion or case or creed—that has nothing to do with the business of the state." Jinnah had spelled out a vision for religious pluralism in a secular Muslim-majority democracy, where Muslims and non-Muslims were equal citizens. He did not speak of an Islamic state, not even of an Islamic republic. But his vision for tolerant diversity was never fulfilled. He died a year later, and though his successors tried to uphold this nuanced narrative, they soon fell back on the more straightforward raison d'être of the country: Islam.

Pakistan was born amid horrendous violence and indescribable dislocation—around 6.5 million Muslims moved from India to Pakistan, while 4.7 million Hindus and Sikhs left for India. Activist, revivalist Islam had grown in British India in part as a reaction to colonial rule, but also in opposition to Hindus, the majority. The name Pakistan was an acronym combining the first letters of the different provinces that made up the new country. But in Urdu, the language of the new nation, it also means "the land of the pure," and there were many who wanted to purify it further. In 1956, Pakistan's constitution declared the country an Islamic republic and prohibited non-Muslims from holding the office of head of state. In the 1960s, military dictators used religion as a rallying cry against India, feeding further intolerance against Hindus and appeasing Islamists. Social and cultural life continued unperturbed, but some now brandished Pakistan as a citadel of Islam.

The architect of that citadel would be Abu A'la al-Mawdudi, the man who had inspired Qutb in Egypt and Khomeini in Iran. Mawdudi had not always been a religious fundamentalist. Born in 1903 in British India, he was a journalist, a poet, and newspaper editor whose intellectual, mystical, theological journey made him the twentieth century's greatest revivalist Islamic thinker. He transformed from a young man in a suit with a round face and a mustache to a preacher with a traditional *karakul* (curly lambskin) hat and a beard. Mawdudi dabbled in Marxism and Western philosophy, and was inspired to become a writer by a poet friend. He admired Mahatma Gandhi and was even briefly an Indian nationalist. But like his contemporary Egypt's Hassan al-Banna, the founder of the Muslim Brotherhood, Mawdudi was dismayed by the fall of the Ottoman Empire in 1924 and the secularism of the founder of modern Turkey, Mustafa Kemal Atatürk. Mawdudi's ideas about Islam and Muslim identity reflected his own existential questioning

and evolved at a time of deep flux for Muslims in India. In a landscape littered with the vestiges of a collapsed Muslim power, the Mughal Empire,
Muslims were caught between the uncertainty caused by a departing colonial power and growing Hindu nationalism. Mawdudi believed that the
rise of the Western concept of nationalism among Muslims had led to the
downfall of the Ottomans, allowing European powers to enter the region.
He believed the answer lay not in more nationalism, or in a new country for
Muslims, but in reviving Islam and implementing true Islamic rule.

In 1932, Mawdudi was still writing very earthly poetry, rejecting the
promise of heavenly rewards.

> Give to the drinkers, O wine bearer, the wine that promotes
>   rapture.
> Disturb the wine shop with every drunkard slip . . .
> We believe in cash, not in credit
> So why narrate to us the story of paradise?

By 1941, in Lahore, he had founded Jamaat-e Islami, the vanguard of
the Islamic revolution of his dreams. His followers would deny he had ever
written such heathen verses. Mawdudi had opposed the creation of Pakistan.
But once it came into existence, he worked relentlessly to turn it into his utopian Islamic state. From philosopher and ideologue, he became a strategist, a
politician with a program. The Jamaat organized a highly structured network
of activists to spread the message, pushing to institutionalize Islamic values
at every level of society and public life, including politics. According to Mawdudi, no ruler, no system had ever been truly Islamic, because Muslims had
become estranged from the true precepts of their religion, and governments
that did not strictly apply the shari'a, Islamic law, were apostates. The jahiliyya, the pre-Islam age of ignorance, therefore continued, and Mawdudi's
response was the *hukm*, sovereign rule, of God over earth through the rule
of shari'a. In its Arabic root declination, the word *hukm* led to the word and
concept of *hakimiyya*: an Islamic state that was the result of the Islamization
of society and state through education, the Islamization of private and public
life, a totalitarian model in which God's law was supreme and elected officials
governed only under the guidance of clerics.

These were the ideas that would later be attributed to the Egyptian
thinker Qutb, but they were unmistakably Mawdudi's. He was the missing
link between Banna's vague vision for an Islamic society and Qutb's urgent

political manifesto, *Milestones*. Novel and radical in their day, Mawdudi's ideas are at the root of modern-day political Islam, radical Salafism, and jihadism. He inspired his contemporaries and the generations since, both Shia and Sunni. His profound influence on Pakistani politics is the bridge that connects the mujahedeen of Afghanistan in the 1980s to the jihadists of the Middle East. Decades later, when Western authors and journalists went looking for the clues that led to 9/11, they would settle on Qutb as the source of much of the evil, providing only a partial understanding of what had happened and why. Mawdudi's key influence would be mostly forgotten, including his connections with revolutionary Iran.

Mawdudi's work had begun to appear in Iran, translated into Persian, in the early 1960s. The Pakistani scholar and Khomeini met in 1963 in Mecca, where Mawdudi delivered a lecture about the duties of Muslim youth that impressed Khomeini. The two men talked for a half hour at their hotel with a translator. Khomeini explained his campaign against the shah. This was the year of protests against the White Revolution, and Khomeini would soon be exiled to Iraq. Mawdudi did not believe in a revolution for Pakistan; he preached for the Islamization of society as the natural path to an Islamic state. But the majority of Pakistanis were indifferent to his message. He was also unpopular with the country's leaders. Mawdudi was jailed four times, only narrowly escaping a death sentence thanks to the intervention of Saudi Arabia in 1953. During the elections of 1970, the Jamaat won only four of the three hundred seats in the National Assembly. But in Zia's Pakistan, Mawdudi was suddenly useful. The pious general sought his advice, and the scholar's views were now published on the front page of newspapers.

Just as in Egypt, the rise of Islam as a political force and a social trend in Pakistan was not the result of one moment, or even the work of one person—it was a slow build that came in waves and ebbed and flowed. It was sometimes bolstered by weak leaders who used the Islamists to shore up their own legitimacy, like Sadat in Egypt, or even secular, socialist Bhutto, who first introduced the ban on alcohol and instituted Friday as the weekly holiday instead of Sunday. In both Egypt and Pakistan, leaders used religion as a balm after the national trauma of a military defeat. For Pakistan it was the 1971 loss of East Pakistan, today's Bangladesh. And just as in Egypt before the assassination of Sadat, the relentless work of Islamists in Pakistan had not yet delivered a sea change—they toiled on the margins, and they converted people to their cause one by one.

Even when Zia spoke, in the spring of 1978, about his mission to purify the country, Pakistani society was far from being gripped by Islamic fervor. For this to happen it required the incredibly powerful, violent, and moneyed convergence of a number of people and events: Mawdudi's groundwork over decades, Zia's rise to power and brutal rule, but also the generous support of Saudi Arabia.

—

Saudi influence in Pakistan was not new. So far it had taken the form of benevolent generosity for grand projects, like a national mosque for which King Faisal had donated $120 million in the 1960s. But the subcontinent was steeped in Indo-Persian culture, and Pakistan's heritage was layered with centuries of Persian influence, from literature and poetry to food and music—and also its national language. Urdu is filled with thousands of Persian words and the national anthem is almost entirely in Persian. Historically and culturally, Pakistan felt closer to Iran, on its western border, than to the countries across the Arabian Sea. Religious scholars with connections in Mecca and Medina, like Mawdudi, felt differently. The scholar had long impressed Saudi kings, his books had been read in the kingdom since the 1950s, the Jamaat had long-standing ties with Saudi clerics, and Mawdudi sat on the board of the Islamic University of Medina, where the blind sheikh Bin Baz was vice rector.

On September 25, 1978, as the revolution was taking hold of Iran and Khomeini was about to head to France, a small item appeared in Pakistan's biggest English-language daily, *Dawn*, announcing the arrival of the "special assistant to King Khaled of Saudi Arabia" to advise the Council of Islamic Ideology on the "Islamization of laws in Pakistan" at the special request of Zia. Maarouf Dawalibi was a former Syrian prime minister, ousted from Syria and jailed in 1963. He had also served as a foreign minister and struck up a friendship with his Saudi counterpart Prince Faisal. Released from prison in 1964, Dawalibi was invited to serve in the Saudi royal court by his friend Faisal, who had become king. A statesman and a professor of Islamic law, educated at the Sorbonne, Dawalibi was exactly the kind of learned man that Saudi kings surrounded themselves with at the time, from Egypt and the Levant, eventually appointing some as governors, emissaries, or ambassadors. Dawalibi, married to a French woman he'd met while studying in Paris, was pious but progressive, and King Faisal had often used him to reason with retrograde clerics like Bin Baz. Dawalibi despised Bin Baz and thought of him as nothing more than a mediocre village preacher. And yet, in 1978, Dawalibi, then serving as an adviser to King Khaled, was about to play a key role in imposing on Pakistan a system of life closer to Bin Baz's vision for society, propelling Pakistan into its darkest decade.

Newspapers reported on Dawalibi's meeting with various officials, including the justice minister, the members of the Council of Islamic Ideology, and of course Mawdudi. There was flowery coverage of the "renowned Muslim jurist" coming from the land blessed with the message of Islam and with the riches of oil, the land where several hundred thousand Pakistanis now worked in everything from construction to mining to services, sending millions of rupees back home in remittances. But for most Pakistanis reading the news, there was not much more to it. The context was clear only in private, during meetings and at a reception held by the Saudi ambassador for Dawalibi. At those, there was grandiose talk as Dawalibi described "the elimination of secular systems and of their replacement by shari'a law as the greatest hope for all mankind." He praised Zia as a sincere Muslim and expressed his hope that countries like Egypt could emulate Pakistan. In their missives back to Washington, somewhat perplexed American diplomats described what seemed to be a fad to them, "Islamania," adding that there were no concrete proposals: "implementation remains elusive."

Behind the scenes, Dawalibi was in fact very busy putting pen to paper and turning this nebulous vision into a reality. He helped the Council of Islamic Ideology frame the new Islamic laws, writing them in Arabic at the council's offices. The laws were then translated into English and Urdu by a team of fifteen. By early 1979, everything was ready.

In Iran, the government of Bakhtiar had fallen on February 11, 1979, and the Islamic revolution had been declared victorious. But just a day earlier, on February 10, Zia had made a forty-eight-minute speech and announced he was imposing Nizam-i-Islam on Pakistan, effective immediately—in other words, Pakistan would now be governed by shari'a (Islamic) law. *Nizam*, the Arabic word for "system," is also often used to mean a regime, and so, appropriately, Zia's dictatorial regime would now rule with an Islamic system of government. This meant changing the country's legal code and introducing harsh punishments for offenses that violated the boundaries of behavior set by God in the Quran: intoxication, fornication, false allegations of fornication, and theft. The ordinances, known as *hudood*, Arabic for "boundaries," were very detailed and took up whole pages in the Pakistani newspapers. From then on, drinkers would be flogged, adulterers would be stoned to death, thieves would have their hands chopped off.

More was coming: Zia wanted to Islamize the entire economy, the legal system, society, everything.

The announcement stunned Mehtab, the young television anchor. She had seen the incremental changes around her, she had sensed the fear, she knew there had been public floggings, but it all felt temporary, like an unpleasant dream. And though most of the country was probably equally stunned, it appeared as though Pakistan was celebrating because Zia, an expert stage master and manipulator, had chosen the joyous occasion of the prophet's birthday to make his announcement. *Eid-e-milad-ul-nabi* in Urdu, or *mawled al-nabi* in Arabic, the occasion was just as colorful in Pakistan as it was in Morocco or Indonesia. In big cities and small villages of Pakistan, green flags and bunting hung on the streets, which were lined with food stalls and cultural events. Garlands of bright lights lit up the walls of mosques. The preparations for the celebrations had started days before. On the day itself, the prayers, processions, and children playing on the streets distracted Pakistanis and filled the silence as the nation slipped further into darkness. King Khaled of Saudi Arabia sent a cable to congratulate Zia, saying he was moved and looked forward to "seeing the application of Islamic laws in all Muslim countries."

Despite the press coverage of Dawalibi's visits to Pakistan, the extent of his involvement in writing the laws was not made public. There was much secrecy around his role, and only years later would a Pakistani jurist doing a review of the work of the Council of Islamic Ideology uncover what he described as the "revolting" details of what had happened in its offices as Saudi Arabia imposed itself on Pakistan, effectively writing a defining chapter of the country's history. On February 11, the day after Zia's announcement of Nizam-i-Islam, the same day that Khomeini declared his victory in Iran, bars, brothels, and breweries were officially shut down in Pakistan. Murree Brewery in Rawalpindi, founded in 1860, had to close its doors, its stock confiscated. Until then, foreigners and non-Muslims had been allowed to consume or produce alcohol, and hotels still served it. But in a flash, ten thousand licenses were revoked across the country. In Khomeini's Iran, there was still chaos and street battles, but there, too, zealots were destroying bottles of champagne and fine wine.

On February 14, Zia spoke to CBS television and was asked if there were parallels between what he was trying to achieve and what was happening in Iran. "Yes," replied the general, "there were parallels in that we were first off." Pakistan had even managed to impose Islamic law with less violence and upheaval than Iran, he added proudly. From Egypt to Pakistan, there seemed to be a desire to emulate or outdo Iran. Perhaps Mawdudi had even accelerated the push for Islamizing Pakistan's laws when he had seen Khomeini's revolution picking up steam at the end of 1978 and the ayatollah becoming a media star in Paris. Had he quickened the pace even further after Khomeini had returned to Iran on February 1? After all, Mawdudi had known of the ayatollah's grand ambitions ever since they had met in 1963 and had inspired some of Khomeini's vision.

A week later, Mawdudi received the first King Faisal International Award for services to Islam, a prize that carried a cash gift of $200,000, which the Saudis went on to award every year, often to scholars and clerics with radical views. Dawalibi paid Mawdudi a home visit in Lahore to congratulate him on his work. The Saudis would never really acknowledge their role in the transformation of Pakistan, one that they had helped to start before 1979. This was in line with their own worldview, which had nothing whatsoever to do with Iran or Khomeini's movements. But Iran's revolution meant that trends that had been simmering, separately but simultaneously, across the Muslim world were now being celebrated and turbocharged, and would start to become entrenched. The ramparts were falling away.

For Pakistan, the impact of the events of 1979, especially the Soviet invasion of Afghanistan, meant that Zia was becoming an indispensable ally of Saudi Arabia and the United States and would be able to withstand the repeated challenges by his own people to his oppressive zealot rule.

—

Mawdudi died in September 1979. He did not get to see the result of what he had ignited in Pakistan, but his work was done. Since independence, Pakistanis had debated the role of Islam in their country, their government, and their daily life. That debate was over, and the Islamists had won—even though they were still a minority. Within a year, Islamic scholars would be bickering over the gruesome details of punishments to be meted out: should the young thief of a mosque clock have his whole hand amputated or just his fingers? Would the amputated limb be the property of the thief or the state? A bus driver sentenced to be stoned to death for adultery was languishing in jail while the background of the four required witnesses was being reviewed—were they pious enough?

In the early spring of 1979, Mehtab was still hopeful. She was back to presenting a television program on local Sindhi television, interviewing singers, philosophers, poets. The show was lively and popular, a reflection of millennia of Sindhi culture, born in the Indus valley, still alive and thriving in modern Pakistan. She loved those encounters, she drank every word of her guests, her heart swelled with pride. She felt that the soul of Pakistan, born on the same day as she was, was stronger than the dictator. She was still on television.

But on the morning of April 4, 1979, Mehtab wept for her country. At 2:04 a.m., former prime minister Zulfiqar Ali Bhutto was hanged in the courtyard of the Rawalpindi District Jail. Bhutto had been put on trial for allegedly ordering the murder of a political opponent. The verdict at the end of a controversial trial was split, yet he was still sentenced to death. Despite appeals through the courts and pleas for clemency from leaders around the world, Zia sent his opponent to the gallows. There were clashes with the police as Bhutto's supporters came out to protest in Liaqat Park in Rawalpindi. Women screamed "Death to Zia, death to Zia's children." In government offices in Islamabad, men wept. "We are just like Iran now," said one.

There was something so extraordinary about 1979, with its cascade of events from the ayatollah in Tehran to the fake messiah in Mecca, from massacres in Aleppo to executions in Islamabad, that to some it felt as if the sky were falling to earth. Bizarrely, in a way, it did. That summer marked the demise of NASA's Skylab space station, in orbit since 1973. On the afternoon on July 12, the 77-ton station crashed through the atmosphere, disintegrating in a blaze of fireworks and scattering its debris over the remote Australian desert. Meanwhile, on earth, whole systems of thought were being altered: in the UK, in May 1979, Margaret Thatcher, leader of the Conservative Party, became the first woman to serve as prime minister. In China, Deng Xiaoping was consolidating his rule and opening up Communist China. They introduced a market revolution on opposite sides of the planet. In the United States, Republican Ronald Reagan would become president in 1981, ushering in a decade of social conservatism in the United States and marking the end of America's own era of leftist revolutionary fervor. Big events, like the Zia coup and the Bhutto hanging, obscured the smaller ways in which life was being transformed. Over time, imperceptibly, people's memories of their own culture and history would be altered. Looking back, they would struggle to pinpoint the exact moment when everything had changed.

But Mehtab would never forget: it was when she was first told she had to wear a veil on television. She felt a chill in her bones. She had been naive and wrong. Not only was Zia staying, but he really was changing the country. The instructions had come from Islamabad in the early months of 1980 and were slowly filtering down to the provinces: the traditional dupatta had to be wrapped tightly around the head as a veil. Mehtab was Muslim and pious but secular: in the world she had grown up in, religion was one's private business. Her relationship with Islam was suffused with Sufi traditions: visits to the shrine of the eighteenth-century saint Shah Abdullatif Bhittai, evenings spent listening to the poetry of Rumi. Since it was launched in 1964, Pakistani television had shown ballet performances and folk dances, women wore everything from saris to bell-bottoms and sleeveless tops. Mehtab wore a traditional *salwar kameez*, her dupatta draped around her neck, the two ends hanging down her back. She told her co-presenter, "I'm not going to cover my head because some dictator wants me to cover. He has his own idea of what Pakistani women should look like, he wants to tell the world: 'Look, our women are so modest, they cover their head.'" Like Khomeini, Zia wanted a visible expression of the country's alleged newfound piety, what he thought was its true identity. But Mehtab felt strongly: this was not who she was, nor who her family or her friends were, and her dupatta would stay right where it was, on her shoulders. Far from the capital, on provincial Sindhi programs, broadcast after prime time, she got away with it for a while.

She was a rising star, her smile was infectious, her manner easy, and one day she was asked to present an evening program from Karachi on national television. She warned the producer: "I am not veiling." He agreed. Fear had not yet become pervasive in Pakistan; there were still acts of defiance everywhere, small and big, and there was much eye-rolling at some of the instructions from Islamabad. When Zia banned makeup for female newscasters, they refused to read the news for a week until the rules were eased. Now, in front of an audience in a studio, Mehtab was asking about the hopes and dreams of young Pakistanis: the young journalists with their aspiration for the truth, the architects with their visions for better urban planning, the poets with their verses about freedom. The program was a national sensation, and somehow she got away with it again.

By the fall of 1980 she was anchoring alone, reading and answering letters from viewers on national television. She dominated the screen. With her high cheekbones, her hair pulled up in a tight bun, her delicate earrings, and her barely-there makeup, Mehtab had an Audrey Hepburn quality. For a few months, she presented her show undisturbed by any remonstrations about the dupatta. She never found out whether her bosses had been stalling Islamabad or whether the instructions from the capital were slow to arrive to Karachi. One day, a call came from the presidential office: Mehtab should veil now or be removed. Her producer called her at home in Hyderabad ahead of the next show taping. "We are in trouble," he told her. "These are the instructions. Please help us." She didn't need to think very long. "Okay, I will help you," she said. "I will not come anymore."

The producer was so relieved, he thanked her profusely. No one had the heart to fire her, but no one could refuse direct instructions from the dictator any longer. There was no explanation about her sudden departure. For weeks, television viewers wondered what had happened to their favorite presenter. One day, a journalist friend called on Mehtab at her home in Hyderabad. He had traveled three hours from Karachi just to see her. She gave him a cup of tea and told him her story. The following day, the *Evening Times* printed a front-page story about her with a picture and the headline LA DUPATTA—no dupatta. (Although *la* is an Arabic word, which was perhaps a mischievous nod to the Arab influence that was introducing these changes.) Mehtab became known in Pakistan as "the woman who said no." Her family, especially her father, was proud of her. For months, outraged viewers wrote letters: they wanted Mehtab back. One of them complained that the "best lady compere ever produced by Pakistan TV" had been removed for a "very frivolous and petty matter." Another complained that the television authorities clearly had no regard for the thousands of "viewers young and old, children and women, educated and non-educated who wish to see Mehtab." The letters were not signed, that would be too dangerous. But they were printed—a small act of defiance by the paper. Mehtab was replaced by a woman who dutifully put on the veil. Who was this mediocre man, Mehtab thought, telling women how they should behave as Muslims? What did he really know about Islam? She hated Zia and promised herself she'd never meet him. She continued to teach. The university also tried to force her to veil but she refused. She told her superiors that her students listened to her and respected her with or without a piece of cloth on her head. She had guts and she knew her religion, her culture. But she was also lucky: she was not the breadwinner for her family and could afford to lose her television job. The university let her stay.

In 1981, the woman who had said no to Zia said yes to the love of her life, Akbar Rashdi, from a well-established Sindhi family from Larkana. The wedding was a big event, and everyone who was anyone in Sindh province came to the celebration in Hyderabad, including the area's most famous family: the Bhuttos, who lived in near-seclusion under the dictatorship. The evening paper the *Star* ran a four-page special in full color about the wedding, headlined MEHTAB GETS MARRIED. Mehtab Channa was now Mehtab Rashdi, and she bowed to tradition—not to Zia's Islam—by lightly placing her red, embroidered dupatta on her head for the ceremony. Pakistanis still had a sense of humor, and the caption for her picture read "Mehtab, don't let the dupatta slip!" Under another picture of Mehtab and a woman dressed in green with uncovered hair, the caption was "Mehtab and her guest." The mystery guest was Benazir Bhutto, daughter of Zulfiqar, who carried the political mantle of her family but whose name was not allowed in print in the papers. Though he'd had his former boss killed, Zia still feared the Bhutto name. Benazir and her mother lived under virtual house arrest in Karachi, their 1930s house in the Clifton area surrounded by barbed wire.

Copies of the *Star* sold like hotcakes. People wanted to know all about the life of their favorite television anchor. But they were also hungry for any news about the Bhuttos, a glimpse of Benazir's face, a confirmation she was still there, still alive. All criticism of her father—his excesses and mistakes in power—had been forgotten now that he had been made a martyr by Zia. Under the yoke of dictatorship, Pakistanis yearned for the Bhutto days. The authorities were apoplectic. They sent orders to the provincial government to buy up all the copies of the paper and arrest the editor. He went underground for a while, and the paper stopped publishing for some days.

Pakistanis were starting to suffocate. Darkness was enveloping the country, but also silence. The silence was hard to penetrate from the outside world. Fear kept people from speaking, the local press was muzzled, and news coverage of Pakistan was dominated not by the abuses of Zia's regime but by laudatory reporting of his role in promoting and supporting the war against the Soviets next door in Afghanistan—America's war. Decades later, when they thought back to the 1980s, the memory of that time would make Pakistanis shudder. Censorship was intensifying; journalists were being lashed, some were hanged. People started to disappear, picked up in the dead of night by the police, their relatives and friends left with no recourse under martial law. There were no more cafés, no more clubs, only deepening fear. Save for the occasional folkloric performance, most stage dancing was banned. Scores of performers left the country, taking with them parts of the country's memory and heritage. Under the weight of censorship, the vibrant Pakistani movie industry was shrinking and cinemas were shutting down. No new ones were built for decades. Life retreated indoors.

Invisible walls were also rising among communities, between neighbors, and even within families. The seeds of intolerance had been there at the outset of Pakistan's creation, though they'd been kept mostly buried. Now, Zia was watering them generously, and the Saudis were adding fertilizer. Mehtab had grown up with Hindu neighbors; they visited each other and played together. Soon, some Sunni Pakistanis refused to even have a Hindu cook in their house, because they considered the food impure. As more Pakistanis started to adhere to the puritanical ideas spread under Zia, tensions grew within families. Sons criticized their mothers, grandchildren chided their grandparents and refused to join the centuries-old tradition of religious celebrations infused with local folkloric customs, like visits to shrines of saints, or the Shab-e-Barat, known in Arabic as Laylat al Bara'a, the night of salvation, when prayers are believed to be especially fruitful. Children had always set off firecrackers at dusk on the occasion, and candles stayed lit for the nightlong prayers. This was now heresy for those who were being wooed by hundreds of ultraconservative orthodox clerics, fanning across the country, newly empowered by Zia. They were a mix of local revivalists, like the Jamaat-trained clerics and preachers from the Deobandi school of thought, the subcontinent equivalent of Wahhabism. And there were, of course, constant winds blowing from Saudi Arabia.

Clerics were gaining influence everywhere: In the bureaucracy, civil servants sought promotions with overt expressions of religiousness; the army now held Quran study groups. Women were banned from playing sports in public; the national women's hockey team, one of the world's best, was forbidden from leaving the country. History was also being rewritten. Jinnah, the secular father of the nation, had a makeover: he was no longer shown in Western clothes in official portraits, only in traditional dress. References to pluralism and freedom of faith in Jinnah's 1947 speech were scrubbed from the record. The methodical, relentless, systemwide changes were akin to a cultural revolution, unparalleled in the history of Islam in the subcontinent but cleaving closely to what was happening in Iran and Saudi Arabia. Although the Jamaat had been in awe of the Iranian Revolution, its leader saw Saudi Arabia as the more perfect model to emulate, with full segregation, banishment of women from the workplace, a ban on women driving, and the male guardianship system.

Zia had caused worldwide consternation when he had Bhutto hanged. He drew rebukes from the West over the abuse of human rights in his first years in power. But once the war against the Soviets began, none of it mattered anymore. Zia was now an essential partner to America and money flowed into the country—official aid from the West and covert assistance from the Gulf funded the Afghan mujahedeen. The survival of Zia's regime was ensured, its longevity a sin helped by the outside world—a sin that Pakistanis would struggle to forgive, especially its women. Mehtab had perhaps been right—Zia would not have lasted in feisty, boisterous Pakistan had it not been for the geopolitics that dictated his survival.

No one really knows how many thieves had their hands amputated, perhaps none; or how many people were flogged during those years—many, too many. Information was scarce. In the first years of Zia's regime, floggings and hangings were a public affair in the village square or city stadiums, but within a couple of years, the national outcry forced the authorities to conduct this grim business out of the public view. One thing was certain and documented: women were the biggest losers under Zia. During the 1960s and early 1970s, Pakistan had adopted very progressive laws ensuring a woman's right to divorce, restricting polygamy, and even prohibiting discrimination on the basis of sex. National literacy rates were still low, even more so for women, but they were rising steadily for everyone. Enrollment of girls in schools and universities was skyrocketing in cities. Women were beginning to participate in politics, they were rising as judges. This is why, despite the long road ahead for a deeply conservative society, Mehtab had believed she was part of a forward-looking country, where the future of women looked brighter. Neither she nor her friends had been looking for Western-style women's rights; they did not speak in the radical terms of American feminists. "We have to exist with men," Mehtab would tell those around her—with men and within their own society and its conventions. The uncompromising attitudes of the "women's libbers" she had met in America was "an extreme position, confrontation was no good." Gradual change had paid off. Now Zia was threatening to yank women back into purdah.

—

The women fought back. They started organizing, early and often. Activism was driven mostly by urban elites, but women of all classes soon joined as they chafed under the weight of the hudood ordinances that were being abused by men to settle scores and send defenseless daughters, wives, or sisters to jail on bogus allegations of adultery or other sins. In 1983, Zia and the Council of Islamic Ideology worked to introduce a number of laws that would reduce women to half citizens based on the shari'a: their testimony was equal to only half a man's in court; their lives were worth half a man's in blood money. The protests started, small at first, then swelling all year long, spreading across the country, bringing together women of all classes: peasants and teachers, activists and housewives.

On March 3, 1983, two hundred women protested in Lahore. They faced off with the police in a huge melee that lasted hours. Some of the women seized clubs from the hands of the police and beat them back. In another protest, which would produce an iconic picture, women burned their dupattas. Men joined too, like Mehtab's husband, or Salman Taseer, a rising star in Bhutto's People's Party of Pakistan and a confidant of his daughter Benazir. He had been thrown in jail by Zia in 1977 and then gone into exile for a few years. But he was back in Lahore with his young wife, Aamna, and he would end up back in a prison repeatedly, for months at a time. In three decades, he would become governor of Punjab, and his continued resistance to the insanity unleashed by Islamization would get him killed, not by Zia but by the monstrous forces the dictator had created. For now, Taseer protested, with almost naive hope that the dictatorship could be toppled.

There were more demonstrations throughout the year. Thousands of women and men, Pakistanis of all classes and faiths, set fire to government buildings, disrupted rail lines, and clashed with police endlessly. By October, four thousand people had been arrested across the country. The tale of how Pakistanis tried to resist Zia barely made international headlines, drowned out by the war in Afghanistan. One day the world would awaken to a changed country and believe it had always been like that. But Zia barely survived the relentless pressure of protests and had to use every stratagem not only to remain in power but to make colorful, vibrant, diverse Pakistan conform to the monochrome image of the perfect Islamic society he had envisioned with the likes of Mawdudi.

Zia promised he would finally organize elections in 1985, but first the cunning dictator held a quickly organized referendum with a convoluted question: in summary, he asked Pakistanis whether they wanted Zia to continue making Pakistan a model Muslim country, in accordance with the Quran. This was a trick question. There was no one else but Zia on the ballot to carry out this task, but who could really cast a ballot and say no to Islam? The opposition was not even allowed to run a no campaign. In saying yes, voters were asking Zia to stay on. The result, on December 20, 1984, was a resounding 97.2 percent yes vote. But the polling stations had been deserted all day. Zia claimed a turnout of 62 percent; the opposition put the number at 10 percent, with multiple irregularities.

One of Pakistan's greatest Urdu poets of the twentieth century, Faiz Ahmed Faiz, had spent the first few years of Zia's time in power in prison and then in exile in Beirut, preferring the chaos of Lebanon's civil war to the darkness of repression. An uncle and mentor of Taseer, the leftist poet of love and revolution had embraced the intellectual effervescence of Lebanon and found kindred spirits among the Palestinian revolutionaries sitting on café terraces during cease-fires. But the Palestinians kept attracting worse and worse Israeli retaliation and, in the summer of 1982, Israeli tanks reached Beirut. Faiz and his wife were forced to flee and return to Pakistan. He died in his home country a month before Zia's referendum, perhaps in anticipation of the unbearable realization that the general had found a way, yet again, to stay in power. Faiz's revolutionary poetry was still banned by the regime, but one woman, a singer, defied Zia. It was always the women of Pakistan who gave the dictator the most grief.

A year after the poet's death, Iqbal Bano, a national icon, obtained rare permission to hold a concert in Lahore. There were some things even Zia couldn't refuse. And there was a way of getting around the ban of singing and dancing: asking for permission to hold a "cultural event." Bano wore a sari, a dress forbidden under Zia both because it was associated with enemy India and because it showed a woman's midriff. And then she lent her voice, powerful but melodious, controlled but emotional, to the most defiant of all of Faiz's verses, written in 1979 in protest at Zia's authoritarian Islam. *Hum dekhenge,* she sang, we shall witness. For ten long minutes she sang the verses as the emotions of the crowd of fifty thousand Pakistanis rose and swelled with her, applause punctuating every pause.

> *We shall witness*
> *It is certain that we too, shall witness*
> *the day that has been promised*
> *of which has been written on the slate of eternity*
> *When the enormous mountains of tyranny blow away*
>   *like cotton.*
> *Under our feet—the feet of the oppressed—when the earth*
>   *will pulsate deafeningly*
> *and on the heads of our rulers when lightning will strike.*
> *From the abode of God*

When icons of falsehood will be taken out,
When we—the faithful—who have been barred out of
  sacred places
will be seated on high cushions,
When the crowns will be tossed,
When the thrones will be brought down,
Only Thy name will survive.

Faiz's verses were deeply subversive. And they seemed directed not only at Zia the oppressor but also at those who proclaimed themselves the guardians of sacred places: the Saudis. There were screams of *Inqilab zindabad* at the concert: long live the revolution, in Urdu, long live the fight against Zia. A live recording of the song was smuggled out, and copies made on cassette tapes were passed around secretly and copied again until they had traveled well beyond the country's borders. The Pakistan that Faiz had known was dying. So was the Beirut he had loved and left. The Lebanon of Musa Sadr and Hussein al-Husseini was no more.

7

KARBALA IN BEIRUT

We are from Beirut, alas, we were born
With borrowed faces and with borrowed minds
Our thoughts are born whores in the marketplaces
Then spend their lives pretending to be virgins.

—Khalil Hawi, *River of Ashes*

In the summer of 1982, Beirut witnessed an invasion, a massacre, an evacuation. Ideas and ideologies died. And then came a black wave. But first, the Beirut of old had to perish. That summer, before he was forced to leave, Faiz wrote a farewell ode to the city that had sheltered him for five years from the wrath of Zia. The Pakistani poet had arrived in 1978, three years into Lebanon's civil war. He had preferred it to the strangulating darkness descending on his home country. The darkness in Beirut was mostly made of gunfights and power cuts, which felt like mere interruptions to morning walks on the seaside corniche or coffee- and cigarette-smoke-filled evenings in the cafés of Hamra Street, on the western side in Ras Beirut—literally, Head of Beirut—the tip of the city jutting into the sea. Often likened to the Champs-Élysées, Hamra was more of a Greenwich Village, a place of intellectual and artistic experimentation since the 1950s, where each political or artistic trend had its café.

With the arrival of the Cold War's proxy wars to the shores of the Levant, ripping open Lebanon's internal cleavages, Beirut was slowly being torn apart, the ravaged downtown splitting it into east and west, Muslim and Christian. Despite the deadly daily fireworks, the city had so far maintained its status as the capital of Arab modernity, a shelter for exiles and émigrés like Faiz, a platform for debate. On Hamra Street, vendors still sold newspapers and magazines printed by every single possible party or ideological camp in the region: pro-Iraqi, pro-Syrian, Nasserist, atheist or pro-Khomeini, communist or pro-American. The displays were a testament to an Arab world that still bubbled up ideas and dreams in a city that provided the liberty to think them, offering enlightenment at the crossroads between modernity and tradition. In a region that was now an authoritarian wasteland, Beirut, even at war, still offered freedom and ferment for intellectuals from Egypt to Pakistan. Faiz was deeply engaged in the Third World and revolutionary politics, and he became immersed in the Palestinian cause, writing odes to Palestinian guerrilla fighters and dedicating one of his final collections to Yasser Arafat himself, whose freedom fighters were murderous terrorists in the eyes of the United States, Israel, and others. In Beirut, Faiz became editor of *Lotus* magazine, a trilingual quarterly of international literature funded by the Soviet Union, Egypt, East Germany, and the PLO. With his Arabic degree, Faiz was the first non-Arab editor of the magazine. He and his adventurous British wife, Alys, settled into a city that allowed them to defy Zia from a distance. For decades, Lebanon had lured not just revolutionaries but also poets, ideologues, artists, and all types of opposition figures and plotters. A weak state was both a blessing and a curse. In Beirut, there was no dictatorship to muzzle opinions—or your guns. The war had made the small Mediterranean country even more of a haven, a live training ground with a casino and restaurants that still served smoked salmon and caviar during cease-fires. There were breadlines and economic hardship, massacres and literary conferences. Every spy agency was in town: the CIA, the KGB, the Mossad.

Arafat, his men, and a plethora of Palestinian splinter factions were still running around like they owned half the country, the tentacles of their presence extending well beyond their staging post in the south on the border with Israel. Supporters of their cause in Lebanon were oblivious to this abuse of the country's sovereignty. Their foes were many, ruthless and bloodthirsty in brutal massacres to eliminate the Palestinian banner from Lebanon.

But first, in the summer of 1982, Beirut died, emptied of its soul, losing its shine and whatever innocence had survived five years of fratricidal war. Husseini, the Shia politician, had already quit the leadership of Amal, unable to accept that the party he had founded with Imam Sadr was a party to such killings. At eleven in the morning on June 6, hundreds of Israeli

Merkava tanks and armored personnel carriers rumbled into Lebanon. Operation Peace for Galilee had begun. The Israelis had tried a clean-up operation before in 1978, invading Lebanon during a weeklong incursion that displaced tens of thousands and killed hundreds on the Lebanese side of the border. The Israelis left behind a border zone controlled by an allied, mostly Christian, militia. They tried to engage with the Shias of the area by allowing them to work in Israel, organizing Ashura celebrations, and arranging for several thousand Shias to visit a shrine located in Israel. The villagers resented the Israelis but they hated the Palestinians more. The Palestinian guerrillas remained undaunted, launching rocket attacks and even crossing into Israel for deadly operations against Israeli civilians. In the summer of 1981, a cease-fire had been declared, which held for many months. The trigger for Operation Peace for Galilee was the assassination of the Israeli ambassador in London, which Israel considered a breach of the cease-fire agreement on the border with Lebanon.

Ostensibly, the goal was to push the Palestinians back twenty-five miles from the border. In reality, the invasion would end up going all the way to Beirut with the goal of helping to shore up Israel's Christian allies in the country. The capital of Lebanon would be besieged, bombed, starved, and parched for weeks until Arafat and his men agreed to leave the country where they had provoked a civil war, splitting nationalists against revolutionaries, left against right, Muslims against Christians. They were evacuated through northern Lebanon and eventually landed in Tunis where the PLO set up its headquarters. In southern Lebanon, Shias greeted the Israelis with handfuls of rice and cheers, relieved to be rid of Arafat and his men. Amal had initially instructed its fighters in the south not to resist and to hand over their weapons if requested. For a while, Israeli soldiers would walk around, shop, and go to the cinema in the southern cities of Tyre and Sidon. Israeli businessmen would drive up across the border to explore business opportunities in Lebanon. None of it would last. The liberators would become hated occupiers very quickly.

But first, at 10:30 on that evening of June 6, one of Lebanon's greatest poets, Khalil Hawi, took a hunting rifle and shot himself in the head on his balcony in his home in West Beirut, near the sprawling green campus of the American University of Beirut, where he was a professor. In the cacophony of war, no one heard the shot. A Greek Orthodox Christian, born in 1919 in Shweir, a small village in the Lebanese mountains, Hawi had written about love and desire but mostly about the yearning for political and cultural change in a region struggling to find a path out of setbacks and despair. The Arab renaissance, cultural and political, of the nineteenth and early twentieth centuries had faded into the distance. A reaction against the intellectual stagnation under the Ottoman Empire, a call for reform in the face of European military superiority, the renaissance, known as al-Nahda (the awakening), had produced endless literature and poetry, cinema and music, media, new approaches to education, as well as modernist thinkers, secular and religious scholars, including modernist Salafists like Muhammad Abduh. From Cairo, intellectual effervescence had moved to Beirut in the second half of the twentieth century. But no new, better order had emerged. There were many reasons why the period of enlightenment ultimately faltered, including colonial repression but also repeated American-instigated coups that helped bring strongmen to power across the Middle East. The political and cultural maturing of the region was thwarted. Hawi's generation of al-Nahda luminaries was still hoping to provide a bridge to the younger generation to find their way forward when he wrote, in his 1957 poem "The Bridge":

> They cross the bridge blithely in the morning
> My ribs are stretched out as a firm bridge for them
> From the caves of the East, from the swamps of the East
> To the New East
> My ribs are stretched out as a firm bridge for them.

But on that June evening, with Israeli tanks rumbling toward Beirut, Hawi had either concluded he could not be that bridge or accepted that there was no New East. A deeply sensitive and brooding man, consumed by his poetry, he had embraced Arab nationalism and was crushed by its failures. From disappointed grand Arab dreams to the torment eating his own country, Hawi was growing old and somber. At sixty-two, his heavy shoulders could not carry the final affront that was the idleness and powerlessness of Arab leaders in the face of an Israeli invasion. "Where are the Arabs?" he had asked his colleagues that morning on the campus of the university. "Who shall remove the stain of shame from my forehead?" Hawi was found the next morning, on his balcony.

As though they understood that the invasion was about to birth something even more alien to them than what they had seen so far, Hawi departed for the heavens while Faiz and Alys decided to return to the hell of Zia's dictatorship, spirited out of the besieged city that summer, leaving behind a love letter to the Beirut they had both embraced so passionately.

Beirut, jewel of the world
A virtual heaven on earth!
When the mirror of
Children's smiling eyes
Was smashed to pieces
These little stars now
Illuminate the city's nights,
And brighten the land of Lebanon.
Beirut, jewel of the world . . .
This city has been here forever,
Will exist forever
Beirut, jewel of the world
A virtual heaven on earth!

Beirut was hell on earth that summer. Faiz titled this poem "A Verse for Karbala in Beirut," a tribute to a city martyred by injustice. Although he was deeply secular, Faiz was no atheist. He was spiritual in the practice of his religion; Islamic imagery and allegories permeated his writings. Unknowingly, his reference to Karbala in Beirut foreshadowed the arrival of the cult of martyrdom and eternal mourning for Imam Hussein. Some believed this was the answer to Hawi's question about who would erase the shame from his forehead.

—

When Sheikh Sobhi Tufayli heard the news about the column of Israeli tanks crossing into Lebanon on that June morning, he felt neither fear nor foreboding—only excitement. He was sitting in the Damascus airport waiting for a flight to Tehran to attend a conference organized by the Revolutionary Guards and their Office for Liberation Movements. Tufayli was contemplating the possibilities that the invasion would provide. A heavyset man in his midthirties, serious-looking, with full lips and a white turban, Tufayli hailed from the small village of Brital near Baalbek, always lawless, tribal, and rebellious in an area famous for cannabis plantations. He had studied in Najaf for almost a decade with Mohammad Baqer al-Sadr, the founder of the Shia Da'wa Party, the Iraqi cleric who had endorsed Khomeini's wilayat and was executed in 1980. Tufayli had been in Najaf at the same time as Khomeini, along with other Shia clerics also from the Beqaa area, Sayyed Abbas Mussawi and Sheikh Mohammad Yazbek. Another one of the students was eighteen-year-old Hassan Nasrallah, who would rise as a militant leader one day. He was in awe of the ayatollah and his "radiant presence," a man in whose company "time and space no longer existed." Ever since returning to Lebanon, around the time of the Iranian Revolution, the more senior clerics had been talking to the Iranians about building an Islamic resistance against Israel. There had been various attempts but nothing concrete had come of them. The war with Iraq was a drain on Iran's resources and there was nothing left for other adventures. There had also been the internal tug of war between the nationalist modernists whose focus was Iran and the radical Khomeinists who believed in revolution across borders. But by 1982, the radicals had won: the Bazergans, Yazdis, and Chamrans were all dead or out of power. And that year, Iran was feeling victorious against Iraq. The time was ripe, thought Tufyali—and the Israelis had obliged with an invasion. At the conference, he and other like-minded clerics asked for help.

Six days later, Iranian soldiers began to land at Damascus airport, hoping to make their way to the front in Lebanon. The man to greet them was the Iranian ambassador to Syria, Ali-Akbar Mohtashamipur, a loyal Khomeini disciple who had studied with the ayatollah in Najaf and was one of the few clerics who had accompanied him to Neauphle-le-Château. In total, some five thousand Iranians flew to Syria. They did not end up fighting the Israelis in Beirut or in southern Lebanon; most of them went home or back to the front with Iraq. But fifteen hundred Revolutionary Guards from the Office for Liberation Movements stayed behind and established a base of operations in Syria on the border with Lebanon. From there, they initially went in and out of the Beqaa Valley, where they rented houses in Baalbek and the surrounding areas; later they would take over the Lebanese Army's regional barracks and a fancy hotel as their headquarters. One of the Guards was Mahmoud Ahmadinejad, the future president of Iran.

The Revolutionary Guards wore military uniforms, but they weren't doing any fighting either: they were missionaries, bringing Khomeini's Islamic revolution to the Mediterranean. For many residents of Baalbek, those who did not see the world like Sheikh Tufayli, it felt like a foreign invasion. For others, the men were a welcome change from the unruly militias that dictated the law almost everywhere in wartime Lebanon. Most important, the Iranians provided services where the state had failed, not just since the war, but since what felt like the beginning of time. Decades later, those who had witnessed the arrival of the Guards would still have vivid memories of how their town changed almost overnight. Baalbek, a mixed city of Shias, Sunnis, and Christians, became Little Tehran, the Tehran of Khomeini. The international festival of Baalbek had paused with the outbreak of the Lebanese civil war, but now music was banned altogether, as were wedding celebrations. A new radio station, the Voice of the Iranian Revolution, began broadcasting sermons, religious songs, and interviews with supporters. The statue of President Nasser that had stood at the entrance of the town was blown up and posters of Khomeini were plastered on the wall. Iranian flags fluttered from lampposts. The walls were covered with slogans about Imam Hussein, about Jerusalem and martyrdom. The town's archbishop was kidnapped and released after two days, but the message was clear. Christians left the area. Alcohol was banned. Women began to veil in large numbers, either coerced or by choice or out of precaution: walking outside without a veil was a recipe for trouble. The Iranian-style black chador, the large cloth wrapped over the head and body, suddenly appeared. Some reports talk of families being paid between $100 and $150 if their daughters put on the veil—a hefty sum in those days in a poor city and community. The Iranians came with a lot of money: they distributed cheap gasoline during the harsh winters, they set up a hospital (named after Khomeini), they took over schools and provided scholarships to study in Iran. They taught classes on the Quran and Khomeini's vision of Islam. They were slow and methodical, quietly overwhelming the town and its surroundings. New ideas and new imagery enveloped people, seeping into their minds, settling into their consciousness over time.

There was also military training. Iranians never did any fighting against the Israelis, but they began to recruit and organize Shia youths in the Beqaa Valley. They attracted the radicals, still a minority: those who looked to Khomeini with awe, or felt that Amal was too moderate, and had defected to found Islamic Amal. Some had trained alongside the Palestinians but had tired of their secular ways, like Imad Mughniyeh, a slim, earnest-looking twenty-year-old, devout, with a good sense of humor, who had been part of Arafat's elite Force-17. Many of the young Shia recruits came from the Beqaa, others including Mughniyeh came from Beirut's southern slums, a poverty belt filled with refugees who had fled the south in waves with every Israeli attack. The ferment of poverty, frustration, and a deep sense of injustice in the face of Israeli occupation would prove propitious for Iranian plans. There had been no Islamic revolution after the assassination of Sadat in Egypt. In Iraq, the Shias had not risen to topple Saddam, and the Shia uprising in Saudi Arabia's Eastern Province had been quelled quickly. In Syria, Khomeini had seen no point in backing an uprising against Assad. The Syrian dictator had also sided with Iran against

Saddam. But in Lebanon, in the chaos of war, in a forsaken, forgotten corner of the country, the Islamic revolution was taking hold with no one to
counter it.

In the training camp set up by the Revolutionary Guards near Baalbek,
the young men received religious instruction from clerics like Tufayli and
Mussawi, now wearing military fatigues under their clerical robes. The
men learned to handle AK-47 rifles and rocket propelled grenades, they
were taught hand-to-hand combat and the art of camouflage. In the same
Beqaa Valley where just a few years ago Palestinian guerrillas had trained
Iranian revolutionaries, Iranians were now training Lebanese Shias, birthing a new movement that would forever change Lebanon's Shia community
and America's relationship with the Middle East. Soon the Lebanese would
run the training camps themselves. The still amorphous movement would
remain unnamed for a couple more years. But this was the founding of
Hezbollah, the Party of God, molded after Iran's own Hezbollah, and it
would be the revolution's most successful export. Still a loose movement,
the group coalesced around clear tenets: Islam was a complete program for
a better life. It provided the intellectual, religious, ideological, and practi-
cal foundations for their new movement. Resistance against Israel was the
priority, its total obliteration the end goal. Crucially, the movement submitted to the wilayat al-faqih and the leadership of the faqih, Khomeini. In
its official manifesto published in 1985 as a forty-eight-page Open Letter,
Hezbollah made clear it desired an Islamic state in Lebanon, a Shia one
just like in Iran, though the group was careful not to explicitly threaten to
impose it. Society would embrace it, they believed, including Christians,
because it was the righteous path.

The story that would be most widely told in the decades to come about
the birth of Hezbollah is that it was born from the ashes of Israel's invasion
of Lebanon in 1982. After rose petals came bullets, and then car bombs.
The story is not entirely wrong. Without the Israeli invasion and occupation, Hezbollah may not have been able to take root in the country. But this
is not the whole story. Sheikh Tufayli's eureka moment at the Damascus
airport preceded the rage of occupation. Even before 1979, Khomeini's
disciples had identified Lebanon as fertile terrain for their revolutionary
projects.

Mostafa Chamran and the LMI were not the only ones who had used
Lebanon as a staging ground for their anti-shah activities. Iranian leftists
and Marxists were there too, training with the PLO before helping to bring
down the monarchy. But the other group of Iranians who had come to

know Lebanon in the decade leading up to the revolution were the hard-line Khomeinists, and they had often clashed with the LMI. One of them was Mohtashamipur. He had trained with the Palestinians in Beirut and spent time in the Beqaa, so he knew the terrain. As Iran's ambassador to Damascus, Mohtashamipur would become crucial in helping the formation of Hezbollah and establishing the conduit of arms through Syria to Lebanon.

Another Khomeinist was Mohammad Montazeri, a young, aggressive, gun-toting cleric nicknamed Ringo who had trained in the Fatah camps in Lebanon before the revolution. The son of Khomeini's closest disciple, an ayatollah and jurist who had played a key role in drafting and implementing the new Islamic constitution, Montazeri was a typical radical-internationalist who had been making contacts with Muslim liberation movements from the Philippines to the western Sahara throughout the 1970s. In December 1979, a week after the start of the hostage crisis at the American embassy in Tehran, he had organized a group of three hundred volunteers to travel to Lebanon. Some of the volunteers were teenagers, others appeared to be in their thirties. Some wore fatigues, others were in civilian clothes. There were fifteen women among them. Bizarrely, the group had neither cash nor valid tickets. Some didn't even have valid passports. They waited for hours to board a plane at Mehrabad airport, chanting "Glory to Khomeini, peace to Arafat." Their cries of *"Allahu Akbar"* echoed through the departure area. They did not carry guns, but they were on their way to Lebanon to fight with the PLO against Israel. Or so they hoped. More chanting: "Today Iran, tomorrow Palestine."

As news of this unsolicited help reached Lebanon, the Lebanese government closed the airspace to Iranian planes and ordered consulates abroad to refer all visa requests by Iranians to Beirut. The president obtained assurances from Syria that no Iranians would be allowed to cross overland. In Beirut, Husseini declared Montazeri mentally deranged. A Shia scholar wrote to Ayatollah Shariatmadari in Qom to tell him that the Shias of south Lebanon did not want Montazeri's volunteers because their arrival would only provoke the Israelis further and sign the death warrant for Lebanon's Shias. Montazeri cared little what the Lebanese or the Shias wanted. With one hundred of his followers, he staged a sit-in and a hunger strike at the Iranian foreign ministry, demanding money to fly. Somehow, he did make it to Lebanon in January 1980, entering illegally, possibly through Syria. In total, two hundred Iranians arrived. During a press conference in Beirut, Montazeri announced hundreds more Iranian volunteers were on their way. Lebanese security officials threatened to resign if Montazeri was allowed to stay. These early forays by radical Iranians, and the local connections they made, were the groundwork for what would become the founding of Hezbollah. From the Beqaa, to the southern suburbs of Beirut and to the south of Lebanon, the movement spread.

While Iran was exploring war, Saudi Arabia was exploring peace. In the fall of 1981, the Saudi Crown Prince Fahd had put forward an eight-point peace plan to settle the Israeli-Palestinian conflict. While the plan offered neither concessions nor recognition to Israel, it was an admission that negotiations were an option. In Tehran, thousands marched in the streets, calling for the death of the Crown Prince. Banners declared him an enemy of Islam. Iran was now cast in the role of the ultimate defender of Palestine and the Arab homeland, and it was building an Islamic resistance movement against the enemy.

———

It began in a spectacularly violent fashion, with plumes of smoke, twisted metal, and mangled bodies. In November 1982, the Israeli command post in Tyre was blown up, killing seventy-five Israeli military personnel. In April 1983, the American embassy in Beirut was bombed: sixty-three people were killed. The following October, the Marine Corps barracks and the French paratroopers' headquarters were blown up. The Americans and the French had come to Lebanon as part of a multinational force for peace in the wake of the Israeli withdrawal. More than three hundred were killed, including 241 Americans, in the worst disaster for the United States since the Vietnam War and the deadliest single day for the Marine Corps since the battle of Iwo Jima in World War II. Each of these attacks was conducted by a young man driving a truck laden with explosives, ramming himself into a building: the first suicide bombers ever seen in the Middle East, a novel, deadly weapon. A combination of a car bomb technique that Israel itself had first used in Lebanon in early 1979 and the Japanese kamikaze concept against American targets in World War II, these suicide bombings were carried out by devout Shias, humiliated by their own state and by Israel and driven by a newfound fervor for martyrdom. Their recruiters were more canny operators, like Mughniyeh, the former member of Arafat's elite force. Mughniyeh had come up with the idea of a suicide bombing against the Israelis in Tyre. His fellow militants thought the idea was ludicrous: Who would be crazy enough to blow themselves up? But he had found someone—a childhood friend—and sent him to his death.

Mughniyeh would become the most devilish Hezbollah military master-mind. With his brother-in-law Mustafa Badreddine, they would hijack and kidnap their way through the 1980s and develop the armed wing of Hezbollah, turning it into a highly efficient and sophisticated militia, with ample help from Iran. Hezbollah would always officially deny any responsibility for the suicide bombings against the Americans and French in Lebanon and for all the Western hostages held in Lebanon during the 1980s and into the 1990s, claiming that Hezbollah didn't even exist in 1983. A group calling itself the Islamic Jihad claimed credit. But people like Sheikh Tufayli would later admit, proudly, that members of Hezbollah's early nucleus were indeed responsible.

By the first half of 1983, the influence of Hezbollah was seeping from the Beqaa Valley into the slums of Beirut—waves of Shia refugees fleeing the south had settled at the bottom of the city, close to the airport, layers of families and clans, villagers converging in neighborhoods. Where you landed determined under whose influence you fell: the more moderate Amal or the Islamist Hezbollah; temperate clerics or firebrand conservative ones. Extended families would evolve in totally separate directions and years later find that one side had espoused the chador and the beard while the other drank wine and wore ties. By 1984, the division of Beirut into east and west sectors had solidified, the Lebanese army had split up, and its Muslim brigade was in charge of keeping order on the western side of the city. But they were no match for the gunmen roaming the streets, young Shias avenging years of exclusion and discrimination by asserting their authority over the streets of West Beirut. Black banners of mourning were raised from lampposts on the streets where Faiz and Hawi had wandered, banners summoning young men to sacrifice themselves in the fight against Israel. The chador appeared on Hamra Street. When people in Ras Beirut first heard the name Hezbollah, many laughed. Hazem Saghieh, a journalist and towering intellectual of Lebanon's left, wondered: "The party of God? And who's the secretary-general? God himself?" A Greek-Orthodox Christian, he had been an ardent advocate of the Iranian Revolution and its promise of justice but was rapidly cured of his enthusiasm.

Very quickly, people stopped laughing. Graffiti appeared on the walls of the shell-shocked city proclaiming *Kulluna Khomeini*, We are all Khomeini. Every night, explosions began to hit bars and shops that sold liquor in West Beirut, around Hamra Street and on Phoenicia Street, the hub of Beirut nightlife, where clubs and bars had been swinging through the 1960s and '70s. One evening, a band of a hundred women in chadors went on a rampage on Phoenicia Street, smashing bottles and furniture in restaurants and bars. Gunmen barged into hotels, shooting up every bottle in the bar. Men with beards harassed women near the American University, demanding that they veil. Posters appeared, plastered on walls and trees. Just a few lines, printed in black, with a call to join a holy cause and a promise of worldly rewards. "A large flat, a fast car, an obedient wife." The puritanism of Khomeini's Iran was flattening Beirut's joie de vivre. Hezbollah was taking hold within the Shia community and building what it would call a "resistance society" by proselytizing, recruiting, or violently coercing Shias in ways that would change the identity of the community, a relentless, methodical campaign that would go almost unnoticed until it was too late. Hezbollah was seen as the embodiment of God's will on earth, the party of God according to the Quran itself, standing against the party of Satan, less a political party than a movement—and anyone who believed could adhere. In Iran, leaders addressed crowds with "O Party of God!" Hezbollah would quote the Quran in their propaganda and logos: "And whoever takes Allah and His Messenger, and those who believe, for friend—surely the party of Allah, they shall triumph." Hezbollah would adopt a variation of the Revolutionary Guards emblem as its party symbol: a raised fist holding a Kalashnikov rifle.

While Hezbollah was making inroads within the community, the armed resistance against the Israeli occupation in the south was still dominated by a coalition of leftist and communist militias as well as Amal, which was entrenched across the south. Even after the dramatic suicide bombings of 1982 and 1983, the Islamists were not yet the dominant force. The Lebanese National Resistance Front had battled alongside the Palestinians when the Israelis had invaded but they were now on their own, carrying out small attacks against the Israeli occupation across south Lebanon. There were more suicide bombers, a whole wave of them in 1985. Not Shias dying in the name of God, but secular nationalists dying for the nation, including a seventeen-year-old girl from West Beirut, Sana Mohaydali, who drove off in a Peugeot and blew up Israeli soldiers at a checkpoint. There was a communist woman who carried a suitcase through a checkpoint; there were Christian leftists and Sunni communists. And unlike the Islamic Jihad group that had blown up the French and Americans but remained in the shadows, these suicide bombers *wanted* the credit and the theatrical, morbid prestige of martyrdom. They wanted to show they were as valiant as—if not more valiant than—the religious fanatics. And so they introduced a new phenomenon to the world of guerrilla warfare and suicide bombers: they videotaped their farewell words and made posthumous appearances. After school, the young Sana had worked in a shop selling VHS tapes, and she had helped a suicide bomber record his farewell message. "The Bride of the South," as she would be called after her death, also taped her farewell message. "I am a future martyr. I do what I've decided to do with my soul at peace," said the young woman from beyond the grave. "I do my duty for the love of my people and my country."

The French magazine *Paris Match* ran a two-page color spread about her titled "La Kamikaze." Publications across the Middle East published pictures of her sweet, smiling face, framed by long dark hair, a red beret on her head. The goal, according to one politician at the time, was to prove that secular national resistance against the Israeli occupation was the alternative to a religious fanatic jihad. Hezbollah was just a momentary craze, a strange phenomenon in the chaos of war. But in the end, the left was no match for the zealousness with which Hezbollah applied itself to the battle, not just against the Israelis, but against their own rivals. The left in Lebanon would soon be eliminated ruthlessly, just as they had been in Iran.

Hezbollah itself used the tactic of suicide bombers very sparingly—it did not want to waste able-bodied men. Suicide was also forbidden, haram in Islam, but willingly making the ultimate sacrifice in battle and dying a *shaheed*, a martyr, was a quest that Hezbollah recruits began seeking with enthusiasm. Khomeini inspired a frenzied, exalted zealotry and obsession with martyrdom that was profoundly changing Shiism, in Iran and in Lebanon. Four years into the war with Iraq, Iran was sending waves of weaponless young boys to their death. Wearing red headbands and armed only with a metal key supposed to open the gates of heaven, thousands of teenage boys walked across minefields to clear the way for tanks, their bodies hurled into the air by the explosions. Volunteers or forcibly rounded up, these human waves were breaking enemy lines. Religious fervor permeated Iranian troops and the volunteer Basij forces, willing to die for the nation, for Khomeini, and for Imam Hussein. As ideological resolve took hold and death in martyrdom became desirable, Ashura was every minute of every day—at least for Khomeini, who insisted on war until victory. This was not an understanding of the Shia faith that Husseini could recognize, neither was it the one that Imam Sadr had preached. Even the martyrdom of Imam Hussein had been disfigured by Khomeini, according to former Iranian prime minister Bazergan, who wrote a celebrated open letter to the ayatollah in 1986 decrying how the revolution had made martyrdom a goal into itself.

Out of power, Bazergan was still in Iran and remained a member of parliament until 1984. He continued to fight for a different Iran, more democratic and less theocratic. He was unsuccessful of course, but in his letter he took Khomeini to task on political and theological grounds. In Fouad Ajami's book *Dream Palace of the Arabs*, which explores the demise and failure of Hawi's generation, Ajami delves into the letter, detailing how Bazergan reminded Khomeini that Imam Hussein had not marched willingly to a certain death. In fact, the Hussein of Bazergan's rendition, just as in Imam Sadr's, was a wise man who decides to return from whence he came when he realizes that the men who have called on him to help fight Yazid have withdrawn their invitation. He tries to avert a clash with his enemies, but it's too late. His war, then, was a defensive war, not a quest for martyrdom. Therefore, Karbala cannot be used to justify "war, war until victory," against Iraq or others. Bazergan said that Khomeini had strayed from "the objective realities and the lessons of the apostles and the imams."

The letter would be forgotten, its message of moderation irrelevant in the midst of war with Iraq, drowned out by the systematic indoctrination, the frenzied fervor of those seeking martyrdom on the battlefield, and the chants for Imam Hussein, a fervor that was washing over the Shia community in Lebanon.

In 1985, Israel pulled out from most of the territory it had occupied since 1982, including the large towns of Sidon and Tyre. It began to set up a buffer zone along its border, a few miles wide. Tens of thousands of Lebanese, Muslim and Christian alike, would continue to live under Israeli occupation for another fifteen years. In the villages that were now free of Israeli soldiers, Hezbollah got busy. The pattern was the same as in Baalbek but harsher and wider-ranging: rampaging against shops selling alcohol, closing down cafés, banning music, banning all other political parties. Fear descended onto people as Hezbollah imposed its law and a wave of assassinations began. Critics and rivals, especially leftists and communists, were eliminated ruthlessly. The crimes were not investigated; no one was caught. But everyone knew. Hezbollah recruited and organized: many joined willingly, others were rounded up. The more men fought in battle against the Israelis, the more there were martyrs, and the more martyrs there were, the more families became indebted to a system of patronage that looked after widows and orphans, ensuring loyalty to Hezbollah. Posters announcing the death of those who had died fighting the occupation began to look different: gone were the smiling faces of young women or clean-shaven men with sideburns who had died for the nation. The battle was now fought in the name of Islam; the men had beards, and the colors were black for mourning and green for Islam—signed: "Islamic Resistance." Many of the posters were exact copies of those on the walls in Iran—designed with the help of artists who had come specially from Tehran to help train local artists to produce public obituaries that were also used as propaganda.

In 1986, the oppressive, ruthless darkness in Iran had become too much for the Fahs family, and they decided to leave Tehran. The truth of what his dreams had helped birth had become a crushing burden for Sayyed Fahs. Nothing had changed; everything was worse: Khomeini's embrace of the Palestinian cause had delivered no victories; a radical Islamist militia was on the rise in his country; and friends were being executed in Iran. The purge that had first targeted the secular left and other opponents of Khomeini was extending its reach, silencing former committed revolutionaries. A whole new wave of executions was under way. It wasn't easy to leave, and it wasn't a clean break. Sayyed Fahs went back and forth for a few years, until he cut all ties in 1988. Just like severing ties with a loved one, the extrication process was hard, drawn out, as one hangs on to slivers of hope that perhaps the other can still change. In the case of the Iranian regime, there was always this hope that perhaps the sage Khomeini simply wasn't aware of the abuses being committed in his name. But he was.

Fahs was shaken to his core when one of his closest friends was defrocked, jailed, tortured horribly, and then executed. Beyond the horrific details, there was the shattered grand dream. Fahs had envisioned a borderless Muslim community, and had gone to Iran believing the wave would start from there. Instead, he had found Shia sectarianism and Persian nationalism. The combination was toxic. He rediscovered his own identity, his Arab belonging, his Lebaneseness. Sitting in Tehran, listening to Fairuz, he cried. The family returned to Lebanon only to find that darkness had preceded them. In their village of Jebsheet, the only woman to wear the full black cloak in the 1970s had been Fahs's wife, as was incumbent on the wife of a cleric. Now there were chadors everywhere. Relatives who had never veiled were covering their hair. His daughter Badia felt as if there had been a coup in their absence, an overnight takeover. She had left Iran a country where there were still daily acts of defiance against the new regime despite the dangers. She came home to find that villagers had fully absorbed the ideas that Khomeini was peddling. Far from the heart of the revolution, unaware of its abject horrors, people wanted some of its shine. There were benefits. With generous funding from Iran, Hezbollah was creating a copy of the Iranian system in Lebanon: schools, charities, martyrs' associations, Mahdi scouts, religious seminaries attached to Qom instead of Najaf. And there were reciters. Professional chanters of religious eulogies for Imam Hussein or others came from Iran to teach and spread a specific style among the Shias of Lebanon.

Badia could hardly believe her ears when she first heard the chanting blaring from loudspeakers mounted on the roof of a car driving around the village. Rhythmic, repetitive, entrancing. But nothing she'd ever heard in Lebanon before. In Iran, yes, but not here. Badia had spent a year studying in the Qom hawza for women but had found it too heavy to bear, almost neurotically devotional. There were too many fables and too much Persian haughtiness. She moved to a hawza set up for Arab students and found an even worse environment, surrounded by students who had left everything to join what they thought was a utopian Islamic state. They were detached from reality, drowning in a fanaticism that would make it hard to return to their home countries. She left there, too.

In Lebanon, Ashura had always been an occasion for reciting poetry and retelling the story of Imam Hussein. Men cried and gently thumped their chests with an open hand, sitting on the floor of a *husseiniyya*, a congregation hall specifically reserved for ceremonies mourning Imam Hussein. The gesture of grief and self-flagellation was known as *latmiya*. In various corners of the world, there were Shias who engaged in a more forceful, sometimes bloody latmiya, self-flagellating with chains, cutting their foreheads and beating them with their hands to make the blood flow—just as Easter passion processions run the gamut from parades through villages in Italy to actual crucifixions in the Philippines. Lebanon had been on the tamer side. But now Ashura, and every funeral of a Hezbollah fighter, was an occasion for mobilizing, indoctrinating, and forcefully thumping one's chest.

A famous religious chanter from the Arab Ahwaz region of Iran had come to Lebanon to propagate the Iranian-style latmiya. Known as Asa-kiri, it was his voice blaring from the cars driving around villages, chanting, rhythmic, militaristic—the new soundtrack to life. He stood in hussein-iyyas as acolytes, men with full beards in military fatigues, led the crowd and demonstrated the gestures: arms swinging above the head, crossing over the chest, and open palms thumping over the heart. Asakiri chanted in Arabic:

> O lover of jihad
> O lover of jihad

Swing, cross, thump. Swing, cross, thump. "All together now, all together!" Some in the crowd looked lost, clapping instead. Some used one hand only, thumping gently as they had done all their life. The most enthusiastic seemed to be the youngest in the front row, swinging their arms energetically.

> O lover of jihad, O lover of jihad
> Ruhollah Khomeini, Ruhollah Khomeini
> On the battlefield of jihad
> O lover of jihad, O lover of jihad
> Grab your weapons, Grab your weapons
> Let's go to the battlefield, Hezbollah calls you
> Hezbollah calls you, to remove all sedition
> Make war against the enemy

Even the soundtrack of revolution had changed. The left had hummed other songs and strummed guitars. Their bard was the Lebanese composer Marcel Khalifeh with his *oud*, the lute-like pear-shaped stringed instrument that is central to Arab music. Khalifeh sang verses of the most famous Palestinian poet of all, Mahmoud Darwish.

> Between me and Rita is a rifle and those who know Rita
> Prostrate themselves and pray to the amber in her eyes.

Khalifeh still sang, but he couldn't fill stadiums anymore. His public had become a target of the Islamists, a campaign to ruthlessly silence those who could offer an intellectual alternative to the Shia community: Shia-on-Shia violence, opposite worldviews clashing.

In Pakistan, the time had come for a new phenomenon that had no precedent in recent history: systematic Sunni-on-Shia killings.

8

SHIA KAFIR

PAKISTAN

1980–88

I went to the West and saw Islam but no Muslims;
I got back to the East and saw Muslims but no Islam.

—Muhammad Abduh,
nineteenth-century modernist religious scholar

In the summer of 1987, Pakistani Sunnis went into a village on the tribal areas bordering Afghanistan and killed Shias, fellow countrymen. Then Shias killed Sunnis. Almost two hundred people died. The violence was not the result of communal riots, nor a feud between tribes. Neither was it a war between nations, as was unfolding between Iran and Iraq. The two neighboring countries had been fighting each other for almost seven years by now, but Iraqi Shias were fighting loyally under their country's flag against Iran, and the narrative of a Persian-Arab clash was only just beginning to take sectarian overtones. No, the bloodletting in Pakistan was the first premeditated, state-sponsored attack by one sectarian militia against another sect, the first such killings that the Muslim world had witnessed in modern times. The sectarian killings were born out of the seeds of the Iranian Revolution and its clash with Saudi Wahhabism, with a dose of provocative zealotry from Zia ul-Haq, still in power thanks to his 1985 referendum appointing him as the upholder of the country's piety.

Each camp had its foot soldiers. But before the blood and the sectarian militias, there were the evangelists: two Pakistani *allamas*—religious scholars with rival worldviews—one aligned with Iran, the other with Saudi Arabia. The two men met only once, but the parallel tracks of their lives tell the tale of the proxy war that the House of Saud and Khomeini began to fight in Pakistan in the 1980s. Their words chart the radicalization of their respective communities, and their brutal deaths mark the start of modern-day Sunni-Shia sectarian violence that would spread across Pakistan before making its way to the Middle East. The two men lived in a separate world, almost a separate country from the one that the television anchor Mehtab was living in, but over time, their Pakistan would come to dominate hers.

Allama Ehsan Elahi Zaheer had studied at the Islamic university in Medina and was a protégé of its powerful vice rector, the blind Saudi sheikh Bin Baz. Allama Arif Hussaini had studied in Najaf and was one of the first Pakistani religious students to embrace Ayatollah Khomeini, attending his evening prayers and lectures in his place of exile and pressing fellow Pakistani students to show support to the Iranian reactionary.

Allama Zaheer had a perennially angry voice and wore the uniform of a nationalist: a karakul hat, worn most famously by Pakistan's founder, Jinnah, and a salwar kameez with a waistcoat on top. With his trimmed dark brown beard and his gold-rimmed glasses with tinted lenses, he looked more like a rabble-rouser than a theologian.

Allama Hussaini was tall and stood out in a crowd, dressed in the long cloak of a cleric, his black turban a mark of his lineage as a sayyed, a descendant of the prophet. His speeches were fiery, but not angry. They both mastered Arabic, Hussaini with a soft, Persian-inspired inflection, Zaheer with the more strained, guttural accent he had picked up in the Gulf.

Zaheer and Hussaini were born a year apart, on either side of the country, just as the 1947 partition of British India was giving birth to an independent Pakistan. Hussaini came from the small village of Paiwar, in the Kurram district of the tribal areas bordering Afghanistan—the only district with a large Shia minority, estimated at around 40 percent. He hailed from the Shia Turi tribe; other tribes were mixed Sunni-Shia, like the Bangash. Zaheer came from the Punjab, where the rich landowners were often Shias and the workforce Sunni.

Pakistan's Shias were the largest minority in the country, the second-largest Shia population outside Iran, but unlike Shias in the Arab world they had never felt downtrodden. Anti-Shia sentiment existed on the sub-continent, even in pre-partition India, but just as in the rest of the Muslim world until then, its expression was limited to a minority of clerics and their followers, a strand of thought that did not pervade the general popu-lation or undermine a country's stability. Communal violence flared every now and then, especially around religious festivals. Sometimes it erupted over petty disputes, like the height of a minaret or the path of a procession, or more serious (but not deadly) matters, like land disputes. Shia leaders spoke out for the rights of all Pakistanis but their demands as a minority community were also heard.

The Shias of Pakistan had been key players in the founding of the country, alongside the father of the nation, Muhammad Jinnah, a Shia himself. Pakistan was not envisioned as a homeland for Sunnis only, but as an inclusive Muslim homeland. And in the first decades of its existence, the sectarian identities of its leaders were of no relevance. Shias were rich landowners in the Punjab, but they also became generals and prominent politicians. Zulfiqar Ali Bhutto married an Iranian Shia. He did not shy away from Shia symbolism—his own name, *zulfiqar*, was the name of Imam Ali's sword with its split tip.

But Zia was putting an end to inclusive Muslim nationalism with his Nizam-i-Islam. When he imposed the new laws in February 1979, he also promised he would set up a state-run zakat fund before the end of that year. One of the pillars of Islam, zakat is a charitable contribution of 2.5 percent of one's wealth over a certain amount, mandated by God but rarely imposed by governments (except for a handful, like Saudi Arabia). With $225 million in seed money from Saudi Arabia, the United Arab Emirates, and the Pakistani government, Zia was planning to make mandatory deductions from personal and corporate bank accounts of all Muslims in the country. He said this would help alleviate poverty and beggary and turn Pakistan into a more just society. The announcement caused much consternation among Pakistanis. Some began to withdraw their money from banks to evade this extra taxation; others complained about the forced piety, wondering whether the government would next distribute punch cards that people would have to show to prove they'd gone to the mosque to pray five times a day. Pakistanis began to refer to the zakat tax as a "Zia tax," joking that all the money was going into the pocket of the biggest beggar of them all.

But for Pakistan's Shias, the plans for mandatory zakat were no joke; they were a sign that Zia wasn't just Islamizing the country, he was "Sunnifying" it. Sunni and Shia Islamic law differ in certain aspects, and by imposing shari'a as he was doing, Zia was mandating a Sunni reading of Islamic law. For Shias, ever since the partisans of Ali had opted not to pay allegiance or taxes to the first caliph after the prophet, zakat could only ever be a voluntary individual act, it could not be levied by the state. Small differences in the reading of Islamic law, which had never been an issue in decades of communal life, were suddenly causing a major rift in Pakistani society. It's not clear whether the Saudis or their envoy Dawalibi were oblivious or indifferent to the reaction in a country with such a large Shia population.

On the same day in February 1979 that Zia had made his announcement about Islamic law, Sunni groups in Karachi held protests demanding the immediate enforcement of Sunni Hanafi Islamic law across all of Pakistan and the appointment of Sunni judges to all the shari'a courts. Shia clerics decided to get organized, worried that this was only the beginning of a campaign against them. On April 12 and 13, 1979, thousands of Shias from various organizations flocked to the town of Bhakkar in Punjab province for a convention. They formed the Tehrik-e-Nifaz-e-Jafariya (TNFJ), the Movement for the Implementation of Jaafari (Shia) law. The TNFJ wasn't demanding to apply Shia law across Pakistan, but wanted, among other things, that it be recognized by courts and that more Shia judges be appointed to the Council of Islamic Ideology. Zia did not impose zakat. Months went by.

Then, on June 20, 1980, Zia finally announced that the zakat ordinance would be officially implemented. The next day, banks across the country were closed for immediate collection of the 2.5 percent tax on all accounts. Enraged by Zia's disregard for their rights, Shias from across the country descended onto Islamabad in early July. The TNFJ, Shia student organizations, and radical clerics gathered a crowd of a hundred thousand that laid siege to government buildings. Braving a rainstorm, tear gas, and beatings by the police, they stayed put for three days. Never before had Pakistan's Shias mobilized or needed to mobilize in such a way. Suddenly awake to their street power, Zia had to relent within a few days and exempt them from the mandatory zakat. The Shia activists were exhilarated: they were the first group in Pakistan to successfully defy the dictator and his martial law on any issue. Their protests had also scored a victory specifically for their community. But Sunni clerics and activists were seething: by giving in to Shias, Zia had undermined their vision of Pakistan as a model Islamic state. Lines were being drawn within Pakistani society, between those who paid zakat and those who didn't, between the Sunnis and the Shias—the "other" Muslims.

With their Islamabad siege, the Shias had committed another first: as a community, they had called on outside support. And Khomeini had answered, warning Zia that if he continued to persecute Pakistan's Shias, he would meet the same fate as the shah. Modern-day Iran and Pakistan were close friends. As a young country, Pakistan had looked to Iran as a model while writing its constitution, and it had rushed to compose a national anthem for the shah's visit to Pakistan in 1950. The shah had positioned

himself as the benefactor of his younger neighbor, though sometimes lord-
ing himself over it, to the resentment of Pakistanis. But there had never
been direct interference in each other's affairs.

Revolutionary Iran did things differently—it positioned itself as the
protector of Shias everywhere. Khomeini saw Shias both as a conduit to
export the revolution—as in Lebanon with groups like Hezbollah—but also
as subjects of his borderless wilayat. Students in particular were targeted.
The Shia Imamiyat Student Organisation (ISO) became a revolutionary
outfit, promoting Khomeini's vision and agenda in Pakistan. Within a few
years, the ISO would be directly linked to the office of the Supreme Leader.
Pictures of Khomeini went up in its offices; young students hung his posters in their bedrooms. Religious students were aggressively courted: in the
past, Pakistanis had mostly gone to study in Najaf, but within a year of the
revolution four thousand students received scholarships from the Iranian
government to study in Qom for up to a year. By the time they returned,
many had fully embraced the concept of the wilayat, preaching it to others
in Pakistan.

There is no telling how receptive Shias in Pakistan would have been
to Khomeini's message of revolution if Zia had not provoked them, but
the provocation gave clerics like Hussaini a powerful rallying tool. Allama
Hussaini was a revolutionary at heart, a rabble-rouser who irked the Iraqis
with his protests about the oppression of Shias while he lived in Najaf.
While he was in Qom, he had sent letters of protests to the shah. When
the zakat siege took place in 1980, he rallied thousands of volunteers from
his home in Kurram. At that time, Hussaini was still a relatively unknown
figure outside Kurram, but by 1984, the thirty-seven-year-old cleric had
become the head of the TNFJ. He went to visit Khomeini to receive official
support. Hussaini had previously been appointed as Khomeini's representative, a *wakil*, but official recognition carried more weight. It also meant
he could collect *khums*, a Shia religious tax, some of it for the benefit of the
Shia community in Pakistan and some to send to Khomeini. The Iranian
Supreme Leader was also a *marja'a taqlid*, an object of emulation for followers. Most of the high-ranking clerics who hold the position of marja'a
are in Iraq and Iran, and their representatives around the Muslim world
collect a portion of the khums tax from the faithful on their behalf. In the
1980s, Pakistan became a huge source of such revenue for Iran.

Hussaini was in awe of the ayatollah. He thought Khomeini was
blessed, the real representative of the Hidden Imam on earth, and the only
man who could break the dominance of the great powers—both the US

and the USSR—on other countries, including Pakistan. Copying revolutionary Iran, Hussaini tried to introduce the new tradition of "Jerusalem Day" in Pakistan in 1984; later he added a "Death to America" day. For Hussaini, only an Islamic revolution modeled after Iran's revolution would solve Pakistan's woes, although he was careful never to give the impression he wanted to bring down the regime with violence. Zia may have been his "near enemy" but Hussaini had "far enemies," the same ones that Khomeini despised so much: Saudi Arabia and Wahhabism. He spoke of them with disdain, those "Wahhabis who wrap themselves in the mantle of Islam," and ranted against the House of Saud, attacking them where it hurt most: parroting Khomeini's favorite line, Hussaini said the Saudis were bad custodians of Mecca and Medina. The task, he insisted, should be given to a committee of Islamic countries. Hussaini's rise provoked fissures in the community; clerics who followed the more quietist tradition didn't approve of his Iranization of Pakistan's Shias.

The more Hussaini and the TNFJ agitated and showed off their newfound power, the more they aggravated Sunni radical groups—a local tit-for-tat mirroring the mix of petulant and sometimes violent reactions the Saudis were having to Iran's export of revolutionary zeal. At the time, Hussaini was running a religious seminary in Peshawar, spreading Khomeini's gospel. He wasn't the only one to settle in the city. Those "Wahhabis in the mantle of Islam" that he hated so much were there now too. The Arab fighters joining the war against the Soviets had converged on Peshawar. They drove big cars, carried big guns, and threw a lot of money around.

—

They trickled in at first, but they stood out immediately. By the mid-1980s, they had taken over whole neighborhoods and were renting dozens of houses on the pine-lined streets of University Town, a quiet part of Peshawar, just outside the nineteenth-century walls of the gated citadel city, a prosperous area filled with whitewashed one-story bungalows and flowering bougainvillea. They ran charities and religious seminaries, they had brought their wives and children, and the wives had more children. They were not all Wahhabis, they weren't even all Saudis, but "Wahhabi" was the blanket term used derogatorily by men like Hussaini and Khomeini to rile up their followers against those Sunnis who espoused the Saudi practice of Islam. For the Arab fighters, Peshawar was the perfect base—Afghanistan was just an hour and a half away, past Torkham Gate and through the famed Khyber Pass, immortalized by Rudyard Kipling in "The Ballad of the King's Jest."

> When spring-time flushes the desert grass,
> Our kafilas wind through the Khyber Pass.
> Lean are the camels but fat the frails,
> Light are the purses but heavy the bales,
> As the snowbound trade of the North comes down
> To the market-square of Peshawur town.

Peshawar's fate was to be located on the Grand Trunk Road, Asia's oldest and longest route. From Alexander the Great marching to India, to the British colonizers who made it their administrative headquarters for the province; from the caravans of traders on the Silk Road to the hippies traveling to India in the 1960s, Peshawar could be everything to everyone: *purushapura*, in the old Sanskrit, a "city of men." The diverse city had a layered past where Sikhs and Hindus had lived among the tribal Pashtuns before independence. A city of flowers, it still had beautiful, lush gardens at its entrance, a leftover from Mughal and British times. Conservative but inclusive, this was a city and a region of famed Pashtun warriors who could recite the verses of two books by heart: the holy Quran and the poetry of their very own Peshawari Sufi saint Rahman Baba. Hundreds of daily visitors thronged the shrine of the seventeenth-century poet, while grandmothers lulled children to sleep with Baba's poetry of love and peace.

Long misunderstood by outsiders, Peshawar had been reduced to a "city of evil countenances" by Kipling and other orientalist writers and journalists who perpetuated the myth with references to "cold black eyes" peering "out of narrow alleys" and fearsome tribal warriors who were "inarticulate" and expressed themselves in the ancient Peshawar way (according to such writers, by firing their rifles). True, there had always been guns on sale in Peshawar's markets, and drugs too, but in the 1980s, the "city of evil countenances" finally earned the reputation Kipling had bestowed on it. Peshawaris didn't see it happening at first. Without their say, their city became a petri dish for ideological experiments that would one day produce an explosion of hatred on the other side of the world. But they were its first victims. Peshawar's fate was also to be the headquarters of the Afghan mujahedeen leaders in exile, home to several hundred thousand Afghan refugees, hundreds of Western aid workers, charities, and UN agencies—and the growing contingent of Arab Islamist activists, fighters, and journalists, lured by the siren call of jihad and the thrill of action.

The Egyptian contingent was the biggest. The doctor Ayman Zawahiri was there; released from jail after the Sadat assassination and now leader of the Egyptian Islamic Jihad, he would rise to number two in al-Qaeda in the years to come. Mohammad Islambouli, the brother of Sadat's assassin, also out of jail, had traveled to Peshawar for jihad after his brother had killed the "near enemy." He played a key role in channeling fighters to Peshawar and would later try to assassinate the Egyptian president Hosni Mubarak. Issam Berqawi, aka Abu Muhammad al-Maqdissi, a Palestinian who had grown up in Kuwait, arrived around 1985. He had studied in Medina, where he had come in contact with Bin Baz and rejoiced in the access to books on Wahhabism. Maqdissi's brother-in-law was Abdellatif al-Derbas, the associate of Juhayman al-Otaibi, who had helped print Juhayman's incendiary pamphlets in Kuwait in 1979. Maqdissi greatly admired Juhayman, and in Peshawar he would write books that took the zealot's vision even further, lambasting the Saudi state and inspiring a new generation of fanatics. For now, he was in the shadow of people like Osama bin Laden. Still young and shy when he first showed up in Peshawar, Bin Laden was flush with money, as the scion of a wealthy family that ran a large construction company and was close to the royal family. At first, he only made trips from Jeddah, but he finally settled in Peshawar with his family in the mid-1980s.

The Arabs kept to themselves in clusters of houses; they paid good rent. Though many Peshawaris resented them and their haughty ways, it was hard to turn down their money. Shop signs in Arabic went up around the area, and they were good customers, so grocers catered to their needs. They drove around in cars with tinted windows, ran schools and mosques, and published books in Arabic that would feed generations of violent militants. They were establishing a small Arabistan in the middle of Pakistan (just as Iranians were setting up a Little Tehran in Baalbek).

Jamal Khashoggi, the young Saudi graduate of Indiana University, was there, too. Now a journalist writing for Saudi publications, he sent excited dispatches from the front about the daily life and the exploits of the Arab fighters, who, in his eyes, represented the unity of the Islamic nation—this Afghan war was a good war, a war of the faithful against the unbelievers. This was also a war that served everyone's interests: the Saudis who needed to rebuild their reputation after the debacle in Mecca, the Americans who wanted to give the Soviets their own Vietnam, and Zia who used it to hold on to power.

Until the early 1980s, Islamist revolutionaries and militants were still focused on the struggle against their respective governments, confined by national borders, as in Syria or Egypt. Although their goals were roughly the same—to bring about an Islamic government in their country—there was no bigger, unifying cause. (Arab fighters had joined the ranks of the PLO on occasion, but it had never become a real transnational legion of fighters.) They had watched the success of the Iranian Revolution and marveled at the power of the spoken word and the ability of Islam to bring millions to the street. With the war against the Soviets in Afghanistan, they discovered the battlefield—and one another. Islamist jihadists of every nationality and creed came together and got high on power.

If Beirut was the supermarket of the left in the 1970s, where Marxists, communists, Egyptians, Iraqis, and all the Palestinian factions debated and theorized, published and drank in bars arguing over ideas and then fought in the streets, Peshawar was the supermarket of the Islamists in the 1980s without the drinking: there the discussions were about Islamic law, fatwas, the war of the believers, the unity of the Muslim nation, and the humanitarian needs of Afghan refugees.

There was actually alcohol available in Zia's Pakistan, bootlegged or smuggled, served in hidden speakeasies or hotel bars, including in Peshawar, which had always evaded full government control and where spies, journalists, and Western aid workers sought a break from the nearby war in the city's watering holes. Some bars were for foreigners only, like the American Club, which opened in 1985 and served drinks and cheeseburgers, and held aerobics classes. Bin Laden was its most famous neighbor. The Intercontinental Hotel, overlooking the Pakistani Armed Forces' eighteen-hole golf course, inaugurated in 1975, was where mujahedeen leaders, journalists, and Westerners now all rubbed shoulders, uncomfortably. On one reporting assignment in Pakistan, Jamal sat in the garden of the Intercontinental Hotel with the mujahedeen as they discussed their day and their next moves and looked sneeringly at the Westerners sitting at the bar. One of the fighters called to the waiter: "Close the curtains, we don't want to see these people inside." There was no violence, no ransacking of bars, no attacks against Westerners, not yet. The bar still managed to serve alcohol until well into the 1980s, but the tension was building. Jamal was young and excited to be part of something greater than himself. He posed for pictures with a Kalashnikov, and he spent days, sometimes weeks, with the Arab fighters, bonding with them and pouring his heart into his dispatches. But in that fleeting moment in the garden, he sensed the arrogance of the Arab fighters, the friction between worlds and cultures. One of his Islamist friends had once criticized him for helping a European aid agency unload a shipment for Afghan refugees—why was Jamal helping the *kuffars*, the infidels? "Because these kuffars are giving millions of dollars of goods to the Afghan refugees," he replied. "Are you?"

The Arab men who were making their way to Peshawar were a strange assortment: renegades unwanted by their governments, true believers looking for a just cause, thrill seekers on a short jihad vacation, doctors treating wounded mujahedeen. They were a mix of holy war fighters, Peace Corps volunteers, and a Muslim version of the Spanish Civil War's communist International Brigades. The inspiration for them all, or at least most, was Abdallah Azzam. A charismatic Palestinian from the West Bank with a trademark beard with two white streaks, Azzam was one of the first Arabs to arrive in Pakistan, and he set up the logistical and theological foundations for more to follow.

Devout from a young age, Azzam had some experience fighting in Jordan with the PLO against Israel. A graduate of Egypt's Al-Azhar University, he went on to teach in Jeddah, where his yearning for jihad pulled him closer to the war in Afghanistan, and to Pakistan, where he started teaching Arabic and the Quran in 1981 at the Islamic University in Islamabad. The newly inaugurated King Faisal mosque, as well as the university, were both Saudi-funded. Azzam soon settled in Peshawar and persuaded Bin Laden, whom he had met in Jeddah, to make the trip. The two men wanted to open the spigot of Arab fighters that had started trickling in 1980. Bin Laden provided the money; Azzam took care of the rallying cry. Bin Laden started by raising a fortune for the mujahedeen in Jeddah in 1984, up to $10 million, contributions from relatives and princes. He announced he would offer a ticket, housing, and living expenses for every Arab (and his family) who joined the fight. Then Azzam issued a religious edict that turned modern tradition upside down: his fatwa argued that the jihad in Afghanistan was *fard ayn,* an individual obligation for every Muslim.

This had not been done before; fard ayn mostly applied to duties like praying or fasting, the pillars of Islam. The fard ayn could apply to a struggle against one's own leader, as Farag had declared it against Sadat in Egypt. But Azzam was making it an obligation for Muslims to defend Muslim land not their own against the non-Muslims. Greater causes usually fell under a different category, *fard kifaya,* a duty met by the community as a whole and therefore not binding on the individual. Clerics ridiculed Azzam's fatwa. Bin Baz fudged his words, calling for financial and moral support. Over time, the lines blurred and the ridicule disappeared when clerics saw that Arab fighters were answering Azzam's call.

Around 1985, Azzam and Bin Laden set up the Maktab al-Khadamat, the Services Bureau, in Peshawar: half guesthouse, half office, the large, one-story house with a big garden in University Town became the nerve center of the Arab jihad. They used the Bureau to fund-raise and offer money to refugees, recruit and deploy mujahedeen, and distribute weapons. Bin Laden paid $25,000 every month to keep it running. In later years, the two men would part ways over Bin Laden's plans to take the jihad global; Azzam would be assassinated in 1989 in Peshawar, and the Maktab al-Khadamat would turn into the nucleus of al-Qaeda.

The bulk of the fighting against the Soviets was done by the Afghans, a quarter of a million full- or part-time fighters throughout the war. Official and covert American support went to them, $3 billion over the course of the eight-year war, with the Saudis matching every dollar. The Arab fighters, or Arab Afghans, as they would become known, were a minority, a few thousand at any one time, an estimated total of thirty-five thousand over the course of the war. Thousands more came as volunteers of all types, including medical, to taste not the thrill of battle but the exhilarating atmosphere of Peshawar and the bonds of this new transnational jihad. No state systematically funded or organized the Arab Afghans; they raised money privately and organized themselves. Unofficially, they were a Saudi pet project, a national cause. The head of Saudi intelligence, Prince Turki al-Faisal, son of the late king, was a frequent visitor to Peshawar. So was his chief of staff, with bags of cash for the mujahedeen. The lines between what was government and what wasn't were indistinguishable in an absolute kingdom. Saudi Airlines gave huge discounts on tickets to Peshawar. Azzam's salary was paid by the World Muslim League. The league also had an office in Peshawar that operated as a front to funnel money and recruit volunteers. In Cairo, the office of the Bin Laden family construction group, which hired local skilled labor for construction in the kingdom, became a pipeline for those seeking to join the battle. Saudi individuals raised and donated money in all shapes and sizes: businessmen wrote fat checks, women donated jewelry. The governor of Riyadh, Prince Salman, the future Saudi king, was in charge of raising private funds for the mujahedeen and funneled millions to the cause. Charities like the Saudi Red Crescent and the International Islamic Relief Organization, all connected to the state, set up offices in Peshawar, working closely with Saudi-backed mujahedeen groups that ran refugee camps. Jamal worried about where the Saudis were spending their money. The funds were going to marginal sectarian groups that were not popular with the wider Afghan population but honed closer to the kingdom's interpretation of Islam. Bin Baz had reportedly thrown a fit when there had been moves early on to promote a popular Sufi-leaning Afghan rebel to the top leadership of the mujahedeen. Jamal thought that no good could come of the promotion of the more sectarian, puritanical Afghan groups, and he made his views known to Prince Salman.

In 1980, there were already more than a million Afghan refugees in Pakistan, then a country of 80 million. By 1990, the number of registered Afghan refugees reached 3.27 million. In those first years, refugees in Pakistan had to sign up with one of the seven official mujahedeen parties backed by Saudi Arabia, the Peshawar Seven, to qualify for food and supplies. With sustenance came loyalty. The refugee camps became recruiting centers for foot soldiers while the religious seminaries indoctrinated the young with a new worldview.

With Zia's approval, Saudi charities built hundreds of *madrassa*s, religious seminaries, along the border with Afghanistan, and they favored the exclusionary teachings of fundamentalist schools of thought from the subcontinent that were closest to Saudi puritanism—like the Deobandis and Allama Zaheer's Ahl-e Hadith. Afghan students filled the classroms but Pakistani enrollment in religious schools was also on the rise. Across the country, but especially along Pakistan's western border with Afghanistan and Iran, funds from zakat collection and Saudi money paid for the mushrooming of religious schools. The rise in the number of graduates in the 1980s outpaced the population growth by an estimated 300 percent. The quality of teaching could not keep up, and the character of the schools' teachings changed: this was no longer about excellence in religious knowledge, but about indoctrination and mobilization, producing either militant activists for the war or Islamic bureaucrats for the continued Islamization of the country. *Madrassa*, the Arabic word for school of any kind, secular or religious, Christian or Muslim, took on a dark, ominous meaning in this context. Some of the graduates of these religious schools became founders of the Taliban movement, which terrorized Afghanistan in the 1990s. The Saudi sponsorship of the Arab Afghans would lead to the rise of al-Qaeda. The problem with Saudi imperialism, cultural or other, was that they were bad managers. More often than not they lost control over their product—then feigned ignorance or innocence.

As often, the Western media focused on the fanaticism of a few in the religious seminaries but ignored a much bigger problem: even the minds of those who did not espouse violence were closing, being molded into something more doctrinaire, less tolerant than what had shaped their parents' understanding of the world. Bigotry was being inculcated in regular schools across Pakistan too, where the curriculum was changing. Textbooks on all subjects became laced with religion, and history was distorted to fit the current ideology, defining Pakistani nationalism as exclusively Muslim, and increasingly portraying minorities as subhuman. The Saudis were helping to create an environment in which ideas and actions could be taken to the extreme, and they were blinded to the consequences of their creation because they could not recognize the intolerance of their own ideology.

—

Of all the cities that were being transformed by the impact of 1979, plunged into fear or darkness, Peshawar suffered the most, and most quickly: a deluge of refugees, of guns, of hatred. The city was being brutalized by Zia's Islamization, the fervor and the quest for martyrdom of the Afghan mujahedeen who were based there, the arrogance of the Arab fighters who walked around like they owned the city. The Friday sermons grew increasingly angry. "Kill in the name of God," screamed the preachers. "Jihad in the name of God." The venom spouted from the mosques' loudspeakers echoed across the city, coming into people's homes through open windows or cracks in the doors, impregnating people's consciousness. Allama Hussaini was still there preaching in his Peshawar mosque where his religious school was popular, full of adepts of Khomeini's message. Two worlds were clashing, at first only in words. From the loudspeakers of Peshawar's Sunni mosques came words the locals had not heard before, or if they had, only in whispers: "Shia *kafir*," screamed the preachers, "Shia kafir." Shia infidels . . .

Jamal Khashoggi had heard those words before, or variations of them, not just because he'd grown up in Saudi Arabia, but because in December 1981 he had agreed to display an anti-Shia, anti-Iran pamphlet at the Muslim Arab Youth Association book fair he helped organize in Springfield, Illinois. Someone had come to him with copies of a newly released Arabic book titled *And Now the Magi's Turn Has Come*, which argued that the Iranian Revolution was nothing but a ploy for Shia domination of the Middle East. The author was signaling that Iranians weren't really Muslims but Zoroastrians (*magi* being a term for Zoroastrian priests) who had infiltrated Islam since the days following the death of the prophet. They therefore posed a real danger to the unity of the Muslim nation. The book was full of historical and theological inaccuracies, but none of that mattered to those who were wary of revolutionary Iran. Egyptian students protested against such a divisive book being sold at the fair. Khashoggi thought long and hard but chose to go ahead—there were values, and there were interests. In 1981, the Arab world was a year into the Iran-Iraq War, and awe about Khomeini's success in bringing a theocracy to power had subsided in the Sunni world. Geopolitics now dictated that everything should be done to undermine Iran. Though it was Saddam who had invaded Iran and started the war, Arabs saw Khomeini as the aggressor.

The author of the anti-Shia pamphlet had first tried to get his book printed at the beginning of 1980, but no publisher in the Arab world would take it, no one wanted to touch such a sectarian polemic. Anti-Shia writings were not new in the Muslim world, but their audience had always been limited, their message—coming from the fringes of fundamentalism— shunned by the majority. The historical, theological Sunni-Shia schism did not preoccupy people in their daily lives. In fact, the author of the *Magi* book was so fearful of the reaction that he wrote under a pseudonym. But in September 1980, just as the Iran-Iraq War was kicking off, the author had found a publisher and a most excellent patron: Bin Baz. The vice rector of Medina University was now the head of the Saudi Council of Senior Ulama. He asked a committee to review the book and became an instant fan: he ordered three thousand copies and helped promote it. Soon 120,000 copies had been printed, making their way around Saudi Arabia, Kuwait, and other Arab countries. The widespread distribution of the *Magi* book was a watershed moment, giving permission to a flood of anti-Shia publications in the 1980s. The author of the *Magi* book would reveal himself two decades later as Mohammad Zayn al-Abidin Surur, a Syrian Muslim Brother in exile, who had lived briefly in Saudi Arabia before settling in Kuwait. His anti-Shia views were driven by his hatred of Assad and Assad's alliance with Iran. Surur's writings and influence would ripple for decades, feeding a surge of reactionary militants that would eventually turn against the Saudi state. But initially, Surur's books served a strategic purpose.

The other anti-Shia author that the Saudis eagerly promoted was Bin Baz's star student, Pakistan's own Ehsan Elahi Zaheer, described as the most influential cleric in aggravating Sunni-Shia tensions and violence in South Asia. A student at the newly opened Islamic University of Medina from 1963 to 1968, he graduated with high honors and was encouraged by Bin Baz early on to publish his views. He wrote anti-Shia polemics even before the Iranian Revolution. Zaheer was schooled in the Ahl-e Hadith tradition, which rejected Shiism. His years in Saudi Arabia likely cemented those

views, and the revolution added fuel to his fire. Zaheer, who later started
the Jamiat Ahl-e Hadith political party, amply fulfilled the hopes of his
Saudi patrons and published fourteen anti-Shia books, which drew a wide
audience. He wrote many of them in Arabic, only later translating them
into Urdu. The heart of his argument was similar to Surur's but without the
politics: Shias were not real Muslims, they were infiltrated by Jews, magis,
and others. Just as with Surur's book, this was new language, not a theological debate, but an attack against Shias as people. Mainstream, moderate
Sunni clerics tried to resist the slippery slope toward such an unbending
attitude against fellow Muslims, but the radical voices grew louder and
louder. Increasing numbers of books were published with titles like *The
Shias' Revolt Against the Quran* or *Shias Rebel Against Islam*. The Saudis not
only encouraged such vitriol but helped translate the books into multiple
languages and distribute them around the Muslim world. Saudi embassies
from Islamabad to Washington kept copies available to hand out. This was
no longer about persuasion but political condemnation.

Although Zaheer didn't delve much into politics in his writings, he did
his bit to rally the faithful as the Iran-Iraq War dragged into its third year.
Iranian propaganda labeled the Iraqi government as an infidel regime, and
Saddam sought cover from the Islamic world. As a secular Baathist, he
had little experience with the world of Islamic organizations, so he turned
to Saudi Arabia. The Saudis sent their favorite man: Maarouf Dawalibi.
The Syrian adviser to the Saudi king, who also served as the head of the
World Muslim Congress, was instrumental in gathering the who's who
of the Islamic world for the Popular Islamic Conference (PICO) held in
April 1983: 280 religious scholars showed up, as well as activists from fifty
countries. The Pakistani delegation was the largest. Islamists who had ini-
tially hoped Khomeini would back their own Islamic revolution, like Syrian
Muslim Brother Sa'id Hawwa; those who were anti-Iran because they saw
Khomeini as a threat to the Arab nation; those who were close to the Saudis; those who saw the Iranians as nothing but infidel magi—they all came.
It made for a strange sight as they sat in their turbans and cleric's robes
in a conference hall whose front row was occupied by avowedly secular
Baathist men in uniform.

Zaheer, who by now had quite the following in the Arab world thanks to
his books, gave a speech denouncing the Iranians and calling on the Muslim
world to rally behind Saddam: "Those people only understand the language
of the sword, these people need to have a sword hanging over their neck, not
just the sword of Saddam and not just the sword of his heroes." Speaking in

fluent Arabic, without notes, Zaheer described the Iranians as evil people allied with other evil leaders, the Syrian and Libyan presidents. But the conspiracy would fail, Zaheer insisted, waving his fist and almost screaming by the end of his speech. In the front row, Saddam listened, impassive, before getting up for a long handshake with Zaheer at the end.

After the pamphlets, the books, and the conferences came the fatwas and the militias. In 1985, the Army of the Companions of the Prophets, the Sepah-e Sahaba Pakistan (SSP) militia, was formed in the Punjab, with the tacit approval of Zia and his security services. The SSP's only purpose was to denounce and attack Shias, the first overtly sectarian militia in the Muslim world, with the chilling rallying cry "Kafir, kafir, Shia kafir"—infidels. In 1986, a series of fatwas began to circulate widely, banning Sunnis from eating food cooked by Shias or attending their funerals. Then came more fatwas explicitly declaring Shias kafir—a true license to kill. Apostatizing non-Sunnis was not a new phenomenon in Pakistan or the Muslim world—it had been done to smaller Muslim minorities—but now it was becoming common currency against Shias, Pakistan's minority of millions.

What happened next was inevitable. In 1986, the sectarian poison that Zia and the Saudis had been injecting into Pakistan collided with the Afghan jihad, on Allama Hussaini's home turf, in Kurram district on the border with Afghanistan. Hussaini's Shia tribe, the Turis, were upset with the influx of refugees from Afghanistan and resented their area being used as a launching pad for attacks into Afghanistan, a passage for fighters and weapons across the border. They were on the receiving end of the retaliation from inside Afghanistan. The local tribes mobilized to block fighters and disarm them, amid reports that the government wanted to turn Kurram into a permanent base for the mujahedeen. Zia could not afford to let anyone stand in the way of his jihad, a lucrative business that was keeping his economy afloat and keeping him in power. Sporadic clashes took place throughout 1986, until July 1987, when Zia sent Afghan and Pakistani Sunni militants to attack Shia Turi villages. The fighting lasted for two weeks; the Shias fought back: 52 Shias and 120 Sunnis were killed, and 14 villages were partially or fully destroyed. Here then was the epicenter of modern-day sectarian bloodletting, the first of its kind in modern times. Sectarianism had been weaponized.

Targeted assassinations came next. On the morning of March 23, 1987, Zaheer was giving a lecture to a packed audience of the youth wing of his party in Lahore. He was interrupted midspeech by the explosion of a small bomb planted at his feet. Eight people were killed on the spot and

Zaheer was severely injured. Both Saddam and King Fahd offered medical care. The Saudis chartered a special medical plane to fly him, accompanied by his father, to Riyadh for treatment. He died at dawn on March 30 at the King Faisal hospital. He was granted two supreme honors: his funeral prayers, attended by thousands, were led by Sheikh Bin Baz himself, and he was laid to rest in Medina. In Pakistan, protests erupted over his death; thousands took to the streets in Lahore, clashing with the police and burning cars, chanting "Blood for Blood" and "Zia Killer." Zaheer had had his differences with Zia—he thought the general was using religion as a tool to stay in power. Like many fundamentalists, he felt the dictator had undermined Pakistan's identity and ideology by caving in to the Shias on the zakat issue. Did Zia dispose of a powerful cleric who was becoming inconvenient? Or did Shias want to silence a man spewing hate against them? Bin Baz personally tried to follow up and push for an investigation. No one would ever be caught for Zaheer's killing, the first high-profile assassination of a religious scholar in Pakistan. But in the years to come, the narrative would put the blame squarely on Shias, those magi kafir.

Just over a year later, after dawn prayers on August 5, 1988, several gunmen barged into Hussaini's madrassa in Lahore and shot him. He died on the spot. His bodyguard apparently tried to kill himself for having failed to protect him. In death, Hussaini was also granted two honors: the Iranians sent a delegation, and a representative of Khomeini delivered a eulogy at the funeral. Iran later issued a postage stamp in his honor. Zia came to the funeral and was also met with chants of "Zia killer, Zia Killer." This time, the killers had in fact been hired by the governor of the province, General Fazle Haq, a key figure of the Zia era, who was working with a member of Zia's security team on the assassination plot. Several members of the plot landed in prison. Haq would later be assassinated. The president's direct involvement was never proved.

Zaheer and Hussain had nothing and everything in common: their violent deaths, their efforts to radicalize their respective communities, and the role they each fulfilled in the proxy war between Saudi Arabia and Iran. Pakistan had now been a witness to the first two major sectarian-motivated assassinations in modern history.

—

Zia was trying to play a dangerous game of sectarian politics without igniting a civil war in his own country. He was also walking a tightrope between Iran, his neighbor, and Saudi Arabia, his generous patron. In the early 1980s, when it became clear the Iran-Iraq War was not going to be a quick affair, Pakistan sent a contingent of around eleven thousand soldiers to Saudi Arabia, including a highly mobile elite tank unit and fighter jet pilots, to help with the internal security of the kingdom and the royal family. The Saudis had no experience fighting conventional wars with modern armaments, but they had money, and the Pakistanis were good soldiers. In 1987, the Saudis became wary of Shia soldiers in the Pakistani contingent, questioning their loyalty. They asked Zia to send only Sunnis. No Saudi official ever confirmed this publicly, and no Pakistani official or officer would ever answer a question about this matter in a straightforward way—all they would say was that if Zia had received such a request, he would have known that operating the Pakistani army on a sectarian basis was a recipe for civil war. The official story was that the contract had come to an end. The Pakistani troops went home.

Two key things had happened in the preceding twelve months that had spooked the Saudis: the Iran-Iraq War was reaching an unprecedented paroxysm of violence, with Iran launching a large-scale offensive, massing six hundred thousand troops on the border with Iraq in the summer of 1986 and warning of attacks against other countries. But even more worrying for the Saudis was the carnage in their own territory, in Mecca on July 31, 1987. Iranian pilgrims had clashed with Saudi police forces, resulting in the death of four hundred people. The Saudis feared there had been an Iranian plot to take over the Holy Mosque. Khomeini was now calling on Muslims to wage war against the House of Saud, and the Saudi embassy in Tehran had been ransacked.

The Saudis wanted to ramp up protection of their throne and their Islamic leadership. To do so, they needed to close Arab and Muslim ranks. In November 1987, during an Arab League summit in Jordan, Saudi Arabia pushed for a strident communiqué against Iran. Newspapers remarked that such a tone was usually reserved for Israel. The Saudis even used the occasion to resume ties with Egypt, ostracized since the March 1979 Arab League summit in Baghdad.

But violence in the birthplace of Islam, and in the house of God, was always a harbinger of turbulent change. At least that's what the Saudi architect Sami Angawi believed with all his heart. The head of the Hajj Research Center, who had witnessed the unfolding siege on the Holy Mosque in Mecca in November 1979, was once again in the holy city when hundreds of pilgrims died on what would become known as Bloody Friday.

9

MECCA IS MINE

SAUDI ARABIA
1987

O pilgrims of the hajj, where have you gone, where?
The beloved is here, come, come,
Your beloved is the next-door neighbor;
Why are you wandering the desert searching?
If you see the faceless face of the beloved
You are then transformed as the Lord of the House and become Ka'aba.

—Rumi, *Divan*, 648

Mecca had already changed. Not just the city, but the Holy Mosque
itself. The most sacred place for all Muslims, God's throne on earth,
was no longer that of Sami Angawi's childhood and certainly not of his
father's days as a mutawwif, guiding the pilgrims. The Al-Sauds saw the
Holy Mosque as the source of their power and leadership of the Muslim
world. Their goal was to attract as many pilgrims as possible to the hajj. To
do so, they needed more roads, more hotels, more space in the mosque
itself. Sami thought that the whole city of Mecca should have been a
sanctuary, but the Al-Sauds were planning a veritable metropolis around
the Ka'aba.

With his Hejazi turban, Sami still stood out just as much as he had
in 1979 in the country with an unofficial dress code. On this day, July 31,
1987, he hovered over Mecca in a helicopter doing aerial photography, doc-
umenting the changes in the city. His time-lapse photography was tracking
the flow of pilgrims to determine how to expand access to the mosque and
improve the religious rituals within and without the inner sanctum. From
up high in the sky, he could see a crush of people, a crowd massing just a
mile from the mosque. In the years since evil and violence had disrupted
the sanctity of the Holy Mosque in November 1979, Sami lived in fear that

violence could erupt again. Was this what he saw unfolding down below? He could tell there was serious trouble. Maybe even blood. His heart tightened in his chest. More than a million pilgrims were converging on Mecca. The hajj would officially start in a few days.

Sami was nostalgic for the old Mecca, for the simpler times when the *mizan*, the balance, between modernity and tradition was easier to attain and maintain. His eternal quest for spiritual harmony was constantly disrupted by construction cranes, bulldozers, generators, and loudspeakers. Sami believed in an evolution that respected the continuity, but Mecca's connections with the past were being physically severed. The future of the sanctuary of Islam was in danger. The aim of his research center was to make further expansions to the mosque and its surroundings more in tune with history, more respectful of tradition. It was a Sisyphean battle.

Every king had tried to put his imprint on the city and the mosque; some were worse than others. King Faisal had been a parsimonious man and the expansion works reflected as much—measured and reasonable, nothing too ostentatious. The current ruler, King Fahd, was a spender who disliked all that was old. He loved glitz and gold. More ancient neighborhoods were being torn down, and Mecca's classical Islamic architecture was vanishing rapidly. Ugly modern buildings were rising, and more chain hotels were being built to accommodate yet more pilgrims. Sami wasn't against modernizing the city, but did it have to mean the destruction of its history? The most painful thing for the architect was the continued disregard for historical Islamic sites, even those dating back to the days of the prophet. The royals had no appreciation of history, while the clerical establishment, obsessed with keeping idolatry at bay, cheered the destruction. Sami's latest heartbreak was his failure to stop the destruction of the house of Abu Bakr, the prophet's companion and father-in-law, and the first caliph. In its place rose a Hilton Hotel. "The past is never dead. It's not even past," goes the William Faulkner line in his *Requiem for a Nun*. But in the kingdom of the House of Saud and for the heirs of Muhammad ibn Abdelwahhab, the past did not exist; history was dead, its relics buried.

There were more and more pilgrims coming to the sacred mosque for the yearly hajj and the minor pilgrimage, the umra, which can be performed at any time of the year. In 1987, 1.8 million pilgrims participated in the hajj, up from 232,971 in 1954. That was an eightfold increase, though the world's population had increased by only two and a half times during that period. The kingdom kept expanding the Holy Mosque and enlarging the highways so more pilgrims would come to Mecca, where they would be presented with a unified version of Islam, stripped of all embellishments, all accretions, all diversity of thought. The Saudis even had the Quran to go with it: in late October 1984, King Fahd launched the King Fahd Holy Quran Printing Complex. One of the largest printing plants in the world, it had a capacity to print eight million copies of the Quran and produce thirty thousand audio and video cassettes of Quran recitations, every year. The complex was built by Rafiq Hariri, a Lebanese contractor who would make a fortune in the kingdom during the 1980s, become a friend of the House of Saud, and return to his country to become prime minister after the end of the civil war. A committee of scholars had worked for months to produce a supposedly "perfect," error-free Quran in its annotations and commentary. All other copies were confiscated, and the "perfect" version was distributed instead. Another committee was working on an English translation. Millions of copies were given to pilgrims and distributed abroad through various channels, including through the embassies' Islamic affairs sections, which had replaced the cultural affairs sections in Saudi diplomatic missions in several major cities.

The Saudi-endorsed translations came with egregious modifications or footnotes, turning those editions into polemics against Jews and Christians. The most widely distributed Quran published in 1985 relied heavily on the explanations of medieval thinkers, including students of Ibn Taymiyya, inserting their commentary into the actual verses. A verse in the "Fatiha," the opening of the Quran, had the words "Jews" and "Christians" inserted in parenthesis, making them the target of hate in an otherwise general call to the faithful to stay on the right path: "Guide us to the Straight Way, the way of those on whom You have bestowed Your Grace, not [the way] of those who have earned Your anger [such as the Jews], nor of those who went astray [such as the Christians]." Contemporary politics was also injected into this version of the Quran, with the addition of the word "Palestine" in a verse about the Holy Land, for example: "O my people! Enter the Holy Land that God has assigned unto you" became "O my people! Enter the Holy Land, Palestine." The Saudi-endorsed versions remain the most widespread, offering non-Arabic speakers a very specific, one-sided reading of Islam, which is hard to question without Arabic knowledge. These strict, polemical, medieval explanations of verses of the Quran were also the basis of religious studies in Arabic and were favored by the likes of Bin Baz as the best readings of the Quran. There was much to learn from these readings if presented with a variety of others for comparative study, but brandishing them as the only acceptable version was problematic.

Sami despaired at the closing of minds around him. Minds could always be retrained, hearts could be retuned, he tried to convince himself. But the history destroyed in the inner sanctum of the Holy Mosque could not be rebuilt. The arched gateway, known as Bab al-Salam, Gate of Peace, through which the prophet had walked to pray by the Ka'aba, had long since been removed. Even the frame of black marble that had been inlaid in the stone floor to mark the gate's historical location was gone. The *mataf*, the open, circular area where pilgrims circumambulate around the Ka'aba, had been enlarged, again and again, repaved with heat-reflecting white marble. To allow this extension, historical pulpits, ancient gates, everything had been removed, including the building covering the miraculous well of Zamzam, which had quenched the thirst of Hagar, Abraham's concubine, and their son Ishmael. The water of the well had been diverted underground and the original opening paved over, its location marked with a black circle on the white marble. The buildings around the mosque were growing taller, the view from the Ka'aba to the hills surrounding the holy city was slowly being obstructed. Sami kept thinking of a hadith that seemed to warn about this: "If you see buildings surpass the [Mecca] mountains, then beware that the hour has cast its shadow." There were a few variations to the wording in various hadiths, but they all pointed to the nearing of Judgment Day.

Every gouge in the bedrock, every move by a bulldozer was a stab to Sami's heart, as though his body were being ripped apart. "This is not God's will," he thought. "This is part of his testing."

—

Now the House of Saud was being tested again. What Sami had seen from the helicopter flying above the city was not another Juhayman episode; it was the embodiment of the Saudi-Iran competition for global leadership of the Muslim world, playing out at the holiest site of Islam. The Iran-Iraq War was in its seventh year, and the Saudis were still paying Saddam generously for his efforts, with billions of dollars in civilian and military supplies: $10 billion up to December 1981, then (along with Kuwait) another $20–$27 billion by the end of 1982. Saudi Arabia itself was being drawn into the conflict. Iran wanted to prevent tankers transporting Iraqi oil from passing through the Strait of Hormuz. It had targeted a Saudi tanker; Iranian and Saudi jets had faced off in the skies.

Despite all the resources they'd received, the Iraqis were unable to win the war. Although mostly friendless and stuck in the trenches, the Iranians dug in their heels, refusing to accept a cease-fire. Whenever the Iranians sounded more belligerent or looked as though they were gaining a slight upper hand on the battlefield, the Saudis scurried to push for a cease-fire. They once offered the Iranians $25 billion in war reparations. They tried secret negotiations, then attempted open ones. In 1985, the Saudi foreign minister, Saud al-Faisal, even traveled to Tehran. His Iranian counterpart, Ali Akbar Velayati, visited Riyadh. In February 1986, when the Iranians seized the key Iraqi oil port of Al-Faw, the Saudis tried again, frantically, to reach a cease-fire through backroom deals, desperate to avoid an outright Iranian victory. But Khomeini and his hardliner henchmen wanted nothing less than the immediate departure of Saddam. This was a nonstarter. Even more egregious to the Saudis was an Iranian request for "observer rights" over Mecca and Medina. This kind of language always induced deep panic in the Saudis. They quickly approved another $4 billion loan to Iraq.

Ever since Khomeini had triumphed over the shah in February 1979, he'd had his eyes on Islam's holy sites—he saw the Al-Sauds as usurpers, unworthy custodians, the "camel grazers" he had written about decades ago. Mecca, God's throne on earth, the gateway to paradise for Muslims, was layered with religious but also political and financial importance. For centuries, the city had been at the heart of Islam but on the periphery of power. No caliph had reigned from either Mecca or Medina since the founder of the Umayyad caliphate, Mu'awiya bin Abi Sufyan, had chosen Damascus as his capital in the second half of the sixth century and made plans to convert an ancient church into a stunning mosque to rival the one in Mecca. The Umayyad Mosque had, not a Ka'aba, but a relic of Saint John the Baptist. The wider Hejaz slowly developed more autonomy, as its own emirate, under a noble overlord, a *sharif*, who was always either a Meccan or a descendant of the prophet's family through his other grandson, Hassan, brother of Hussein. Removed from the politics, the scheming of caliphs, and the internecine conflicts, Mecca developed its aura of a mystical, celestial city. For centuries, the sharif of Mecca had been a servant of the caliphs, who derived legitimacy from the holy sites while receiving financial gains from levying taxes on the pilgrims.

Khomeini recognized the hajj as a unique opportunity to reach millions of Muslims and spread his revolution. He had been methodically chipping away for years. In 1981, there were violent clashes between the Saudi police and Iranian pilgrims who were distributing pictures of Khomeini and chanting *"Allahu Akbar va Khomeini rahbar"* (God is great,

Khomeini is the leader). Khomeini wanted to change the nature of the hajj itself, turning a spiritual event into a political protest to undermine the House of Saud. By 1984, Khomeini had set up the Organization for Hajj Endowments and Charity, which operated under his direct supervision. The leaders assigned to guide the caravans of Iranian pilgrims underwent extensive ideological training and were in charge of disseminating the Supreme Leader's message via booklets (printed in various languages) and by holding meetings with non-Iranian pilgrims and foreign officials. The goal was not only spreading the revolution's message, but actively proselytizing and converting pilgrims to Shiism. Within two years the Iranians, or at least the more radical faction of the leadership, felt emboldened in their designs on Mecca. In 1986, 113 Iranian and Libyan pilgrims were arrested in Jeddah upon arrival, accused of carrying huge quantities of explosives. The Iranians among them were accused of being Revolutionary Guards. The Saudis believed they had planned to take over the Holy Mosque.

King Fahd had had enough of the constant challenge to the House of Saud's legitimacy as the guardian of the two holy sites. In October 1986, in front of an assembly of royals and clerics, sitting on a baroque-style, gold-painted armchair, King Fahd announced he was officially replacing the title of His Majesty the King with that of Custodian of the Two Holy Mosques. First introduced by Saladin during the Crusades, the title had never been officially used, until King Fahd, who—with his reputation as a gambler and playboy—needed its shine more than any of his predecessors. But no title could fend off Khomeini's messengers. Ahead of the 1987 hajj, Khomeini exhorted the Iranian pilgrims to turn it into a "battlefield," to march "with as much ceremony as possible during the hajj" and to "express their hatred toward the enemies of God and mankind." Iran had reached the limits of its military capabilities and was sinking in the battlefield. The Saudis had just crashed the oil market with overproduction, bringing the price of a barrel from $30 to $13, bleeding the Iranian economy even further. Khomeini needed a boost, something to reenergize the faithful.

On July 31, 1987, just a few days before the official start of the hajj, Iranian pilgrims leaving the mosque after prayers gathered for a march. There were reports of a tacit understanding with the Saudis that they would tolerate a peaceful march with no political slogans. The intelligence chief Prince Turki al-Faisal, who oversaw security for the hajj, denied that such an agreement had ever been reached. Either way, the procession clashed with a cordon of Saudi police trying to stop the marchers. At 6:30 p.m., the protesters burned American flags. Just before seven, an altercation occurred.

Saudi police used tear gas to push back the protesters. The crowd of sixty thousand retreated, but the exit alleys were blocked. Witnesses said pilgrims attacked the Saudi police with knives. Shots were fired. Prince Turki described pilgrims carrying bats and sword-like machetes, hidden under their white pilgrim ihram, ready to strike the police. The Iranian version has the Saudis resorting to excessive and unwarranted violence. The Saudis always denied firing into the crowd, but witnesses spoke of people with bullet wounds to the chest, arms, and thighs. "Shots could be heard loud and clear," and "cartridges were found on the main street." By eight in the evening, it was all over. More than four hundred people had died, 275 of them Iranian, according to Saudi officials. The Iranians put the toll at four hundred Iranians killed and four thousand injured.

Sami was devastated once again by what had happened in what was supposed to be a sanctuary of peace. Politics had no place here—neither Iran's politics nor anyone else's. For three days, official Saudi state media said nothing—as usual. Even the pan-Arab *Asharq al-Awsat*, read by thousands around the region, kept up the pretense of a successful, calm hajj, with headlines that ignored the tragedy. By August 2, there was a brief mention of an official warning against all protests, after Iranians had caused minor disturbances, according to the paper. Then the reporting suddenly shifted to highlighting the support the kingdom was getting from around the Arab and Muslim world in the face of the "Iranian mob." But there was no hiding the bloody debacle that had leaked into global headlines and was being retold in all four corners of the world, by tens of thousands of pilgrims close enough to have witnessed or heard about the carnage. Here was yet another stain on the record of the House of Saud as custodians of the holy sites.

The Iranians were apoplectic. A crowd of more than a million gathered two days later in Tehran, chanting "Revenge" and "Death to the Saudi rulers." The speaker of the house, Ayatollah Akbar Hashemi Rafsanjani, called on the faithful to avenge the blood of the martyrs, "uproot the Saudi rulers," and "divest the control of the holy shrines from the contaminated existence of the Wahhabis, those hooligans." "The true revenge," he added, "is to remove the colossal and precious wealth belonging to the Islamic world which lies under the soil of the Arabian Peninsula . . . from the control of criminals" and use it to fight "infidels, paganism, and arrogance." A mob ransacked the Saudi, Kuwaiti, French, and Iraqi embassies in Tehran. A Saudi diplomat was killed.

For months, the Iranians and Saudis worked to rally the world's Muslim opinion, each to their respective side, blasting their messages through the media and organizing competing conferences. The Saudis gathered six hundred supporters from 134 countries for a conference organized by the World Muslim League in Mecca. It cost over $400 million. The Iranians held theirs under the title "International Congress on Safeguarding the Sanctity and Security of the Great Mosque," bringing together three hundred participants from thirty-five countries. The accusations they hurled at the Saudis revealed historical grievances that had mostly lain dormant while Saudi Arabia and Iran had been friendly allies, during the reign of the shah. Rafsanjani called for the "liberation" of Mecca, while another cleric accused the House of Saud of being "a bunch of English agents from Najd who have no respect either for the House of God or for the pilgrims who are the guests of God." This was a reference to the way that the founder of the Saudi state had relied on British help to edge out his rival Sharif Hussein from Mecca.

When King Abdelaziz ibn Saud had launched his first raids to recover his ancestors' land in Najd in the early 1900s, he'd also had his eye on the rest of the peninsula, especially Mecca and Medina, holy places that would add Islamic glory to his crown. Those were still under the rule of Sharif Hussein, descendant of the prophet, longtime ally of the British. In 1916, as the Ottoman Empire faltered during World War I, Sharif Hussein proclaimed himself king of Hejaz. The British and French acquiesced. But Abdelaziz had also been courting the British, hoping to convince them he was the better option to rule not only the Hejaz but the whole of the Arabian Peninsula. With his warriors, he was conquering more and more terrain, defeating another rival dynasty, the Al-Rashid, that had ruled over large parts of the peninsula for almost a century. In March 1924, after the collapse of the Ottoman Empire, the secular founder of modern Turkey, Mustafa Kemal Atatürk, dissolved the caliphate, sending the last caliph of the Ottoman dynasty, Abdulmejid II, into exile. Sharif Hussein briefly laid claim to the title of caliph but soon lost the support of the British (one of his sons became king of Iraq, the other founded the monarchy that still rules in Jordan). Abdelaziz sent his troops to conquer the Hejaz, starting with a brutal massacre in Taef. When the Al-Sauds reached the holy sites in December 1924, Wahhabi zealots destroyed the cemetery of Jannat al-Baqi in Medina, the resting place of many of the prophet's relatives and companions, including his daughters and wives. Such destruction and desecration caused consternation across the Muslim world, but Shias were especially incensed. They called on Muslims to rally and expel the Al-Sauds from the Hejaz.

Abdelaziz moved quickly. He invited delegations from Persia to inves-
tigate the alleged damage. One of the delegations reported that Mecca was
in better shape than it had been under Sharif Hussein. The other group
left Medina disheartened by the destruction it had witnessed. Yet another
delegation came from India, demanding that control over the holy cities
be handed to a committee representing all Muslim countries. Abdelaziz
swiftly sent them on their way. Other travelers described terrible damage to a site described as so rich in "the remains of great saints that they
have almost lost their individual importance while the relics of just one of
the persons mentioned would be sufficient to render celebrated any other
Moslim town."

The zealot warriors had wanted to make sure that the cemetery and
its domes would never be rebuilt—this was the second time that the forces
of Wahhabism had tried to obliterate it. The first wave of destructive zeal
had happened in the early 1800s, when the descendants of Muhammad
ibn Saud, the original founder of the Al-Saud dynasty, had pushed to conquer more territory outside their emirate of Najd. They conducted bloody
raids into the territories of Qatif and Bahrain, which were dependencies of
Persia, and into Iraq, which was under Ottoman rule. In 1801, they sacked
Karbala, in Iraq, in one of the worst massacres in Islamic history, killing
two thousand people (according to the account of one of their own chroniclers). They plundered the city and stripped the shrine of Imam Hussain
of its treasures, its cloth embroidered with pearls and gems. In 1803, one
of the Al-Sauds was assassinated at the mosque in Dir'iya, their hometown,
as revenge. Two centuries later, when Saudis would be asked about the
bloody history of their ancestors and their plunder of Karbala, they would
immediately point out it had really all started with a dispute about trading
routes, in which Iraqis had been the first to attack, "killing 300 Wahhabis." Few historians recorded that event, but Saudi chroniclers of the time
mention it, and it frustrates Saudis that this sequence of their ancestors'
rightful quest for justice is ignored. The reality remains that the sack of
Karbala was disproportionately atrocious. The plunder was used to build
the Al-Sauds' campaign to conquer Mecca and Medina, which they occupied briefly, looting the treasures of the tomb of the prophet and destroying the Jannat al-Baqi cemetery. The Muslim world was horrified. Meccans
saw the men as dangerous fanatics, infidels dressed as Muslims. By 1810,
the Ottomans had had enough of the Wahhabis and sent their army to
crush them. Dir'iya was reduced to rubble. Abdallah ibn Saud, descendant of the founding father, was captured and taken to Constantinople to

be decapitated. A renowned jurist and scholar in Damascus at the time, Muhammad Amin ibn Abidin, a Sufi and a *mufti* (Islamic jurist) from the Hanafi school, had nothing but scorn for "those who followed Abdelwahhab." In his seminal book *Radd al-Muhtar ala ad-Dur al-Mukhtar* (Guiding the Baffled About the Exquisite Pearl), he wrote about the demise of those who thought that they alone were the true Muslims, killing fellow Muslims and scholars until "God had finally neutralized them and destroyed their country."

During the second half of the nineteenth century, Ahmad ibn Zayni Dahlan, a mufti in Mecca belonging to the Shafi'i school, wrote at length about the seditious Wahhabis, describing how Egypt had marked the news of Abdallah ibn Saud's arrest with one thousand cannon shots, decorating towns and celebrating for seven days. Dahlan had little good to say about Ibn Abdelwahhab and his followers, describing them as sly. He devoted two books to repudiating the Wahhabis: one telling the story of their demise and one refuting their thought, titled *al-Durar al-Saniyya fil Rad ala al-Wahhabiyya* (Resplendent Pearls in the Refutation of Wahhabism). Dahlan was deeply worried that the singularity of opinion and creed preached by someone like Ibn Abdelwahhab would be the undoing of the Muslim nation.

The founding of the kingdom of Saudi Arabia must have felt like sweet revenge for the House of Saud and their allies from the Al-ash-Sheikh. Scorned for two centuries, annihilated by the Ottomans, exiled to Kuwait, they were back, with help from the British, and they were flush with money. They could silence everyone.

In 1987, Sofana Dahlan sat in her art class in a Jeddah middle school and traced a thick black line through the neck of the figure she was drawing—in essence, slitting his throat. The ten-year-old didn't have violent tendencies. She was only doing what she was being told by her primary school teacher. She also had to black out any faces in her books. Creativity was being murdered on a daily basis in Saudi schools. Sofana was a descendant of Mufti Dahlan, whose predictions had come true.

The young girl lived with the double legacy of Ibn Abdelwahhab's fundamentalist teachings on one side and, on the other, the forgiving, inclusive vision of her ancestor Mufti Dahlan. At school, Sofana learned all about Ibn Abdelwahhab's unitary version of extreme Salafist, Hanbali Islam. Her parents told her to study it for her school tests and then forget about it—to retain only what she was getting in private tutoring in Shafi'i Islamic teachings. At school, she was taught that you could not be friends with Jews and Christians; at home and on travels, her parents socialized with all kinds of non-Muslims. At school, she was taught that all human representations were a sin, even photographs, which were described as *al-shirk al-asghar*, the lesser idolatry. But at home, there were family portraits and pictures on the wall. There were too many contradictions for a child to comprehend and reconcile. She was too young to fully grasp this separation of the private from the public, but it produced intense inner turmoil. She would outgrow the confusion and would eventually challenge the system to become one of the first Saudi woman lawyers. But the one teaching that she couldn't leave behind, that would remain seared in her mind, was the notion that music was haram, forbidden. "Listen to music," the teacher had told Sofana when she was just six years old, "and you will have melted iron poured into your ears on Judgment Day." She could never outgrow that frightful image. She would always startle when she heard music, even as an outspoken lawyer who had traveled the world, even as a grown woman in her forties, when a young, powerful crown prince would become the de facto ruler of Saudi Arabia and confuse her even more by opening concert halls, bringing John Travolta and the Cirque du Soleil to the kingdom.

———

A decade after the sky fell to earth, after revolutions and uprisings, a whole new series of dramatic events were about to unfold, ushering in a new decade and setting the stage for the next phase of the Saudi-Iran rivalry. Wars would end and dictators would die, but the new peace could not undo the deep transformations that had taken root in the pysches of nations and people during the 1980s.

10

CULTURE WARS

What happens when you win?
When your enemies are at your mercy:
How will you act then?
Compromise is the temptation of the weak;
this is the test for the strong.
—Salman Rushdie, *The Satanic Verses*

On August 17, 1988, a four-engine C-130 plane carrying Zia ul-Haq crashed. It was 4:30 p.m., just a few minutes after takeoff from Bahawalpur in Pakistan's Punjab province, close to the border with India. All thirty passengers perished, their mangled bodies scattered over a large, sandy plain just miles from the airport. There was talk of a ball of fire that had engulfed the plane before it crashed. Was it sabotage? A missile attack? An internal malfunction? Sabotage was the most likely answer, but the investigation was never allowed to reach any conclusion. There was one certainty: the dictator was dead.

At home in Karachi, the former television anchor Mehtab Rashdi wasn't even sure of that. Not at first. Could it be true that Zia, the man who had silenced Pakistan's women and abused the country, was really gone? The woman still known for having said no had been waiting for years for news like this. She hadn't known how or when the country would finally be rid of the evil buffoon, but she had been waiting. Now the radio and television channels were playing Quranic recitations. She felt no sadness. But she didn't dare feel joy yet, either. The streets were quiet, her heart was still. By evening, she could breathe again, maybe for the first time in years. She felt like a boulder had been lifted off her chest, off the whole country. He truly was gone.

Condolences poured in, even from India. The US secretary of state,

George P. Shultz, described Zia as "a great fighter for freedom." Vice President George H. W. Bush called him "a great friend," his loss a tragedy. But
there was no sense of tragedy in the country—foreboding perhaps, but
not tragedy. In their homes, many Pakistanis celebrated quietly, some even
with bootleg whisky. Along the border with Afghanistan, in the Kurram
district, home of the assassinated Shia cleric Arif Hussaini and tragic birthplace of modern-day sectarian killings, Shias celebrated loudly, by firing
rockets and bullets into the sky, enraging their Sunni neighbors, who saw
Zia as their champion and defender. More sectarian clashes ensued and
twelve people died. Shiite shops were burned and looted.

In the eyes of most Pakistanis, the dictator had gotten what he deserved.
He was no fighter for freedom. This was God's wrath, thought Mehtab. A
man who was everything had been turned to ashes in an instant.

"I do not regret the death of Zia" was Benazir Bhutto's first reaction
when she heard that the man who had sent her father to the gallows was
dead. She had been in Pakistan for just over two years now, since a triumphant return from exile in April 1986. Zia had announced he was finally
going to hold elections, and he had allowed her to fly home, not expecting
the crowd of hundreds of thousands who thronged the streets to greet
her and chant "Zia dog." The dictator decided to place obstacles in her
way. He maintained the ban on political parties, which meant Bhutto and
her Pakistan Peoples Party couldn't be on the ballot, despite the Supreme
Court's ruling they should be allowed to run. He scheduled the general
elections for November 16, 1988, when Benazir would be days away from
delivering her first child. But now that the dictator was dead, Benazir
would run practically unopposed. Fate had interverened and there was
justice after all, Mehtab kept thinking.

A few weeks later, the former anchor received a phone call from the
Islamabad headquarters of Pakistan television. Would she like to cover
the general election? "How would you like me to appear on-screen?" she
asked. Her question was met with lighthearted laughter. "Any way you
want," came the response. There would be no dupatta imposed on women
anymore. She agreed. This was her victory over darkness, over the man
who thought he was a better Muslim than she. Her first appearance on television in eight years would signal that change had arrived. Benazir Bhutto's
party, the Pakistan Peoples Party, won enough seats to form a government.

For five days, there was dancing and music on the streets of Pakistan,
a public eruption of joy after years of fear, a celebration of life after everything but religion had been banned. Were people celebrating the first dem-

ocratic elections in over a decade, or was it a belated celebration of Zia's demise? Probably both, but another, more amorphous dictatorship was taking hold of the country, born from seeds planted there by Zia, with generous help from Saudi Arabia and the United States.

Benazir was now prime minister, the first-ever female Muslim head of government anywhere—and one of the rare women leaders on the world stage, still a small club. But she would never again appear in public—in Pakistan or overseas—without a veil, a loosely wrapped white chiffon scarf that became her trademark. She would try to undo Zia's Islamization and carry forward her father's dream of a progressive country where there was no discrimination on the basis of sex, race, or religion. But she would fail, assailed by the now entrenched religious and security establishment bristling at a woman leader and her secular rule. With the encouragement of Saudi clerics, there had even been fatwas against her run for office.

She would be removed from power by August 1990, outdone by the military establishment's maneuvers against her, and plagued by allegations of corruption. Most Pakistanis had hoped her rise to office would yield a return to normal life, to the pre-Zia era, with no screaming clerics or gangs of armed gunmen—religious or criminal—ruling the streets. They looked forward to a full return of civilian rule. But Pakistan's army, powerful before, was now so entrenched in politics that they didn't even need a general in the presidency to rule the country. Bhutto was replaced by a Zia protégé and friend of Saudi Arabia, Nawaz Sharif, a soft-spoken forty-year-old with a round face and a balding head. Sharif appeared bland, a nondescript-looking man, but he was a ruthless, cunning politician who would dominate Pakistani politics for the next three decades, in and out of power, in and out of political exile in Saudi Arabia, yet always pushing to continue Zia's Islamization and sectarianization of the country.

—

When Zia ul-Haq died in the summer of 1988, the war between Iraq and Iran had just ended. The summer had devastated Iran's armed forces. Saddam had unleashed hell and fury, not to mention chemical weapons, on Iranian cities. Missiles had rained on Tehran the previous winter, emptying the city of a quarter of its inhabitants. On the morning of Sunday, July 3, the USS *Vincennes* shot down Iran Air flight 655 over the Strait of Hormuz as the plane made its way to nearby Dubai. There were 290 civilians on the plane, including sixty-six infants and children. No one survived. Their lifeless bodies floated in the sea amid the wreckage of the plane.

A US Navy spokesman said the *Vincennes* had mistaken the Airbus A300 for an Iranian F-14. An hour earlier, one of the *Vincennes*'s helicopters, flying over the strait, had come under fire from an Iranian boat. The Americans returned fire and sank two Iranian boats. US president Ronald Reagan said no one could minimize the horror of what had happened and described it as a "great tragedy" but an "understandable accident." At the UN, Iran sought condemnation. There was none. There was no apology either. Iranian diplomats described the downing of the plane as "a premeditated act of aggression and a premeditated cold-blooded murder." Iran vowed revenge. Some anti-American demonstrations in the country followed, but overall the reaction was muted. Iranians were too exhausted to even protest, but mostly they were devastated by the lack of international sympathy for the tragedy, as though this was just part of the cost of being at war, the cost of being Iranian. The country could take no more. The plane shooting was a notable turning point for the Iranian leadership, including Khomeini. For months, those closest to him, including his son, had argued it was time to accept a cease-fire. They argued that the war against Saddam could not be won without years more of blood and treasure. Now came proof that the outside world cared little how many more Iranians died, in a war or a plane crash. Survival of the regime and the revolution itself was on the line.

In a radio address on July 20, Khomeini endorsed a cease-fire with Iraq. "Happy are those who have departed through martyrdom. Happy are those who have lost their lives in this convoy of light. Unhappy am I that I still survive and have drunk the poisoned chalice." The deadly debacle in Mecca and Khomeini's repeated failure to rally the Muslim world to internationalize Islam's holy cities were still weighing on him. The ayatollah needed another tool to revive revolutionary fervor.

—

Another war was drawing to an end, in Afghanistan. The Soviets were tired by a conflict they too couldn't seem to win or lose. They were pinned to the wall, outmatched by the money and weapons that the Americans, Pakistanis, and Saudis were pouring into the conflict. Stinger missiles that could bring down a plane were the latest addition to the arsenal of the mujahedeen, altering the balance of power. With fifteen thousand troops killed, several hundred thousand wounded, and tens of thousands dead from disease, President Mikhail Gorbachev wanted out. No one knew it quite yet, but the Soviet Union's collapse had just begun.

Before he blew up in the sky, Zia had signed on to the Geneva Accords of April 15, 1988, which ended the Soviet involvement in Afghanistan and provided for the withdrawal of 150,000 Soviet troops by February 1989. On February 15, 1989, after weeks of slowly drawing down their forces, the last Soviet troops crossed the Termez Bridge over the Amu Darya River in the opposite direction than the one they'd driven in December 1979—out of Afghanistan and back into the Soviet Republic of Uzbekistan.

The CIA's post in Islamabad sent a cable to the agency's headquarters: "We WON." At headquarters, they popped the champagne. At the US embassy in Pakistan they celebrated. The Saudis also felt they had won. Their money had paid for what they saw as the victory of Islam. There were no champagne celebrations, just a quiet sense of accomplishment. Khomeini wouldn't have it. He wanted a say in the future of Afghanistan. Two days before the final Soviet withdrawal, the headlines in the pan-Arab newspaper *Asharq al-Awsat* read, IRAN THREATENING THE MUJAHEDEEN AND SIDING WITH THE SHIAS. Shias represented only 15 percent of the total population of Afghanistan, but Iran pushed for a bigger representation during negotiations taking place in Peshawar for the formation of the government in exile and the *shura*, the consultative council. Iran had backed mujahedeen groups as well, mostly Hazara Shias, though they hadn't done much fighting. This was a Saudi show and the kingdom's work over the years, pouring money and arms into the pockets of loyal Afghan mujahedeen, was paying off. The radical Sunni Islamist groups had the upper hand. The Tehran-backed groups walked out of the talks and Iran was left empty-handed. Still Khomeini wouldn't give up. The day before the Soviets crossed the bridge out of Afghanistan, the very day before Saudi Arabia's quiet victory, Khomeini started a cultural war that would deeply transform the Muslim world for decades to come.

—

On Valentine's Day 1989, right before the 2:00 p.m. news, the newscaster on Tehran Radio read out a statement Khomeini had dictated: "I inform the proud Muslim people of the world that the author of *The Satanic Verses*, which is against Islam, the Prophet, and the Koran, and all those involved in its publication who were aware of its content, are sentenced to death. I ask all Muslims to execute them where they find them." Any Muslim who might die in the process, Khomeini added, would be considered a martyr.

We may never know whether Khomeini timed his move with cunning precision to overshadow the headlines of the Soviet withdrawal on February

15 and the Saudi victory, or whether he seized the opportunity when he saw it. The biggest irony is that he was finishing off what the Saudis and their friends had in fact started.

The author of *The Satanic Verses*, the British Indian writer Salman Rushdie, was already the acclaimed winner of the 1981 Booker Prize. *The Satanic Verses* was his fourth book, published in September 1988, about two Indian Muslim immigrants to Britain who die on a hijacked plane that explodes over the English Channel. They fall to earth and are magically transformed into living symbols of good and evil. Their stories are intertwined with that of a prophet called Mahound, in a place called jahiliyya. Rushdie described the book as a work about "migration, metamorphosis, divided selves, love, death, London, and Bombay." Muslims saw references to their prophet Muhammad and his wives, whose names were given to prostitutes in the book. Khomeini's edict to kill Rushdie sent shock waves through the literary and publishing world. That same night, Rushdie got police protection and went into hiding. Khomeini had become the spokesperson of Muslims who felt aggrieved and slighted, even those who had not read *The Satanic Verses*. Six hundred pages and a quarter of a million words long, the book may have been a masterpiece, but it was a maze. Yet someone had gone through it very diligently in India, Rushdie's native country. And within a month of publication of *The Satanic Verses*, in the fall of 1988, he had called a friend in Leicester, telling him there was a campaign to ban the book in India, urging him to do God's work in the UK.

In Leicester, Faiyazuddin Ahmad, a jovial-looking man, got to work, photocopying extracts of the book and sending them around to Muslim organizations and to the embassies of forty-five Muslim countries in the UK. A recent arrival in the country, Ahmad had previously worked in East Pakistan and Saudi Arabia as a managing editor of newspapers, and was now at the Islamic Foundation in Leicester, a local chapter of the Pakistani Jamaat-e Islami, which received funding from Saudi Arabia. Ahmad, who also had ties with the Saudi-funded World Assembly of Muslim Youth, traveled to Jeddah in October to brief members of the Organization of Islamic Cooperation. At the Saudi embassy in London, the head of the Islamic affairs section, Mughram al-Ghamdi, helped set up the UK Action Committee on Islamic Affairs to campaign against the book and get it banned. Only a few Muslim countries answered the call. But by December, British Muslims were protesting, burning a copy as they marched through the small town of Bolton. The subcontinental rivalry between Deobandis and Barelvis was mirrored in the Muslim community in Britain, fueling a competition for bigger and bigger protests. A month later, in January 1989, a larger one took place in Bradford, just an hour away from Bolton. The anger rippled back to the subcontinent. Not to be outdone, the Jamaat organized its own demonstration in Islamabad on February 12, bringing a massive crowd to protest outside the US cultural center in Islamabad. More than eighty were injured, five were shot dead. The story goes that Khomeini was watching the news that evening and was moved enough by the deaths of the Pakistani youths that he issued his fatwa. The book had been translated into Persian and had been on sale in Tehran—no one seemed exercised about it until Khomeini spoke out.

The Saudis couldn't let this pass. They went the legal way. Sheikh Bin Baz declared that Rushdie should be tried in absentia to determine whether his book was blasphemous. Sheikh Gad al-Haq, the head of Egypt's highest religious authority, Al-Azhar, came out against Khomeini's fatwa. But they were not standing up for freedom of speech and writing, no—Al-Azhar's view was simply that no one could be put to death before there was a fair trial to determine whether blasphemy had indeed been committed. Any verdict in such a case would have to be handed out by a head of government.

Rushdie did not stand trial, and he survived the death threats. But the Japanese and Turkish translators of his book, and the publisher of the Norwegian one, were all assassinated for their association with Rushdie. Others with no connection to Rushdie would soon be felled or have their lives wrecked by accusations of blasphemy, from Egypt to Pakistan. Death by blasphemy had now been introduced to the Muslim world by a strange twist in the competition between Iran and Saudi Arabia to position themselves as the standard-bearer of global Islam. But Saudi Arabia's role in this dynamic would be forgotten, and the fatwa against Rushdie would become solely an Iranian story.

On June 3, 1989, Khomeini, eighty-six years old and ailing, died of heart failure. In his will, he left a parting shot against the Saudis. The twenty-nine-page document was read by Ali Khamenei, the president and soon-to-be Supreme Leader. "Muslims should curse the tyrants, including the Saudi royal family, these traitors to God's great shrine, may God's curse and that of his prophets and angels be upon them . . . King Fahd spends a large part of the people's wealth every year on the anti-Qorani totally baseless super-stitious faith of Wahhabism. He abuses Islam and the dear Qoran."

Khomeini's death would in fact allow a détente to begin between Iran and Saudi Arabia. The president, Ali Khamenei, became Supreme Leader; the speaker of the house, Ali Akbar Rafsanjani, was elected president.

Despite the vitriol Rafsanjani had spouted at the Saudis during the 1987 hajj crisis, he was a pragmatist, eager to rebuild the country's economy after the war with Iraq. In August 1990, Iran's enemy Saddam Hussein invaded and annexed Kuwait; his troops were on Saudi Arabia's border. The Iranians and the Saudis were suddenly united in fear of the same madman. By September, the foreign ministers of both countries were talking in New York on the sidelines of the UN General Assembly.

The invasion of Kuwait ushered in another geopolitical change in the Middle East. As President George H. W. Bush put together the largest possible military coalition, he was eager to involve as many Arab participants as possible, including Syria. Hafez al-Assad agreed to participate. In exchange, in a quid pro quo that was never explicitly stated, the United States turned a blind eye when Syrian troops invaded the Christian areas that had remained outside their control in Lebanon, on October 13, 1990.

The Syrian tanks silenced everyone's guns and imposed the Pax Syriana. Alliances and proxies had shifted over the course of the war in Lebanon. Syria had invaded several times and was in control of dominantly Muslim areas of the country and West Beirut. The Palestinian Liberation Organization was gone; the Palestinian refugees were still there. Christians had slaughtered one another. Israel still occupied large parts of southern Lebanon. Hezbollah's rise had continued, and its ruthless campaign to eliminate intellectual opponents within the community had reached Beirut, claiming the lives of well-known writers and journalists. One of the most prominent, Hussein Mrouweh, was shot dead at home on his sickbed. The power of ideas was simply too much for Hezbollah to bear. And still the critics were not silenced. They never would be. Just as in Pakistan, where Zia had to repeatedly, continuously subjugate critics with violence to stay on top, so Hezbollah would have to repeatedly beat down opponents. In July 1990, just months before the official end of the war in Lebanon, thousands demonstrated in Tyre. "We want to speak the truth!" they chanted. "We don't want to see any Iranians!" Lebanese Shia clerics called for the end of the "Iranian invasion" and the departure of the Revolutionary Guards who had come to the Beqaa Valley after the 1982 Israeli invasion and still maintained a presence. But the Guards could in fact leave; Hezbollah, their local affiliate, was in place. And by allowing Assad to send troops into Lebanon, America had unwittingly provided a way for his ally Iran to maintain its foothold on the Mediterranean. The black wave from Iran would not recede. The other one, from Saudi Arabia, was rushing along the Nile.

11

BLACK WAVE

EGYPT

1992–95

These fools, by dint of ignorance most crass,
Think they in wisdom all mankind surpass;
And glibly do they damn as infidel,
Whoever is not like them, an ass.

—Omar Khayyam, *Quatrains*, 156

Nasr Abu Zeid never wanted to be Egypt's Salman Rushdie. He had never wanted to give the impression that he "was against Islam. Far from it." Among his worst fears was that Westerners would look at him and see a critic of Islam. That's not what he was. The progressive professor of Islamic studies and Arabic at Cairo University was born a Muslim, raised a Muslim, and, as he liked to repeat, *inshallah*, he would die a Muslim. He only wanted to make his religion more accessible in today's world, gentler, less doctrinaire.

When Nasr was accused of apostasy in Egypt, just a few years after the Rushdie fatwa, the comparison to the British Indian novelist came easily to Western media reporting on a foreign country. But Nasr's supporters in Egypt preferred to compare him to the Italian physicist and astronomer Galileo. Some 350 years earlier, the Catholic Church had persecuted Galileo as a heretic during the Roman Inquisition for asserting that the earth moved around the sun. He had to recant his discoveries, which caused him much anguish until his death. Over time, the Church walked back its condemnation, and in October 1992 the pope closed a decade-long investigation into the condemnation and published a formal acknowledgment of the Church's error. Nasr's ordeal began around the time of that apology, and just like Galileo he believed in science and reason, insisting he would continue to "struggle in support of Islam, armed with scientific reasoning and solid methodology."

Nasr's critics dismissed him as a rotund, quiet man, as a "little" secular writer, an infidel. His supporters scoffed: Nasr was their Galileo, the only difference was that the Vatican had apologized to the Italian savant, whereas "some in our universities still believe the earth does not move." That was the fear of progressive thinkers in Egypt, that the darkness spreading outside, "terrorism dressed in the garb of religion," was now scaling the walls of universities to turn them into courts of inquisition. Reason and faith, science and dogma—all locked in battle in Cairo. For a while, Egypt's intellectuals were defiant, buoyed and invigorated by the challenge. "Liberalism till victory or martyrdom" declared Mohammad Said al-Ashmawy, a senior, progressive judge on the court of appeals.

There would be many deaths.

For Nasr, it all began in 1992, with a straightforward request for a promotion to the position of full professor in the Arabic department of Cairo University. The tenure committee submitted his file, including all his publications, to three professors for evaluation. One of them, Dr. Abdel Sabour Shaheen, was a fundamentalist preacher at Cairo's seventh-century Amr ibn al-As mosque, the first mosque built in Egypt. Shaheen did not like what he read.

Exegesis, the critical interpretation of scripture, is not an Islamic tradition, and for Orthodox Muslims like Shaheen, the Quran is the uncreated, eternal, inviolate word of God. Nasr, meanwhile, was the author of books titled *Critique of Islamic Discourse* and *Rationalism in Exegesis: A Study of the Problem of Metaphor in the Writing of the Mu'tazilah.*

The socially timid, bespectacled scholar was a freethinker who challenged the orthodox tradition in Islam and argued that the Quran had to be understood both metaphorically and in its historical context. He was a man of his time, eager to help his fellow Muslims apply the teachings of the Quran to the modern world. To do that, he believed that "the human dimension of the Quran needs to be reconsidered." So although the Quran was indeed the word of God, Nasr's argument was that it had been revealed to the prophet Muhammad through the use of a language, a local dialect even, rooted in a specific context: the Arabic language of the Arabian Peninsula of the seventh century. If the word of God had not been embodied in human language, how could anyone understand it?

Nasr was not starting from scratch: he was building on a great inheritance that went back to the eighth century. His master's thesis had been about the Mu'tazilah, the rationalist Islamic movement drawing on Greek philosophy that had first stirred a big debate between reason and dogma barely two hundred years after the founding of Islam.

The Mu'tazilah first emerged in the eighth century, in Basra, in today's southern Iraq. They believed that while God's speech was uncreated and revealed to the prophet, the writing of the Quran was an earthly phenomenon: words, ink, paper. Furthermore, the writing had happened well after the revelation and the death of the prophet. The Mu'tazilah applied reason to the study of the holy book and believed in free will. Their movement reflected the times they were living in — the Abbasid era was the golden age of Islam, the time of science and philosophy, of Abu Nuwas's libertine poetry about love and wine, the thousand and one days and nights of Scheherazade, and the Abbasid caliph Haroun al Rashid. Baghdad's famed library, the House of Wisdom, became the repository of world knowledge, overflowing with original and translated works. At the same time in Baghdad, also under the Abbasid caliphate, was Ahmad ibn Hanbal, founder of the Hanbali school of jurisprudence: resolutely orthodox, literalist, and opposed to the Mu'tazilah doctrine, which had become state doctrine. His opposition landed him in jail, and his following surged. Hanbalis believed Muslims had lost their way, and as the Abbasid caliphate weakened, the followers of Ibn Hanbal became more organized, leading the fight against rationalism and anything that could distract from the purest form of the original faith, including music. They "set up in fact a kind of 'Sunni inquisition.'"

As the four major schools of jurisprudence slowly crystallized, orthodoxy also settled in. Some Sunni religious leaders believed most major religious matters had been settled and began to restrict the gates of *ijtihad*, independent reasoning, to give precedence to emulation. Reading, understanding, and explaining the Quran would have to rely on the body of knowledge accumulated up until then—the Mu'tazilah period was over. Hanbalism would later soar and spread to Persia and the area around Palestine, where Ibn Taymiyyah was one of its stars, before declining again during the Ottoman era, under the weight of its own rigidity and intolerance. Its geographical influence would slowly be reduced to the austere interior of the Arabian Peninsula, the arid plateau of Najd, home of the first Saudi kingdom—where Muhammad ibn Abdelwahhab took it to another level.

Fast-forward twelve centuries, and Nasr was pushing his foot through that door of ijtihad. Shaheen's takedown was vitriolic: he accused Nasr of an "atrophy of religious conscience," passing judgment over his faith rather than his work. Shaheen described him as a heretic, an atheist

leading a "Marxian-secularist attempt to destroy Egypt's Muslim society."
The preacher also hoped that "God would make a place for him in paradise
because of his good work against the academic who had lost his way." The
desire to be rewarded by God for showing others the right path in Islam
would become a recurrent theme in years to come in attacks, verbal and
physical, against progressive thinkers or anyone labeled an apostate, no
matter the reason. In Pakistan, it was being used as the justification for
forced conversion of Hindus and Christians to Islam.

By early 1993, the university had caved and denied Nasr's promotion.
On Friday, April 2, using his pulpit at the Amr ibn al-As mosque during
midday prayers, the victorious Shaheen declared the scholar an apostate.
Like a pinball, the word "apostate" bounced from minaret to minaret
across Cairo, and by the following Friday, in sermons across the country,
preachers went after Nasr—even in his own village. As an apostate, under
Islamic law, he had lost the right to live and—perhaps even more precious
to him as a newlywed—the right to be married to a Muslim woman. His
wife was Ebtehal Younes, the French literature student who had silently
approved of the killing of Sadat in 1981.

Theirs was a story of unconventional love in a traditional society,
rebellious in an age of conformism, quiet in an age of simmering turmoil.
They were an unlikely couple in more ways than one. Ebtehal was now
an assistant lecturer in French literature at Cairo University. Nasr was all
about Islamic studies and the Quran. He was a poor village boy, she was
an upper-class Egyptian; his father was a grocer, hers a diplomat; she was
petite, he was big. She was fiery and, at thirty, already a spinster by Egyptian standards; he was fifteen years older and divorced, still a stain on anyone in a conservative society.

She didn't care. They were different but they spoke the same language,
dreamed the same dreams. Their friendship grew into love, and when they
married, just before his troubles started, Nasr felt as though his life finally
made sense, that he had finally arrived at his destination. Suddenly, fundamentalists who didn't know them or their love for each other were ripping
them apart. The charge of apostasy wasn't even on the books in Egypt, so
Nasr was sued for separation in the family affairs court under a principle
in Islam known as *hisba*, which allows any Muslim to sue in court if he
believes Islam is being harmed—a loophole Islamists had just discovered
and would abuse for years. Under Islamic law, a Muslim woman cannot
marry a non-Muslim, and Nasr was now considered an apostate, which
meant Ebtehal had to be separated from the heretic.

The legal battle dragged on for two years. Never before had such theological debates taken place. It was a turning point for Egypt and Islamists, with the Muslim world watching. Meanwhile in Cairo, there had been a run in the bookshops on all of Nasr's publications. The headlines were focused on Nasr, but Ebtehal was deeply wounded, too. She felt morally raped, reduced to an object that Islamists were using to hurt Nasr, an object that was back on the market: Shaheen had even offered to find her a new husband.

Ebtehal's devotion never wavered. If anyone was serving Islam, it was her husband, she insisted. They were both devout, practicing Muslims, so who were these people to declare him an apostate, to judge who was a good Muslim and who wasn't? In some ways, "these people" were part of the same movement that had paved the way for Sadat's assassination. She understood now it had never been about Palestine. Sadat's killing was a religious assassination dressed up as a political act, and now she was a victim of the very trends it had unleashed and the fundamentalism that was sweeping the Egypt of the 1990s.

Farag Foda, Egypt's most vocal secular intellectual, had seen it coming well before she did. While Nasr came to the debate about Islamic fundamentalism from a historical, theological, and linguistic angle, Foda was an agronomist, a scientist with a methodical approach to the defense of a secular state in the face of creeping fundamentalism in Egyptian society. A decade prior, in 1985, his bestseller *Before the Fall*, a short but incisive political essay, had neatly summarized the trends that were shaping the rising Islamic fervor in a society searching for answers after the repeated, searing defeats of Arab nationalism in the face of Israel.

Foda had identified three Islamic trends in Egypt. The first was the traditional political one of the Muslim Brotherhood, with historical roots in Egypt—it was the weakest but the most pragmatic, according to Foda. Then came revolutionary Islam, inspired by Iran, the kind that wanted to overthrow systems wholesale, the one that Nageh Ibrahim, Abdelsalam Farag, and other young Egyptians had embraced in the 1970s. In Foda's view, this was the most dangerous but the least widespread because it relied on a specific demographic: young hotheads. And finally there was what he described as the moneyed Islam, the Islam of riches—the Islam of petrodollars.

That third, moneyed Islam was the most powerful, according to Foda, because it *looked* modern and contemporary but was actually insidious, slowly infiltrating all aspects of society. Violence could be quelled, militants imprisoned, but once people's minds had been altered by a new worldview, it could take generations to undo the damage. Moneyed Islam flaunted its wealth to promote new, supposedly more righteous ways: introducing Islamic banking and then demanding that female employees wear the veil; setting up publishing houses and offering huge sums of money for authors to write books, but only those who promoted a specific outlook, a specific, puritanical understanding of religion; or hiring journalists to write for Saudi-funded pan-Arab publications like *Asharq al-Awsat*. A regular contributor to the paper could earn $3,000 per month, more than a year's salary for the same job at Egyptian publications. But with the paycheck came political redlines, intellectual censorship, and self-censorship, the kind that atrophies the minds of vibrant societies. The strategy, according to Foda, was to make people dependent on those petrodollars, tying their financial security to the servicing of a Saudi vision for society and politics.

In 1990, the Syrian poet Nizar Qabbani, in self-imposed exile in London, penned a ruthless, prophetic poem, "Abu Jahl Buys Fleet Street," a critique of the rich men from the Arabian Peninsula in flowing white robes who had descended on the city and seemed to be buying it up. *Abu Jahl* means "father of ignorance" in Arabic, and the title of Qabbani's poem was a nod to a contemporary of the prophet named Abu Jahl, a pagan who had fought Muhammad and rejected Islam.

In his poem, Qabbani asked: "had England become the capital of the Caliphate? And oil walked as a king on Fleet Street?" Mostly, the poem was a warning to Arab journalists and intellectuals not to become enslaved to philistine paymasters. Leftist intellectuals had "turned their backs on Lenin and were riding camels," those who wanted to be successful editors "had to kiss, day and night, the knee of the prince." Qabbani appealed to an unnamed ruler to take anything they wanted but to spare the word, the letters:

> O long-lived one, you buy pens by the barrel,
> We want nothing of you,
> So keep on fucking your slave women as you wish
> And go on killing your subjects as you wish,
> And encircle the nation with fire and steel . . .
> No one wants to steal the cloak of your caliphate,
> So keep on drinking the wine of your petrol,
> But leave us our culture, our letters.

Foda was deeply concerned about Saudi cultural imperialism setting the tone across the region. But the trends he identified were not operating on separate, parallel tracks. They reinforced each other: local attitudes and dynamics fueled by new factors, exacerbated by regional trends. Members of the Muslim Brotherhood were returning from Saudi Arabia and working to change the system and society from within, adding a new layer to the understanding and practice of religion in their home country. The Gama'a Islamiyya and the Islamic Jihad were a product of local factors, frustrated with the quiescent approach to those in power—they believed in violence; they had gone to fight in Afghanistan, where Saudi money and influence also reigned, and some were coming back. The two trends, moneyed and revolutionary, were now mixing in Egypt.

Foda was relentless in his attacks against all types of Islamists. A big man with a booming voice and worry beads threaded among his fingers, he harangued and mocked them, deconstructing their arguments piece by piece. He was a skilled debater, always ready to take them down, in interviews and in his acerbic writings. On January 8, 1992, he did it publicly, in front of fifteen thousand people—it was a fatal turning point.

The twenty-fourth annual Cairo International Book Fair had organized a public debate featuring Foda and three other speakers: Mohammad Khalafallah, who was a secularist, like Foda, and two Islamists. One of them, Mohammad al-Ghazali, was a leading Islamic scholar and graduate of Al-Azhar, a charismatic preacher who had taught at Islamic universities in Mecca and Doha as well as in Algeria during the 1980s. The other, Ma'moun al-Hodeibi, had lived in Saudi Arabia in the 1970s and 1980s. He was the son of the Brotherhood's second Murshid A'am (general guide) Hassan al-Hodeibi and would one day become general guide himself.

Even the event's title had been hotly debated: "Egypt, a Secular or Islamic State?" was the Islamists' preferred version. They wanted to box in their opponents as atheists. The book fair had settled for "Egypt: a Civil State or Religious State?" Egypt had never seen a public debate on this subject. The mood was febrile, the audience of men and women agitated. There were chants of *"Allahu Akbar wal Jihad sabeeluna"* (God is the greatest and jihad is our path). The conference hall was overflowing, and the doors to the fair itself had to be closed. Inside, it was standing room only, with people squeezed along the walls and even behind the speakers. There were no security precautions.

Ghazali and Hodeibi argued in favor of what they described as an Islamic democracy, ruled by the shari'a, as they decried the cultural invasion of the West. Foda defended his identity as a Muslim: "I can accept that communism be insulted, I can accept that socialism be insulted, but I cannot accept that Islam be insulted." But, he asked, which Islamic state were his opponents suggesting as a model? There were no successful examples; Iran, Saudi Arabia, and Sudan had been failures. He went further: Why this sudden obsession with an Islamic state? "For thirteen hundred years [since the first century after the prophet] only one percent of people have advocated for a religious state, while ninety-nine percent have advocated for what we are calling for, which is a civil state." Even that idealized, halcyon time of the early days of Islam was imperfect, mired in disputes and violence, he continued. Three of the first caliphs, close companions of the prophet, known as the Rightly Guided Caliphs, had been assassinated.

Foda had been a thorn in the side of the Islamists for a decade at that point, ever since he'd made headlines with *Before the Fall*. He was working to build a secular political party, Al-Mustaqbal, the Future, bringing together Muslims and Christians. Now Foda was shredding the Islamists' credibility in public. The time had come to get rid of him.

They couldn't even face him when they killed him. It was a Monday afternoon, June 8, 1992, six months after the book fair debate. He was coming out of his office with his son and a friend, in a residential suburb of Cairo. Two illiterate men who had never spoken to him or read his work sped by on a motorcycle and fired seven bullets into his back. They shot and injured his fifteen-year-old son, too. They were simply following orders. Safwat Abdel Ghani, detained but never charged in the plot to kill Sadat, had passed on a message through his lawyers to recruit the killers.

Egypt had seen political violence and assassinations, but this was a first: intellectual terrorism. The country was shaken, the Arab world shocked. There would now be a before Foda and an after. The fearless agronomist and intellectual was described in newspapers as the martyr of the nation. Thousands of Egyptians attended his funeral. President Mubarak sent a representative; ministers, governors, the mufti of the republic, intellectuals, ambassadors all joined the procession through the streets of Cairo. As they carried the casket, draped in a green cloth embroidered with verses from the Quran, mourners calmly sang the national anthem. "My country, my country, to you I dedicate my heart and my love." The sadness soon gave way to anger and the procession turned into a protest against terrorism. "No to the Jihad, to the Brothers," "Long live the crescent, long live the cross."

The country was split. And it was perhaps Foda's sister who first expressed it in a heartfelt, anguished cry after his funeral: "Why did they kill him? He was a Muslim! How could they declare him an atheist divorced from his religion? Who gave them the right to divide us between Muslims

and infidels?" That was precisely what was happening. Hardline Sunni Islamists were no longer simply separating Muslims from non-Muslims, or
Sunnis from Shias, an approach that was already leaving a trail of dead
bodies, ripping apart small communities with sectarian violence. They were
now also asking within their own community: Are you a good Muslim?

Nonviolent, or political, Islamists deflected responsibility after Foda's
murder. The Muslim Brotherhood claimed the government was partly
responsible, because it had allowed him access to the airwaves, to "stab
Islam in the heart . . . [a] provocation of Muslim sentiments at a time when
the whole world is hounding them with war." Al-Azhar had condemned
the killing when it happened, but earlier it had also criticized Foda's plans
for a secular party, describing the move as a danger to the Muslim nation
and denouncing secularists like him as enemies "of everything that is
Islamic." His assassins would later say that Al-Azhar had spoken, so they
had acted. The Sunni world's highest religious authority had shown, trag-
ically, how words could be an invitation to murder.

Even more shocking was the appearance of an Al-Azhar scholar as a
defense witness for Foda's assassins during their trial, in July 1993. Mohammad al-Ghazali, who had sparred with Foda at the Cairo book fair and
inspired thousands of Islamists in Algeria, condoned the killing. His argument echoed in part the one made by the head of Al-Azhar in the Rushdie
case: it was up to the state to carry out the sentence of death against apostates after a trial, but since the state had failed to curb Foda, the sentence
could be carried out by righteous Muslims. Chillingly, Ghazali declared
there was no punishment for a Muslim stepping in to carry out this deadly
duty. Ghazali was the 1989 recipient of the King Faisal award, the prize first
bestowed on Mawdudi, the founder of the Jamaat in Pakistan.

The Egyptian government had been trying to separate violent Islam
from moderate, political Islam, the militants from the preachers, those
wishing to overturn the system and those working within, like Al-Azhar.
But Foda himself had warned that the government's attempt to placate the
radicals—for example by giving more airtime to those who appeared to be
moderate Islamists—was feeding intolerance and playing with fire.

—

Since the mid-1980s, under its Grand Imam, Gad al-Haq, Al-Azhar had
become much more activist in its promotion of a conservative Islam, pushing back against secular values. It had banned books before, including
Nobel Prize winner Naguib Mahfouz's 1966 novel *Adrift on the Nile*, but it

was now increasingly involved in the censorship of literary works, films, anything cultural. The group issued fatwas condoning Islamic banking and female genital mutilation while banning organ donations and tinted contact lenses and condemning women who didn't cover their hair.

There were endless speculations and rumors about the extent of Saudi influence in pushing this latest trend. The Saudi-Egyptian relationship was full of contradictions. Al-Azhar University taught all four schools of jurisprudence, giving them equal importance. Many of its teachers and students and even grand imams belonged to Sufi orders. Al-Azhar still considered Wahhabism to be a deviation from true Islam, and yet the Grand Imam was close to Saudi Arabia. He, too, would be awarded the King Faisal International Prize. Rich individuals from the Gulf donated money to the institution, and many of its preachers and scholars had studied or trained in Mecca. The influence was elusive but pervasive. Proud Egyptians simultaneously refused to acknowledge the influence of Saudi Arabia on their country, insisting that they were the teachers in this relationship, at all levels, from jihad to political Islam, while also complaining that the kingdom was corrupting their country. With its new wealth, Saudi Arabia was overwhelming and convincing. Saudi Arabia—the birthplace of Islam—had also been blessed with the riches of oil: surely, then, God smiled upon that country; surely theirs was the true Islam.

That's what millions of migrant workers from Egypt, Pakistan, Syria, and other Muslim countries thought when they went looking for jobs in the young kingdom that was booming in the 1980s. In 1968, there were ten thousand Egyptians in Saudi Arabia; by 1985, there were 1.2 million. They were lower-class and lower-middle-class Egyptians, in awe of the wealth of their Saudi paymasters. Construction workers, drivers, salespeople, gardeners, and migrant workers practically ran the country, then returned home from the kingdom for visits or to settle back home permanently, with new money and new mores. They could afford to buy things that had been out of reach before, from television sets to cars and houses. Immersed in the Saudi lifestyle and worldview, many kept the habits they picked up there—the flowing white robe, the niqab or face veil for the women, the more assiduous praying, and the denunciations of Sufism, intercession of saints, and Shias. In Pakistani villages, the Syrian countryside, or rural Egypt, migrant workers who had struck it rich in the Arabian Peninsula built mosques to show off their new wealth and piety, installing preachers trained in Saudi Arabia. This submergence in the Saudi way of life covered everything, including women.

Egypt had always been a conservative, traditional society, but the veil did not dominate, nor was it a source of tension or debate; it was neither banned nor imposed by the state. The Gama'a had had some success in promoting the veil on university campuses, but 1979 ushered in a real wave, with women emulating the exhilarating example of Iran, covering their hair in a symbolic rejection of imperialism and the West. In the 1990s a second wave arrived, fed by Saudi money and proselytizing, which specifically targeted the middle class. In the 1970s, 30 percent of Egyptian women wore the headscarf; by the mid-1990s, it was 65 percent.

The veil was the new chic; it was a status symbol. In the past, middle-class and rich Egyptians may have looked to Europe for the latest fashions. Now they looked to Saudi Arabia and adopted not just the veil but even the niqab, which was previously an unknown phenomenon in Egypt.

The most dramatic visual of the black wave crashing over Egypt was the veiling of dozens of its beloved, beautiful actresses who had delighted generations of Egyptians and Arabs. One after another, they had their come-to-Islam moment. The first was Shams al-Baroudi, who had played the role of the working woman following her love interest to Australia. She went to Mecca on the pilgrimage in 1982 and returned veiled. She stood out as someone finding faith after a deeply spiritual experience. But Baroudi went on to actively encourage others to repent and leave behind their sinful lives as actresses.

By 1993, dozens of well-known actresses had donned either the veil or the niqab and were explicitly spreading their message in weekly religious lectures known as "Islamic salons" in the homes of Cairo's elite. They impressed other women, who were mostly uninformed about religion, with these sermons, and they encouraged them to urge others to wear the veil and distributed booklets, some printed in Riyadh. Moved by their faith and injunctions, some of those attending the lectures decided to veil on the spot. Over time, hundreds of women passed through these salons, and most of them spread the message further. The "repentant" actresses, as they were known, were highly visible and public in their proselytizing. They were a curiosity, but they also set an example.

The influence of Saudi money was difficult to prove but on everyone's lips. Several Egyptian stars, including the dainty Faten Hamama, who had appeared in the landmark Egyptian film *I Want a Solution*, alluded to the fact they had been offered vast sums of money to abandon acting and wear the hijab but had refused: one million dollars and a monthly salary of $150,000 was among the top offers one of them received from a man suspected to be from the Gulf.

The actresses who veiled vehemently denied they had been paid. But they did have connections to Saudi Arabia. Baroudi lived in Jeddah for a while, another traded in Islamic-style fashion and lived in both Jeddah and Egypt. Others spoke at events in Saudi Arabia about their born-again experiences in return for high speaking fees. Still others were driven by the necessity of keeping their job: the Saudis were setting up satellite television channels and production houses, they funded films and serials, and they didn't want to see too much skin. Some of the repentant actresses renounced their art completely, but others wore the veil specifically to stay on-screen. Saudi Arabia was a big market for Egyptian cinema, and whereas in the 1960s and 1970s Saudis had enjoyed watching actresses in short dresses and big hairdos, the mood and the market in the kingdom had changed after 1979. There was endless speculation, disparate bits of evidence, and connections made—but no paper trail. None of the actresses would ever conclusively deny or prove the Saudi connection. But the suspicion about the Saudi role in funding this trend was the source of many jokes.

"Who are the second-best-paid women in Egypt?"

"Belly dancers, because Saudi tourists throw banknotes of a hundred dollars at their feet while they are dancing."

"And who are the best-paid women in Egypt?"

"The converted belly dancers, because Saudi sheikhs transfer banknotes of a thousand dollars to their account if they stop dancing."

Egypt's famous filmmaker Youssef Chahine believed that religious fundamentalism was alien to Egyptians and described it as a "black wave" from the Gulf: "The Egyptian has always been a very religious person, but at the same time he is also a lover of life of art and music and theater." He trusted that his countrymen would find a balance between secular modernity and traditional religious forces.

They didn't.

Foda's assassination marked the violent beginning of the siege of Egyptian intellectuals. For the years to come, secular, liberal, progressive writers and thinkers would be hounded, banned, harassed, and assassinated. The long target list included journalists, intellectuals, and plastic surgeons. Even the Nobel Prize–winner Mahfouz, a national symbol, as Egyptian as the Nile, came under attack—stabbed in the neck by two assailants in October 1994. He would survive, but his writing hand was severely impaired.

Religion took over everything, rapidly. In 1985, barely 6 percent of books published in Egypt were religious. In 1994, it was 25 percent, and by 1995, 85 percent of books sold at the Cairo book fair were religious. In the mid-1980s, there was a mosque for every 6,031 Egyptians; by the mid-2000s there would be one for every 745. Taxi drivers played less Umm Kulthum and more Quranic recitations. Family photographs came off walls and mantels and were stored in drawers, especially photos of grandmothers wearing short sleeves and low necklines, or sporting the big hairdos of the 1960s. Modesty was the new norm, and pictures could lead to *shirk*, idolatry. The most orthodox, literalist concept of *shirk* and *al-shirk al-asghar*, the one that the young Sofana Dahlan had been taught in school in Jeddah, seeped into the consciousness of Egyptians, though it was a foreign concept in centuries of Egyptian traditions, art, and culture. Drawing nudes in university art classes was a thing of the past. Everything was now determined by *halal* or *haram*, permitted or forbidden in religion. Every second of people's lives became regulated by religious edicts, the search for heavenly salvation. The beliefs and practices of Islamists, once on the margins, had entered the mainstream.

Decades later, once society had settled into its new cultural and religious references, a speech given by President Nasser in 1965 to mark the anniversary of Egypt's victory in the Suez crisis would resurface and circulate as people asked themselves, "What happened to us?"—because of a passage in which Nasser had spoken irreverently about the veil. He was the greatest orator the Arab world has ever had, and his speeches—broadcast on the radio—enthralled audiences across the Arab world as he fluidly moved from rousing exhortations to serious explanations to jokes, all delivered in an easy, man-of-the-people style. He was a masterful storyteller.

In front of his usual massive crowd of supporters, a mixed audience of men in suits and women in skirts hanging on his every word, he came to the subject of the antagonism with the Muslim Brotherhood. Some of its members had tried to assassinate him, hence the brutal crackdown. He recounted how he had met with Hassan al-Hodeibi, the leader of the Brotherhood, in 1953. Hodeibi had made a number of requests, including apparently making the veil mandatory. The crowd, men and women, erupted in laughter and applause at such a preposterous idea. One person in the crowd screamed: "Let *him* wear it!" leading to more riotous laughter. Nasser said he had tried to explain to Hodeibi that this was a personal choice, but Hodeibi insisted: Nasser was the leader, he had to set the tone. Nasser continued: "I told him, you have a daughter in the faculty of medicine, she's not wearing a veil, why? If you can't make one woman, your own daughter, wear a veil, you want me to go down to the street and force ten million women to wear a veil?" By now, even Nasser was laughing as the crowd roared with delight.

Nasser's legacy and his repression of the Muslim Brotherhood set in motion a dynamic that contributed, decades down the road, to the toxic mix of fundamentalism, Salafism, and Wahhabism in Egypt and beyond. A nationalist modernizer, he was also an observant Muslim who had performed the pilgrimage to Mecca twice—no one could argue that his views were the expression of a mind corrupted by Western values. They reflected perhaps his city upbringing and the condescension of the urban middle class toward the rural class, who still wore *gallabiya*s, traditional peasant robes, and still kept their women covered or inside the house. Those who made it to the city discarded what they saw as the backward attire of village life, choosing instead to embrace modernity. Islamists claimed that it was the influence of the corrupt West that pushed women to unveil. But such assumptions overlooked the fact that Egypt was the birthplace of Arab feminism, and that Egypt's own emancipation from the West was symbolized in a famous statue of a peasant woman removing her headscarf as she leans on the mythical sphinx. That 1920 sculpture by Mahmoud Mokhtar became a metaphor for national independence and still stands not far from Cairo University, by the Nile.

Egypt had a long history of enlightenment, which gave hope to those living through the dark days of the 1990s. Foda's last sentence in his 1985 *Before the Fall* was a rallying cry to other intellectuals, the expression of his own conviction that Egypt could still get back on track if only more moderate voices spoke up. It had worked in the past. "Dialogue is the only way out of this crisis," he wrote, "because sometimes the word can stop a bullet, because it is of course stronger, and definitely longer lasting." Foda's incisive analysis had misjudged the extent of the social transformation happening around him. His faith in Egypt and in the pen had not saved him.

—

This was the environment in which Nasr, the scholar, was fighting for his own survival and that of his marriage in 1994, just a few years after Foda was killed. He couldn't quite square his ordeal with the Egypt that he loved, for he knew that this was not the Egypt of his youth. Westerners looked at Nasr and others like him who stood up to Islamists and saw someone "like us," an exception who shared their values. Nasr would come to resent that outlook—they didn't grasp his deep Egyptianness. His was not a story about a Westernized, secular member of the Egyptian elite rejecting the ways of the rural folk. Nasr was a village boy, a man of the people, of the land; the waters of the Nile coursed through his veins.

There was room for tolerance in small villages like Quhafa, in Tanta, where Nasr was born. It was a village of believers, both Christians and Muslims. Tolerance was not a learned concept; it was how people lived. Nasr's father had a strange friend from another village, a Christian Copt who came to Quhafa for work. The family hosted him for years, and when he died he was buried in the family cemetery. No one minded that he was a Christian.

There was room for modernity alongside religion in Quhafa. Nasr's father, a grocer, had sent him to the village school to learn reading and writing, arithmetic, and the Quran. By the age of eight, Nasr had memorized the Quran. His father had big dreams for his eldest son: he wanted Nasr to continue his religious studies and become a sheikh in the tradition of the great religious scholar Muhammad Abduh, the nineteenth-century founder of Islamic modernist thought. But from a young age, Nasr had become enamored with another reformer: Taha Hussein, his generation's most influential modernist, the figurehead of Egypt's intellectual renaissance, and the blind dean of Arabic literature. A village boy from Upper Egypt, Hussein made his way to the classrooms of Al-Azhar and all the way to the Sorbonne in Paris, where he married a Frenchwoman and returned to Cairo. He, too, had argued that the Quran was full of metaphors and allegories, and while also full of historical facts it should not be read literally. He, too, had been accused of apostasy. The debates between literalists and modernists were not new—the difference was in how they ended.

Unlike Foda and Nasr, Hussein had stared down the Islamists repeatedly and won, every time. When women gained the right tó enter universities in 1929, "religious reactionaries sought to drive them out" a few years later, but their "male colleagues confronted [them] and scattered the ranks of demonstrators who had stormed the college." Hussein had mobilized students to defend women's education, like a military commander going to battle for a "just cause" that was a "raging sea," which could not be held back by "throwing a few pebbles into it."

When charged with apostasy, Hussein had to leave the university for a few years, but when he returned, his students carried him on their shoulders triumphantly, all the way to his office. He eventually became minister of education in the 1950s and was nominated for the Nobel Prize in Literature. When he died in 1973, he was mourned as a great figure of the country's intellectual renaissance.

Having aspired to walk in Taha Hussein's footsteps all these years, Nasr was perhaps hoping he might be vindicated as well. But the tide of fundamentalism had come in; there was no rampart for Nasr. "Taha was accused of apostasy by people from outside the university, and the university defended him," Nasr would later say. "In my case, I was accused of apostasy inside the university, and some people from outside are defending me. Taha Husayn was never called a kafir. What's most telling is how the conception of apostasy has now been transplanted into the university."

By the spring of 1995, Ebtehal and Nasr were exhausted. They were mostly confined to their apartment, armed guards standing outside. She had aged ten years; her eyes were puffy. She wore a pendant with a picture of Nasr on it like an amulet. She didn't care if the militant Islamists killed them; something had already died inside her.

June of that year was dizzying in contradictions and upsets. Cairo University promoted Nasr to full professorship despite all the controversy. Any elation was short-lived. On June 14, the Cairo Court of Appeals ruled that Nasr's writings proved that he was indeed an apostate and declared his marriage to Ebtehal null and void. The Islamists had managed to subvert the legal process. They had taken their fight from the mosque to the courts, and they had won their first big case. Egypt was setting a precedent.

Sheikh Youssef al-Badri was one of the Islamist lawyers who had brought the case against Nasr. Like Shaheen, he was also a preacher, but in a small, neighborhood mosque. His sermons seethed with anger against the academic: "This is the religion of a third of the world's population! How can you attack Islam and pretend you are a Muslim?" The faithful, barely one hundred of them, listened to the sermon as Badri exploded the day after the verdict. The ruling was not enough: Nasr was an apostate, a "*murtad*, and a murtad is a dead man." To make things worse, Ayman al-Zawahiri reared his head from Sudan, where he and Bin Laden were by now, and issued a fatwa: killing Nasr was an Islamic duty.

On July 23, 1995, Ebtehal and Nasr left their homeland on a plane for Spain, then onward to Leiden in the Netherlands, where the university was welcoming him as a professor of Arab and Islamic studies. Within months, his books would be removed from Cairo University's library. In exile, Nasr and his writing slowly faded from the minds of Egyptians, along with the names and legacies of Farag Foda, Mahmoud Mokhtar, Taha Hussein, Muhammad Abduh, and so many others who represented the era when Cairo and Egypt were the mecca of Arab culture and they were leaders in the region's intellectual renaissance. For years, Nasr yearned to return home. Egypt came to him in his dreams. But it would be more than a decade before he saw the Nile again.

—

In August 1993, the Egyptian minister of the interior, Hassan Alfi, had survived an assassination attempt carried out by the Islamic Jihad. The attack made big headlines because of the high-profile target and the method used. Zawahiri had approved a new weapon: suicide bombings. Sunni jurisprudence was even stricter than Shiism on the issue of suicide. But just as the Iranian Revolution had inspired ideas among Sunni fundamentalists, the actions of groups like Hezbollah were provoking a deadly competition. The suicide bombing against the marine barracks in 1983 had achieved a key goal: the American troops had left. Palestinians took note. In 1987 Palestinians had rebelled in the West Bank and Gaza, after twenty years of life under Israeli occupation, arbitrary detentions, and land expropriations. Neither freedom nor peace was in sight. The First Palestinian Intifada (uprising) was a grassroots popular movement with mass protests that lasted six years but resolved nothing. Peace talks that began in 1991 in Madrid and then Oslo brought only slow, barely tangible progress. And so, just a few months ahead of Zawahiri and the attack on Alfi, Palestinian militants had opted to try suicide bombings in the Israeli-occupied West Bank, targeting a restaurant in the Jewish settlement of Mehola. That attack made few headlines. But Palestinians would continue to carry out countless suicide bombings against Israelis, both civilians and soldiers, in the Occupied Territories and inside Israel. Beyond fighting occupation, Zawahiri's endorsement of suicide bombings had opened a treacherous door. In less than a decade, Zawahiri and Bin Laden would send nineteen hijackers on a suicide mission to crash their planes into buildings in the United States.

12

GENERATION 1979

SAUDI ARABIA

1990–2001

In the dark times
Will there also be singing?
Yes, there will also be singing
About the dark times.

—Bertolt Brecht, "Motto to the Svendborg Poems" (1939)

Mansour al-Nogaidan had been guilty of violence before. Barely twenty years old, he'd done a few short stints in jail for spouting radical views, like calling on people to take their children out of public schools—only religious schooling was acceptable, anything else was an infidel model. In 1991, under cover of darkness, he and his friends had firebombed video stores and a women's support center in his hometown of Buraidah, three and a half hours northwest of Riyadh. For that, he had spent almost two years in jail. The way he saw it, he was being punished for trying to align the world he saw around him with the world as it should be, according to the teachings of the clerics, teachings he imparted to his flock as an imam in a small neighborhood mosque. Those teachings did not stand out in Saudi Arabia; they were very much the mainstream line of thinking. The small, round man with protruding eyes and the beard of a devout Salafist had nothing to do with the bomb that exploded in Riyadh on November 13, 1995. He ended up back in jail anyway. The Saudi authorities were taking no chances.

On that day, just three months after Nasr Abu Zeid and Ebtehal Younes had fled Egypt, the Saudis discovered they were not immune from the wave of rigid intolerance they had cultivated at home and helped promote outside the kingdom. At 11:40 a.m., a car bomb exploded in a parking lot just outside a building that housed the offices of American military trainers. The powerful explosion shook the capital as a fire engulfed the structure. Black smoke billowed across the city. The building was just off a main thoroughfare in the busy district of al-Olaya. Six people were killed and sixty wounded. Most of them were eating an early lunch in the building's snack bar on the ground floor. Four of the five Americans killed were civilians. Americans had come under attack in Beirut, tourists in Egypt had been killed, Algeria was being ripped apart by a civil war after the army canceled an election in which the Islamic Salvation Front was assured victory, all of this following the Juhayman events of 1979. But in the kingdom, this was the first such act of violence: foreigners targeted with a car bomb.

The Americans were there as part of a long-established mission to train the Saudi National Guard. The attack was a signal to the royals that their alliance with America was still a sin in the eyes of the most conservative of Saudis, just as it had been for Juhayman. There had been threats faxed to the American embassy in the spring demanding that the "crusaders" leave the "land of Islam" by June. The embassy staff said they had taken the faxes seriously but had never heard of the group who made the threat and could not find any further information. "This was not something you think would ever happen here," said Raymond E. Mabus Jr., the US ambassador to Riyadh.

The alliance between Saudi Arabia and the United States had grown only stronger since the first handshake between President Roosevelt and King Abdelaziz in 1945. None of it was ever very visible to the naked eye or in the heartland: a military base operated by the US Air Force until 1962 was located in Dhahran, far away from the capital, in the oil-rich Eastern Province. ARAMCO also had its headquarters there, its large gated compound housing several thousand foreign employees and their families. That was the kingdom's first compound for foreigners, a universe unto itself that would be replicated in smaller versions across the country. The kingdom welcomed foreign expertise but kept the foreigners behind walls everywhere, especially in Riyadh.

The compounds were small oases of normality for the foreigners: women could work and drive on the compound; there were mixed swimming pools, club bars, and music. For conservative Saudis, the compounds were cities of sin they didn't want to know about; for radical Saudis, they would soon become targets. Over time, as the number of foreigners grew into the millions, those enclaves only cemented the divide between Saudis and foreigners, between those who belonged to the pure land of Islam and those who didn't. Other than in elite circles, there was little social interaction between Saudis and foreigners. Some well-off Saudi families with the right connections, looking to escape the suffocating atmosphere of life in Riyadh, would find a way onto the compounds—but they would end up paying a high price for doing so.

The building that was targeted in November 1995 was not on a compound; it wasn't even behind a wall. It was (in security parlance) a soft target, the kind that radicals in the country had been looking for to express their ire at the dramatic, in-your-face expansion of the military alliance between Saudi Arabia and America just a few years earlier. In 1990, when Saddam Hussein invaded Kuwait, King Fahd had called on America for protection and President George H. W. Bush was quick to respond. On August 8, just six days after Saddam sent his troops across the border into the small emirate, some fifteen thousand American troops headed to Saudi Arabia, along with two aircraft carriers, as the United States began to corral an international coalition to dislodge Iraqi troops from Kuwait. The king had set off a storm: calling on the West for assistance and bringing even more infidels to the birthplace of Islam was both a demonstration of weakness and an affront to the pride of every Muslim. The Al-Sauds were pragmatic when they needed protection. They'd relied on the British to cement their hold on the peninsula in the 1920s, even calling in the Royal Air Force to squash an uprising within the ranks of the king's warriors. They had enlisted the French to quell the rebellion inside the Holy Mosque in 1979. This time, they needed all the might of the Americans against the man they knew could be their undoing. After all, they had armed him to the teeth for years against Iran.

In 1990, Osama bin Laden was in Jeddah. Following the Soviet withdrawal, he was done for now with Afghanistan. He didn't want America's help on the Arabian Peninsula and believed it was possible to defeat Saddam by "organizing battalions of righteous Islamic volunteers." He wanted to meet the king and put his plan to him: a sixty-page plan outlining his strategy for a guerrilla war. Bin Laden insisted he had some eighty thousand fighters at his disposal, all battled-tested Afghan war veterans. He also claimed he had all the weapons he needed. He never met the king, and the minister of defense who did meet him, Prince Sultan, dismissed his plan: there were no caves in Kuwait like there were in Afghanistan; Bin Laden could not fight a traditional army that would lob missiles at him. But he was unperturbed: "We will fight him with faith."

The royals did not take him up on his offer, but yet again, their role as defenders of the faith and the holy sites was thrown into doubt. On January 9, 1990, Saddam convened a repeat of the Popular Islamic Conference that had gathered the who's who of the Islamic world in 1983 and bestowed Islamic legitimacy on his war against Iran in the 1980s. This time, Saddam declared war on the Saudis, those who had "put the Mecca of the Muslims and the tomb of prophet Muhammad under the spears of the foreigner." He added the words *Allahu Akbar* to the Iraqi flag.

The Saudis hit back. They convened their own Popular Islamic Conference at the same time in Mecca. Needless to say, it attracted more people, and of course Maarouf Dawalibi was there, not in Baghdad. King Fahd also leaned on the man who never failed to help the Al-Sauds out of a bind: the blind sheikh Bin Baz, the same one who had nurtured Juhayman and his coterie before sanctioning the use of force in the Holy Mosque. Against the advice of some of his Saudi colleagues, Bin Baz issued two fatwas, in 1990 and again in 1991, sanctioning the unsanctionable: he declared that in certain emergencies, a Muslim state could ask for help from a non-Muslim state. He then blessed all those, Muslim and non-Muslim, who were participating in the "holy war" against Saddam, who was now declared an "enemy of God." By the end of January 1991, half a million American troops had descended on the kingdom to protect the oil fields and use the kingdom as a launching pad to liberate Kuwait. There were female soldiers driving trucks. Foreign correspondents, including women, were flocking to the country, staying in hotels, unaccompanied.

Saudi citizens were taken aback by the developments: Why did the kingdom need outside help for its protection? Why didn't it have its own professional army ready for the job? Saudis had been tolerant of their government's failings and even the corruption of the royals when they were told that budget cuts in the 1980s were paying to build up the country's defense as the Iran-Iraq War raged. Where had all the money gone? Two strands of society were pulling in very different directions as the kingdom appeared to be opening to the outside world by the force of war. There were those, educated and progressive, who saw an opportunity to push for social and political reforms that had been shelved after 1979. There was still no constitution, although the king had said in 1980 that it was ready; the shura council (an appointed, consultative, and nonlegislating parliament, first introduced in the 1930s) had been retired years ago and had still not been revived. Whatever modern luxuries and subsidies Saudi citizens enjoyed in the kingdom, they were no longer enough to make up for the social restrictions that had become only harsher, making life even grimmer in the kingdom. Holidays abroad provided an easy escape, but people, especially women, wanted more.

Women had been most affected by the rolling back of the limited social freedoms they'd had before 1979. Hundreds had already graduated from universities abroad and bristled at the closeted life they had to lead in the kingdom, the only country in the world where women were not allowed to drive. On November 6, 1990, seventy Saudi women gathered in the parking lot of the al-Tamimi Safeway supermarket in Riyadh in their cars. They dismissed their drivers, took the wheel, and drove through the city. The convoy of plush automobiles—Buicks, Mercedes, Lincoln Continentals, and the like—broke down into smaller groups at every intersection, until they were all intercepted by the Saudi police about half an hour after the protest began. The women, who all had the support of their husbands and male relatives, were briefly detained and made to sign pledges that they wouldn't repeat their protest. Those who had government jobs (teaching at the university, for example) were dismissed by order of the king. This was the paternal side to the misogyny of the system, the soft tone with which the king dealt with unruly female subjects. The zealots were not soft.

From their pulpits, clerics denounced the protesters as "dirty American secularists" and "fallen women." Their names and addresses were printed on leaflets distributed around mosques, one leaflet accusing them of having renounced Islam; inherent in that accusation was the threat of death for apostasy. Bin Baz issued a decree formally forbidding women to drive, but he could not undo the damage of his acquiescence to opening the door to half a million Americans. A war of words had begun; fiery speeches spread around the country on what was still the favorite propaganda tool of the time, the same one that Khomeini had used to spread his revolutionary message: cassette tapes.

Two clerics led the protestations: Safar al-Hawali and Salman al-Audah. Hawali was a forty-year-old, taciturn-looking man, with deep-set eyes and a long, untrimmed, jet-black beard. Audah was younger and more jovial, and he kept his beard short. The two men had opposed the jihad in Afghanistan, disagreeing with Azzam's call on all Muslims to fight the Soviets. But they could not abide the arrival of the infidels on the peninsula. Their tapes sold like hotcakes, under the table, in the back of shops, passed around after prayers at the mosque. They decried the influence of the West on their country, warning that the war with Iraq and the arrival of infidel troops in Saudi Arabia were part of a larger plan by the West to dominate the Arab and Muslim world. "It is not the world against Iraq," said Hawali in one speech, "It is the West against Islam. If Iraq has occupied Kuwait, then America has occupied Saudi Arabia. The real enemy is not Iraq. It is the West."

The speeches became increasingly political and fiery, enraging Saudi youth already discontent and bored, or frustrated after returning from the jihad against the Soviets. Some were now traveling to fight in Bosnia and Chechnya. Hawali and Audah also petitioned the king for reforms in two letters: they demanded the establishment of the long-promised shura council, and they called for domestic and foreign policies that complied fully with the shari'a. There was no outright call for the removal of the royal family or any questioning of the legitimacy of the House of Saud. Instead, theirs was a call to embrace Islamic values more truly, and to reject servitude to the West. This was a reform movement working within the confines of the state, but the king saw it as a betrayal by his subjects. By 1994, Hawali, Audah, and dozens of their followers had been thrown in jail, where they would stay until 1999. But the tapes of their sermons still circulated, others were still preaching, and dissidents spread the word from exile by fax.

The House of Saud felt betrayed for another reason. The two clerics had something in common: they had both been students of prominent figures connected to the Muslim Brothers, the Egyptian Mohammad Qutb, brother of Sayyid, and the Syrian Surur, author of the book about the Shias as magi. The two men had arrived in Saudi Arabia in the 1970s. Qutb had supervised Hawali's dissertation on secularism at the Umm al-Qura University in Mecca in the 1980s. Audah had been deeply influenced by Surur, who taught and preached near his hometown, in the city of Buraidah.

The first wave of teachers from the Arab world had come to the kingdom in the 1930s and 1940s with secular texts: the history of the French Revolution, the poetry of the great Arab masters, the writings of reformers of the Arab renaissance. Then came the Muslim Brothers with their religious teachings, more in tune with the needs of the kingdom, though there were key differences between the Brotherhood and the Wahhabis. Initially, the Brothers worked within the framework of the state, focused on shaping a model, conservative Islamic society. But as Egyptians or Syrians, they had politics in their DNA, and by 1991, their ideas had transformed Wahhabi Salafism, traditionally obedient to the ruler, into a more activist Salafism. Some described it as Qutbist or Sururi Wahhabism, following either Qutb or Surur. Injecting political activism into an absolute monarchy, they had unleashed a protest movement that was challenging the king. The House of Saud would never forgive the Brotherhood, and would conveniently blame the group for all the extremism and violence that was about to be unleashed. But the local grievances were very real. Surur, Qutb, and others had simply given them the tools to protest.

The royals decried this sahwa, this Islamic awakening, which was not what they'd had in mind when they had encouraged a sahwa after 1979, believing it would remain focused on religion and education, on proselytizing and enforcing prayer times. The uncomfortable truth for the House of Saud was that they also had long used the Muslim Brotherhood to their advantage, to lend legitimacy and respectability to institutions like the Islamic University of Medina.

Founded by King Faisal in 1961 as a gift to the Wahhabi establishment, the university had an explicit mission: to train, proselytize, and extend the reach of the kingdom's religious establishment beyond the country's borders. Before that, efforts to send Wahhabi scholars from Najd to proselytize in neighboring Iraq and Syria had been met with scorn. Attracting non-Saudi scholars to the university (with the help of big paychecks) would show that it was not a purely Wahhabi establishment, but a legitimate endeavor with broad Islamic appeal. The syllabus was still shaped by the Wahhabi creed, focused on the works of Ibn Abdelwahhab, Ibn Taymiyyah, and the Hanbali school of thought. There were limited comparative studies. The powerful vice rector was none other than Bin Baz. Mawdudi sat on the board. Mohammad Qutb was on the university's founding advisory council, and the sahwa leader Hawali had been a student. The Brothers had influenced their Wahhabi colleagues, and had themselves absorbed Wahhabi ideas—but the product was still made and facilitated in Saudi Arabia. Until 1979, the kings had bent that product and the clerics to their will, keeping them in check. After 1979, the Wahhabi religious establishment had become king.

Mansour, the young man who had set the video stores on fire, had not gone to Medina University, but he had lapped up Surur and the Qutb brothers' writings, which were widely available in Saudi Arabia, in schools and at universities. What set Mansour apart was that he questioned everything, even the presence of God. This initially led him down the path of extremism. Assailed by doubts, Mansour made a deal with his creator: he would give up everything and live the way the prophet and his companions had lived fourteen centuries earlier if God helped him get rid of his doubts. At the age of sixteen, he joined a hardline Salafist group that tried to re-create the mythical time of the prophet, living with no television, no radio, no newspapers, and barely any modern amenities. The community of three hundred had its own schools, focused solely on religious teachings. Mansour grew his beard and stopped speaking to his family. He later compared it to living like the Amish. He began to outdo his fundamentalist teachers: he issued a religious edict against the 1989 FIFA World Youth championship being held in the kingdom—football was haram. He landed in jail for fifty-five days for daring to oppose the royal family's games. Mansour and men like him were frustrated by the hypocrisy around them, big and small: Why had the Custodian of the Two Holy Mosques invited the infidels into the kingdom? Why did government sheikhs say that Western films were propagating un-Islamic values, yet still allow them to be sold? Why did Mansour end up in jail for firebombing a video store when he was doing exactly what the Taliban were doing in Afghanistan?

In 1996, the Saudi government recognized the Taliban government and its Islamic Emirate of Afghanistan. They, too, were destroying video and cassette tapes, banning music and sports, and enforcing prayer time. The Saudis supported the growth of the Taliban, seeing kindred spirits in these revolutionaries who embraced an Islamic purity that the House of Saud perhaps aspired to, but could never attain as a kingdom allied to the West. The Saudi Committee for the Promotion of Virtue and the Prevention of Vice, the religious police, helped train and support the Taliban's version, and Saudi charities provided them with "humanitarian relief." Though the Taliban were Deobandi, they were as close as possible to Saudi Wahhabi orthodoxy, and the kingdom hoped they would grow into a mature state, just as their own country had done after King Abdelaziz united it by the sword.

The most radical Saudi youths thought that even Hawali and Audah were too soft. They were reading Abu Muhammad al-Maqdissi, the Palestinian scholar and intellectual heir of Juhayman who had published his books while in Peshawar. In a later book in 1989 he had specifically targeted the Saudi kingdom: *Al Kawashif al-Jaliyya fi Kufr al-Dawla al-Saudiyya* or *The Obvious Proofs of the Saudi State's Impiety*. In 1994, he landed in a Jordanian jail. But just before, he had met several times with a twenty-four-year-old Saudi, Abdelaziz Mu'atham—the mastermind of the bombing in Riyadh against the National Guard training facility on that November day in 1995.

Mu'atham confessed to the crime on television with his co-conspirators, describing several meetings with Maqdissi and the influence of his writings.

He said he was also inspired by Bin Laden. Saudis were in shock. How could young, devout Muslims, some of whom were covered in the glory of the war against the Soviets, engage in such violence against their own country? There was no ability or willingness to recognize that these young men were a product of their environment, of a youth spent learning about the enemies of Islam and glorifying the mujahedeen. For those who only preached, the anger stopped there. For those who had any propensity for violence, or who had tasted war and witnessed death, the battle continued when they returned home. They were dismissed as deviants, just like Juhayman. Bin Baz said such extremism needed to be fought with preaching the rightful da'wa, the path to salvation for Muslims.

When the Saudi authorities jailed hundreds of extremists in the wake of the 1995 bombing, it was the end of the political sahwa. But the violent streak it had produced would continue and grow into al-Qaeda on the Arabian Peninsula (AQAP). Mansour was still full of questions, about God, about religion, even about the Quran—had it really existed since the beginning of time, or had it been written by humans? These had been the questions at the center of Nasr Abu Zeid's writing in Egypt and the Mu'tazilah before him. But these were not questions that anyone dared ask in Saudi Arabia. In prison, Mansour got his sister to bring him books about Sufism, considered heretical by Wahhabis, then got his hands on books by Western philosophers.

While he was isolated in his cell, alone on his intellectual and spiritual journey, the détente between Iran and Saudi Arabia, begun in the wake of Iraq's invasion of Kuwait in 1990, continued and produced moments that were hard to fathom for some. In 1998, Rafsanjani, no longer president but still a top leader, was in Saudi Arabia for a ten-day visit. He was the highest-ranking Iranian to visit the kingdom since the 1979 Revolution. This was not a quick diplomatic trip by a foreign minister. This was a high-profile, red-carpet affair. Rafsanjani had called for the liberation of Mecca from the Al-Sauds during the 1987 crisis at the hajj. The pragmatic Iranian now posed for pictures with King Fahd and went to Mecca for the umra. How could this be? How could the Custodian of the Two Holy Mosques be having a friendly chat with the magi of all magis? This could not pass without denunciation. The clerical establishment would not swallow the royal realpolitik. While Rafsanjani was attending Friday prayers at the Prophet's Mosque in Medina, Crown Prince Abdallah by his side, the resident preacher sheikh Ali al-Huthaifi angrily denounced the Shias, using the pejorative word *rafidha*, derived from the Arabic "to refuse"—those who had refused to recognize the first caliph, Abu Bakr, and had followed Ali instead. The episode caused deep embarrassment for the Saudis, and Sheikh Huthaifi was removed as a preacher from the mosque (albeit for only a year).

The détente, which had begun with a low-key meeting between the Saudi and Iranian foreign ministers in New York in 1990, had evolved steadily, thanks to the personalities of both Rafsanjani, the pragmatist, and Crown Prince Abdallah, always a great believer in accommodation and Islamic solidarity. Abdallah was, after all, the one who had praised the Iranian Revolution in April 1979 for its Islamic credentials. After the end of the Iran-Iraq War in 1988, Rafsanjani had gone shopping in the Soviet Union, but he knew it would not be enough to overcome a war that cost the economy $1 trillion and killed an estimated one million Iranians. Iran needed to sell more oil and needed more of a say in the Organization of the Petroleum Exporting Countries (OPEC). For that, it needed Saudi Arabia. When Saddam invaded Kuwait, Iran pointedly did not criticize Saudi Arabia's call for help from America—the Great Satan.

In early March 1991, soon after Kuwait was liberated, Iraq's Shias in the south and Kurds in the north seized on the momentary weakness of their dictator. They had been encouraged to rise by President Bush, and the uprisings had come close to bringing down Saddam. But America, Saudi Arabia, and even Iran failed to come to their help. Saddam survived. On March 18, the Saudi and Iranian foreign ministers met in Oman for three hours and followed with a startling announcement: their countries had settled their dispute about the hajj and would be resuming diplomatic ties within forty-eight hours. Saudi Arabia pledged to increase the quota for Iranian pilgrims, not quite back to the level preceding 1987's Bloody Friday, but up from 45,000 to 110,000. The rapid and unbelievable reconciliation was hailed in the Arab world. This was a NORMAL RETURN TO NORMAL RELATIONS, headlined the Kuwaiti newspaper *Al-Seyassah* on March 19. This was proof, the paper wrote, of the civilizational ties between Iran and its Gulf neighbors, which went back centuries. The Kuwait crisis, the editorial added, had shown what Iran was really made of, and Iran had stood up for what was right. Rafsanjani's efforts to open up to the rest of the world were also paying off: the World Bank had given Iran its first loan since 1979. Britain had renewed diplomatic ties. France and Germany were already doing brisk business with Tehran. A ban on Iranian oil sales was lifted.

Saudi Arabia and Iran both had reasons to want this détente, which was proof, if ever there was one, that their common interests could trump

any ideological differences—even to the extent of silencing doctrinal disputes and religious hatreds. Rafsanjani was especially keen to defuse the
Sunni-Shia tension that had built up since 1979. He was also determined to
find an agreement that would allow more regular Shia visitations to what
was left of the cemetery of Jannat al-Baqi. Access to the cemetery, with its
rows of unmarked graves, was restricted and open only to men. Rafsanjani
believed that keeping it off-limits fueled continued resentment of Shias
toward the House of Saud, a festering wound that never healed because the
relief of crying over the graves was out of reach. On a later visit by Rafsanjani, Crown Prince Abdallah made sure that Jannat al-Baqi was opened to
the Iranian delegation, men and women, for three days.

The rapprochement was so successful that it worried the Americans,
who were wary of Abdallah, a more conservative, less pro-Western royal
than his half brother Fahd. He had limited education but more vision.
Saudi Arabia and Iran were suddenly speaking with one voice on various
regional issues, including Iraq and the Middle East peace process. Nothing
seemed to get in the way of the honeymoon—not Iran's missile tests, not
even another bomb attack in Saudi Arabia with Iranian fingerprints on it.

—

In June 1996, a massive explosion tore the face off an eight-story building
housing American Air Force personnel in Al-Khobar Towers, in Saudi
Arabia's Eastern Province. Nineteen American servicemen died, and more
than four hundred people were injured. The explosives packed in a sewage tanker truck were the equivalent of twenty thousand pounds of TNT,
more powerful than the 1983 marine barracks bombing in Beirut. The
first suspect was al-Qaeda. But suspicion quickly turned to a Shia group,
Hezbollah al-Hejaz, affiliated with Hezbollah in Lebanon. The Saudis were
reticent in their cooperation with the FBI. Even after an indictment in
June 2001 named several Shia Lebanese and Saudi members of Hezbollah
al-Hejaz as having connections to Iran, the Saudis were reluctant to join
the chorus of condemnation of Tehran. The priority was preserving their
rapprochement with Tehran. The Saudis justified it by insisting there was
a difference between the pragmatist moderates they were talking to—like
Rafsanjani and his successor president, Khatami, a moderate elected in
1998—and the hardliners who were trying to derail the relationship. No
one in Saudi Arabia or the Gulf was naive about Iran. There was clearly no
trust, but there was a desire to somehow make it work, a Saudi belief that
over time shared interests could moderate revolutionary ardor. In time, the

Saudis would come to believe they had been fooled and that the moderates and the hardliners were in fact the same, or at least acting in concert.

But forces beyond Abdallah and Rafsanjani were at work, forces that both sides had been grooming for years. For the Iranians, these forces were the zealous upholders of Khomeini's revolution, the hardliner believers, and the Revolutionary Guards. In Lebanon, Hezbollah was transforming from a mere militia into a political party with an organized armed wing. For Iran, ideology was a tool of state power and the allies and proxies that Tehran groomed answered to the Supreme Leader. On the Saudi side, the dark forces were the product of Saudi money, both private and from the government, that had made its way to the Afghan mujahedeen, the Deobandi seminaries in Pakistan, even the coffers of Al-Azhar in Egypt and the pockets of hundreds of clerics from around the Muslim world who had trained in Saudi Arabia. From militancy to intellectual terrorism, the forces fed by Saudi Arabia had no return address; they were not state-run, and they could not be controlled. Some moderated themselves but others mutated into even more violent versions.

Mansour al-Nogaidan knew very well the danger they represented to his own country and the world, though he could never have imagined the magnitude of what was about to happen. Out of jail, he had traveled far in his mind and his heart—too far for those who attended the mosque where he preached in Riyadh; too far for the Saudi state. In 1999, Mansour still had questions. He wrote in a Saudi newspaper that he thought everyone should have the right to ask questions, including of religious leaders. He was shunned at the mosque, as people refused to pray with him. He moved to the south of the country, where he continued to write about the need to question clerics and their interpretations. The authorities banned him from writing. He would end up back in a cell for a while. Mansour was now part of a small circle of former jihadis who had discovered critical thinking and consequently found themselves in the crosshairs of the powerful clerical establishment. He was among a handful of Saudi men who had the distinction of having been jailed for being both too radical, then too liberal.

On September 11, 2001, at 4:46 p.m. in Saudi Arabia, Mansour was visiting his parents in his hometown of Buraidah. He was sitting in the living room watching Al-Jazeera, the Arab CNN, beaming out of Qatar since 1996. State-funded but much freer than the stale, state-controlled news on offer in Arab countries, the channel was quickly making a name for itself—it had already broadcast two interviews with Osama bin Laden. Al-Jazeera was reporting that a plane had just crashed into the North

Tower of the World Trade Center in New York City. Mansour was transfixed by the horror unfolding in front of his eyes on the screen. The second
plane crashed into the South Tower three minutes after 5:00 p.m. Like the
overwhelming majority of the rest of the world, Mansour tried to make
sense of it, his mind racing. As news emerged about a plane crashing into
the Pentagon and then another into a field in Pennsylvania, there was no
doubt that America was under attack—and he had a sinking feeling that
he understood exactly what had happened and what it meant. Within a
day, fingers were pointing at al-Qaeda. On September 13, Secretary of State
Colin Powell identified Bin Laden as a prime suspect. By September 15, it
had become clear that more than a dozen of the attackers were Saudi. On
September 27, Robert Mueller, the head of the FBI, made public the faces
and names of all the attackers.

The kingdom had a schizophrenic reaction. Silently, many Saudis had
come to understand that the repressive culture and closed society they
lived in produced men like the hijackers. They knew they had collectively
allowed intolerance to grow and flourish around them, and they had done
nothing to stop it, not as a society and not as a government. But there
was also denial, including at the highest level: this had to be a Western or
Zionist plot to frame Saudi Arabia. Even a year later, the interior minister,
Prince Nayef bin Abdelaziz, was still stating that it was impossible that fifteen Saudis could have participated in such an attack—he blamed a Zionist
conspiracy. "We still ask ourselves, who has benefited from the attacks?
I think that they [the Jews] were the protagonists," he told the Kuwaiti
newspaper *Al-Seyassah*.

Again, the hijackers were described as deviants who had lost their
way and did not represent either their society or the true Islam. But the
Saudi hijackers were not outcasts, they weren't even living on the far margins, not even the way Mansour had done. They had gone to school and
learned the Quran, grown up in mostly middle-class, deeply religious
families, and gone to university to study law. Some were school dropouts;
only one of them had mental difficulties, for which he found solace at the
mosque. They were imams in neighborhood mosques, or *hafiz*, men who
had learned the entire Quran by heart. Most of them had gone briefly to
Afghanistan, Bosnia, or Chechnya in 1999 or 2000, although few had made
it to an actual battlefield. Bosnia and Chechnya were wars deemed righteous by Saudi officialdom, a fight in the name of Islam, a battle to protect
Muslims from slaughter. Prince Salman, governor of Riyadh and future
king, had fund-raised for Bosnia just as he had done for Afghanistan.

In the mid-1990s, dismayed by Western inaction in Bosnia, Saudi Arabia reportedly channeled $300 million worth of weapons to the Muslim-led government of Bosnia, on top of $500 million in humanitarian aid. The jihad against the Soviets may have been over, but the flow of men to Afghanistan had continued. Saudi Arabia was one of only three countries that had recognized the Taliban's Islamic Emirate of Afghanistan, which was now sheltering Bin Laden. He had been on the wrong side of the Saudi authorities since he called for attacks against the House of Saud, but he was still a folk hero to many Saudis. The 9/11 hijackers did not stand out in their country; they were unremarkable, representing the average Saudi man of that generation, the generation of 1979, the fateful year around which most of them were born. It was as though they had been born and raised for nothing else but death in the fireball of a raging hell, victims and killers at once.

One Saudi who was not in denial or silent contrition was Mansour. He had spent a few weeks deconstructing the path that these men had been on, and he believed that he had been vindicated in his warnings against the closed, oppressive, intolerant system in which young Saudis were being raised with no outlet for the anger being whipped up inside them in mosques across the country. He began to focus his newspaper articles on challenging the current thinking in the kingdom. He "tried to give a new interpretation to the verses that call for enmity between Muslims, and Christians and Jews." Those verses did not apply to modern times, and he called for friendship among all faiths. He was shunned by friends, labeled blasphemous on Internet forums. Then he was fired from the newspaper. But Mansour wasn't cowed; he kept writing.

In 2003, two major bombings targeted residential compounds in Riyadh, in May and November. There were fifty-six dead and almost four hundred injured, including children. Among them were Jordanians, Egyptians, Lebanese, and even Saudis. This was not some Zionist plot, a faraway tragedy, or an attack against infidels. The bombers were Saudi members of al-Qaeda and they had killed civilians in the kingdom—including Muslims. More than anything, it was this detail that seemed to awaken the Saudis to the threat of terrorism. There was a large crackdown on extremist suspects. The May bombing became known as Saudi Arabia's 9/11. There had been many predictions over the years about the end of the House of Saud, but this time it was almost palpable; an atmosphere of *fin de règne* hung over the kingdom.

Mansour thought the authorities were going after the wrong culprit, and he wrote as much in a brazen opinion piece in the *New York Times* titled "Telling the Truth, Facing the Whip": "I cannot but wonder at our officials and pundits who continue to claim that Saudi society loves other nations and wishes them peace, when state-sponsored preachers in some of our largest mosques continue to curse and call for the destructions of all non-Muslims." Mansour ended up in jail for five days. He had committed the unforgivable sin not only of openly attacking the clerical establishment, but of going to a Western paper to do so. By 2004, the mufti of the kingdom had pronounced him an infidel.

After the attacks of September 11, Saudis were forced by the United States to exercise more control over where their money for charity and proselytizing was going—a lot of it was outside state control. There were some three hundred private Saudi charities sending $6 billion a year to Islamic causes around the world. Every day, wealthy Saudi individuals donated an estimated $1.6 million to charity, and some of it ended up in the wrong hands. According to one estimate, almost $60 million donated to legitimate Saudi-based charities went astray, with $2 million per year going into the coffers of al-Qaeda. The Saudis set up a government commission to oversee charity money going abroad, dissolved some charities, and shut down the Islamic affairs section in the five main embassies in the West. Reluctantly, the Saudis also promised to review the school curriculum, but they never did much—either because, at their core, the royals espoused some of the same beliefs as the clerical establishment, or because they didn't dare challenge the clerics.

Jamal Khashoggi, the journalist who had written excited dispatches from the front lines of the Afghan war, was back in Jeddah, working as the deputy editor of the English-language daily *Arab News*. He still believed in political Islam, but he had never espoused violence and he especially opposed Muslims killing other Muslims. This was what divided the world of Islam: those who believed in letting others live and those who didn't. Osama bin Laden had been Jamal's friend; they had spent time together in Peshawar and in Afghanistan. Jamal had been one of the first to interview the tall, lanky, rich Saudi. In 1995, Khashoggi, acting as a kind of unofficial intermediary for Bin Laden's family back in Saudi Arabia, had tried to persuade Bin Laden to publicly renounce his campaign against the Saudi establishment and denounce violence inside the kingdom. The violent sahwa was just beginning. Bin Laden, who was living in Sudan by then, running a training camp for militants, refused. Jamal left, exasperated. After 9/11, Jamal described Bin Laden as living in a fantasyland of terror.

He wrote a mea culpa on his personal website, saying the kingdom wasn't even trying to understand what had led fifteen Saudis to become hijackers.

A week after the May 2003 bombings, Khaled al-Ghannami, an ex-jihadi—like his friend Mansour—published an opinion piece in the progressive *Al-Watan* paper, calling into question the legacy of Ibn Taymiyyah, the spiritual father of Wahhabism. He identified the fundamentalist medieval cleric as the source of much of Saudi Arabia's troubles. Ibn Taymiyya's words, wrote Ghannami, were a true disaster, leading people to take it upon themselves to impose virtue on others. For Salafists and Wahhabis, Ibn Taymiyya's words and edicts were unassailable. Khashoggi had just been appointed as editor in chief of the newspaper two weeks prior. He was promptly fired.

Of all those who tried, in the wake of the September 11 attacks, to wake their compatriots to the dangers of exclusionary thinking and the intolerance that the Saudi system fostered, Sami Angawi, the architect from Jeddah, had the most daring and visually provocative approach. Now in his fifties, he was still speaking out against the destruction of the Islamic heritage in Mecca and Medina—of some three hundred sites, only ten remained. He had resigned in 1988 from the Hajj Center he founded, perhaps forced out by his own integrity, his unwillingness to accept that money was the new God in Mecca. If there was any trauma in his life that most pained him it was the fact that he had never managed to stop the bulldozers. Every stone that was dug up, every building that was torn down felt like a stab in his heart. For Sami, there was a connection between the destruction of buildings and of Islamic heritage and the terror that had been wrought in New York: a monopoly on religion by those who dictated that only their way was right, erasing everything else. The religious authorities endorsed such destruction by stating that it was not permitted to glorify buildings. Sami put together a private lecture for small groups in his Jeddah home, itself an ode to ancient Meccan architecture that he had built himself, with inner courtyards and hanging gardens. The slide projection showed three images: the Saudis dynamiting a minaret in a holy shrine in Medina in 2002; the Taliban blowing up the colossal sixth-century Buddhas carved into a mountain in Afghanistan in March 2001; and finally the World Trade Center engulfed in flames on 9/11. Saudi officials dismissed his lecture as an extreme extrapolation.

—

During the 1990s, the Middle East had witnessed a decade of relative calm, in part thanks to the détente between Iran and Saudi Arabia but also as a result of Pax Americana—post–Cold War, the United States was the unchallenged hegemon. The Saudi-Iran rapprochement had yielded more than anyone expected, including a security agreement. When Saudi Arabia's defense minister visited Tehran in May 1999, his Iranian counterpart declared: "The sky's the limit for Iranian–Saudi Arabian relations and co-operation as the whole of Islamic Iran's military might is in the service of our Saudi Muslim brothers." President Bill Clinton was basking in the glory of a unipolar world and America was prospering as the indispensable nation. Throughout his presidency and until his very last months in power, Clinton was working on peace between Arabs and Israelis—succeeding only with the Jordanians. Even though people like Nasr in Egypt had their lives upended, Iraq was under UN embargo, and bombs had gone off in the Saudi kingdom, the decade carried some promise. It all came to an end on 9/11. President George W. Bush went to war against the Taliban, who were sheltering Osama bin Laden. After liberating Afghanistan, America declared a global war on terror, a frenzy of liberation. Bush decided to finish what his father had begun—he went after Saddam.

PART III

REVENGE

PART III

REVENGE

13

CAIN AND ABEL

IRAQ

2003–2006

I am not alone: many children of my homeland
Escaped to Iran along with their suffering too.
In their exile, they are my family, in our loss we are all brothers
I am the son of Baghdad, whenever you meet me,
I am the son of Baghdad, wherever you see me.

—Ibrahim Ovadia,
"A Guest in Tehran," *Baghdad: A City in Verse* (1951)

There was no time to rejoice. There was freedom, reunion, and then murder, a dizzying succession of events, intense emotions, and nauseating savagery. In exile in Iran, Sayyed Jawad al-Khoei heard the news from family back home in Iraq, gruesome details slowly trickling from his hometown of Najaf, the horror too big to grasp. Sitting in Qom, he listened to commentators on the evening news describe the murder of his uncle in the holy city as the well-deserved end of a traitor. Hacked to pieces, left bleeding on the street. Then shot. Not even the black turban and clerical robe had protected the forty-year-old man who'd met such a cruel end in the shadow of the holiest Shia site of all, Imam Ali's shrine.

On April 9, 2003, invading American troops had reached Baghdad. Saddam was on the run. His statue on Firdous Square was toppled by an ecstatic crowd, drunk on the sudden rush of oxygen, as though a block of concrete had lifted from their chest, breathing in the possibilities and imagining new horizons after more than three decades of dictatorship. On April 10, Jawad's uncle, Sayyed Abdulmajid al-Khoei, was killed by fellow Shias. But he was no traitor. How could freedom be so inexplicably deadly, so full of contradictions? How could his uncle have survived the treachery of Saddam, the pain of exile, only to return and be killed in a free Iraq?

From a distance, Jawad was reliving years of trauma. He was only twenty-three, but his dark brown eyes were those of an old man. Tall and heavyset, he wore his beard neatly trimmed and short. His father, Sayyed Mohammad Taqi al-Khoei, had sent him out of Iraq at the age of just thirteen, soon after the 1991 uprising of Kurds and Shias, to save him from Saddam's claws. Jawad wanted to stay. He cried for days before his departure and throughout the twelve-hour drive through the desert to Amman. He would never see his father again. In exile, Jawad became an orphan. In 1994, Sayyed Mohammad Taqi was on his way back from prayers in Karbala on a Friday evening when his car crashed into a truck that appeared out of nowhere. It was no accident. He and two others in the car survived the initial impact but were left bleeding by the side of the road. Government officers at a nearby roadblock forbade anyone to offer help.

At the time, Jawad was training as a seminarian in Qom, the next-best place after Najaf. Jawad loved the city; he felt safe there and was an eager student. But it was not home. He was always made to feel that he was an Arab, a stranger, a lesser Shia even. He resented the potent combination of Iranian nationalism and fierce Shia sectarianism—exclusionary and imperial. He studied with graduates of Najaf's hawza and Iraqi clerics in exile who taught religion in Arabic and in the Najaf tradition. There were many differences between the hawza in Najaf and the one in Qom, in their teachings and school of thought. The biggest divide had been Khomeini's doing.

Jawad's grandfather Grand Ayatollah Abulqasim al-Khoei had been one of the most popular and revered Shia spiritual leaders in recent times since his accession to the position of grand ayatollah in 1970, until he died under house arrest in Najaf in 1992. If Najaf was the Shia equivalent of the Vatican, then the grand ayatollah was something of a pope. Al-Khoei had a huge worldwide following as a marja'a taqlid, an object of emulation. A marja'a is a reference point for Shias everywhere, across borders and oceans, for all their questions about religion in daily life, but also about social and political issues. Whole families can follow the same marja'a, individuals can choose to follow someone different, but being a marja'a is a huge source of soft power and financial income, the kind that Khomeini had tried to divert by declaring himself Supreme Leader in a wilayat al-faqih, requiring fealty and emulation from Shias everywhere. Neither Khomeini nor Khamenei ever attained the level of popular following as a marja'a that Khoei had enjoyed. His student and successor Grand Ayatollah Ali Sistani inherited most of al-Khoei's following and his popularity.

Sistani had survived life under Saddam; in a free Iraq, he would have to weather Iran's efforts to swallow Najaf into the Supreme Leader's orbit. Although Sistani was Iranian, he was loyal to Najaf's centuries-long tradition of independence from politics.

When Khomeini first arrived in Najaf in 1964, al-Khoei had done his duty as a grand ayatollah and hosted him for a week. But beyond the initial hospitality, the Iranian political agitator had found a frosty welcome in Najaf. Al-Khoei and the senior clergy in Najaf did not believe that the original concept of wilayat al-faqih could extend beyond guardianship of widows and orphans. Crucially, al-Khoei believed that in the absence of the Mahdi, the wilayat could not be held by only one faqih, for no one was that wise—assuming so was a recipe for religious dictatorship. Like Imam Musa Sadr in Lebanon, he instantly recognized the dangers of Khomeini's politics. In the fall of 1978, as Iran was boiling and Khomeini was already in Paris, the empress of Iran had visited Najaf alongside Saddam hoping to enlist Khoei's support for her husband, the shah. Khoei had given her a ring inscribed with the words "God's power is superior to theirs." He thought the Iranians were crazy to try to get rid of the shah. Iraq's Shias had sometimes appealed to the Iranian monarch for help in appeasing Saddam's oppressive ardors, and they worried about life without this recourse. Khomeini never forgave al-Khoei, neither for that moment nor for his theological criticism that undermined the foundation of the Islamic state that Khomeini wanted to build in Iran and beyond. And he never forgave Najaf for having spurned him. Decades later, an American invasion was clearing the way for revenge.

In 1991, Sayyed Abdulmajid, son of the grand ayatollah and uncle of Jawad, fled Iraq with his family to London. There were two imperatives in those turbulent days: the thousand-year-old hawza needed to be preserved and protected, so some had to stay, including the aging grand ayatollah and his older sons. But the continuity of the al-Khoei name also had to be ensured, so other family members had to take shelter abroad. The youngest of the ayatollah's sons had disappeared during the uprising and its aftermath, most likely killed by the regime, along with some two hundred Shia clergymen. Mohammad Taqi, another son and Jawad's father, would die next. Saddam continued to eliminate Shia clergymen for years. In London, Abdulmajid, a smiling, shy cleric with deep green eyes, ran his father's charity foundation. He tried, with his interfaith outreach, to soften the image of Shiism in the West, after a decade that had been marked by the hostage taking in Tehran, the rise of Hezbollah, and plane hijackings.

He also had conversations with Western officials about returning one day to an Iraq free of Saddam.

During the 1991 uprising, instructed by his father, Abdulmajid had traveled south to meet the Americans entering Iraq from Kuwait to ask what help they would provide to the Iraqis after they had encouraged them to rise up against the dictator. But the meeting was called off at the last minute. The Americans retreated. Abdulmajid understood instantly the uprising was doomed. He couldn't return home and crossed into Saudi Arabia and then brought his family out. The Shias had been left to fend for themselves—and die by the thousands, bodies lying on the street, eaten by dogs. The Shias of Iraq felt betrayed. More than a decade later, Abdulmajid was convinced things would be different and that this president Bush, the son, would go all the way to Baghdad. He felt it was important for him to be there early on, for many reasons. He believed the 1991 uprising had failed because there was no coordination among different towns, groups, and rival clerics. With the gravitas of the Khoei name, he was hoping he could help coordinate efforts from Najaf for another uprising against Saddam in parallel with the US military campaign.

Abdulmajid also wanted to be there because he worried about the anger and resentment that had built up in the Shia community, not just against Saddam and the Baath Party but against the oppression that had become synonymous with Sunnis as a whole. He worried too that the Shias, betrayed by America before, might reject a US occupation outright and find themselves excluded from a post-Saddam government. He wanted everyone to talk to everyone; he wanted Shias to work with Sunnis and allow them to open religious schools even in Najaf. He wanted Sunnis to feel proud to vote freely for a president whether Sunni or Shia. Iraq's Sunnis had suffered under Saddam, too; his jails did not discriminate. But if Shias had come to see the state as nothing but a sectarian institution used by Saddam to oppress them, Sunnis still believed in the legitimacy of the state itself, regardless of their feelings about the dictator—and they felt the ground shake under their feet when the Americans invaded. A hairline fracture appeared in their inner being. Jarred by endless American missteps, the fracture would soon widen, splitting the country open, birthing new demons.

Whatever Washington's misguided reasons for going to war, Iran saw an opportunity to change the score in the Iran-Iraq conflict to its advantage. Abdulmajid was wary about Iran's ambitions in his country, specifically in Najaf. Saddam had worked hard to constrain the power of the

Najaf hawza, and in 1991 it had become mostly inaccessible to Shia students from outside the country. Meanwhile, Qom was rising as the center of religious learning for Shias. Abdulmajid and other Najaf clerics like him hoped that in a free Iraq, the holy city could reclaim its leading role as a center of learning and impose itself as a voice that counterbalanced the state-run Shiism of Qom. Beyond its designs on Najaf, Tehran was betting on networks of exiled Iraqis in Iran, Islamists who espoused Iran's politics, some of whom still saw themselves as the vanguard of a new phase of the Iranian Revolution. "But the Shia of Iraq are not happy with that role," Abdulmajid had said. "We are different from them even culturally, not to mention serious differences of religious doctrine." He believed strongly that clerics had no business running a country. The dangers would be many in the post-Saddam vacuum, but Abdulmajid told his family: "I must go because the risks of not going are even greater." On April 1, 2003, Abdulmajid flew with American troops to the southern town of Nassiriyah, near Basra.

There was one danger he had not foreseen or had certainly underestimated: internal Shia rivalries and the folly of those who thought they were more righteous than others.

By around April 4, he had arrived near his hometown, camping on the outskirts of Najaf in an abandoned factory with a group of American Special Forces, who accompanied him in and out of the city. People everywhere recognized him instantly, leaving their cars in the middle of the street to greet him, rushing in disbelief to touch his cloak. He wore a bulletproof vest under his clerical robe, because he was, after all, in the middle of a war, but he declared: "I have never felt so safe as I do here." When he finally made it to the Imam Ali shrine, he walked into the courtyard through one of its monumental doors and looked up to the large golden dome scintillating in the spring sun, a minaret on each side, built of thousands of gold-painted bricks. He was mobbed by well-wishers; as he walked into the inner sanctum, they followed him as he prayed and kissed the silver lattice enclosure of Imam Ali's tomb.

A crowd had gathered as Abdulmajid walked to the back of the courtyard, up some steps, into a large room bedecked and bejeweled on the inside: the al-Khoei family vault where his father, the great ayatollah, was buried, along with his brother Mohammad Taqi. He could finally pray for their souls in their presence. After thirteen years away, he couldn't get enough of the spiritual sanctity of this holiest of sites for Shias, a space imbued with so much pain, ancient and more recent, and yet so deeply moving in its quietude and breathtaking beauty that he returned to pray by Imam's Ali shrine a few days later, on April 10, just before nine in the morning.

He had gone into the shrine, leaving behind the Americans who had been protecting him on the streets. Soon after noon prayers, as he sat in the office of the keeper of the shrine, an angry crowd formed outside chanting: "Long live Sadr! Long live Sadr!" They were not calling out for the vanished Imam Sadr but for a distant Iraqi cousin of much inferior caliber. Moqtada al-Sadr was a young hothead thrust into a leadership position in 1999 at barely twenty-five, when his father, a popular ayatollah, was assassinated by Saddam. Ayatollah al-Sadr had been an activist cleric who gave fiery speeches and rallied huge crowds at Friday prayers in the slums of Baghdad. The regime allowed it because he railed against America and Israel, Saddam's favorite enemies. A nationalist, he also emphasized the Arab identity of Iraq's Shias, as opposed to Persian Shias. But when he became too popular, Saddam had him killed, along with his two eldest sons.

His youngest prankster son, nicknamed Ayatollah Atari because he loved playing videogames, suddenly inherited the mantle, and found himself the leader of tens of thousands of Shias. Moqtada's black turban had barely settled on his head. He had a mediocre rhetorical style and a limp handshake that belied the rage within him. But he had ambition and believed that he—not anyone else—deserved to lead the Shias of Iraq after the demise of Saddam. To achieve his goals, he would even betray his father's nationalism and accept Iranian training and weapons. Before the fall of Baghdad, Moqtada had already begun organizing a militia that would become the feared and ruthless Mahdi army. They would kill American soldiers but also anyone in Iraq who did not submit to Moqtada. Those were his men shouting outside the office where Sayyed Abdulmajid was sitting on that April morning.

A window was smashed. Shots were fired. Everyone had a gun—the mob outside but also the men inside. One of Abdulmajid's bodyguards was mortally wounded, shot right below his bulletproof vest, and bled to death. Abdulmajid took off his turban, held it to his chest, and pleaded for calm and mercy. The shooting went on for ninety minutes. A grenade was thrown into the room and Abdulmajid was wounded. Soon, the men inside were out of ammunition and surrendered. The mob tied their hands and pushed them outside. "We are taking you to Moqtada al-Sadr for him to pass sentence," one of the captors reportedly said. Outside, the prisoners were stabbed repeatedly, and one of them died. Abdulmajid was bleeding profusely. He was dragged to the outside of Moqtada's home near the shrine. A message came from inside, from Moqtada: "Don't let them sit in front of my door." He was dragged down a street and shot again. In the eyes of Moqtada, Abdulmajid was a rival with real credentials who would show up his own intellectual weakness and his meager theological achievements. But the young hothead who had never left Iraq also resented those who had lived in exile, branding them as agents of the West and traitors to the nation, even the Khoeis, who had sacrificed so much for their country and their faith.

In Qom, Jawad wept for his uncle, and relived the searing loss of his own father. One man killed by religious violence, the other killed by secular violence; one assassinated in the name of God, the other in the name of nationalism. Jawad had been planning to join his uncle in Iraq within days. Instead, he stayed in Qom, fearing for his country, free from one kind of horror only to sink into another. His mind wandered back to the events of 1991. He had been just a teenager but he remembered the thrill of hope, and the savagery that followed. Freedom had been so close; the uprising had almost succeeded.

In January 1991, the US-led war to dislodge Saddam from Kuwait began with a massive air campaign, and a few weeks later, on February 15, when it became clear that Saddam was a strawman in the face of American firepower, President George H. W Bush called on Iraqis to rise up against the dictator: "There is another way for the bloodshed to stop: and that is, for the Iraqi military and the Iraqi people to take matters into their own hands and force Saddam Hussein, the dictator, to step aside and then comply with the United Nations' resolutions and rejoin the family of peace-loving nations."

Within days, the Saudis invited exiled Iraqi politicians to Riyadh in the hope of assembling an Iraqi government-in-waiting. They were also talking to different groups of officers and former officers who were plotting to move against Saddam. But the Saudis were disorganized and sending mixed messages. Iraqi politicians described receiving one call from the Saudis and then never hearing from them again. The Saudi efforts amounted to nothing. The Iranians were also looking to seize the moment, and they had more success on the ground.

One of the Iraqis in exile in Iran was Ayatollah Mohammad Baqr al-Hakim, who had fled Iraq in 1980 when his friend Mohammad Baqr al-Sadr, the founder of the Islamist Da'wa Party, was executed by Saddam. In Iran, al-Hakim set up the Supreme Council for the Islamic Revolution in Iraq, a religious, political group with an armed wing: the Badr Brigades. Over time, the ranks of the Badr Brigades swelled to an estimated ten thousand Shias who defected from the Iraqi army ranks or were taken prisoner by Iran and pressed to join. From the start, the Badr Brigades operated under the supervision and control of Iran's Revolutionary Guards, conducting small cross-border and sabotage operations. There is footage of its founding commander Hadi al-Amiri on the front lines talking about their operations against the Iraqi army and Saddam, the "crazy enemy." When the 1991 uprising started, the Badr Brigades were on the move quickly, infiltrating Iraq from the south and connecting with underground cells in the country.

The popular rebellion started spontaneously in late February with small acts of defiance and sabotage. From the Shia south to the Kurdish north, an oppressed people seized on a moment of weakness in the dictatorship. On the highway out of Kuwait, littered with burned tanks, a demoralized, humiliated army was rebelling against a leader who had yet again sent them into a losing battle. On March 3, an Iraqi tank commander fired a shell through a huge portrait of Saddam in the main square of the southern city of Basra. Onlookers and nearby soldiers applauded. The wall of fear crumbled, and courage spread like wildfire. By March 5, Karbala had risen up; in Najaf, a protest near the Imam Ali shrine turned into a gun battle. Five days later, Saddam's regime seemed close to collapse: he had lost control of fifteen out of eighteen provinces. While the Shia leadership inside Iraq tried to organize the civilians and grand ayatollah al-Khoei called for a peaceful uprising, Ayatollah al-Hakim weighed in from Iran and appointed a representative in Basra to help establish an Islamic republic. Pictures of Khomeini appeared on the streets. As regime forces began to fight back, desperate men, women, and children sheltered in mosques. Makeshift surgery rooms were set up inside the Imam Ali shrine. The dead piled up. Cornered and fearful, the crowds chanted "Iran help us" and "There is no ruler other than Ali, we want a leader who is a Ja'afari (Shia)."

Just as the uprising was starting, the Americans were discussing conditions for a cease-fire with the Iraqis. In a bizarre episode, the US commander of the military campaign, Norman Schwarzkopf, agreed to allow the Iraqis the use of helicopters to ferry military officials across the country, away from the front line, since the country's infrastructure had been so heavily damaged. His Iraqi counterpart asked specifically whether helicopter gunships would be allowed to fly, since they would be used as transport helicopters. Schwarzkopf acquiesced, as long the helicopters did not fly over areas where American troops were located. "In the following weeks," the general wrote in his memoirs, "we discovered what the son of a bitch really had in mind: using helicopter gunships to suppress the rebellion in Basra and other cities." It's hard to believe that the general did not anticipate this. Perhaps he did, but was unconcerned as long his troops were safe. But few Iraqis were aware that they were also victims of a treacherous moment of diplomacy: while Saddam's troops shot fleeing refugees from the air and rounded up people in mass executions, the Saudi and Iranian foreign ministers were in Oman talking reconciliation. On March 22, the Saudis and the Iranians announced that they would resume diplomatic ties, broken off in 1987. Ayatollah al-Hakim's Badr Brigades packed up and went back to Iran. America and Saudi Arabia had come to fear the breakup of Iraq in a chaotic civil war or—worse—the rise of a Shia theocracy loyal to Tehran. But the Islamic Republic of Iran, defenders of Shias everywhere, had abandoned Iraq's Shias for the sake of realpolitik. On March 24, the *Al-Hayat* newspaper's front-page headline screamed AMERICA DECIDES NOT TO CONFRONT IRAQ HELICOPTERS.

The carnage in 1991 was unprecedented. Saddam's rule had not been specifically sectarian before. Shias had been a target when they overtly opposed him. Now, he went after them with determination. The shrines in Karbala and Najaf were shelled in an act of arrogant, vengeful spite. Thousands disappeared. Two million people were on the move, in the south and the Kurdish north. Young Jawad saw his father and grandfather dragged out of the house and taken for a humiliating televised audience with Saddam in Baghdad, a forced show of reconciliation. The Khoeis were under surveillance around the clock. Security guards stood outside the house, trailing them everywhere, even riding with them in the car. Fear permeated everything: people's days, their dreams, the air they breathed. Sayyed Abdulmajid was on his way to London. Jawad was sent away. Soon his father would die, without a goodbye. Shia commemorations like Ashura were banned. Years went by and thousands more died, disappeared in the darkness of Saddam's dungeons or swallowed in the misery of a country now under embargo and cut off from the rest of the world, a people punished for the madness of their leader.

—

In mid-March 2003, just days after the start of the US "shock and awe" bombing campaign that preceded the ground invasion, Saddam's regime still found the time to arrest dozens of pilgrims as they tried to reach Karbala for Ashura. Then, suddenly, Saddam's statues were being toppled and the dictator was on the run. By the end of April, hundreds of thousands of Shias were marching to Karbala from across Iraq to mark the Arba'een, the fortieth day of mourning for the martyrdom of Imam Hussein. They were celebrating the end of their own martyrdom. In Iraq, the land of Imam Hussein's sacrifice, the rituals had always been more passionate than elsewhere in the Muslim world. Men, women, and children walked for days, and some crawled on their hands and knees to reach the shrine. They waved green or black flags, beat their chests slowly, rhythmically, flinging their right hand up and down—*thump*. Up and down—*thump*. Some whipped their backs with chains. The hypnotic ritual was simultaneously a renewed communion with faith and a Shia show of force in the new Iraq. Year after year, the pilgrimage to Karbala would attract more and more people, millions after millions, the human mass swelling to five times the size of that performing the yearly hajj to Mecca. Najaf and Karbala were now open to the world, at least to all those who dared make the journey into a country that was still occupied and slipping into violence. The first to come were Iraqis-in-exile and Iranians. The Iranians traveled with an assigned guide on each bus, driving across the border. The men were old enough to remember the Iran-Iraq War just fifteen years ago and the chant that had accompanied them on the buses to the front line.

We'll give our lives to conquer Karbala.

Rise up brave warriors, take your homeland from the enemy.

The road to victory passes through Karbala.

Now, some Iraqi exiles returned to Karbala and their homeland not just to pray but to finish what they had hoped to achieve in the 1980s along with the Iranians. Ayatollah al-Hakim, leader of Supreme Council for the Islamic Revolution, was back in Najaf. So were his colleagues in fatigues Hadi al-Amiri and his Badr militants. Al-Hakim seemed to have moderated his views: he had acquiesced to cooperation with the Americans and counseled patience with the occupation. After all, his triumphant return would not have been possible without the Americans. He called for unity.

—

Just after he led midday prayers on Friday, August 29, 2003, Ayatollah al-Hakim walked out of the Imam Ali shrine in Najaf and onto the street through the courtyard's southern portico. In his black cloak and black turban, he walked to his car. Suddenly, day turned into night. People went momentarily deaf. The sky rained blood, sandals, dried fruits, body parts, candy, and brick debris.

"The Sayyed is dead. They killed the Sayyed," one man screamed.

The car bomb had been so powerful and so close to al-Hakim that people said his body had been totally vaporized. There was a three-foot crater in the ground. The mosque was damaged. A two-story mall nearby was leveled. Ninety-five people were killed, almost five hundred injured. The closest hospital was a scene of utter chaos as relatives crammed the lobby and the hallways. A group of young men in pressed shirts, carrying shiny new AK-47 rifles and walkie-talkies, showed up and began to bring order to the crush of people. Their leader stood out: in his fifties, wearing gray trousers and a white button-down shirt. He asked the nurses if they needed supplies, he comforted doctors who broke down. He acted like an Iraqi government official but he wasn't. He spoke Arabic, but with a very distinct accent: he was Iranian, and his men, young Iraqis in pressed shirts, were Badr militants. Some of their colleagues were among the wounded, probably bodyguards of al-Hakim. The Iranian was their commander, most likely a member of the Iranian Revolutionary Guards. He was consoling an Iraqi doctor, who was repeatedly asking why anyone would do this.

"Don't you see?" the Iranian responded. "They have declared war on us."

He seemed to sense or know that this killing was the work not of Moqtada or other fellow Shias but of Sunnis. Not a Sunni state exercising oppression through extra-judicial executions, no—this was the work of Sunni militants, sectarian killers, Shia haters . . . This was war. It was also the first time in the Arab world that Sunni fighters had specifically set out to kill Shias since the 1801 Wahhabi raid against Karbala. In Pakistan, sectarian killings had begun under Zia with the massacre in 1987 on the border with Afghanistan, when the Pakistani dictator had let Sunni militants loose on Shia villages. From Peshawar all the way to Iraq, hate and sectarian violence had mutated into ever more violent iterations, inhabiting men who each wanted to outdo their mentors.

The attack that had killed Ayatollah al-Hakim was the work of Abu Musab al-Zarqawi, a protégé of Abu Muhammad al-Maqdissi, the Jordanian ideologue who had spent time in Peshawar and written the anti-Saudi pamphlets that inspired the first bombings in Saudi Arabia in the 1990s. Abu Musab

al-Zarqawi was the nom de guerre of Ahmad Fadeel al-Khalayleh, a Jordanian high school dropout, bootlegger, and bully from the Jordanian town
of Zarqa who had found his raison d'être on the battlefield of Afghanistan
at the tail end of the war against the Soviets. Thrown in jail in Jordan 1992,
he had met Maqdissi and matured under his mentorship into a leader and
recruiter. Out of jail, he had gone back to Afghanistan in 1999, where he
set up his own camp of fighters thanks to start-up money from al-Qaeda.
The rebellious Zarqawi had first refused to pledge allegiance to Bin Laden,
but al-Qaeda saw him as a potentially useful conduit into certain countries.
After 9/11 and the US bombing campaign to bring down the Taliban in
Afghanistan, Zarqawi fled through Iran to northeast Iraq where he arrived
in the summer of 2002 and set up a camp for his group, Ansar al-Islam,
Supporters of Islam. Outside a small circle of jihadists, no one had heard
of Zarqawi. On February 5, 2003, he was catapulted to world fame.

The US secretary of state, Colin Powell, was speaking at the UN to
make the case for removing Saddam. The US administration was using
all the excuses and all the tools it could to justify the march to war—Iraq's
alleged weapons of mass destruction, the need for democracy in the Middle East, and now Saddam's alleged ties with al-Qaeda. "Iraq today harbors
a deadly terrorist network headed by Abu Musab al-Zarqawi, an associate
and collaborator of Osama bin Laden and his al-Qaeda lieutenants," said
Powell. Zarqawi's bearded face appeared on a large screen. Powell alleged
that al-Qaeda and Saddam were cooperating through Zarqawi. In one
speech, Powell mentioned Zarqawi's name twenty-one times. Although it
was not beyond an avowed secular dictator like Saddam to use religion or
cooperate with Islamists if it helped his agenda, there were no formal links
between al-Qaeda and the Iraqi regime. Zarqawi was there not to assist
Saddam but to further his own jihadist ambitions. And the Americans had
just removed all the obstacles on the way to Baghdad for him.

As the US-led military campaign got under way, young men lined up
in front of the Iraqi embassy in Damascus, just a few blocks from the US
embassy. They came from Algeria, Jordan, or Saudi Arabia for a chance to
participate in what they hoped would be a repeat of the Afghan jihad or
Chechnya, except this time it would be war against the greatest infidels—
the Americans. Syrians joined too. At the Iraqi embassy, they were all
issued fake Iraqi passports to facilitate border crossings. They boarded
buses and crossed into Iraq, ready to fight and die. Syrian officials, including the grand mufti, were openly encouraging this jihad, hoping the Americans would sink into a quagmire that would keep them too busy to plan

the toppling of other dictatorships. Iraq was fertile ground for a Sunni insurgency, more so than even Zarqawi had ever anticipated.

—

Under embargo throughout the 1990s, Iraq had been mostly shut off from the world and turned inward. The land of biblical Eden and cradle of civilization that had given the world one of its seven wonders, the Hanging Gardens of Bablyon; the Arab country with the first woman cabinet minister in 1959 and where women were given equal rights in the constitution of 1970; the birthplace of the renowned architect Dame Zaha Hadid; the nation where artists at the Fine Arts academy painted nudes and masterpieces—that Iraq was no more. Food shortages, decaying infrastructure, growing infant mortality, thousands leaving for exile—the 1990s had hollowed out the country. Despair drives people to faith, and in Iraq they were flocking to the mosques as more and more women were putting on the veil.

Saddam both encouraged and controlled the trends. A cigar smoker whose favorite drink was said to be Mateus rosé wine, he tried various tactics to brandish his credentials as a devout Muslim. During the 1980s, to fend off Iran's accusations that he was an infidel, he had hosted the Popular Islamic Conference (PICO) with Saudi help. During and after the 1991 Gulf War, Saddam tried to rebrand himself as a believer president fighting the infidel West. But Saddam was worried: he had begun to recognize and fear the growing influence of Salafists, some of whom had direct links to Saudi Arabia, his new enemy. Iraqi intelligence had documented attempts by Saudi clerics to smuggle Wahhabi religious propaganda into Iraq. In 1993, in an attempt to mollify the masses but also to counter the spread of Wahhabism in Iraq, he launched his very own Faith Campaign to promote state-sanctioned Islam.

Religious education was made compulsory in schools, alcohol was banned, Qurans were mass printed, more mosques were built. As the mosques got busier, intelligence officers were sent to keep tabs on clerics and their followers. Scores of them were dominated by Salafist clerics, a strand that had been growing under Saddam's nose since 1979.

That year, Saddam had briefly jailed members of the Muwahidoun group, the absolute monotheist Salafists modeled after Wahhabism. Some of the key members were army officers. Removed from their positions, they were held in Abu Ghraib jail, where they met like-minded Islamists. Released in the mid-1980s, they continued to proselytize and recruit in mosques across the country. The men who referred to Saudi Arabia's

Sheikh Bin Baz as the "father sheikh" and professed admiration for Juhay-man al-Otaiabi went on pilgrimage to Mecca and brought Wahhabi liter-ature back with them. After 1993, they used the Faith Campaign to their advantage. By keeping their most radical thoughts private, they posed as servants to the state, ready to help spread Saddam's gospel. Over time, many army officers and Baath officials, broken by years of war, ended up embracing a more puritanical piety. Hanging out in the mosques they were supposed to report on, they absorbed Salafism by osmosis.

While some of Iraq's Muwahidoun and other Salafists were focused solely on proselytizing, others had more jihadist tendencies. Underground cells formed, where militant literature was passed around, including the writings of al-Maqdissi. Around 1999, fearing the Islamization trend was getting out of control, Saddam executed dozens of people and jailed hun-dreds more. From far-flung villages or cities, store clerks, police, and army officers met in prison and expanded the network of Salafists. In October 2002, as the drums of war were beating, Saddam emptied his jails. This was a trick in the well-worn dictator playbook: preemptive sabotage. If he couldn't stay in power, he would make sure no one else could rule by planting the seeds of chaos. The Salafist jihadists were now on the loose. When Zarqawi had arrived in Iraq, he expected to find a country of secular heathens, or at least a place where he would need to expend much effort on spreading the message of Salafism before he could recruit active fighters. Instead, he found a country with an extensive Salafist network connected to people in high places in the Iraqi state. Saddam's Faith Campaign was the cauldron in which Salafism and nationalism had melded, a curious development and indirect result of the Saudi-Iran rivalry that would con-tribute in the years to come to the creation of the Islamic State in Iraq and Syria.

In the chaos following the fall of the regime in 2003, hardened Salafists found common ground with disgruntled soldiers and officers who were out of a job after the American administrator of Iraq disbanded the four-hundred-thousand-strong Iraqi army. They were then joined by the Arab fighters traveling by bus to Iraq. The Sunni insurgency against US troops was under way. It consumed policymaking in Washington for years and destroyed Iraq's chances to recover from dictatorship in the short term. More than half a million Iraqis died. More than four thousand American soldiers were killed, almost forty thousand wounded. There were splinter groups and competitions, street battles and car bombs. There were those who simply wanted to resist the occupation and those who saw an opportunity to establish an Islamic state—a Sunni Islamic state, one that would undo the deep wound of seeing Shias and Iran become powerful in post-Saddam Iraq. The headlines about the surge of Shia power dominated the news. The ranks of the Sunni insurgency swelled. Dozens of young Saudi men joined the fight, the latest generation in the "caravan of martyrs" that had started in Peshawar with Abdallah Azzam and Bin Laden.

In the first few years following the invasion, Saudis made up almost half the foreign fighters in the insurgency and Saudi jihadists carried out more suicide bombings than any other nationality. Though it was a small number per capita for Saudi Arabia, compared to other nationalities, Washington was frustrated, complaining to Riyadh that this was undermining efforts to rebuild Iraq. The United States accused the Saudis of failing to stem the flow of fighters coming from the kingdom and of financing militant Sunni groups. The Saudis flatly denied that their citizens were heading to Iraq.

Unofficially, the Saudis were not displeased, and as always, they had plausible deniability; the state was not organizing anything. But individual Saudis were donating money to the cause, just as they had during the Afghan war, and fiery preachers in the kingdom were not silenced even while they exhorted their brothers to fight the infidels in Iraq. Across the kingdom, people were excitedly retelling stories they'd heard from the front line. The Internet was abuzz with memorials for the valiant martyrs. For a while, the kingdom looked away: it was rather convenient that young hotheads were going to die in Iraq at this point in time. The start of the insurgency in Iraq coincided with the first wave of bombings against civilian housing compounds that rocked Riyadh in 2003 and 2004. Iraq was a welcome release valve.

The Saudis had warned the Americans not to invade, telling them it served no one's interests and would cause a resurgence of fundamentalism that would reach the United States and Europe. They warned about the destruction of Iraq, but what they really worried about was a Shia-ruled Iraq where Iran called the shots. A Sunni insurgency was the deadly antidote.

—

On February 22, 2006, five minutes before seven in the morning, a huge explosion rocked Samarra. The city was home to two famous mosques that are more than ten centuries old: one with an unusual cone-shaped minaret with an outer ramp spiraling up its 170 feet, and another with a golden dome. Just over an hour away from Baghdad, on the eastern bank of the river Tigris, Samarra was layered with millennia of history, the history of all humankind, dating back to ancient Mesopotamia. Samarra had once served as a lavish capital for a brief period during the Abbassid caliphate before the caliphs moved to Baghdad in 892. But Samarra's urban planning and architecture had survived the passage of time—a rare example of an ancient Islamic capital still intact in modern times. There were also layers of sectarian coexistence that went back centuries.

The spiral Malwiya minaret belonged to the city's Great Mosque, built by the Abbasid caliph. A Sunni mosque in a dominantly Sunni city, its minaret was still standing that morning. But inside the Al-Askari mosque, with its golden dome, dust and rubble was everywhere, the steel beams were exposed and the blue sky visible through the gaping holes blown through the onion-shaped structure. There lay the remains of the tenth and eleventh Shia imams, and it was where the last imam, the Mahdi, was said to have gone into occultation. The mystical legacy of the shrine had lived on for more than a thousand years, making it one of the most revered sites for Shias. But Al-Askari was part of the collective experience of the city: Sunni clerics had looked after it for centuries, and the Sunnis of Samarra swore by it, just as Shias did. Sunni families highlighted their lineage back to the Shia imams—sectarian belonging could change over time, but the proud heritage remained as identities overlapped.

One such family was the middle-class Badri family. The pious father taught Quranic recitation. Some of the uncles were Baathist officers. One son, Ibrahim Awwad Ibrahim al-Badri, led neighborhood children in chanting the Quran. In 1996, al-Badri enrolled in Saddam's Islamic University and obtained a master's degree. He loved soccer but became increasingly intolerant, virulent in his puritanism. After the invasion he was jailed by the Americans but kept his jihadist views quiet and was soon released. In jail, he had met more jihadists and disgruntled army officers. Outside, he connected with al-Qaeda in Iraq, which sent him on a mission to Syria. In Damascus, he also finished his PhD dissertation in Islamic studies. All of this would serve him well in a few years, when he would inherit Zarqawi's mantle, taking over the mission of establishing an Islamic state in Iraq and adopting the nom de guerre Abu Bakr al-Baghdadi.

The magic and the mythical tragedies of Badri's hometown of Samarra have endured millennia and traveled beyond the region, from the scribes of Solomon in the Babylonian Talmud to John O'Hara's *Appointment in Samarra*—ranked as one of the best modern English-language novels— and the tale of the merchant's servant in W. Somerset Maugham's 1933 play

Sheppey. The tale is the same: trying to slip through the fingers of Death, people travel to Samarra, only to find that the appointment is inescapable and Death has followed them to the city.

On that morning of February 22, 2006, a young Iraqi woman set off from Baghdad to Samarra. Atwar Bahjat was fearless but not reckless. She was always pushing boundaries, gently but resolutely, until she became one of three women in a newsroom of more than a hundred men at the Al-Jazeera bureau in Baghdad and then at another channel, Al-Arabiyya. The thirty-year-old woman with a sweet smile loved fashionable, colorful veils, which she often wore with a big knot to the side, like the flowers of a flamenco dancer. She was a poet at heart, a graduate of Arabic literature studies from the University of Baghdad. She had begun by writing in Iraqi newspapers under Saddam and then moved on to state television. With the US invasion came media freedom. International newspapers and television channels were not able to operate freely in Iraq without government minders, so all sorts of Iraqi newspapers and television stations sprang up. Wedding photographers became war photographers; English literature students became translators for foreign correspondents; poets became recognized faces on Al-Jazeera television. Atwar had first been assigned cultural stories, biding her time, building her contacts, and pleading with her editors until she was sent out on the big stories. She peppered her sentences with the customary terms of endearment that Iraqis—as well as others in the region, like Lebanese or Syrians—use equally with men and women, old and young. "Yes, my dear," "What do you need, my heart," "Of course, my eyes." Born in 1976, fed a steady diet of Baathist propaganda in school, struggling through the embargo of the 1990s, she was now eager to do her bit for her country by telling Iraq's story to Arabs across the region watching her on television. She was also a living symbol of the Sunni-Shia coexistence that comes naturally outside the arenas of politics and war. Her father was a Sunni from Samarra, her mother a Shia from Karbala.

When news came that a bomb had gone off in Samarra, she pleaded with her editors. She had to go. This was her hometown. It was dangerous, but she could handle it. Off she went with her two-man team. The city itself was too tense to enter, so they reported from the outskirts. She phoned in to the news desk a few times. Her television report, recorded and transmitted to the main station, aired at six that evening. It ended with the words: "Whether you are Sunni or Shia, Arab or Kurd, there is no difference between Iraqis, united in fear for this nation. Atwar Bahjat, from the outskirts of Samarra, al-Arabiyya."

Within half an hour, gunmen came looking for her in a pickup truck, firing shots in the air to disperse the crowd that had gathered to watch the television star in action. "We want the correspondent," they shouted. Atwar and her team were snatched and taken away. Their bullet-riddled bodies were found the next day. There were conflicting reports about who had killed her: Shia gunmen or Sunni? Was it al-Qaeda because she was reporting about the bombing of a Shia shrine? Or the Mahdi army because her father was Sunni? If there was one thing the killers on the loose across Iraq could agree on, it was that people like Atwar did not belong in Iraq, and neither did the ideals of coexistence that she embodied.

Iraq's educated middle class, its intellectuals, artists, progressive thinkers, empowered women, veiled and unveiled, would all become the victims of a systematic purge. Zarqawi and his ilk mostly blew people up indiscriminately, hoping to cause maximum death and destruction. Moqtada would send death squads, hunting people down at universities, medical clinics, and in their homes.

Atwar's death on February 22, 2006, was overshadowed in the news by the fury that the bombing of the Al-Askari shrine had set off. From Kirkuk in the north to Basra in the south, from Najaf to Karbala and Baghdad, Shia militiamen and mobs went on a rampage. By the end of the day, twenty-seven Sunni mosques had been shot up, set on fire, or destroyed with rocket-propelled grenades or machine-gun fire in the capital alone—sixty in total across the country. Three Sunni clerics had been shot dead, a fourth had been kidnapped. In Basra, a dominantly Shia city, the police took ten foreign Arab fighters jailed in connection with the Sunni insurgency out of their cells and shot them dead in apparent retaliation.

Iraq had simmered with rage and violence since the US invasion: there was the Sunni insurgency and there was the Mahdi army. The two were mostly focused on fighting the Americans. Sometimes, they killed each other. The assassination of Ayatollah al-Hakim was intended to provoke sectarian strife but had not yet unleashed hell. With the bombing of the Al-Askari shrine in 2006, it was all-out civil war. Years of savagery ensued as people redefined their identities around sect and Sunni-Shia hatred began to take hold beyond Iraq's borders. And there were bigger shifts happening in how Sunnis and Shias perceived their place in the Arab and Muslim world. Iran was taking revenge for the suffering and humiliation it had endured during the war with Saddam. This, in turn, would lead to counter-revenge by Sunnis.

14

FRACTURE

From the time of Adam to this day
humans have been created equal like the teeth of a comb,
with no advantage for the Arab over the Persian,
the red-skinned over the black, except in their piety.
—Hadith of the prophet Muhammad

The era of revenge had begun in 2005 with an assassination. Then an air strike. Finally, a hanging. Each act of violence killed a man of influence, with far-reaching consequences. All three were Arab, Sunni, and self-made. Yet their worlds and ideals were so utterly different that, in reality, the three men had nothing in common. One was a loser turned terrorist bent on wholesale destruction; the second was a revolutionary who became a megalomaniacal dictator and hollowed out the soul of his nation; the third, the son of a vegetable vendor, made billions in Saudi Arabia, then rebuilt his country and became known as Mr. Lebanon. Sunni strongmen each in his own way, Abu Musab al-Zarqawi, Saddam Hussein, and Rafiq Hariri lived very different lives with very different purposes. Their deaths, all occurring within two years (at the hands of very different killers), produced an imperceptible fracture in the collective psyche of the Sunni world—a long, drawn-out moment when realities flipped and historical identities were switched, when the strong began to feel like victims and the oppressed began to subjugate.

Since 2003, Iran had been working hard to reap the benefits of the American invasion of Iraq. Saddam, its nemesis, was gone, and so were the Taliban, the enemy to their east in Afghanistan. Iran was unleashed.

The country was acting imperial. Tehran's allies and proxies were feeding off the chaos and consolidating their gains on the ground, from Iraq to Lebanon. The elimination of the three men during this particular span of time fed Sunni insecurity, the kind that pushes people to embrace, or silently approve, the most vicious form of violence in revenge for the loss of power, a ghastly balm for the humiliation of defeat, perceived or real.

First came the assassination, a declaration of war on Valentine's Day in 2005, just outside Beirut's famed Saint George Hotel. Once a den of beauty queens and spies with an outdoor swimming pool overlooking the glistening Mediterranean Sea, it was now a pockmarked empty shell, one of the jewels that had not yet been rebuilt since Lebanon's civil war ended in 1990 with the Pax Syriana.

When Syrian troops took full control of Lebanon that year (with US acquiescence), in exchange for Syria's participation in Operation Desert Storm, Hafez al-Assad was building on the 1989 Taef Agreement, the power sharing arrangement between the different Lebanese sects that the Saudis had helped broker. The Syrians would keep the peace with forty thousand troops—a Syrian soldier for every hundred Lebanese. All militias had to disarm, but an unwritten exception was made for those fighting against the continued Israeli armed presence in southern Lebanon, seen as a legitimate resistance against the occupation. Hezbollah, still a young organization, was quick to take over that loophole, rebranding fully as a resistance movement. By then, it had also eliminated or outgunned everyone else. It was also holding Western hostages, and the outside world could not risk endangering their lives by putting pressure on the group to disarm. Hussein al-Husseini, the Shia politician and friend of Imam Sadr, had been elected speaker of parliament in 1984. He had helped father the Taef Agreement. His goal was to end the bloodshed—more than 150,000 Lebanese and non-Lebanese had already died. He still believed that with the end of the civil war, the anomaly that was Hezbollah in Lebanon and within the Shia community would disappear. But he too had, unwittingly, helped ensure their survival.

Hezbollah had become a useful tool for Assad. The wily Lion of Damascus posed as the good guy, helping with the release of the Western hostages thanks to his relationship with Iran. He made Washington happy by agreeing to negotiate peace with Israel, but then used Hezbollah to poke the Israelis on the border between Lebanon and Israel, giving him leverage in the negotiations. He made sure Iran understood that while Hezbollah could operate in Lebanon, *he* was the boss of the country. Assad used that alliance with Iran to keep Saudi Arabia and the Gulf countries on their toes: eager to defuse his potential mischief, they provided him with huge subsidies. For years, Assad walked the fine line of being close to Iran but not opposed to Saudi Arabia, a strange modus vivendi that filled his pockets and helped Hezbollah entrench itself in Lebanon, building its arsenal and its "resistance society"—a modus vivendi that flourished during the Saudi-Iran détente of the 1990s and was maintained by Assad's son and successor, Bashar al-Assad, until it exploded on February 14, 2005, at exactly 12:55 p.m., as a six-car motorcade drove past the Saint George Hotel.

Black smoke billowed in the blue sky over Beirut, windows were shattered miles away, bodies were incinerated in a fireball in the ten-meter-wide crater blown into the asphalt just outside the Saint George. Four thousand pounds of explosives had targeted the man who embodied the Saudi-Syria-Iran triangle: Rafiq Hariri, whose body had been incinerated in the fire. Lebanon was changed forever. Few assassinations have provoked such a dramatic shift in the trajectory of events across an entire region. But that day, the Middle East shifted on its axis. The détente was over. Iran had declared war on Saudi Arabia. The dead man was like a son to King Fahd and Crown Prince Abdallah. His killers, an international investigation would find, were Hezbollah operatives. The assassination had been sanctioned by Damascus, and probably Iran.

A big, portly man with a full head of salt-and-pepper hair and a thick mustache, Hariri had made a fortune in the desert kingdom turning the fantasies of the royals into reality almost overnight by building lavish palaces, conference centers, and the printing presses that churned out thousands of Qurans in Mecca. His fortune provided him with a rolodex whose contacts spanned the globe. He was a personal friend of presidents and prime ministers everywhere. With Syria's blessing, Hariri had become Lebanon's prime minister for the first time in 1992, the same year that Hezbollah decided to go into politics, fielding candidates in the legislative elections. That same year Hassan Nasrallah, one the young Shias who had studied in Najaf in the 1970s, became Hezbollah's secretary-general. Iranian and Saudi allies, side by side in the hallways of parliament, with Syria as the kingmaker—everything seemed possible in the 1990s. The ambitious Sunni construction magnate helped rebuild Lebanon and downtown Beirut with glitz and pizzazz—but with little consideration for those who had long felt excluded and had tried during the war to smash their way into Hamra Street and Beirut's clubbing district.

Shias still felt left out, consistently on the outside looking in, even though the community was more powerful and wealthier than ever. Their insecurity was fed continuously by Hezbollah, which reminded them constantly that without the guns of the Party of God, the Shias of Lebanon would again be downtrodden. Hezbollah had sunk its claws into the community by providing all the services that Lebanon's weak state did not: hospitals, schools, after-school activities, subsidies for widows of militants killed fighting Israel. But those who tried to turn their backs on the party were harassed, beaten, eliminated ruthlessly. Others, like the former Khomeini enthusiast Sayyed Hani Fahs, were branded as traitors.

The shift that brought an end to Hariri's life was set in motion by the death of Hafez al-Assad in the summer of 2000, keeper of the modus vivendi. His son, Bashar al-Assad, inherited the presidency but none of his father's gravitas. Tall, lanky with a receding chin, Bashar was in search of ways to assert himself, and he was in awe of Hezbollah and its leader Nasrallah, who had succeeded where even Assad's father had failed. Hezbollah, with the generous help of Iran, had achieved a victory that every Arab army had dreamed of since Israel was established in 1948: it had liberated Arab land.

In May 2000, exhausted by the relentless guerrilla warfare of Hezbollah, the Israelis had withdrawn from southern Lebanon, putting an end to more than two decades of occupation. They took their checkpoints, prisons, and torture cells with them, along with several hundred of their allies from the local proxy militia that helped enforce the occupation. Hezbollah was celebrated in Lebanon by Christians and Muslims alike; the party was feted across the region. Just as another round of peace talks between Israelis and Palestinians faltered, Nasrallah said he offered "this lofty victory to our oppressed people in occupied Palestine . . . The road to Palestine is through resistance and uprising, serious resistance and real uprising . . . like in Lebanon. To the Arab and Islamic nation, [I say] shame, defeat, and humiliation are a thing of the past."

Nasrallah paid tribute and thanks to Khomeini, to Khamenei, and to Syria. Not a word about any Lebanese leaders. There was one man he didn't mention but who also saw the Israeli withdrawal as his victory: Qassem Suleimani, head of the al-Quds force, the IRGC arm in charge of exporting and upholding the revolution. He was known as the "living martyr" for all the frontline battles he had survived in the war with Iraq. He was working ever more closely with Hezbollah operatives and Nasrallah. They had grand plans. Looking across the border into Israel, even Jerusalem seemed within reach. Once an eighteen-year-old student in awe of Khomeini in Najaf, Nasrallah was now delivering a victory for the Supreme Leader and the wilayat. Nasrallah had also become an Arab hero, polling as the most popular leader in the Middle East, and an alternative to the Arab rulers who kowtowed to America. In 2000, a Shia leader could still be adulated by Sunni crowds, but not for much longer.

Shia leaders like Hussein al-Husseini or Sayyed Fahs were hoping that Hezbollah would now retire its fighters and loosen its grip on the Shia community—after all, its job was done. But Hezbollah did not lay down its weapons. In October, barely five months after the Israeli withdrawal, Hezbollah kidnapped three Israeli soldiers along the border and detained an Israeli businessman in a sting operation. The soldiers had died during the abduction, but their bodies and the businessman were later traded for four hundred Palestinian and thirty Lebanese prisoners who had been held in Israeli jails for years. The Arab world was jubilant: Hezbollah had done it again—Israel was being made to kneel. And yet somewhere in the back of the minds of many remained a recurrent, nagging question: Why are the Shias scoring such victories? Why aren't the Sunnis? Hariri had just become prime minister again, after a couple of years out of power. He was frustrated by Hezbollah actions—this was not the image of Lebanon he wanted to project on the globe—but his hands were tied.

—

Hezbollah was only gaining in stature, and after the Israeli withdrawal, it now controlled even more territory in southern Lebanon: miles of craggy hills overlooking northern Israel, villages and towns that its men in black could patrol on their motorbikes, more walls on which it could plaster pictures of its martyrs, rooftops on which it could fly its flags and the black banners of mourning for Imam Hussein. Beards, once regarded suspiciously under Israeli occupation, now grew long, and women in chadors arrived from Beirut to visit their long-lost relatives in liberated villages. Hezbollah were the liberators, embraced by most Shias but regarded more warily by Christians and Sunnis living along the border. Having matured since its early years, Hezbollah worked to win over its new subjects with more subtlety. There were no reprisals, no assassinations, and no smashing of liquor bottles—not yet.

The Lebanese state, unable to impose itself where Hezbollah held sway, was mostly absent from a region in dire need of help after years of occupation. Hezbollah had millions it could spend every month, courtesy of Iran and rich Shia supporters from the diaspora. Imam Khomeini schools and Mahdi scout groups sprung up; more husseiniyyas were built. Ashura commemorations became bigger, bolder, and longer. In an effort to maintain constant mobilization of its followers, Hezbollah emulated

Iran's growing number of religious commemorations. Ashura extended over more days. One bled into another and soon Ashura and the fortieth commemoration, the Arba'een, felt like one long period of wailing and chest thumping. Shias who did not adhere to Hezbollah felt even more alienated and began to describe the transformation of their community as the Iranization of Shiism. All of the south of Lebanon began to feel like Hezbollah's fortress, with pictures of Khomeini and Khamenei hanging on walls just miles from the Israeli border. Hezbollah's reconstruction arm, called Jihad for Construction, rebuilt hospitals and stocked dispensaries, paved roads and repaired electricity pylons. Children in particular were preyed on—through them, Hezbollah's beliefs, slogans, and imagery could invade the homes of families, regardless of their political affiliation. Hezbollah set up summer camps and kids returned with stickers and caps bearing Hezbollah logos. The children thought it was cool. Parents who were not religious or political were wary but relieved there was something to do for their kids during the summer period. Over time, tensions arose within families, with teenagers who wanted to join the ranks of combatants or don the chador. The sale of liquor was banned, with some shops acquiescing in fear, as others resisted. Backgammon and card games were frowned upon. Cafés closed. There was nothing cultural on offer—except Hezbollah programming of all mediums. It created a milieu that was as all-enveloping as it was inescapable—not even Badia Fahs had managed to resist it, perhaps because when she had just returned to Lebanon from Iran in 1986, it was still unclear what Hezbollah would become, beyond a militant group fighting Israeli occupation.

Despite the history of her father's disillusionment with the Islamic Republic and Badia's own shock at seeing women wearing the chador in her village of Jebsheet when they returned from Iran in the mid-1980s, she, too, had donned the black cloak. She had fallen in love with a Hezbollah combatant, and there were expectations of the wife of a Hezbollah fighter, so she fell in line. The marriage wouldn't last. There are so many reasons why a marriage falls apart; with Badia there was the added complication of a father who was becoming an active critic of the party her husband belonged to. As a Hezbollah wife, she was an insider, yet she never adhered completely. She knew of their ways, and her brain rebelled against them. As a divorcée, she was victimized twice: by the community that wanted to punish her for her father's positions and by the religious courts that ruled over personal matters in Lebanon and discriminated against women. Badia still lived in the town of Nabatiyyeh, once a cultural bastion of Jabal Amel, a center of Shia learning with a proud tradition of poetry, now a bastion for Hezbollah. She feared for her teenage son. When a neighbor alerted Badia that her son had been seen walking into a mosque known as a Hezbollah recruiting center, she called her father in Beirut. He raced to Nabatiyyeh and demanded that his grandson be handed over to him. No matter the sayyed's politics, no one could refuse a man with a black turban. Sayyed Fahs drove the teenage boy to Beirut and kept him there, far from the claws of the party of eternal war and martyrdom. The weight of the party had already changed the Shia community, and now it was weighing down the country.

⸺

By 2004, Rafiq Hariri was beginning to resent the arrangement that had first brought him to power in 1992. The Syrian occupation and Hezbollah's adventures were thwarting his ambitions for Lebanon. Hariri tried to undercut Syria's stranglehold over the country by secretly helping to draft a UN resolution calling for a Syrian troop withdrawal from Lebanon. The Syrians were furious. When Hariri tried to block plans to extend the mandate of the Lebanese president, a stalwart ally of Damascus, Bashar al-Assad warned that he would "break Lebanon over [Hariri's] head." Hezbollah, on the other hand, was not going anywhere; its members were Lebanese, so Hariri tried to engage its leader, Nasrallah, in a dialogue, hoping to calm the ardors of the militant group. The two men met several times and the discussions went late into the night, over tea and fresh fruit. Both men came from modest origins, both had a good sense of humor, and both had ambitions and a reach that went well beyond the borders of tiny Lebanon, but their lives and worldviews were so different that it's hard to understand what middle ground Hariri was hoping to find. The Lebanon Hariri envisioned was not one that Nasrallah wanted to live in, and vice versa. Despite their cordial late-night conversations, there was definite condescension in Hariri's tone when he spoke of Hezbollah, especially in the month preceding his assassination. He was gearing up for the next elections, and polls suggested his electoral machine would steamroll the Shia group. The way he saw it, he wanted to build, while they wanted to destroy; he wanted to work for peace and prosperity, they wanted eternal war. "Who wants to live like that?" he thought out loud in the company of visitors, just weeks before he died.

Nasrallah and Hariri met for the last time on February 11, 2005. They ate more fresh fruit and chatted into the early hours of the morning. It was their last supper.

On February 14, Hariri was dead. The accusing fingers immediately pointed at Syria. Hundreds of thousands of Lebanese of all faiths and sects descended onto the streets of Beirut, protesting for weeks and demanding that Syrian troops leave the country. Hezbollah organized counterdemonstrations to laud Syria and pledge eternal support. Assad would eventually bring his soldiers home, ending a thirty-year occupation of Lebanon. He knew, however, that—along with Iran—they still had control of the country, thanks to Hezbollah and other allies. A wave of assassinations followed: progressive intellectuals, longtime defenders of the Palestinian cause, communists, members of parliament, Christians, Sunnis, and Shias. This time the assassins reached beyond the Shia community, which had already been decimated by the wave of targeted killings in the 1980s. No one was caught, but everyone surmised who the killers were. The targets were those with a high profile and the intellectual heft and legitimacy to take on Hezbollah's discourse, or offer a progressive path forward for the country. The liberal camp was in disarray, hunted, its politicians forced to hunker down. The country was split sharply into those who aligned with Iran and Syria (the axis of resistance against Israel and the West) and those who looked to the West or Saudi Arabia for support.

Even as they were trying to thwart America in Iraq (allowing jihadis to cross through Syria, propping up Shia militias), or perhaps precisely because they were doing so, Damascus and Tehran had been feeling vulnerable, both wondering whether they were America's next target. After 9/11, Iran had helped the United States by sharing intelligence about al-Qaeda and the Taliban. President Khatami was hoping for a thaw in relations. Instead, in 2002, President George W. Bush lumped Iran into the "Axis of Evil" along with North Korea and Iraq. Iran, Syria, and Hezbollah could not afford to lose ground while America was on the prowl and the region was in such flux. While Iran worked to overpower Iraq, Assad and Hezbollah needed to make sure Lebanon remained theirs, and Hariri was getting in the way. He had to go. Inside Iran, the regime also closed ranks and the next president, elected in August 2005, was a conservative true believer, one of the Revolutionary Guards who'd had a brief tour of duty in Lebanon in the 1980s to help set up Hezbollah, a man awaiting the return of the Mahdi with messianic devotion: Mahmoud Ahmadinejad.

With the killing of Hariri, Iran had unofficially declared war on Saudi Arabia, just as the kingdom itself was feeling fragile, grappling with the wave of al-Qaeda bombings. In August 2005, King Fahd died and Crown Prince Abdallah, de facto ruler for a decade, became king. Despite the proxy war unfolding in Iraq and the killing of his protégé in Lebanon, King Abdallah tried to uphold the détente with Iran. He even hosted Ahmadinejad in Saudi Arabia a few times. But Iran was getting increasingly bolder in Iraq: the Islamic Revolutionary Guard Corps (IRGC) was funding and arming militias, evading US sanctions by siphoning off Iraqi oil, and planting their friends in key positions in ministries. King Abdallah then felt deeply betrayed when it was revealed that Iran had a secret nuclear program, one it had developed during the period of détente with Saudi Arabia. In 2008, after a political tussle in Lebanon about Hezbollah's growing power, there was a showdown in the heart of Beirut between Hezbollah and Sunni militiamen. Everyone still had guns in Lebanon, but no one had a trained fighting force like Hezbollah. Within hours, hundreds of its fighters took over large parts of the city and routed their opponents. The political balance of the country had been tilted in favor of Iran and Syria. King Abdallah would soon begin to rail against Iran and call on the United States "to cut off the head of the snake."

—

On June 7, 2006, at 6:15 p.m., two American F-16s launched a missile strike against a house surrounded by palm trees, fifty-five miles northeast of Baghdad. The aircraft dropped two 500-pound laser-guided bombs on the house. Six people were killed; one of them was Abu Musab al-Zarqawi. Iraq had had a new prime minister since May, leader of the first full-term government since the fall of Saddam Hussein. For the first time in Iraq's history, the country's top leader, chosen after an election, was a Shia. Nuri al-Maliki had fled Iraq in 1979, at the age of twenty-nine. He was a Shia activist and member of the Islamist Da'wa Party. Maliki spent his years in exile between Iran and Syria until he returned to Iraq in 2003. Like almost every Iraqi Shia, several of his relatives had been killed by the regime. Maliki had the honor of making the announcement about the killing of Zarqawi at a press conference alongside the American ambassador and the American commander of US forces in Iraq.

By then, Zarqawi had not only beheaded Western hostages and blown up the UN headquarters and the Jordanian embassy in Baghdad, he had also sent suicide bombers into four-star hotels in Amman one December night in 2005, killing sixty people and injuring more than a hundred. Zarqawi was so bloodthirsty that even al-Qaeda had kept its distance from him, criticizing his gruesome videotaping of the beheadings and counseling him against the wanton killing of fellow Muslims, including Shias. Even

Zarqawi's mentor Maqdissi had never condoned the killing of Shias. But Zarqawi *wanted* a civil war in Iraq; he wanted to kill Shias so they would lash out at Sunnis, and so Sunnis would feel compelled to rise up, join his ranks, and reclaim their country. He was hoping to build an Islamic state in Iraq. Now he was dead. The Americans had killed him, but a Shia prime minister promised this was only the beginning. "Today Zarqawi has been terminated," said Maliki. "Every time a Zarqawi appears we will kill him. We will continue confronting whoever follows his path. It is an open war between us."

In Jordan, in his hometown of Zarqa, condolences were held for the "martyr Abu Musab al-Zarqawi." Several members of parliament visited to pay tribute. Zarqawi's family and tribe had renounced him after the hotel bombings in Amman. But in death, in these fraught times of sectarian tensions and insecurity, he was theirs again. And they promised there would be a thousand more Zarqawis to fight the Americans—or anyone else who threatened them.

—

On December 30, 2006, at dawn, a man in a black suit and white shirt stood on an elevated metal platform, in a dark, dreary room. Tall, with a salt-and-pepper beard, his head almost touched the ceiling as he looked down at the small group of men watching from below. On either side of him stood a man clad in green khaki trousers and a black jacket. The two executioners, faces covered in black ski masks, lowered a thick rope with a noose and placed it around the elderly man's neck. Saddam Hussein was living his last moments. After months in hiding, trying to evade capture by the Americans, he had finally been found in December 2003, cowering in a hole, haggard and disheveled. He was put on trial and received a death sentence. In mid-December 2006, he had lost his appeal. Prime Minister Maliki insisted there should be no delay in carrying out the sentence. After months of court proceedings, the final hours were hurried. Saddam was brought to the gallows, in a former intelligence base of the regime in Baghdad that now served as a US military base. He began to recite the Muslim profession of faith, the *shahada*: "I profess there is no god but God, and Muhammad is his prophet."

"Moqtada, Moqtada, Moqtada!" The men below were taunting him, calling out the name of the hothead cleric leading the Mahdi army. "Long live Mohammad Baqer al-Sadr," others chanted, referring to the cleric that Saddam had executed in 1980. "Moqtada? That's [how you express] your manhood?" snarled Saddam. "Go to hell," came the reply from one of the men.

At 6:10 the trapdoor opened beneath Saddam's feet, just as he was repeating the shahada "There is no god but God and Muhammad is his proph—" The group, which included Shia members of the Iraqi cabinet, erupted in cheers: "The tyrant is dead!"

One man in the audience had filmed the dictator's last moments on a cell phone. The video aired without sound on Iraqi television. But the grainy footage leaked beyond official hands and the taunts were heard by all. Everyone had a different interpretation. Many Sunnis saw an older Sunni statesman heckled by a Shia mob, deprived of dignity in his last moments. Many Shias were relieved, vindicated in their long wait for justice.

Jawad al-Khoei felt deeply conflicted. The young cleric whose own father had been killed by the regime felt some measure of relief. But why had it been carried out in such a disrespectful way? Were past grievances a justification for vengeful behavior? And why execute Saddam on this specific day? Maliki had made a fatal mistake—he'd ordered the execution of Saddam on the eve of an important Muslim holiday, Eid al-Adha, when rulers traditionally issue pardons. Perhaps he had done it on purpose, a spiteful man eager to show his mettle and determination to avenge all those who had been brutally killed or had disappeared in the darkness of Saddam's republic of fear. Saddam issued pardons on holidays, but he also delivered body bags. Every holiday, families grew anxious, never knowing what a knock on the door would bring: reunion with a loved one, bruised and gaunt but alive, or the heartbreaking confirmation of their death. "We have become Saddam," thought Jawad. "We have become him. We have adopted his ways." Jawad thought back to the decades of history of Shias as a minority, always in the opposition, rarely in power, always seeking justice from oppression. Now, at this key moment in their history, they had failed the test of magnanimity, the very test that Imam Hussein would have passed. They had become the oppressors.

━

The death of these three Sunni men between 2005 and 2006 reverberated beyond Iraq and Lebanon, beyond the Arab world itself. They each represented a very different Sunni outlook on the world. Hariri had friends and fans all the way in Pakistan. Saddam's hanging provoked protests in Sri

Lanka and Pakistan-controlled Kashmir. Zarqawi was a hero in a minority circle. In Karachi, Sunni militants would soon complain that *they* were the persecuted ones, while they sat sipping tea in the sun, a gun in their lap, bodyguards roaming freely. Iran, they would say, was coming after them, and Saudi Arabia was their savior. In a Sunni majority country, where Shia mosques were being blown up on a regular basis, it was somehow the Sunni gunmen who felt like the underdog—yet another example of a majority group feeling threatened in its supremacy, unwilling to share long-held power. The backlash would be terrible, the revenge bloody and medieval, unlike anything the Muslim world had witnessed in recent times. The imperceptible fracture was now an open wound and the sectarianization of identities was setting in. In Pakistan, the rising tide of cultural intolerance and political score settling that had started under Zia was reaching new and savage heights.

15

SURRENDER

PAKISTAN
2011–18

When they came into my village
With a weird philosophy to kill
in the name of God
They looted everything . . .
They ruined my schools
Raped my dolls
Orphaned my children
Widowed my sisters
And we kept silent—like stones or tombs.

—Farid Gul Momand, "Surrender,"
Paris Hilton Versus the Poor Poet (2014)

The apostate was dead. Shot at close range in broad daylight in Islam-abad, on the morning of January 4, 2011. The body of the tall man, in a dark salwar kameez, was slumped on the floor, riddled with twenty-seven bullets. His blood seeped into the pavement, near a gray Honda Civic. The crowds came out the next day in the thousands. Not to mourn the dead, but to celebrate his killer.

In all 6,236 verses of the Quran, there is not a single verse calling on Muslims to silence blasphemers by force. Not in 1989, when Khomeini called on believers to kill Salman Rushdie, not in 1992, when the Egyptian intellectual Farag Foda was shot in Egypt, and still not in 2011. The Quran is immutable, and all it does is tell believers to respond to blasphemy with dignity.

But the doctrine of death for apostasy had taken on a life of its own in the previous two decades and had made its way back to Pakistan. The cultural war that Khomeini had started with his fatwa had seriously restrained the boundaries of expression. Worse: in the time that had elapsed since the assassination of Foda in Cairo in 1992, the reference points had moved. No one called it terrorism anymore; no one mourned the victims as martyrs of the nation, as Foda had been mourned. Few dared to protest against those who killed in the name of Islam, afraid they would meet the same fate. Everything had shifted to the right; the old extremes were the new center—or so it felt.

In a few years, the crowds would reemerge, tens of thousands of Pakistanis swarming the cities, shutting down traffic, to mourn the killer put to death by a justice system that felt it had no choice but to condemn him, though it likely would have preferred to spare him, if only to avoid creating a martyr. The apostate, the murdered man, was Salman Taseer, the nephew of Alys Faiz, wife of Faiz Ahmad Faiz, the poet of love, the same Taseer who had continued to protest against Zia in the streets of Lahore during the 1980s, even after he had spent time in the dictator's dungeons. The confidant of the Bhuttos had become a towering figure of Pakistani politics and had been governor of Punjab since 2008. He had just had coffee with a friend in an upscale neighborhood of Islamabad. The killer, police commando Mumtaz Qadri, was on Taseer's security detail that morning, a last-minute addition for the governor's visit to the capital. Taseer's killing was too high profile to drown in the quagmire of Pakistani bureaucracy and willful incompetence. But also, for once, in the land of unresolved assassinations, the killer had willingly and proudly surrendered; the case was resolved on the spot; there would be a trial and a defendant.

"I am a slave of the Prophet, and the punishment for one who commits blasphemy is death," Qadri said with a smile to the news reporters and camera crews that had rushed to the scene after the killing. His hands and legs were bound by nylon rope. He smiled again as he was booked into a police van, delighted by his moment of fame. He seemed confident that he had secured his place in heaven by ridding Pakistan, the Land of the Pure, of a man who had committed a double sin: defending a Christian who had committed blasphemy and a woman at that.

Aamna Taseer was now a widow. She was tall and slender with a big smile, but on this fateful day, she felt alone, and afraid, not only because her husband was gone, but because Pakistan had finally surrendered to the forces of darkness, the forces he had fought against all his life. Zia had succeeded beyond his own expectations in transforming Pakistan. The result was not a model Islamic society, but a country full of zealots. Pakistan had so many problems: there were poverty, gangs, a demographic explosion, crime, and corruption—but the violent forces of radical fundamentalism compounded them all. Since Zia's death, generous funding and constant tending by the Saudi kingdom had continued to nurture those dynamics, keeping the fundamentalist fire alive and the mob agitated.

Aamna felt guilty. It was she who had first told her husband the story of the blasphemous woman, Asia Bibi, just a few months before. The governor was a man of action, trying to fight the forces of extremism, and he immediately set out to help Bibi who, by then, had been in jail for over a year.

—

Bibi's story began in June 2009, when she was harvesting *falsa* berries outside her village of Ittan Wali, not far from Lahore, in the Punjab, in a field belonging to rich landowners. She was hoping to make an extra 250 rupees ($2) on a Sunday to supplement the income of her brickmaker husband. Working under the sweltering sun of the Punjab summer, she went to fetch water from the nearby well, pulling up a bucket and dipping a metal cup into it to drink a few sips. In Bibi's version, another woman set upon her, declaring that the well had been sullied by a Christian and rallying other women behind her. Bibi tried to defend herself. An argument ensued, comparisons were allegedly made between Christianity and Islam, and Bibi was asked to convert to Islam on the spot. The argument eventually died down and the crowd dispersed.

Five days later, working in another field, Bibi found herself face-to-face with the same agitator, who had brought a mob with her. They roughed up Bibi, screaming "Death to the Christian." The police arrived. Bibi insisted she did not insult the prophet, but the women saw it differently. Bibi did tell them that Jesus had done more for humanity than the prophet Muhammad, which was perceived as an insult. She would maintain that story in court and in her autobiography. And for saying as much, she now stood accused of blasphemy. She made her case worse by rejecting what was presented to her as the only way to salvation: conversion to Islam. Thrown in jail, she was put in solitary confinement for her own protection: the mob on the inside was no more forgiving than the one on the outside.

The trial took place a year later. There were many discrepancies in the testimonies, as well as reports of old grudges and years of harassment against Bibi and her family, the only Christians in the village. In principle, the Roman Catholic wife and mother also had the law on her side: article 135(A)(a) in the Pakistani penal code promised to imprison anyone who incited ill-will, hatred, or disharmony between communities on grounds of religion, race, or caste. And Bibi had clearly been the victim of such an incitement. But it was Zia's law that won: the 1986 law that handed out the death penalty to anyone who defiled the name of the prophet. And so, on November 8, 2010, Asia Bibi was sentenced to die by hanging.

The blasphemy law had initially been codified by the British a century earlier, in what was then pre-partition India. The intention had been to punish insults against any religious beliefs in an effort to preserve harmony between the different sects in the British colonial empire: Hindu, Muslim, Christian, and other. While in power, Zia added teeth to the laws, severely criminalizing any perceived insult to the prophet, his companions, the Quran, and basically anything having to do with Islam. In 1986, blasphemy against the prophet became punishable by death or imprisonment for life. Finally, in October 1990, the Federal Shariat Court of Pakistan called on the government to amend the penalty for blasphemy, making death the only punishment possible. The government acquiesced. The new death penalty punishment, with no possibility of bail, opened the floodgates of abuse and vigilante justice. The law became a favorite tool to settle scores for spurned lovers and rapacious businessmen, but by far the largest proportion of its victims were minorities, including Muslim minorities. Christians, Ahmadis, Hindus, and Shias accounted for 50 percent of the cases. And the numbers shot up dramatically. From 1927 to 1985, only ten blasphemy cases were heard in court. Between 1985 and 2011, an estimated four thousand cases of blasphemy of all sorts were tried, from desecrating the Quran to defiling the name of the prophet. More than thirteen hundred Pakistanis were formally accused of blasphemy under various clauses of the law. No other accusation seemed to get the police moving as swiftly as cries of blasphemy: not kidnappings, not threats of violence, not belonging to an outlawed radical group, not even overly zealous behavior on the part of a police officer, such as Qadri.

Governor Taseer was appalled when his wife told him about the verdict in Asia Bibi's case. Together with their daughter Shehrbano, they went to visit the woman in prison and then held a press conference with her. Taseer wanted to reform the blasphemy law and stop it from being misused; he saw it as an existential threat to the identity of Pakistan—or what was left of it. Taseer didn't bow to fear, he never had, not even after months shackled to the floor in solitary confinement in the dungeons of the Lahore fort. "I'm not made of wood that burns easily, don't worry about me, I'll come back to you," he had once scribbled on a piece of paper delivered surreptitiously to his wife through a messenger during the Zia era.

After Zia died, the world moved on, seemingly still oblivious to the impact those years had had on the country. But Aamna and Salman Taseer had trauma inscribed in their every cell, like all Pakistanis—and they kept fighting back. And so, on November 23, 2010, with the confidence

of one who had stared down death, Governor Taseer declared that the
president was a "liberal, modern-minded president" who was not going
to see a "poor woman like that targeted and executed." "It's just not going
to happen," Taseer added. The president was Asif Ali Zardari, widower of
Benazir Bhutto, who had been assassinated in December 2007. The mob
was quick to react to Taseer's words. Religious parties agitated the angry
crowds and thousands protested his comments, across the country and
outside the governor's mansion, even burning Taseer's effigy. His fate was
now tied to the blasphemer.

Taseer did not back down. This wasn't just about one woman. This
was about the soul of his country, a soul that still vibrated to the verses
of Faiz and the music of Iqbal Bano. As matters intensified in December
2010, Taseer quoted Faiz's most beloved and famous poem in a television
interview, offering tenderly patriotic verses that carried both hope and a
sense of self-sacrifice.

> *O burdened hearts, come walk with us again*
> *Come, O friends, for we go to be slain.*

The governor loved Twitter and used the platform to excoriate rivals,
skewer critics, and bemoan the state of the world. On December 31, he
sent out a poignant missive into the ether of social media:

> "I was under huge pressure to cow down b4 rightist pressure.
> Refused. Even if I'm last man standing."

And he was. When he was killed, there was no cohort of outspoken friends and colleagues loudly proclaiming that they would follow
in Taseer's footsteps and continue what he had started. Politicians from
his own party effectively abandoned him in death—as they had done in
life—on the issue of blasphemy. No one denounced his murder as terrorism, the way Egyptians had done two decades earlier. No one was fool-
ish enough to proclaim: "Liberalism till victory or martyrdom," the way a
progressive judge had done after Foda's assassination in Cairo. There had
already been too many deaths. Egypt and Pakistan have much in common in their history and politics, though their social and cultural contexts
belong to different continents. Foda and Taseer, both tall and imposing,
both charismatic, vocal, and fearless, were similar targets for zealots.

To keep up appearances, flags were flown at half-mast and three days of mourning were declared. Taseer was, after all, a governor. But his family did not feel held by the nation in its mourning. A group of five hundred Islamic scholars had warned Pakistanis not to offer funeral prayers for the governor or they could meet the same fate. One militant religious group saluted "the bravery and valor of Mumtaz Qadri." In the media, reactions were mixed. PUNJAB GOVERNOR MARTYRED headlined the *Daily Times*, a left-leaning newspaper owned by Taseer. Another opined that terrorism did not always come with the garb and beard of the Taliban, warning that the future was bleak. But mostly, Taseer was described as a "liberal extremist." Every one of his faults was put back on the table: his secular ways, his divorce, his son with an Indian woman. Munawar Hasan, the head of Mawdudi's Jamaat-e Islami, was unequivocal: "Salman Taseer is himself responsible for his own killing."

Taseer's position as governor afforded him an official funeral, but there were few official representatives and only a thin crowd at the funeral in the Cavalry Ground cemetery in Lahore. President Zardari, a friend of Taseer who had described him as a liberal just weeks earlier, did not attend. Punjab rangers with red and black fantail turbans delivered a military salute. The bugle echoed in the cold January air as "The Last Post" was played, the final farewell to soldiers, a British and Commonwealth regimental tradition. Colored wreaths were laid near the grave. At the end of the service, the governor's sons, Shahbaz and Shehryar, their faces ashen, their eyes swollen, were presented with a big bowl of rose petals. They grabbed a handful, kissed the petals, and scattered them over the black coffin. There was so much of Pakistan being buried in that grave.

Miles away and just hours apart in the city of the crime, roses were also being showered on the killer, who was making his first appearance in court. A smiling, burly Qadri appeared before the bench amid cheers and felicitations. He faced charges of murder and terrorism, but people slapped him on the back and a garland of flowers was placed around his neck. The trial would take ten months, and he would be sentenced to death. In the meantime, tragedy struck again, twice.

In March, Pakistan's minister of minority rights, a Christian who had spoken in favor of reviewing Asia Bibi's case and reforming blasphemy laws, was also assassinated. Shahbaz Bhatti, traveling with only a driver despite years of threat, died on the spot when gunmen sprayed his car with bullets as he was leaving his mother's home in Islamabad. The killers scattered pamphlets on the scene, signing the murder: Taliban al Qaeda-

Punjab. Then a few months later, Shahbaz, Taseer's eldest son, was kidnapped.

On August 26, 2011, Shahbaz was heading to work when a car blocked his
way and five masked gunmen dragged him out of his Mercedes, a gun to
his head. The twenty-eight-year-old spent the next four and a half years
in captivity, subjected to indescribable torture, shot, and kept in solitary
confinement. He was taken across the border into Afghanistan, where he
survived American drone attacks and emotional torture, and through it
all, he thought of those days and weeks that his own father had spent away
from his family, in Zia's jails. "Physical pain touches only the surface, you
must never let it break your spirit," his father had once told him.

Shahbaz was first held by a shadowy, ruthless group, the Islamic
Movement of Uzbekistan, whose focus had migrated from Uzbekistan to
Pakistan and Afghanistan. By November 2015, he was being held by the
Afghan Taliban. The exact details of the affair are still not fully known, but
there was something that felt either divine or coordinated about Shahbaz's
sudden release by his captors at dawn on February 29, 2016, after five years
in captivity. On that exact same day and around the same time, Qadri, the
killer of Governor Taseer, was being led to the gallows in Islamabad. If
Shahbaz had been held as a bargaining chip in exchange for Qadri's release
or the overturning of his sentence, he was of no use anymore. Released into
nowhere, for nine days Shahbaz walked and hitchhiked from Afghanistan
into Pakistan's Balochistan province. This last phase of his ordeal meant he
did not witness Qadri's funeral in Pakistan, a funeral that celebrated his
father's assassin.

On March 1, tens of thousands of Pakistanis came out to protest Qadri's
execution, bringing cities across the country to a standstill. Thousands
more traveled to the capital to attend the funeral. They walked, drove, and
rode their motorbikes, blocking entire highways. The ambulance carrying
Qadri's body was strewn with roses, inching through a human sea toward
Liaqat Bagh Park, in Rawalpindi, Islamabad's adjacent twin city and headquarters of the Pakistan army. This was where Benazir Bhutto had been
assassinated in 2007. Now the killer of her friend Taseer was being honored in the same spot. Several hundred thousand mourners thronged the
park and the surrounding area, holding up Qadri's picture and wearing "I
am Qadri" signs around their necks. The country was tense, fearful of more

violence, and the media were forbidden from broadcasting the funeral. But in the age of mobile phones and social media, there was no way for the state to hide the monster it had bred.

Aamna's stomach churned at the size of the crowd, but she wasn't all that surprised. She knew the country she was living in and how it had changed but, as her husband had done, she persisted in believing that those cheering Qadri were a minority—a loud and sometimes violent minority, but a minority nonetheless, in a country of almost two hundred million people. The state, too often complicit in violence, wasn't helping. The minister of religious affairs declared Qadri a martyr.

By the end of 2016, there was a mosque and a shrine to Qadri on the outskirts of Islamabad in his home village of Athal. With two minarets and a green dome, the small mosque soon became a pilgrimage site for thousands of Pakistanis. It cost almost a million dollars to build, and the money came entirely from donations of supporters, according to Qadri's family. Under a ceiling inlaid with mirrorwork mosaics, visitors knelt to pray by Qadri's white marble tomb, adorned with delicate carved marble latticework. Such visitations are anathema to any fundamentalist orthodox Islam, heresy for the Saudi Wahhabis and their allies in Pakistan, the Deobandi and Ahl-e Hadith religious groups. But Qadri was actually a Barelvi Muslim, the less doctrinaire, more tolerant school of Islam on the subcontinent, which overlaps with Sufism and openly venerates saints and the prophet Muhammad. Rivals of the Deobandis since the creation of their movement in the early twentieth century, the Barelvis had long promoted themselves as a moderate counterbalance.

So what happened? How did one of theirs kill in the name of religion? The winds of extremism blowing in Pakistan for three decades had carried almost everyone further to the right. The center had moved, and everyone reorganized around a new understanding of the norms. The competition for who was a good Muslim was slowly engulfing more and more people, leading to excesses of self-righteousness and the creation of more radical groups and their ever more violent spinoffs. With minorities like Shias and Ahmadis already considered beyond the pale of Islam, the next step in the competition for purity was Sunni versus Sunni. Barelvis were attacked for their beliefs, dismissed as idolaters for their visitation of tombs. Not to be outdone by those claiming to be the standard-bearers of righteous Islam, the Barelvis began to organize in the 1990s to take over Deobandi mosques, provoking a race to the death with bombings, assassinations, and counterassassinations. They, too, resorted to violence to assert their blind devotion to the prophet. And so Mumtaz Qadri had killed Governor Salman Taseer and declared that, in doing so, he was a slave of the prophet.

Since the end of the war against the Soviets in Afghanistan, Saudi influence in Pakistan had become less obvious but perhaps more insidious. Saudi intelligence officials didn't need to fly to Peshawar twice a month anymore with bags of cash, as they had done in the 1980s. Their network of influence was well established, with both formal and informal networks. Even well after 9/11 and the clampdown on radical outfits, American diplomats in Pakistan reported back to Washington that Saudi organizations were still paying around $100 million annually to Deobandi and Ahl-e Hadith clerics, ostensibly with the knowledge or tacit approval of the authorities. The Ahl-e Hadith movement had grown massively since the 1980s and the heirs of Ehsan Elahi Zaheer were busy converting thousands to their side. With generous Saudi and Gulf funding, they had created a publishing empire and were expanding their network of madrassas, religious seminaries. Deobandi religious seminaries were still the majority at 65 percent, but both served the Saudi worldview. Classes were taught in Arabic, and, thanks to donations from the Gulf, school fees were low. In a developing country with huge income disparities and a big youth bulge, low-cost religious schools with full room and board were a relief for families unable to provide for their children. There were now more English, math, and computer skills classes, but they were all inscribed in the activist mission of jihadi Islam. There was nothing diverse or tolerant about the teaching imparted to the children.

Just like the Iranians, the Saudis expected loyalty in return for their largesse and patronage. In their efforts to counter Iran, the Saudis sometimes descended into petty, obsessive minutiae. In 2012, Mumtaz Ahmed, the president of the International Islamic University of Islamabad (established with Saudi funding back in 1981), committed the faux pas of inviting the Iranian ambassador to a VIP reception at the university. The Saudi ambassador requested that the university rescind the invitation. The president declined, pointing out that Pakistan and the university maintained good relations with both Iran and Saudi Arabia. He was promptly replaced with a Saudi. Some of these shenanigans went unnoticed by the wider public. But often they grated on Pakistanis.

"Servility to rich Arabs" called out Pervez Hoodboy, a professor, author, and longtime critic of what he described as the Saudization of Pakistan at the expense of its historical and rich connection to Persian culture and traditions. The protestations against cultural homogenization and the

Arabization of Islam seemed to have been reduced to the whimper of an older generation that insisted on responding with the traditional Persian expression *Khoda hafez,* May God be with you, when someone uttered the Arabized version *Allah hafez.* In Arabic, Allah is used by Muslims and Christians alike to say God, but in Pakistan, where Urdu was laced with Persian words, it had always been *Khoda,* Persian for God. Those taking a stand insisted on calling their prayers *namaz* rather than using the Arabic *salat,* and for them Ramadan was still *ramzan.*

Mehtab Rashdi, the rebellious television anchor, was definitely a *Khoda hafez* person. Now in her early sixties, she said *namaz* and fasted during *ramzan,* and she still wore her dupatta draped on her shoulders. She worried that these small daily acts of defiance were lost on a younger generation that had no memory of the country's more pluralistic past or even the Persian influence on their history. She had been secretary of education in Sindh province at one point and saw firsthand the continued, growing influence of Islamist groups with links to Saudi Arabia. Face veils and the ankle-length overdress cloak called the *abaya* were spreading on university campuses, which puzzled the woman who had defied the dictator's orders to wear the veil. There was no dictator imposing the veil anymore, but the dictatorship of the closed mind had taken root.

One day in 2000, she agreed out of curiosity to attend Quran lessons given by a woman preacher who was all the rage in Pakistan. A relative of Mehtab's sister-in-law had been haranguing her for months, insisting that she attend a lecture by Farhat Hashmi, the founder of the Al-Huda religious schools and institutes. Hashmi was a pure product of the Zia era, just twenty years old when the dictator had come to power. The daughter of a Jamaat-e Islami activist, she became a Jamaat activist herself for a while. Hashmi got her doctorate in Islamic studies from Glasgow University, but she cited prominent Saudi or Saudi-backed scholars, including Bin Baz, as her inspiration. In 1994, she'd established the Al-Huda Foundation, a welfare organization that ran short courses and full-time classes on its bigger campuses in Islamabad and Karachi. Hashmi's teachings were based on the Ahl-e Hadith school of thought and were openly critical of Barelvis and Shias. Al-Huda's headquarters, a large villa in an upmarket neighborhood of Islamabad, was paid for by donations from Saudi Arabia and the Gulf, according to information from bankers in Pakistan.

Mehtab walked into the Regent Plaza hotel in Karachi and up to the foyer outside a hotel conference room, where she was greeted by enthusiastic women, all veiled, giving out books, DVDs, and CDs with religious content, all published by Al-Huda. In the conference room, she sat among rows and rows of women, some four or five hundred affluent Pakistanis with designer handbags and expensive shoes. Some of them were wives of political or defense officials, or local provincial bureaucrats. They were bored, frustrated housewives, Mehtab thought, just like the relative who had brought her here. With grown children, uninterested husbands, and idle mornings, they sought to give meaning to their lives.

Hashmi entered the hall, and though her audience was made up exclusively of women, she continued to hide behind her niqab, showing only her eyes. Tall, heavyset, and wearing round glasses, the televangelist read her lecture off a laptop screen. To Mehtab's ears, the tone was monotonous. What was all the fuss about this woman? But most of the audience seemed enraptured, scribbling notes furiously. Mehtab left before it was over. But she had instantly understood that this was about assiduous proselytizing and recruiting. Each of those women was expected to bring along more women, just as she had been dragged to this lecture. There was no definitive count of how many adhered, but the approach was a force multiplier: by 2017, there would be two hundred local branches of Hashmi's institute across the country, providing short seminars, attended by tens of thousands of women, most of them middle- and upper-class. Another fifteen thousand women had formally graduated with a diploma or certificate. There was a cottage industry of books and tapes, clothes, even halal makeup. Mehtab could see the impact around her. The phenomenon closely resembled the religious salons of the 1990s in Egypt, where middle-class and upper-class women embraced a stricter reading of religion, often donning the veil on the spot, inspired by the pretty former actresses who'd had their come-to-God moment. Among her social circle, Mehtab began to notice not just more veils, but other subtle, insidious changes, like friends hissing at her for celebrating the prophet's birthday, or pulling on her sleeve to make her sit down when she stood to show respect to the prophet's name being read out. In line with Wahhabi beliefs, not even the prophet could be venerated in Hashmi's world, only God.

The women from Hashmi's lectures and classes began hassling their husbands, children, and friends for not being devout enough. Photographs came off the walls of homes and framed verses of the Quran went up. The women stopped listening to music, watching television, reading fiction, and dancing at weddings. Hashmi was setting new social and moral standards for Pakistani society, going even further than what had been achieved by Zia and edging ever closer to full Saudi-style Wahhabi Islam, with a complete rejection of all accretions or even traditional culture in general, in a country where music, poetry, dance, and literature were part of the DNA, where even trucks were decorated with an explosion of artful color. Women who studied full-time at Al-Huda for years, and later managed to step back, spoke of brainwashing, of being pulled into what resembled a cult, with 24/7 prayers, recitations, religious readings, and devotion to Hashmi. There was never any open call for violence, but the women were increasingly isolated from society, encased in a set of rigid rules that made them intolerant of other ways—an unhealthy fanaticism, a kind of latent radicalism.

—

This was not the future that Mehtab had envisioned for Pakistan in November 1988 when she returned to television to cover the election of her friend Benazir Bhutto. Mehtab had considered that moment a personal victory, as she smiled to the millions of Pakistanis who tuned in to the news, her hair uncovered, having outlasted the dictator. She meant it as a message to her country that the nightmare was over, that change had finally come. But Zia's legacy was already too entrenched.

Perhaps the worst leftover from the Zia era was the sectarian intolerance and violence, both of which had grown exponentially since those first killings in the Kurram district in 1987. It continued with a massacre of 150 Shias by Sunni vigilantes in 1988, followed by retaliatory assassinations of militant Shia leaders. In 1996, there were five days of Sunni-Shia fighting in Parachinar that left two hundred dead. Mosques were being bombed, both Sunni and Shia. Iranians were also targeted: in 1990, the Iranian cultural attaché in Lahore was assassinated; in 1997, the Iranian cultural centers in Lahore and Multan were torched and five Iranian military personnel were assassinated in Rawalpindi.

By 2012, one in two Pakistanis did not accept that Shias were Muslims. All minorities were targets. Christians, Ahmadis, and Hindus faced a battery of discriminatory laws and the appalling practice of forced conversion to Islam by vigilante groups who abducted young girls and forced them into marriage or into a madrassa. Shias were still more fortunate and well established in society, a thirty-six-million-strong minority, the largest Shia population outside Iran. But they accounted for 70 percent of the victims of sectarian attacks in the decades since the creation of the anti-Shia group Sepah-e Sahaba Pakistan in 1985, the first overtly sectarian militant group. It was banned in 2002 but produced several spin-offs, like Ahl-e Sunnah

Wal Jamaat. It was banned as well in 2012, but its leaders still gave interviews on the streets of Karachi with no fear of arrests, and still held public
rallies with the screams of "Shia kafir."

Shias had tried to fight back and set up their own sectarian militia. But
they had little outside help; Iran did not invest in this enterprise as it had in
Hezbollah. Sunnis got the monopoly on violence and the Shias became the
hunted. From car bombs against Shia mosques to suicide bombs during
religious processions, the sectarian violence became a systemic campaign
of elimination, at a fast clip. In 2011, the terrorist group Lashkar-e Jhangvi
sent an open letter to the Shia community in Quetta, in Balochistan, home
to around six hundred thousand Hazara Shias. "All Shias are worthy of
killing. We will rid Pakistan of [this] unclean people," read the letter. "Pakistan means land of the pure, and the Shias have no right to be here . . .
We will make Pakistan their graveyard—their houses will be destroyed by
bombs and suicide bombers." Most chilling were the recurrent waves of
targeted assassinations of middle-class Shia professionals: doctors, intellectuals, lawyers, journalists, even officers were shot at close range on the
street, or had small bombs placed under their cars. In a crime-ridden,
gang-infested city like Karachi, one could dismiss all this as just more random violence, but the pattern was clear. Hundreds of Shia professionals left
the country. In August 2012, men wearing army uniforms stopped a bus
traveling in the Gilgit-Baltistan area in northern Pakistan. The gunmen
checked the IDs of passengers, pulled out those who were identifiable as
Shia by their names, and shot them. It was the third time that year that Shia
men had been pulled off a bus and shot. The state did nothing.

The Pakistan that Mehtab had grown up in wasn't perfect, but it was
certainly more tolerant, more liberal, more progressive, and far less ruthless. There were so many reasons for the descent into chaos: local dynamics, corruption, overpopulation, the devious military establishment. But no
matter how she turned it around in her head, it always traced back to Zia
and Saudi money. He was dead, but so were Benazir Bhutto and Governor
Taseer and countless others, in a country now disfigured by violence.

—

When Shahbaz Taseer finally came home in March 2016, his father's killer
was dead and buried. The Taseers' broken hearts, still mourning Salman,
were partly mended by the joy of Shahbaz's almost miraculous survival.
The family home was now cordoned off from the city by a security perim-
eter and police barricades, a metaphor for the ever-shrinking freedoms of

progressive-minded Pakistanis. Aamna had all her children and grand-children near her, but she knew that in that first week of January 2011, when twenty-seven bullets had riddled her husband's body, something had been irremediably shattered, not only for herself and her family, but also for the country. It was the culmination of what had been a long dark road for Pakistan: a dead end.

The same week that Governor Taseer had been shot, hope was surging three thousand miles to the east through the streets of Cairo and Tunis, hope that change was possible, that there was a passageway out of that dead end of life under Arab dictators. But the region was still hostage to the dynamics unleashed in 1979, and the Saudi-Iran rivalry would mutate yet again.

16

COUNTERREVOLUTION

EGYPT

2010–16

I did not wield a dagger
Or even an old weapon
Nothing but a rage born of hunger.
—Amal Dunqul, "Do Not Reconcile" (1976)

Ebtehal Younes was now the widow of an apostate, just like Aamna Taseer in Pakistan. The French literature professor, who had not shed a tear when President Sadat was killed but had found her life upended by the black wave that had followed his death, was back in Egypt after years of exile in the Netherlands. For the first time in decades, she felt hopeful about the future of Egypt. She was a widow, but at least her husband, Nasr Abu Zeid, had not met a violent death; he died in 2010 of a deadly viral infection contracted during a trip to Indonesia. He was gone but perhaps more alive than ever. Young Egyptians had discovered his words, and they were reading him, quoting him, in Cairo but also in the provinces in rural Egypt, where boredom reigned and books were still the cheapest form of entertainment. Egypt's youth were frustrated, restless, boiling; they were thirsty for life, answers, and justice.

At the time of his death, Nasr had reached a reconciliation of sorts with his homeland. In 2002, after seven years in exile, he returned for a short visit to see his family in the village of Quhafa. For years, he had dreamed of going home and he wanted a decent return. Perhaps he even fantasized of having a grand return, like that of his idol Taha Hussein, carried on his students' shoulders back into his office after accusations of apostasy in the 1930s.

But that Egypt was long gone. Cairo University never invited him back; he never taught there again. Nasr made a few more low-key visits. His village, Quhafa, once surrounded by fields, with no running water, had become a suburb of the city of Tanta. Hosni Mubarak was still president, dutifully overseeing the decline and deepening rot of his country since he took over from the assassinated president in 1981. In 2002, the population was around 73 million. There were 40 million people under twenty-five. A conservative estimate put the number of unemployed at 7 million. By 2010, the population was almost 85 million and everything was worse. The black wave from the Gulf appeared to have ebbed, or at least it didn't feel like an aggressive campaign anymore, perhaps because, just as in Pakistan, the changes unleashed in the 1980s and 1990s had achieved their purpose, of molding Egypt into the stifling society that Nasr found on his first visit back to the homeland.

Still, there were small openings, pockets of oxygen. Privately owned satellite television in particular had changed the conversation in Egypt and the region since the proliferation of stations, starting in the 1990s. Stale and sanitized, state television was no longer the only source of information or entertainment. There were now three hundred channels to choose from, with everything from scantily dressed singers contorting in impossible dance moves on Rotana TV to Salafist preachers pronouncing fatwas and discussing the road to salvation on al-Nass TV. In the schizophrenic world of Gulf power and money, it was no surprise that rich Saudis owned both those channels. Television had become a powerful soapbox for Islamists; the channels were split almost equally between religious programming and regular political or cultural programming, although those speaking in the name of religion were louder, and always on a mission.

But it was thanks to television that Nasr was reintroduced to the Egyptian and Arab public. During his years in exile, he had been recognized and celebrated around the world, had won awards, and been in the presence of legends like Nelson Mandela. In the febrile post-9/11 period, where all the talk was of a clash of civilizations, here was an erudite, well-traveled Muslim man who was both a believer and a reformist, a man who did not skirt around the issue of acts of terror perpetrated by Muslims, while making a rational case for why violence was not inherent to his religion. More important, Nasr had thought through the question posed after 9/11 by the British American historian Bernard Lewis: "What went wrong?"

Lewis saw everything as a clash of civilizations, and it was he who coined that term. He believed that Arab countries were sick: "either we bring them freedom or they destroy us."

If Nasr agreed with Lewis about the decline of Islamic civilization because of intellectual stagnation, the kind that had sent him into exile, he disagreed virulently with the idea that Muslim society was intrinsically retrograde. He saw the way forward very differently: salvation did not have to come from the West. Islam's transition to modernity would come from within; renewal was possible. He knew it because he was a product of that intellectual journey and was walking in the footsteps of nineteenth-century progressive Salafist thinkers like Muhammad Abduh, those who took inspiration from the wisdom of the prophet's companions to forge a way forward in the modern world.

Nasr's speeches and writings had been noticed in the Arab world, too, where the attack on the Twin Towers had caused a strange mix of consternation and unspoken satisfaction but mostly had provoked a serious crisis of identity. Friends and colleagues back in Egypt helped pave the way for his return, and on one of his visits to Cairo, in 2005, Abu Zeid was invited to appear on Egyptian state television for an hour-long interview on a popular talk show, *Bayt Baytak* (Our Home Is Your Home). Watched by several million Egyptians, he talked about his life in exile, his thoughts on the Quran, the veil, and freedom. Nasr had not grown bitter in exile, he had softened, because he believed that his personal ordeal paled in comparison to what his homeland was going through. Egyptians watching the show could see he was one of them; he, too, had suffered from poverty, bureaucracy, and cronyism. He was his usual jovial, affable self. He did not look like an apostate—whatever an apostate was supposed to look like.

In 2008, Nasr was invited to give a series of lectures at the Alexandria library and the American University of Cairo. He chose to speak about his favorite subject, the rationalist Mu'tazilah movement of the eighth century. But he also spoke about the need to regenerate the country's highest religious institution, Al-Azhar, and address the stifling of art by religious taboos, as well as the state of affairs in Egypt, where there was no freedom and no democracy and the state still abused religion to outdo the Islamists and maintain its grip on people. He didn't know what type of reception he would receive, but Egyptians answered his call, especially the young, who had rarely heard such public discussions. All the seats were taken. People stood in the back; they sat between the aisles and on the floor in front of the stage. They were young, mostly in their twenties, thirsty for what had been forbidden, eager for a window onto the world of rationality. Here was a man who spoke about the need to renew the understanding of Islam and Islamic tradition; here was a man who had fought for his thoughts and for freedom of thought, a man who stood his ground. By the time Nasr fell ill in 2010, he felt at peace with his homeland, enough that he requested to fly back to Cairo to be treated there. As death neared, he asked Ebtehal to bury him in his village. The funeral was small. There was no large procession, no government representation. But he was home.

Ahmed Naji had gone to Nasr's 2008 lectures though he cared little for religion, despite or perhaps because of the devout home he'd grown up in. But he sat in the crowded auditorium enthralled to listen in person to a man whose writings he had recently discovered, due to his love of literature and the Arabic language. Nasr was a master of the Arabic word; it was his entry point into understanding the Quran. Ahmed loved Nasr's smiling, calm demeanor that defused the criticism of antagonistic questioners in the lecture hall. He was mesmerized by the enduring love between Nasr and Ebtehal, a kind of modern-day, Egyptian Romeo and Juliet who had survived the charge of apostasy and the tragedy of exile.

Ahmed had recently returned to Cairo after a childhood spent between Kuwait and Libya. He studied journalism and joined the staff of *Akhbar al-Adab*, Cairo's literary review magazine. With his short curly hair and Frank Zappa mustache, his patterned Nehru shirts, his vests, and his cigarillos, Ahmed looked like a British dandy. But he was deeply subversive; his writings were political without ever openly discussing politics. He was irreverent and humorous, and he spoke fast. By the age of twenty-two, he was a published author. At thirty, in 2016, he would end up in jail for writing fiction: not journalism or reportage or even activism, but fiction. In Egypt, to write was to resist. Ahmed saw in Nasr a writer who had resisted, and inspired others to do the same.

But before jail, there was revolution. Unrest had been in the air for a few years, but no one recognized the signs or the magnitude of what was about to unfold.

Then on January 25, 2011, Egyptians took to the streets to express a rage that had been building up within them, maybe for decades. They'd had enough of the corrupt, oppressive, inert, dilapidated swamp they were living in. Next door, Tunisians had just rid their country of their president, Zine al-Abidine Ben Ali. On January 14, Ben Ali had fled to Saudi Arabia. Two weeks of protests had put an end to twenty-two years of despotic rule. Now, Egyptians were going after President Hosni Mubarak and his thirty-year rule. Every day, the protests and the rage grew. But so did the elation, as women with coiffed hair and designer bags or tightly wrapped veils and long manteaus, bearded sheikhs and teens in jeans and football jerseys, peasants in gallabiyas and businessmen in suits, all converged on Tahrir Square. They inhabited different planets, but they met as Egyptians for the first time and found one another on a square with a long history as a symbol of patriotism, dating back to British rule. Surrounded by grand buildings telling Egypt's story, from the Egyptian Museum to the Arab League headquarters and the headquarters of Mubarak's National Democratic Party, the somewhat shapeless square had several boulevards converging on it, a rare open space in the heart of Cairo, with a grassy roundabout in the middle, a perfect stage for Egypt's *bon enfant* festival against tyranny. Ahmed drank it all up. He wasn't sleeping. He felt alive, perhaps for the first time in his life. *Tahrir* means "liberation" in Arabic. Ahmed wanted the square to earn its name.

Day after day, millions of Egyptians protested. "The people want the fall of the regime," they chanted. There were violent clashes with the police. More than eight hundred people died. Mubarak promised some reforms, then promised he wouldn't run again for president. It was no longer enough to send the protesters home. They were camped on Tahrir Square; the nights were tense. For courage and reinforcement, they painted the walls with verses and sang poetry.

> *The brave men are brave . . . The cowards are cowardly . . .*
> *Come with the brave . . . Together to the Square . . .*
> *We defeat defeatism and heal the wounds . . .*

Those were the words of Fouad Ahmed Negm, poet of the people, the man who'd praised the Iranian Revolution in 1979, hoping it would usher in a real, social democracy in the region. He'd spent a total of eighteen years in jail for irking all of Egypt's rulers. His old poems mocking the late president Sadat were brought back to life. Finally, this was the revolution of the people that Negm, now eighty-two, had been waiting for his whole life. Or so he thought. As did Ahmed.

Iran and Saudi Arabia were both watching closely. People power made the Iranians nervous. Revolution had brought down the shah in 1979 and the largest crowds since then had come out in 2009 to protest fraud in the reelection of President Ahmadinejad. Dubbed the Green Movement, they almost brought down the Islamic Republic. But there were no Islamic slogans in the Egypt protests: there were flags, music and dancing, families picnicking. Thousands prostrated for Friday prayers on the square, but their demands were for bread and justice. Was this a new dawn for a secular democracy in Egypt?

On February 1, after almost nine days of complete silence, Iran's Supreme Leader, Ali Khamenei, seemed to have made up his mind—or perhaps he hoped that if he said it and willed it, it would be so. He declared that the uprising in Egypt was "like the yell that the Iranian nation let out against America and against global arrogance and tyranny" in 1979. Mubarak would meet the same fate as the shah, said Khamenei; this was the beginning of an Islamic awakening in the Middle East. For Iran, this was an opportunity, the one that had not been fully exploited in 1981 by the assassins of Sadat, Khaled Islambouli, Abboud Zomor, and Mohammad Abd al-Salam Farag.

At 6:00 p.m. on February 11, Vice President Omar Suleiman announced Hosni Mubarak's resignation, putting an end to his thirty years in power. The universe has a dark sense of irony: February 11 was also the anniversary of the Iranian Revolution, the day that the government left behind by the shah had fallen in 1979. The Iranians probably saw this as a sign from heaven. The Saudis weren't amused. They weren't simply fearful that their own people could be inspired by uprisings in the Arab world; they had traumatic flashbacks to 1979 as they watched events unfold in Egypt: streets thronged by millions, America dropping a longtime loyal ally almost overnight, the most powerful army in the Arab world standing by, a regional power paralyzed—the echoes of Iran and the downfall of the shah were overwhelming. The Saudis had been oblivious to the dangers of Khomeini in 1979. Since then, they had lived in constant fear of a repeat of a revolution in the Arab world, Islamic or other. They had tried to warn the Americans, but President Obama believed that the arc of history bends toward freedom, and he saw it bending in Egypt. For Saudi Arabia, this was a nightmare. The time to strike back was now.

—

Just over a year after the fall of Mubarak, in the summer of 2012, Mohammad Morsi, an engineering professor with a PhD from the University of Southern California, was elected president of Egypt. Where the United States saw free and fair elections, the Saudis saw a vital threat, for two reasons. Morsi was a lifelong member of the Muslim Brotherhood, which meant Islamists had arrived at the top, not with a coup, not with an assassination, not with an uprising, but through the ballot box; a successful example of political Islam could feed calls for elections in Saudi Arabia itself. The Saudis were also deeply distrustful of the Muslim Brotherhood generally, since the betrayal of the political sahwa of the 1990s.

A heavyset man with a short-cropped beard, Morsi had served in parliament for a few years. He understood the importance of Saudi Arabia as one of Egypt's key financial backers. His first foreign trip was to Riyadh. But his second trip was to Tehran, in September 2012, to attend the summit of the Non-Aligned Movement—it was the first visit to Iran of an Egyptian president since Sadat had visited the shah in 1976. Iran had tried to meddle in Egypt throughout Mubarak's time in power, reportedly plotting assassinations and sabotage. The only remaining Iranian diplomat in Egypt was expelled in 1992. There had been a thaw during President Khatami's time in power and then tension again: in 2009, Hezbollah was accused of planning attacks in Egypt. There were still no diplomatic relations between the two countries. And now came a visit that had been unthinkable just a year earlier, a turning point, made possible by the continued warmth in the relationship between Iran and the Egyptian Muslim Brotherhood.

Although the Syrian Muslim Brotherhood had felt betrayed by Iran in the early 1980s, the Egyptian Brotherhood had never denounced the Islamic Republic of Iran. In fact, when Khomeini died in 1989, the Egyptian Muslim Brotherhood publicly mourned him as the man who had unleashed an Islamic revolution against oppressors everywhere. The long history between Egypt's Brothers and revolutionary Iran had been forgotten by most in the region, but in newspaper articles and newly published books, its details were resurfacing: Khomeini's admiration for Sayyid Qutb, the 1984 postage stamp in his honor, the visit to Cairo of Navvab Safavi, leader of Iran's Fedayeen-e Islam. Mostly, people were remarking on the similar structure of the rule of the religious jurist, with a Supreme Leader in Iran and a Supreme Guide for the Brotherhood in Egypt.

Then, in February 2013, President Ahmadinejad traveled to Cairo to attend a summit of the Organization of Islamic Cooperation. Morsi rolled out the red carpet for the Iranian leader and all the other heads of state attending. But the rest of Ahmadinejad's visit was troubled—a protester even threw a shoe in his face as he was walking out of a mosque. Ahmadinejad visited Al-Azhar and had a tense meeting with the Grand Imam, Ahmad al-Tayyeb. Afterward, another sheikh from Al-Azhar, Hassan al-Shafie, made a few comments in front of television cameras, Ahmadinejad by his side. After calling the Iranian leader a friend of Egypt, he veered into contentious terrain. "There are people who are spreading the Shiite sect in Egypt and are frequently visiting Iran," said Shafie. Ahmadinejad started to shake his head. "Those people are insulting the prophet Muhammad's companions, who are symbols to Sunnis," Shafie continued. "We reject this, and this has been affecting the relations between the Egyptian and the Iranian people." Ahmadinejad and a Shia cleric accompanying him started whispering to each other. The Iranian president interjected, in Arabic: "This is not what we agreed. We agreed [to talk about] unity, brotherhood." The Azhari sheikh nodded but persisted. He next chided Iran for its involvement in Syria. A popular uprising against Assad had begun there around the same time as Egypt's revolution, but unlike Mubarak, the Syrian dictator was not willing to bend to the popular will and offered no concessions. Within weeks, he was raining a deluge of bullets on the protesters who were calling for democracy. The opposition took up arms to defend themselves and fight back. Within months, Assad had deployed artillery and fighter jets. Iran stood by his side; Hezbollah was helping on the ground. The country would soon be engulfed in war, with multiple fronts and multiple players.

At Al-Azhar, faced with the hectoring sheikh, a tense Ahmadinejad interjected several times, before signaling he would walk away if the lecture continued. Sheikh al-Shafie ended on a more conciliatory note, calling for unity, to which Ahmadinejad smiled broadly and said in Arabic: *ahsant, ahsant,* well done, well done.

Geopolitics had clearly obliterated all sense of history in Egypt. No one even mentioned Al-Azhar's own Shia past. The religious institution dated back to the Fatimids, the fourth Islamic caliphate and a Shia dynasty that ruled from the tenth to the twelfth century over a territory extending from the Red Sea to the Atlantic. They were the descendants of Fatima, daughter of the prophet and wife of Ali. This was the only and last time since Ali's own brief rule in 656 that direct descendants of the prophet had ruled as an Islamic caliphate, and therefore the only time that the caliph and the religious leadership had been one. One of the first universities in the world, Al-Azhar was first built as a center of Shia learning and named in honor of Fatima, who was known as al-Zahraa', the brilliant. Cairo itself had been built by the Fatimids as their new capital in 970. The Fatimid reign was one of flourishing arts and abundant scholarly works. There were no forced conversions to Shiism, but a tolerance for minorities that left a lasting pluralistic legacy. When Saladin defeated the Fatimids in 1170, Al-Azhar was shut down for over a century and Sunni Islam became the state religion once again. Centuries later, in the land of the pharaohs, Islam still stood at the intersection of Sunnism and Shiism; on a popular level, for centuries, and until the very recent past, there had been no divide between them. But for a few decades now, just as in Pakistan, there had been efforts to curb the mawleds in Egypt, the colorful, exuberant celebrations of the birthdays of saints and the prophet. Some of this was the result of state-led efforts to organize the chaotic festivities, or even of Sufi-led reforms, but many Egyptians attributed the changes to the influence of Saudi puritanism.

Ebtehal and her late husband echoed what most thought when they said that Egyptians were Sunni in their faith but Shia in their culture and temperament, and she resented what she described as Saudi cultural diktats. Perhaps those sentiments scared the Saudis at this delicate time in the region, a time of chaotic uprisings from Egypt to Syria and Bahrain, chaos behind which Saudi Arabia saw the hand of Iran and the specter of 1979. Iranians were aggressively courting Egypt, and Ahmadinejad's fiasco at Al-Azhar did not deter them.

Barely two days after Ahmadinejad's visit, Morsi received a letter from seventeen Iranian scholars and officials calling on him to draw on the experience of Iran and impose full shari'a rule in Egypt. The Iranians were offering their experience and knowledge. The media coverage of the letter reflected either Saudi Arabia's deep insecurity or its willful agitation of anti-Iran feelings. The Saudi-run pan-Arab newspaper *Asharq al-Awsat* was the first to publish the letter, claiming it was signed by the Supreme Leader. The letter, according to the newspaper, called on Morsi to implement a wilayat al-faqih in Egypt and to join Iran in building a great new Islamic civilization. Egyptian newspapers quickly repeated the claim, causing furious reactions in Egypt, including from within the Muslim Brotherhood. Iran denied the letter was signed by Khamenei and denied it had made any reference to wilayat al-faqih, threatening to sue *Asharq al-Awsat*. But the seed of doubt had been planted.

Saudi Arabia's fear of Iran and its obsession with conversions to the Shia faith predated Egypt's revolution and Morsi's election. The Saudis, quietly but methodically, had been keeping an eye on Iran's every move there, just as they had been doing in Pakistan, and they would only build further on this: their counterrevolution would be sectarian, an upgraded version of the anti-Shia, anti-Iran rhetoric Saudi Arabia had helped spread in the 1980s. The money spent would be vast and the results deadly. The kingdom had an ally of convenience in its endeavors, the United Arab

Emirates—a small country with the ambitions of a big military power and a staunch ally of the United States.

In 2008 and 2009, the Saudi ambassador was already sending cables to Riyadh detailing Egypt's concerns about how Iran was courting Egyptians through cultural and religious exchanges. In another cable, the ambassador alerted Riyadh to Iran's efforts to "infiltrate" Al-Azhar. The institution had opened its doors to Shia students from Lebanon in 2007 and was responding favorably to an Iranian suggestion to open an Azhari institute in Iran and to welcome students from Iran to Al-Azhar in Egypt.

By 2012, a year after the fall of Mubarak, the tone of the Saudi diplomatic missives had become more alarmist. The Saudi intelligence services were reporting to higher-ups about the "Shia movement" in Egypt, which they claimed was enjoying newfound freedom in post-revolution Egypt, demanding more space to practice their faith, a bigger say in the writing of the constitution, and the right to form a party. Al-Azhar was apparently also sounding the alarm: it shared its concern with Saudi diplomats and asked for help to counter Iran's alleged proselytizing. The number of Shias in the country was hotly debated—most experts put it at several hundred thousand; the state had a more inflated number of one or two million. Even that was minuscule in a country of 90 million, and no amount of conversions could really qualify as a national security threat.

Sheikh al-Tayyeb of Al-Azhar had publicly and forcefully spoken about the dangers of the "rising Shia surge, in the land of Sunnis, in the vicinity of the minaret of Al-Azhar." In May 2012, Al-Azhar launched a campaign to warn against the dangers of conversions to Shiism, with pamphlets, conferences, and lectures in youth clubs.

There was no doubt that the 1980s—with the Iran-Iraq War and alleged Iranian plots to provoke unrest in Egypt—had colored how official Egypt, as opposed to popular Egypt, dealt with its Shia minority, harassing and imprisoning them to the point where Mubarak had declared, in 2005, that Shias could only be loyal to Iran—a fifth column. This was a Saudi line par excellence. Were Al-Azhar's fears in 2012 founded? Were they the result of Saudi whisperings in the ears of its sheikhs and years of carefully cultivating the institution? Either way, Al-Azhar's campaign against Shiism was having an impact—an inadvertently violent one.

—

In the early days of summer 2013, anti-Shia posters went up in the small town of Abu Musallam, twenty miles south of Cairo. They were signed by a Salafist organization under the headline THE CAMPAIGN AGAINST THE SHIA SURGE. In their sermons, the town's clerics denounced the Shias as unbelievers. A procession went through the town, clerics and young men brimming with rage and screaming "No to the Shias." A few weeks later, on June 23, Shia townsmen gathered in the privacy of one of their homes to celebrate a mawled. One of their guests was a well-known cleric, Hassan Shehata, a former Sunni imam for the Egyptian army. Shehata was a rare example of someone who had converted to Shiism in the 1990s and become a vocal critic of Saudi-style Salafism and Wahhabism.

A mob started gathering around the house in the afternoon, dozens and then hundreds, hurling stones at the house, then Molotov cocktails, calling Shehata's name. They scaled the walls, climbed onto the roof of the two-story house, and tore a hole through its flimsy concrete ceiling. Hoping to calm the crowd and save those inside the house, including women and young children, Shehata came out, followed by three others. But the rage of the crowd overpowered them. The mob beat them with metal rods, threw them to the ground, stomped on them, tied their hands, and dragged them through the streets. The police arrived eventually. The four men were already dead.

Where did that blind hatred come from?

On Wesal television, they celebrated Shehata's violent death with glee. Wesal TV was one of the many virulently sectarian satellite channels that had sprung up in the decade since the Iraq War. There were some one hundred twenty religious stations across the region and an estimated twenty of them were spouting anti-Shia or anti-Sunni vitriol. Wesal TV was Sunni, operating out of Saudi Arabia and trying to build a Salafist media empire with news channels in various languages, some of which broadcast out of London. Its stated goal was "to expose the Safavid enterprise," a euphemism for Iran.

Abdulrahman Dimashqieh, a Lebanese Salafist preacher with a minor following, was a guest on one of the channel's talk shows to comment on Shehata's death. "I'm very happy he died, he deserved it . . . Of course, we don't approve of the way he was killed, we didn't call for his killing . . . But I'm joyful. I'm not simply satisfied with God's justice having been carried out, I'm joyful," Dimashqieh told the show's host. Then he looked straight into the camera and smiled. "I'm joyful."

"Praise be to God," said the anchor. This was a typical answer, denying any responsibility for creating the atmosphere in which the killing had become permissible while signaling clearly that it was halal, permissible by religion. In the bottom left corner of the screen, the words "Iran is killing our brothers" flashed under a small Iranian flag, which fluttered and then tore in half.

In 2017, nine men would be sentenced to fourteen years in jail for She-hata's murder. But Egypt had crossed into dark territory. For Ebtehal, as for most Egyptians, it was incomprehensible. She saw the rise of sectarian hatred as a direct result of Saudi influence and politics "This is not our fight," she kept saying. Saudi Arabia left no one indifferent. Its check-book diplomacy, its influence and power, real or imagined, was either praised or deeply resented. There were grand statements about how the whole of Al-Azhar had become a Wahhabi institution, claims that every mosque in Egypt received funding from Saudi Arabia and that every Quran reciter had adopted the purposely monotonous, joyless Saudi-style cadence. The statements were sweeping and often uninformed, but they reflected how many Egyptians had come to view Saudi intentions: negative and nefarious.

The Saudis and the Emiratis were busy working behind the scenes with the army to help bring about Morsi's downfall. Morsi was only helping, by accumulating mistakes and pushing for extraordinary presidential powers, immunity, and a constitution with strong Islamist tenets. The people began to turn on him. The revolutionaries of Tahrir Square had not signed up for a power grab by an Islamist. On June 30, millions of Egyptians took to the street, clamoring for Morsi's departure. Ahmed was among them. His father was a member of the Muslim Brotherhood, but Ahmed had long ago rejected religion and he wanted Morsi out. The army was poised, egging on the protesters, flying its jets overheard in support. The military coup could now be depicted as a response to the will of the people.

The Saudis and the Emiratis cheered when Morsi was overthrown, on July 3, 2013. They quickly pledged $8 billion in cash and loans to help the transitional government. The crackdown on Morsi supporters protesting the coup a month later was bloodier than any past repression of the Broth-erhood, bloodier than anything anyone had seen: at least 817 protesters dead, the largest killing of demonstrators in a single day in recent history, anywhere in the world, surpassing the estimated toll of the 1989 Tian-anmen Square massacre. Ahmed's father, a doctor, had been there, too— the family had frantically searched for him, but he escaped the bloodbath unscathed. He was shocked to find that in his village, he was now being shunned by neighbors and friends, people whose children he had attended to as a doctor. Society was turning on itself.

Morsi and most of the Muslim Brotherhood leadership ended up in jail, hundreds of its members sentenced to die in the course of the following year. In 2019, after six years of solitary confinement and inadequate health care, Morsi would collapse during a court hearing and die from cardiac arrest. The organization was banned. Field Marshal Abdel Fattah Sissi, friend of Saudi Arabia and once a military attaché at the Egyptian embassy in Saudi Arabia, oversaw the crackdown. He was elected president in May 2014.

The power of the people was buried under the rubble—not dead, but barely alive. Cairo was still hell, a city where, in Ahmed's futuristic, fantastical novel, "life is one long wait, and the smell of trash and assorted animal dung hangs about all the time and everywhere . . . Cairo's not what you'd expect from a city of its size. In spite of its teeming millions, this is a city that is hopelessly repressed. A coalition of social, political, and religious taboos conspire to keep everything that ferments in the city's underbelly from rising to the surface." Ahmed had written *Using Life* before the revolution, before the rage rose to the surface, but the book was published in the summer of 2014, by which time the rage had come to naught. The action was set in modern-day Cairo, but a Cairo that had been eviscerated by sandstorms, which had also killed millions and even subsumed the pyramids into sinkholes. Ahmed never mentions Mubarak, Morsi, or Sissi, but his novel is about the dueling instincts of inertia and rage that propelled young Egyptians to the streets and then forced them to retreat.

The protagonist's sexual encounters with his older girlfriend Mona are described in explicit, lightly erotic detail, there's a lot of hash smoking, and the conversations are laced with crude words, the same way they litter the everyday sentences of many Arabs, except the most devout ones. "You're nothing but a cocksucker among cocksuckers. Quit the drama, little one, and enough blaming yourself. In the end, it's not so bad to be a cocksucker in Cairo. Just relax and take it all in." Inertia in a riotous novel, one that unexpectedly landed Ahmed in jail.

The book had been approved by the censors before publication— perhaps his metaphors about modern-day Egypt were beyond their grasp. Most of them were familiar with every curse word on the pages. But an excerpt, published in the *Akhbar al-Adab* literary review magazine where Ahmed worked, had made its way into the home of a prudish citizen, who claimed that upon reading the sexually explicit language, his heartbeat had faltered and he had keeled over. Just as in Nasr Abu Zeid's apostasy case in the 1990s, here was a private citizen coming forward as a censor, this

time as a guardian of society's morals. Ahmed didn't expect a sentenc-
ing and was initially acquitted. But in February 2016, the case came alive
again mysteriously, and an appeals court sentenced him to two years in
jail. Thanks to the prowess of his legal team, he was released early, after ten
months of shivering cold and sweats, of cockroaches and humiliation—
but he remained embroiled in a Kafkaesque bureaucratic limbo, forbidden
from leaving the country for unknown, unknowable reasons.

Ahmed was comforted by the support he received from fellow writers
and artists—650 of them had signed a petition calling for his release. Former officials spoke in his favor, even the policeman taking him to court
told him he didn't deserve the sentence. If Nasr had been tried today,
thought Ahmed, he too would have received a flood of support. Perhaps
the trial would have ended differently, perhaps he wouldn't even have been
exiled. Cairo may have been a hell in Ahmed's novel, but in today's Egypt
he could actually publish it and be supported for doing so. There were no
death threats—though admittedly he had not written about religion.

Ebtehal saw things very differently. There was a generational divide;
the bar of expectations about quality of life and space for freedom of
expression had been lowered almost to the ground. The vigorous debates
of her youth about the role of religion in society were shut down the day
she and Nasr got on a plane to Europe. The rise of religion had pervaded
all aspects of cultural and social life. Just as Mehtab saw it in the small
details in Pakistan, Ebtehal felt it here: the call to prayer as mobile phone
ringtones; the recordings of the traveler's prayer in elevators; the aggressive, violent harassment of women on the streets. As a young woman in the
1960s, her own mother had walked the streets of Cairo in a skirt and short
sleeves and no one had batted an eyelid.

Ahmed's generation had no memory of those days, of the social and
political plurality of the past, the plethora of choices; they had come of age
in the 1990s with the constant din of religion dominating the debate. For
them, it felt as though space was finally opening up for *more* debate, that
the future could still be a more progressive place. Ahmed's book had been
approved by the censors. He had been released early. The young writer saw
the Muslim Brotherhood rise to power and fail, its aura finally burst by
the reality of governing. He saw women removing the veil, disillusioned
by religion; he saw women waiting on him in cafés late at night. If Ebtehal
felt that the past was another country, Ahmed saw a different, better future
in the making.

And so he often wondered: Had he really ended up in jail because he had written about cocks and pussies—or was it because of his columns? Ahmed had strong opinions about Saudi Arabia, and he didn't hide them. The kingdom's diplomats not only kept track of Shias, Al-Azhar, and alleged conversions, but also kept tabs on journalists and their writing. Some journalists did knock on the Saudi mission's door, hoping to be rewarded for favorable coverage. The embassy hired one of them to set up its media relations department in 2012, paying him $200,000 while he was still working as the anchor of a talk show and sat on the board of a major Egyptian newspaper. Except for the number of zeros at the end of the sums, things had not changed much since the 1990s, when Egyptians working for Saudi-owned newspapers engaged in self-censorship to flatter the kingdom. In 2010, Ahmed had received a bizarre phone call from the Saudi embassy, telling him he was banned from visiting the kingdom, even though he had never even applied for a visa and had no desire to visit. But he wrote often about the kingdom, sometimes with disdain, but always with piercing insight.

In early July 2014, while doing some research for an article, he had unearthed an old copy of an Egyptian magazine, *Al Lata'if al-Musawwara*, which had published the report of the Indian delegation returning from the Arabian Peninsula in 1926, the one that had demanded that the Al-Sauds hand over control of the two holy cities, after the warriors of Abdulaziz had conquered the Hejaz province. There were black-and-white pictures from Mecca and Medina, of wrecked shrines and cratered walls, of ancient sites in a heap of rubble at the Jannat al-Baqi cemetery—all this destruction the calling card of ibn Abdelwahhab's descendants and the foundation on which the Saudi kingdom was built. Back then, the Ottoman Empire was crumbling, borders were disappearing, and the British were looking for a strong man to control these desert lands. According to Naji, it was just like now, in 2014, in Iraq but also Syria, where the popular revolution had splintered beyond recognition and any common vision for a democratic, pluralistic future had been bombed into deep retreat. A new mutation of an old demon was making headlines as hordes of men in black, waving black flags, erased modern borders and conquered land, not on horses or camels as in 1926, but in pickup trucks and armored personnel carriers. They leveled shrines, smashed statues, and blew up Shia mosques.

They were not establishing a kingdom but reverting to the times of the prophet and claiming they were establishing a caliphate. The Islamic State in Iraq and Syria was born, with Raqqa in Syria as its capital. The group would often be referred to by its Arabic acronym, Daesh, and Ahmed's article about the founding of Saudi Arabia was headlined THE DAESH OF 1926. He was one of the first to draw the parallel between Saudi Wahhabism and Daesh, better known in the West as ISIS. Ahmed's travel ban would last longer than Daesh's hold on territory, and though there were many differences between the kingdom and the caliphate, the parallels would be drawn by many, and they would stick, much to the frustration of Saudi Arabia.

17

BETWEEN ISIS AND IRGC

IRAQ AND SYRIA

2011–18

Where they burn books, in the end they will also burn people.
—Heinrich Heine (1797–1856)

Yassin al-Haj Saleh had never given up on his hopes for a country free of tyranny. At heart, he was still the idealistic young leftist student thrown in jail in the middle of the night in 1980. Sixteen years in a cell, some of them in Syria's notorious Tadmur prison, had not bent him. On the contrary, after his release in 1996, he moved to Damascus and picked up his pen to document life in prison, his own intellectual evolution, and Syria's transformation under the dictatorship. He wrote article after article, many published in *An-Nahar*, Lebanon's liberal newspaper. He was among a small group of intellectuals who continued to resist and speak out in Assad's Syria. That was how his country was branded by the dictator: *Souri-yya al-Assad*, the Syria of Assad, as though it were private property. Drilled into children's heads at school, written on the walls and on banners hanging from bridges, the phrase made clear there was no escaping the Assads, father and son. Then came 2011 and the Arab uprisings. Timid yearnings for freedom became a flood of people on the streets of Syria demanding the fall of the dictator. Millions took to the street. Yassin glimpsed the contours of a more hopeful future.

So how could it be that when he returned to his hometown of Raqqa, in the summer of 2013, he found himself at the epicenter of a conflict not his own, looking over the ruins of his life, having been robbed of his soul, his love, his family. Yassin and millions of Syrians were rebelling against tyranny, but their country found itself caught between the spiritual heirs of Ibn Abdel-wahhab and the upholders of Khomeini's legacy; between the Islamic State in Iraq and Syria (ISIS) and the Iranian Revolutionary Guard Corps (IRGC).

In the first few months of 2011, when there was still hope, Syrians had discovered each other and their own power as they broke out of the internal prison that had confined them throughout decades of dictatorship. They had even discovered careless joy and laughter, rare commodities in such conditions. Yassin was sharing this experience with the love of his life: Samira al-Khalil, also a former prisoner. They had met in 2000, and the vivacious woman, with wavy brown hair and deep-set dark green eyes, was his intellectual partner, his sounding board, his everything. Yassin and Samira dreamed of a life lived beyond the steel and psychological barriers of the Assad regime. On the streets, Syrians locked arms as they marched, waving flags and chanting, "There is no [president for] eternity, long live Syria, down with Assad." They believed they were succeeding, even when Assad's forces started shooting and sent tanks into cities. Abdul-Baset al-Sarout, Syria's beloved national soccer team goalkeeper, found a new calling: singing for the revolution.

> Paradise, paradise, O our homeland,
> O beloved homeland, and your noble soil
> Even your fire is paradise.

Hunted down within Syria, imprisoned by the thousands, the revolutionaries worked to build the critical mass necessary to bring down Assad. An opposition in exile, inept and divided, was in charge of dialogue with the world, calling for support to help the protesters on the ground grab territory from which they could then set up an opposition government and challenge Assad. In March 2011, President Obama had agreed to US military participation in an air mission, along with NATO and Gulf allies, to protect Libyan protesters from their dictator. So why not Syria?

Yassin was not an organizer. He was an intellectual, an activist, most of all he was a writer, and he documented the revolution relentlessly with his articles. He now wrote regularly for the pan-Arab daily *Al-Hayat*. He wrote an article every week, sometimes twice a week, holding up the torch of hope and bearing witness to the unraveling. He could not have foreseen that some of his articles would one day become a book under the title

The Impossible Revolution: Making Sense of the Syrian Tragedy. Though he knew the genocidal streak that ran in the Assad family, he never thought tragedy was inevitable. Throughout 2011 and 2012, Assad steadily lost his grip on large parts of the country. In Washington and European capitals, presidents and prime ministers believed his days were numbered. But they had underestimated the dictator with no conscience. He was the true heir of his father. He would make no concessions; his approach was "Assad, or we burn the country." And he would do just that.

The Syrian uprising and the subsequent brutal war have been characterized from many perspectives. Most cite big geopolitical events for saving Assad, like President Obama's reluctance to intervene as he had done in Libya, or his backing down from a promise to punish Assad for using chemical weapons against his people in 2013. But the longer the outside world allowed Assad to kill, torture, and imprison with impunity, the more the revolution fractured. The Syrian battle for freedom was in a race against the inexorable radicalization and militarization of any revolution that drags on too long. As rage and despair built up, the revolutionaries picked up arms, rebel factions formed and splintered. The revolution was also in a race against those who saw an opportunity in the chaos—two very different groups of men in black, bearing different flags, enemies in fact, had been scouting the terrain. They weren't even Syrians.

In August 2011, Abu Bakr al-Baghdadi, the Iraqi from Samarra, sent a scouting mission of seven or eight men from Iraq into Syria to assess how ripe the country was for his ambitions. Baghdadi was taking Zarqawi's dream of establishing an Islamic state to another level. His men found a country much like Iraq in the years after the US invasion: outside the large cities, men with guns roamed freely, state institutions were weak, and—most conveniently—Assad had released scores of Islamists from his jails, just as Saddam Hussein had done before the US invasion of 2003. This was a classic move: the dictator appears to show magnanimity at a time of unrest and declares an amnesty for prisoners, but alongside the intellectuals and activists, he releases into the wild those who will inflict chaos, so he can be called upon as the best option to bring peace. In Syria, some of the men released had fought in Iraq, groomed by Assad himself to make life miserable for the Americans in Iraq. Assad would jail the fighters as soon as they returned, letting them rot in prison until he next needed them. As he set them loose in 2011, he deviously warned the international community that the protesters were religious extremists, making him the architect of his own self-fulfilling prophecy. Baghdadi's men traveled west from Iraq into Syria, on desert highways and along rivers, a well-traveled road used by fighters who had gone in the opposite direction to join the insurgency in Iraq. In Syria, courtesy of Assad, they found a ready network of Salafist jihadists they could tap into to serve Baghdadi's grand designs of a borderless Islamic state. But without a revolution for freedom, there would have been no such opportunity.

At almost the same time, in Lebanon, hundreds of Lebanese and Syrian men were undergoing rigorous training under the leadership of Hezbollah in a remote part of the Beqaa Valley. The power of the organization had only grown since the 2005 assassination of Rafiq Hariri, Mr. Lebanon. It had survived the UN inquiry into the killing, although several of its operatives had been tried in The Hague in absentia for their involvement. They included Mustafa Badreddine, brother-in-law of Imad Mughniyeh, the man who had started the wave of suicide bombings in the 1980s. The group had also emerged intact from a devastating war with Israel in 2006. In the years that followed, it incited more political crises that brought down governments and pushed for cabinets more amenable to their needs. Their ambition and arsenal grew in tandem with Iran's work to solidify its stranglehold on Iraq. In the summer of 2011, Hezbollah was training its men to be prepared for everything: self-defense, municipal governance, religion, and how to run the infrastructure of a state. Even before the Syrian revolution had dissolved into an all-out war, Iran and Hezbollah had seen an opportunity to sink their claws into Syria and expand their power across yet more territory. Syria was convenient terrain, with a ruthless yet paradoxically weak president, a member of the "axis of resistance" who would soon need help to maintain power. Iran and Hezbollah were poised to step in.

Within a year of the uprising, Saudi Arabia had begun exploring how to arm the opposition: the Saudis wanted Assad gone so they could contain Iran's ambitions in Syria. In private, Saudi officials began to describe Assad as an occupier, a man with no legitimacy who was oppressing the majority with help from outside forces.

Few who watched the Syrian revolution rise and unfold thought back to 1979, but the echoes would be obvious in hindsight—except everything was worse, as though all the players picked up where they had left off after the jihad in Afghanistan, or the Iran-Iraq War, or the 2003 Iraq War. The son of Sa'id Hawwa, the Syrian Muslim Brotherhood ideologue, was involved; Surur, author of the *Magi* book, was playing a key role rallying the Islamists; even the son of Arif Hussaini, the assassinated Pakistani allama, would show up in Damascus to meet Shia fighters. With appetites sharpened, everyone returned to the battle with renewed vengeance. There would be rivers of blood, millions displaced, millions of refugees. The war in Syria would break the Middle East. It would break the world.

But first, it would destroy the lives of men like Yassin. In the fluid chaos of the revolution, he couldn't know all the details about the forces lurking in the background. He focused on the possibilities, on the Syrianness of the revolution and the goodness in Syrians' hearts; on the belief in the righteousness of their cause and their call for basic freedoms. He had always believed that the country's Islamists had to be included in a future, democratic country. Their exclusion for decades under Assad had solved nothing—in fact, the exclusion of Islamists was a blanket exclusion of all diverse forces, from left to right. He knew it wouldn't be easy to forge a common vision with Islamist parties, but he believed it possible. For two years, he had lived in hiding in Damascus, moving from neighborhood to neighborhood to escape capture. Hundreds of activists were being rounded up and thrown in jails, only to disappear. Evidence of torture and mass exterminations would emerge. At least Samira was not on any wanted list, so she could still move freely.

In the spring of 2013, Yassin was smuggled to areas outside the regime's control, fifteen miles northeast of Damascus, in Douma and Eastern Ghouta. Soon after the regime found out he had escaped, they began searching for Samira. She fled the capital and joined him. Still, they were not cowed. They got to work, helping local civilian committees that were setting up a semblance of self-rule, the template they hoped would prove that a local alternative to Assad was possible. With friends, they documented the regime's abuses, hoping for justice. When Raqqa fell into the hands of the Free Syrian Army and other rebel groups in March 2013, the first provincial capital to be captured by the opposition, there was much rejoicing. Statues of the dictator were pulled down. Yassin began to plan a trip to find out what freedom tasted like in his hometown. He was wary, but hopeful.

One of the rebel groups was an Islamist outfit, Jabhat al-Nusra, the Front of Support for the People of the Levant. In battle, they were one of the most successful. The United States had designated al-Nusra as a terrorist organization with links to al-Qaeda. Its leader was a Syrian who had fought the Americans in Iraq after 2003. But for the sake of bringing down Assad, the much weaker FSA was willing to accept anyone's help. In

Raqqa, the fighters of Jabhat al-Nusra were greeted as liberators; people overlooked their apparent extremism. In the growing chaos of the war, few Syrians believed that such groups would survive peacetime and play a role in Syria's future. But al-Nusra was a Trojan horse. The group's leader was a friend of Zarqawi and Baghdadi, and al-Nusra was acting as a front for Baghdadi's grand project: a foothold in Syria. That spring, Baghdadi himself reportedly moved from Iraq to Syria. He wanted to speed up his project of an Islamic state, a caliphate where borders did not exist and where he would be the leader of all Muslims.

At around the same time, May 2013, Hezbollah sent hundreds of its top fighters into Syria to help Assad's forces recapture the small border town of Qusayr. Hezbollah was already assisting Assad's regime in Syria but had not yet acknowledged its role publicly. The battle lasted seventeen days. Hezbollah lost at least a hundred fighters, with dozens more wounded. But they recaptured the town and, with it, control over a strategic corridor that rebels had been using to bring weapons into Syria. The battle of Qusayr was a watershed moment: Hezbollah tipped the balance back in the regime's favor. It would pour more and more men into the war, becoming a party to the conflict. The head of the IRGC's al-Quds force, Qassem Suleimani, attended some of their funerals, as early as February 2013, when one of his comrades from the war against Saddam was among the first Iranians killed there. "Syria is the front line of the resistance. We will support Syria till the end," Suleimani declared. For him, the Assad regime and Syria were part of his grand ambition to build his own borderless empire, just like Baghdadi, except this one would be loyal to the wilayat al-faqih. Iran was again pursuing "war, war until victory"—even if victory looked like devastation on someone else's land.

From Egypt to Saudi Arabia, clerics were incensed by Iran's daring. So incensed that, for the first time, clerics preaching in the Holy Mosque in Mecca called on Sunni Muslims to help their Syrian brothers, by all means, including arms.

As elite members of the Quds force and Hezbollah fighters fanned out across Syria, al-Nusra set up a shari'a court in Raqqa. They attacked other rebel groups. They assassinated FSA commanders. They berated women who didn't veil. On the outskirts of Raqqa, men with black flags gathered, then streamed into the city in convoys of white pickup trucks. Throughout the summer, more men arrived, most of them Iraqis. They eliminated rivals from the FSA and other rebel groups. Slowly but ruthlessly, Baghdadi's men seized control of Raqqa, even taking over most of al-Nusra. In

April 2013, Baghdadi announced that a new organization was formed: the Islamic State in Iraq and Syria.

By the time Yassin made it to Raqqa that summer—an arduous, nineteen-day journey through empty desert land and under the scorching sun to evade the authorities—he found a black flag planted at the entrance of the city, signaling conquered territory. Most of the men in black with guns and long beards were foreigners: Iraqis but also Tunisians, Saudis, Egyptians, even Europeans. They walked around like they owned the city. Yassin wanted to go for a stroll, smell the gardens, hear the nearby river. Instead, he had to hide indoors, coming out only briefly at night. He had become a stranger in his hometown, a potential target on the very streets where he had roamed freely as a teenager. Worse, he had arrived to devastating news: his two brothers had been kidnapped by ISIS. One was a local council member, and as ISIS took control, it detained men who resisted its agenda, men like Yassin's brothers. By the summer of 2013, ISIS had taken up a large building in Raqqa as headquarters. Yassin stayed in touch with Samira, who had remained in Douma. They had initially planned for her to join him once he established a safe route, but the situation Yassin found in Raqqa did not permit that. They spoke often over Skype video calls as she updated him about how life was getting harder in areas that were free of government forces but now under siege—Assad was starving them into capitulation.

On August 21, 2013, Yassin almost lost Samira forever. The Syrian regime forces had launched an attack with chemical weapons against Eastern Ghouta, the opposition-held area outside Damascus that included Douma. Up to fourteen hundred people died. The sight of children gasping, foaming at the mouth, and whole families killed in their sleep galvanized world opinion again—two years into the rebellion. But only briefly. President Obama had previously warned Assad that the use of chemical attacks was a redline. Missile strikes against Damascus seemed imminent for days, until Washington and Moscow made a deal under which Assad would give up his chemical weapons. America did not want to go to war and Assad survived. The message seemed to be that he could kill his people with any weapon he wanted, except chemical weapons. Samira and her friends had witnessed everything and they had survived. That episode was an inflexion point for Syria and the world. Assad had broken international law with no consequences; left to die by the world, sensing that Assad would feel emboldened, thousands more Syrians fled the country, on foot and by sea. Trying to get as far away as they could, they headed to Europe. Assad's allies, Russia and Iran, would now pour even more effort into shoring him up, and by 2015 Russia would intervene militarily with air strikes and special operations forces on the ground to help Assad further. And so the ranks of jihadist groups swelled with rage and recruits: more foreigners arrived, more Syrians joined, even men who had never been religious and preferred a drink to prayer. In their despair there was nothing left to hold on to but guns and religion. Early on in the revolution, Sarout, the Syrian goalkeeper, had joined the ranks of the Free Syrian Army. But the FSA was disintegrating. There were no good options for good men. So Sarout joined an Islamist rebel group. He grew a beard. He stopped singing.

—

In Raqqa, Yassin pondered the strange fate of his city, which could have been the capital of free Syria, or the headquarters of the IRGC. When Yassin was released from prison in 1996, he had returned to Raqqa to embrace his parents, brothers, and sister. Deep in the Syrian hinterland, both neglected and exploited by the state for years, the city of his youth was conservative but not Islamist. Society was patriarchal and traditional, but men and women mixed somewhat freely; more women were going to college. They wore T-shirts and dresses, or long flowing abayas and a loose veil if they were more conservative. But Yassin also noticed something he had never seen during his youth: women covered in a black cloak from head to toe, their faces behind niqabs. One of his relatives was among the thousands of Syrians who'd worked in the Gulf. A failure at school, this man had amassed a bit of wealth and Saudi customs: his wife, in turn, had adopted the Saudi garb. At the time, Yassin didn't pay it too much mind. It all felt like a fashion that people would grow out of, just a passing fad.

What felt very permanent was the construction site funded by Iran. A huge new structure was rising on the southeastern edge of the city, where the cemetery used to be. In 1988, local residents had been given three months to move the tombs of their loved ones to a new location. Left behind were two simple concrete tombs, long believed to be the burial site of two companions of the prophet, both killed in battle in 657. For centuries, the tombs had been a site of veneration by Raqqawis and local tribesmen. Sufis came too, and women prayed to be granted husbands and children. Over centuries, Shias and Sunnis had alternated claiming the saints as theirs. The new project was funded by Iran, and the architecture was typically Iranian: two square structures, each topped by a dome and flanked by a minaret, on either side of a fifty-meter-long esplanade with arches. When the mosque was completed in 2004, it was not just the largest Shia shrine in Syria, bedecked in beautiful, Persian blue tiles, but also an Iranian outpost in the Sunni hinterland, complete with portraits of Khomeini and Khamenei. Raqqawis had tried to stop the construction—these were their saints, their pilgrimage sites. The complex deprived them of their traditions and collective memory. There were no Shias anywhere nearby, but Iranian pilgrims began to flock to the site, clerics from Hezbollah spoke at the mosque, and the Iranian cultural center in Aleppo organized rallies there. There were attempts to convert locals to Shiism as well. Iran's efforts to invest and lay claim to Shia religious sites in Syria—even going as far as reinventing them—were all part of a strategy to expand its authority beyond its borders. Some of this effort had started as early as May 1979, just months after the Iranian Revolution, when a huge piece of land adjoining the Sayyeda Zaynab shrine in Damascus had been expropriated and turned over to a joint Iranian-Syrian construction company that would build hotels in the vicinity of the shrine to accommodate an ever-growing number of Shia pilgrims. Visited by Sunnis for centuries, the shrine became an exclusively Shia experience, an Iranian project.

—

In January 2014, ISIS declared Raqqa the capital of the new caliphate. In March, ISIS blew up the Iranian outpost in Raqqa. It had long been desecrated, with graffiti on the walls declaring it a Sunni mosque; the portraits of Khomeini and Khamenei were removed and destroyed. After the explosions, Hezbollah and Iran could justify their involvement in the war in Syria by claiming they had to protect Shia shrines. Groups like ISIS and other Islamists could brandish sites as proof that Iran was trying to take over Sunni land. A religious war had been invented by men hungry for power, land, and guns. Sunnis across the Arab world, especially in the Gulf, began donating to support fellow Sunnis fighting against Assad and the Iranian project. Much of the money made its way to jihadist groups. Iran began recruiting more fighters from farther afield: hundreds of Shias from Pakistan and Afghanistan made their way to Iraq and Syria.

Meanwhile, the two hundred thousand inhabitants of Raqqa were suddenly given a gruesome lead role they had never asked for. Yassin's hometown would make global headlines and become synonymous with inhuman suffering. The reign of terror began with a crucifixion: two people shot and crucified in the city's public square, left for days for all to see. Another crucifixion followed. Then came a group execution of men who appeared to be defeated rebels from a rival group. The executioners cut heads off bodies and planted them on fence posts. Raqqa had never seen public violence of this kind; no one in Syria had. Even Assad conducted his torture and executions behind walls. ISIS wanted to instill fear so extreme as to elicit obedience. Women were required to veil and cover their faces. Soon they would hardly dare leave the house. An all-female morality police, the Khansaa brigade, which included foreigners, began to patrol ruthlessly. Schools were closed for months and reopened only when ISIS had redesigned the curriculum to mirror its ideology. ISIS promoted its violence as a spectacle, with a media operation that produced slick videos, grabbing the headlines in the Western media, while Assad's secret industry of torture and executions continued to swallow thousands of Syrians.

That spring and throughout the summer, Baghdadi and his men launched a spectacular offensive that took the world by surprise—especially President Obama and his administration, who had dismissed ISIS as a minor player on the scene, thereby justifying America's lack of intervention. Months of preparation went into the plan as Baghdadi's men fanned out across Syria, setting up local governing infrastructures, hunting down FSA rebels, and recruiting more men. In Iraq, ISIS freed some five hundred prisoners, many of them from the Zarqawi days, men who would swell the ranks of a rapidly growing force. Baghdadi fueled the flames with a wave of shocking bomb attacks that would drive Sunnis into the arms of his organization, seeking protection as the state continued to fail them. The big offensive began on June 5, from Baghdadi's hometown of Samarra. Within days, columns of men, packed onto the back of pickups, or driving military vehicles stolen from the Iraqi army, overran land from Mosul in northeast Iraq across the border and into Syria. The Iraqi army collapsed as Baghdadi's men took town after town, seizing control over territory that stretched from just outside Baghdad all the way up to the Turkish border. It was a stunning defeat: several thousand lightly armed men facing down a national army twenty times larger, much of it equipped by the Americans. The loot was worth millions. The control over oil fields brought in even more. But victory in the name of a caliphate was invaluable for the zealots; it was a victory against history.

The territory had a rich cultural past. Far from re-creating it, Baghdadi brought with him a sledgehammer to smash history into smithereens, trying to eradicate the collective identity of millions. Iraq and Syria, cradles of ancient civilizations, were losing not only their future but also their past. In Mosul, ISIS burned down or ransacked centuries-old libraries, destroying invaluable manuscripts and maps. In the ancient Assyrian city of Nineveh, a pneumatic drill was used to gouge out the eyes of a nine-ton winged bull statue, once a symbol of the power of Assyrian kings. In Syria, ISIS destroyed an ancient Greek settlement that included the world's oldest known church and synagogue. The site had been so well preserved through the centuries that it was referred to as the Pompeii of the Syrian Desert. ISIS destroyed two of its temples and later beheaded the archaeologist who had looked after the site for forty years. There is always looting and wanton destruction in war, but this was purposeful, ruthless, and relentless vandalism. ISIS justified these brutal acts by claiming it was fighting polytheism and idolatry. Baghdadi was also turning his back on the long tradition of caliphs who had encouraged art, history, and literature.

Not since the founding of the modern Saudi state had there been such a cultural rampage in the Middle East, such bizarre, misguided obsession with breaking statues and shrines. And not since the days of Muhammad ibn Abdelwahhab and the first Saudi state had there been such fanatical zeal in eliminating those who were outside the narrow confines of an extremely puritanical worldview. The comparisons with Wahhabism and Saudi Arabia, identified early by Ahmed, the novelist in Egypt, began to abound. In Saudi Arabia, many watched with deep anguish the destruction of Syrian and Iraqi heritage, a violent gesture that was all too common in the kingdom. The Saudi journalist Jamal Khashoggi recognized much of what was happening in Syria from his time covering the Afghan jihad: the eagerness of young men to join a cause, the desire to defend fellow Sunnis against an enemy, a haphazard effort by the government to help, guns flowing freely, extreme ideas taking hold.

Jamal looked at ISIS and he saw Wahhabism untamed, in its purest form.

Indeed, members and supporters of the group wrote pamphlets describing Baghdadi as walking in the footsteps of Ibn Abdelwahhab, continuing his mission of upholding extreme monotheism while fighting idolatry and imposing Islamic law on seized territory.

Saudi Arabia vehemently rejected the comparisons with ISIS and pointed out that the group had in fact declared war against the kingdom. It was true that Saudi Arabia had neither funded nor armed ISIS, and it was also true that ISIS had the kingdom in its sights—but this was because the zealots believed the House of Saud had strayed from the true mission of Ibn Abdelwahhab. ISIS was Saudi progeny, the by-product of decades of Saudi-driven proselytizing and funding of a specific school of thought that crushed all others, but it was also a rebel child, a reaction to Saudi Arabia's own hypocrisy, as it claimed to be the embodiment of an Islamic state while being an ally of the West.

Yassin did not spend much time studying the nuances of ISIS's theological differences with other Salafist militant groups. This was primarily because more than 90 percent of the half million people who had died in Syria had been killed by Assad, while the West was obsessed with the phenomenon that was ISIS. But Yassin also saw most violent Islamists as mere nihilists intent on destruction. So while he understood why Syrians or Iraqis might have joined out of despair after being abandoned by the world, out of necessity, or perhaps out of conviction that this was a righteous path, he had no time for foreign Muslims from Europe or Arab countries who swarmed places like Raqqa, acting like the new colonizers or settlers. And he cared nothing for Saudi Arabia's efforts to distance itself from ISIS—the kingdom may not have directed the rise of this cult of fanatics, but it had done more than enough to feed the various Islamic nihilists who were hijacking the revolution and destroying Syria. One of the men that Saudi Arabia had backed in the Syrian war had ripped out Yassin's heart.

On December 9, 2013, at 10:40 p.m., a group of masked, armed men had barged into the office in Douma where Samira was working along with three friends: Razan Zeitouneh, Wael Hamada, and Nazem Hammadi. Razan was one of the founders of the Violations Documentation Center, which tracked human rights abuses. She had received threats before from a group calling itself the Army of Islam, Jaysh al-Islam, but no one took them seriously. For a while after Samira and her colleagues were kidnapped, Yassin was in denial, hoping they would be released quickly. But days, then weeks, then months passed—and nothing. Yassin was already in exile; in October, he had fled to Turkey. Samira had been worried about his safety in Raqqa and had pressed him to leave. They had been looking for ways to get her out of Syria as well. Now he had lost his homeland, his brothers, his soul mate. He may have felt broken, but he didn't buckle. He kept writing, calling out the monsters. "[Samira's] abductors represent an Islamist re-creation of the cruelty against which the revolution originally erupted," Yassin wrote a few months later in a newspaper article. "The case of Samira and her colleagues represents the case of Syria, trapped between the regime, the embodiment of brutality, and the Islamists, the embodiment of inhumanity. For the two, the prisons were the first thing they cared about in whatever area they control."

The leader of Jaysh al-Islam was Zahran Alloush, son of a Salafist preacher from Douma, who had trained in Saudi Arabia, where he remains to this day. Alloush himself had studied at the Islamic University of Medina. Back in Syria, his Salafist activism landed him in jail in 2009, but he was one of the many Islamists that Assad had released in 2011. Alloush started his own faction, which slowly grew into a brigade and then a small army, thanks to generous funding that flowed to him from his family contacts in Saudi Arabia. He, too, wanted to build a theocracy ruled by Islamic law, an Islamic state, just a bit less brutal than ISIS. He called for a Syria cleansed of Shias. But he had no ambitions outside Syria and he did not behead Westerners, so he made fewer headlines. When it became clear at the end of 2013 that the United States would not intervene on behalf of Syrian rebels, Saudi Arabia decided to throw its weight and checkbook behind Alloush, spending millions to train and arm his group. Alloush even traveled to Saudi Arabia to meet with officials. But while the Saudis knew how to throw money at a problem, they had no real ability to follow through on their strategy. Money was flowing to Syria from other Gulf countries, like Qatar and Kuwait. Instead of working together toward a common goal, rivalries emerged among the Gulf countries as they fought for influence in Syria. America's disinterest in helping bring down Assad continued to function as a rallying cry: hundreds of jihadists and wannabe jihadists, but also losers of all kinds, flocked to Syria. Some joined al-Nusra, others joined ISIS. They came from Europe, from Russia, from Egypt and Jordan. After Tunisia, the largest number of Arab fighters came from Saudi Arabia—although the number was lower per capita in relation to the size of the kingdom's population.

In exile, Yassin watched as these foreigners laid claim to his country and stole the Syrian revolution, not just the Sunni ones but also the Shias—the biggest group of foreign fighters was in fact on Iran's side. Iran had been recruiting actively all the way in Pakistan and Afghanistan. Estimates put the numbers of Shia fighters in Syria anywhere between twenty thousand and eighty thousand. They were Iran's very own transnational army. Iran was also chipping away at its project to build a contiguous area of influence from Iran through Iraq into Syria and all the way to Lebanon. In Syria, it was forcing demographic changes by implanting families of Shia fighters of various nationalities or displaced families from Iraq in areas around Shia shrines; there were population swaps, and Syria's few Shias from villages deep in Sunni areas were moved to villages in areas under Assad and Iran's control. Hezbollah was using the template that had served so well in Lebanon to build a "resistance society" in Syria, setting up Islamic Mahdi scouts, offering public services, and caring for families of martyrs.

In a few more years, Yassin's hometown and vast areas of Iraq, including large parts of Mosul, would be little more than a pile of rubble, devastated by a US-led bombing campaign to defeat ISIS. The destruction would defy belief, with whole city blocks flattened. The toll on civilians was shocking: hostages of ISIS in their own city for four years, they would die in air strikes meant to liberate them. Whole families were wiped out in an instant; sixteen hundred civilians were killed during months of shelling. But by October 2017, America could claim victory against ISIS. The Iranians would be quick to come back to Raqqa, to rebuild the shrines ISIS had blown up.

In the end, the most emblematic confrontation between ISIS and the IRGC happened not in Raqqa but seven hours away on the southernmost point of the Syrian border with Iraq, at the crossing of al-Tanf, in the summer of 2017. ISIS launched a surprise attack against a Syrian government border post where IRGC advisers were positioned. The battle lasted over two hours, leaving only one Iranian alive, Mohsen Hojaji, a twenty-six-year-old officer who was captured and paraded in front of the cameras. He looked stoically at the lens of his captors, resigned to meet his fate. An ISIS fighter with blood on his cheek held Hojaji by the arm, a knife pressed against his skin. Two days later, the young Iranian was beheaded, in a gruesome video that ISIS made public.

In Iran, resentment had been rising about the country's costly involvement in wars outside its borders. Hundreds of Iranians had died in the fighting in Iraq and Syria. Hojaji's death, his haunting face and stoic look, briefly united Iranians. His body was given a hero's welcome. Then Hojaji's widow, clad in a black chador, said the strangest thing: Hojaji had died to preserve a woman's right to wear the veil. He had lost his head, she said, so Iranian women could continue to cover theirs. As though, since 1979, the Iranian Revolution had been about one thing: a woman's modesty. For some in Iran, it certainly was beginning to feel that way.

18

ACHILLES' HEEL

IRAN

2014–19

I think about it and yet I know
I'll never be able to leave this cage
Even if the warden should let me go
I've lost the strength to fly away.
—Forough Farrokhzad, "Captive" (1958)

Masih Alinejad had long since removed her veil and embraced her mane of curls, untamable—just as she was. Hers had been a long journey, from the girl born in 1976 in a poor village near the Caspian Sea, whose father had joined the morality police, the Basij, during the revolution, to the rebellious teenager who asked too many questions, to the confident forty-year-old woman revolting against the system, first in Iran and then in exile since 2009. Growing up, she had been taught that she would have molten metal poured into her ears on Judgment Day if she listened to music—the same threat seared into the brain of Sofana Dahlan, the young woman in Jeddah. Worlds apart, separated by the abyss of the Saudi-Iran rivalry, they had grown up in very different circumstances. They didn't know each other and probably would never meet, but they were the same age, facing similar restrictions on their choices, their minds, and their bodies. They were both a product of 1979, their lives shaped by the intractable dynamics that year had unleashed. In Iran, Masih had also learned that her honor and her family's honor were tied to the piece of cloth covering her hair. Even at school, her teacher had made clear, in no uncertain terms, that she would go to hell if she didn't wear the veil. So she wore it, dutifully, wrapped so tightly around her head it felt like a second skin. She wore it while she slept. All the women of the family kept it on even inside the home: a two-room mud house with no toilet and an outdoor fire pit as a kitchen.

Across Iran, many families had led double lives since 1979—a public one, where they abided by the rules, and a private life, where they broke all of them. Publicly, alcohol was banned, as was music. But there were still private parties where women and men danced together, everyone drank, and music played. Formal concerts were forbidden but there were private performances and garage bands. Satellite television dishes were banned but everyone owned one and hoped the neighbors wouldn't tell. Morality police patrolled the street, but boys and girls found ways to go away on weekends together. The secrecy was schizophrenic. As a result, children, unable to discern this intangible barrier, sometimes outed their parents without realizing it.

Masih's family had not led a double life. They had been true believers. Once clean shaven with a mustache, her father had grown a beard after 1979 and lectured young men about attending prayers. In 1989, at the age of twelve, Masih thought her world was going to end when Khomeini died. And yet, under her veil was not only rebellious hair but also a rebellious mind. The youngest of six, she was a tomboy and had asked her mother why she couldn't ride a bike like her brother. In high school, she asked her teacher why boys didn't wear the veil. Then came small, rebellious acts, like shedding the all-black chador she wrapped herself in to walk to school. Though she was still veiled, her father told her she had dishonored the family and refused to speak to her for two months. She soon began to aim higher, asking for more freedoms in what was the beginning of a lifelong quest to challenge authorities posing as wardens of the law of God. With a group of friends, she started writing and distributing an underground pamphlet; they spray painted the words "Freedom of Speech for All" on walls of a nearby town.

They were just teenagers from a small village, rebelling and pretending to be intellectuals. But in the Iran of the 1990s, that amounted to sedition, and she landed in jail for a month. More shame for the family. In jail, she found out she was pregnant before being officially married to her fiancé. She married and divorced before she was twenty-five. The rebellious streak that kept propelling Masih forward eventually led her to Tehran, where in 2000 she became an intern, later a parliamentary reporter, for *Hambastegi*, a national newspaper that was part of Iran's burgeoning reformist press under president Khatami. Masih wore red shoes and incensed her superiors. But she was good at her job: she knew where and how to dig to uncover scandals in parliament and make front-page headlines.

Despite the oppression ushered in by the Islamic Republic, Iran had never become a fully totalitarian state. Iranians were simply too argumentative, too cultured and cultural: within the sanctioned parameters, there were still surprises in elections, lively parliamentary debates, reformist media that pushed the agenda, and intellectuals of all classes, who kept writing, meeting, and sketching a different future. There was even a bold, controversial magazine, *Kiyan*, which published articles addressing religious pluralism and the role of clerics in politics. The publication had been founded by an intellectual of the revolution, Abdolkarim Soroush, who had played a key role in the cultural revolution that Islamized university curricula. But since the early 1990s, Soroush had been challenging the system from within, asking the same questions that the Egyptian intellectual Nasr Abu Zeid had been wrestling with. Soroush, like Nasr, wrote about hermeneutics and tried to understand the context in which the Quran had come into existence rather than accepting it as the uncreated word of God. And like Nasr, Soroush faced the wrath of those who saw themselves as true believers—he would be harassed and beaten by groups like Ansar-e Hezbollah, armed thugs that operated with the tacit approval of the state.

Kiyan would eventually be shut down, and Soroush would have to leave Iran in 2000. There had been hope that Khatami, a moderate, affable cleric, could steer the country out of its rigidity and transform the system without overthrowing it. But he wasn't delivering. Student protests in 1999 demanding more rapid reforms led to five days of rioting that turned Tehran into a battle zone as thousands of students chanted "Khamenei, shame on you, leadership is not for you." The Basij and other paramilitary groups were let loose into the crowds and beat the protesters. The unrest spread across the country in what was the worst challenge so far to the twenty-year-old Islamic Republic. But the system survived. And despite his failure to deliver change, Khatami was given another chance and reelected in 2001 for a four-year term, because even while he was one of the founders of the Islamic Republic, he was more moderate than his predecessors who had ruled since 1979.

In Tehran, as a journalist, Masih went into parliament, veiled like all Iranian women in public, and exposed a slush fund for legislators. With a black piece of cloth wrapped around her hair and a manteau made of blue denim, she caused a stir when she made public the salaries of legislators, revealing that they had not taken the promised pay cut. She kept pushing the envelope and making the front page. After rejecting the chador, Masih had begun to question the veil, but she still regarded the piece of cloth as a secondary problem in a country beset with more pressing issues. When she had called out for freedom of expression in Iran as a teenager, she was still endowing the Islamic Republic with her dreams. She believed you could fix the system, and then the issue of the veil would take care of itself. But increasingly she found that officials who were trying to deflect her questions would challenge her attire: she had a strand of hair showing, her shoes were red, her manteau was too colorful. They told her they would answer her questions when she practiced "good hijab." The veil was being used to shroud the country with a semblance of homogeneous unity, keeping women docile and silencing those who dared ask questions.

Masih began asking politicians about the veil. From the former president Rafsanjani to Khatami himself, she asked each man what he would do if, on a trip to France, where the veil had been banned in schools, his wife was asked to bare her hair. They responded that it would be an insult not only to Islamic values but to their wives' right to choose the veil. She had trapped them: What about the wives of foreign leaders who visited Iran? Didn't they have the right to choose? The politicians fidgeted. Rafsanjani admitted reluctantly that she had touched on a sensitive issue. Masih understood then that the veil, the hijab, was not a secondary issue, it was one of the ideological pillars of the revolution envisioned by Khomeini, part of the scaffolding holding up the structure—but it was also the Islamic Republic's Achilles' heel, because the women were suffocating. The women who had marched in 1979, chanting "in the dawn of freedom, there is no freedom," were still there, and with them a new generation of daughters, along with all those who had embraced the revolution before being disillusioned by it.

Iran's youth had big dreams, but those dreams were stuck in 1979— this was the legacy the Supreme Leader was trying to uphold and renew. Iran's youth were defying the system daily, even with strands of hair that showed from under a veil that was slipping farther back on their heads. Boys and girls were daring the religious police by holding hands on the street. Masih was pushing even harder, going too far with her questions and her scoops. She was harassed, interrogated, and finally her newspaper was pushed to fire her. She left the country to study English in London. When she tried to return in 2009 to cover the presidential elections, she was told she would end up in jail if she flew to Tehran.

In these elections, Ahmadinejad, Khatami's successor and president since 2005, had been headed for a loss and a moderate candidate, Mir-Hossein Mousavi, was expected to win. But Iran was consolidating its gains in the region in the aftermath of the 2003 US invasion of Iraq, and Ahmadinejad was serving the cause well. In the eyes of the Supreme Leader and people like Suleimani, this was not the time to change course with a softer image. The official results were announced soon after the polls closed: Ahmadinejad had won.

Three days after the election, two million people took to the streets in support of Mousavi, asking, "Where is my vote?" The spirited soul of the Iranian nation was alive and well—but again it was no match for the ruthlessness of a system ready to deploy all its weapons to stay in power. The Green Movement protests went on for three months; at least sixty-nine people were killed and hundreds imprisoned. Mousavi was put under house arrest and would remain so, with his wife, for years. All the while, Masih was unable to return to Iran. She had made waves abroad, writing about the repression inside her country and making a very public quest to interview Obama. In public, and whenever she gave television interviews, she still covered her hair—not with a veil, but with a hat or a cap. She was still unable to fully shed her second skin in public. And she still didn't want to disappoint her parents, who she knew could be watching.

In 2012, almost ten years after the US invasion of Iraq, two years into the Arab uprisings, Ahmadinejad's second term as president was coming to an end and Iran was feeling secure about its regional gains. But Khamenei and the Revolutionary Guards were increasingly worried about the sanctions that were squeezing Iran's economy—not only because they feared popular protests but because there was less revenue for them to siphon off. Khamenei decided to test the promise Obama had made on his first day in office to offer an "unclenched fist" if Iran extended its hand. Secret, direct negotiations between Iranian and American officials began in 2012 in Oman to explore lifting the sanctions on Tehran in exchange for Iran freezing its nuclear program. To help seal that much-needed deal, the Supreme Leader was ready to present a gentler face of Iran to the world. He watched as Hassan Rouhani was elected president in June 2013—another cleric from deep within the system, a centrist with a reputation for running the clock in negotiations with the West, letting talks drag on to maintain the impression of moderation and engagement but without making concessions. Rouhani promised hope and diplomacy and Iran's youth were ecstatic. They honked their horns as they drove around cities across the country. The pace of back-channel negotiations picked up and the talks soon became public.

In September 2013, a month after Obama backed down from launching strikes against Assad to punish him for using chemical weapons, he and President Rouhani spoke on the phone while they were both at the UN General Assembly. The Iranian foreign minister, Javad Zarif, and the US secretary of state, John Kerry, sat down for a tête-à-tête. It was the highest level of contact between the two countries since 1979.

The Saudis were shocked and felt deeply betrayed. They had long since moved on from the era of détente in the 1990s and had a particular aversion to back channels between Iran and the United States. They'd felt betrayed before by such talks, and it made them feel deeply insecure about their place in the Middle East and their role as America's top ally in the Arab world. The Saudi-US alliance, based on oil for security, had its limitations, and the relationship had been sorely tested by events like the September 11 attacks. Meanwhile, there were policymakers in Washington who felt Iran held more promise of turning into a democracy than a desert kingdom with an absolute monarchy. The Saudis were apoplectic when they heard such musings. The Obama administration also believed that if a deal could be reached while the reformers were in power, an improved economy would further strengthen the reformers and show how much the hardliners had failed the people.

Obama was hoping to bring more balance to America's posture in the Middle East. If Iran was less of a threat, the United States could decrease its military presence in the region. American troops had begun pulling out of Iraq in 2009, and there were none left by the end of 2011. Obama hoped to loosen the embrace that America had been locked into with Gulf states. He wanted to step back, to stand at equal distance from both Iran and the desert monarchies. Although the ultimate goal was to freeze the threat of an Iranian nuclear program, there was some merit to the broader approach. But it would ultimately fail—in part because, in its obsessive pursuit of a deal, the Obama administration did not appreciate how much the regional context had changed between the time the talks began in 2012 and the time they concluded in July 2015 and how this had adversely shaped perceptions of the deal and of America's standing among its allies in the region.

—

When the nuclear negotiations got under way, Masih was still in London, writing about repression in Iran and finding ways to connect with prisoners inside Tehran's infamous Evin prison so she could tell their stories. The abuses were continuing under Rouhani, an indication of the limited power of reformers. After living in the West for a few years, Masih was able to finally, fully embrace her wild, curly hair, and even posted a picture on her Facebook page that showed her running down a London street with cherry trees in full blossom. The wind was blowing through her hair, and she had her arms spread out. In the caption, she described how her hair was free after being held hostage for thirty years by those in power in the Islamic Republic. She had unknowingly started a campaign. Soon she was flooded with responses from women inside Iran who complained they did not have her freedom. But Masih remembered the moments of clandestine freedom that she and her friends would steal while she still lived there. So she posted pictures of her younger self with her hair cut short looking like a boy and hiking without a veil. A picture of herself driving from her village back to Tehran, without a veil. Iranians were constantly finding breaches in the fortifications that the Islamic Republic had built. And so Masih called on women inside Iran to send her pictures of their moments of stealthy freedom, *azadi yavashaki*.

The women were creative: they took pictures from behind, with glasses, their faces half turned away, in the shadow, or facing the camera with their heads bent back so only their chins would show, as well as their hair, hanging loose. Although their faces were not visible, the women were still taking a risk. But they had tasted freedom, and it was hard to let go. The pictures kept coming in. By the end of May 2014, the Facebook page that Masih had created, My Stealthy Freedom, had more than five hundred thousand fans. She had started a movement. Clearly, the veil was not a small issue—without a veil, women could not be outside, go to school, or get a job. As she explained her campaign to the Western press and Persian-language media, she kept emphasizing that she was not objecting to a piece of cloth but to the mandatory veil and the lack of choice. She was protesting against the men in power who stamped their ideology on women's bodies, on their hair. She dismissed those who told her about the progress women had made since the days of the shah, thanks to the Islamic Republic—when it came to female literacy rates and university enrollment, Iran had moved at the same pace as most of the region. But new limitations had been imposed since 1979: women judges had all been fired within weeks of the revolution, including Shirin Ebadi, the first female judge in Iran's history, who would go on to win a Nobel Peace Prize for her relentless human rights advocacy. In the 1960s, Iran boasted the first female cabinet ministers in the region; there were none after the revolution, until Khatami came to power in 1997. Although women were elected to the first parliament under Khomeini, segregation limited job opportunities for women. And, of course, the ban on music had severely undercut the art world, keeping divas like Googoosh at home, hoping endlessly for permission to return to the stage. She eventually went into exile in 2000.

The campaign that Masih had inadvertently launched took on a life of its own inside Iran, picking up momentum as women became more daring and sent pictures of themselves with their faces showing. Then they began sending videos, filming themselves walking on the street without a scarf. Often it was a husband, brother, or father filming them proudly, declaring solidarity with the women. There were women who wore the chador and declared their support for those who wanted the freedom to unveil. There were videos of altercations with religious police, clerics, and other women who believed in the necessity of veiling for all. Masih sifted through the videos and pictures and posted them on her social media channels. Soon her Instagram account would have more than two million followers. In one video, filmed in the female-only section of a metro car, a woman clad in black challenged the unveiled woman in front of her: "You're provoking the regime. Our men did not go to war so you could go out naked." Masih knew that argument, she'd heard it when her own brothers went to battle against Saddam's Iraq in the 1980s. The Iranian government had used the sacrifices of the thousands of men who died in a senseless war to silence dissent and demand submission as a show of respect for the martyrs who gave their lives for the nation. Iran's involvement in Syria to help Assad meant that Iranian men were again fighting and dying outside their own borders, and nationalism was once more wrapped up in a woman's modesty. Masih was incensed when she heard the widow of the IRGC officer Mohsen Hojaji, who had been beheaded by ISIS in Syria in August 2017, declare that her husband had lost his head so the women of Iran could keep covering theirs. How ironic, thought Masih, since he had died fighting in a country where women aren't forced to veil. By then, Masih was living in Brooklyn, and her campaign against the veil was beginning to unnerve the authorities. Hojaji's widow was wading in: "I'm asking people, for the sake of a wife of a martyr, a mother of a martyr, a sister of a martyr, to keep their hijabs."

Iran had initially kept its involvement in the war in Syria quiet. Men were dying but there was no official death toll. By 2017, the deaths were

in the hundreds and discontent was bubbling. The timing of Hojaji's gruesome death was fortuitous for the regime: it transfixed and briefly united
Iran, rallying everyone around the flag. His beheading in a desert landscape with smoke billowing in the background provided striking imagery
for posters embellished with Shia iconography. Qassem Suleimani of the
IRGC's al-Quds force made no secret of how Hojaji's execution served the
cause. "In order to glorify the significance of an issue, sometimes God
creates an incident," he said after the funeral. "Martyr Hojaji's death was
meant to provide further meaning and glory to the struggle for the defense
of the [holy Shia] shrines."

—

Six thousand miles away in Virginia, Mohsen Sazegara cried for Hojaji—
yet another senseless death. He cried for his country too, but mostly he
agonized over Syria. Mohsen, the young activist who had flown from Paris
to Iran with Khomeini and helped found the Revolutionary Guards, was
now in exile, just like Masih and so many others. His had been a long
and painful journey out of the Islamic Republic, with a harrowing detour
through its jails. Mohsen had so many regrets that they kept him up at
night. The revolution had been a huge mistake, and his generation had
so much to atone for—could the younger generations ever forgive what
had happened in 1979? Could Syrians ever forgive what Iran was doing
to their country? Iran's hands were soaked in Syrian blood. Iran had saved
Assad, and was just as responsible as the Syrian dictator for the horrors
that had unfolded: more than half a million dead, more than five million
refugees, more than six million displaced within Syria, hundreds of thousands disappeared in jails. Mohsen could not understand how Iran, which
had suffered so much during the war with Iraq, could now help inflict such
devastating pain on another country. And for what—shrines?

After leaving the Revolutionary Guards, Mohsen had spent the 1980s
in various government offices. He knew about the ruthless killings and
hangings of leftists in the immediate aftermath of the revolution but dismissed them as the passing excesses of a revolutionary moment. He had
heard about the torture taking place in prisons, but dismissed that too as
the abuse of power by a few. But in 1984, he was arrested, wrongly accused
of participating in the assassination of a prime minister. Jailed for twenty-
four hours at Evin, he heard the torture with his own ears coming from
nearby cells. When he got out, he went to see Khomeini to tell him what

he thought the Supreme Leader did not know: his subordinates and acolytes were betraying the values of the revolution. The warden of Evin was
removed and Mohsen felt vindicated. He had been right; these were just
isolated incidents by bad individuals. He was jailed again in 1986 for no
clear reason and spent two months in prison, with forty-nine days in solitary confinement.

In the following years, the more he looked around him, the more he
saw evidence that it was the revolution that was rotten. He quit his government job and moved closer to the reformists' circle, joining the *Kiyan*
group with Soroush. He started his own newspaper. He reread all of Khomeini's statements, but this time he read between the lines; he thought
back to that one word, *hichi*, nothing, that Khomeini had uttered on the
plane back to Tehran. He studied other revolutions and understood what
he had not been able to see when he was an eager young revolutionary: the
seeds of dictatorship had been there from the beginning, with the elevation
of Khomeini as the sole leader.

In 2003, while Khatami was president and Soroush had already gone
into exile, Mohsen called for a change in the system and was jailed again.
He spent almost four months in prison and went on a hunger strike for
seventy-nine days. His son was arrested. The hardship of prison and the
hunger strike damaged his eyes and he was given permission to leave
the country for surgery abroad. While he was abroad, he was sentenced
in absentia to more jail time. His family had already left the country, so
Mohsen decided not to return. He settled in the US and tried from afar
to bring down the system he helped create. With frequent interviews on
television and his own YouTube channel, he appealed to his fellow Iranians
to oppose the government with nonviolent means, to erode support for the
regime. But from the violent clampdown of protests in 1999 and 2009 to
the war in Syria, the regime never shied away from using force to silence
dissent and expand its power. When Mohsen had helped found the Revolutionary Guards, he never once considered that the paramilitary group
would have a role outside Iran's borders.

Hojaji's death in Syria in 2017 briefly helped Iran make the case that
it was on America's side in the war against ISIS. Iran would point to Saudi
Arabia as the source of all Sunni extremism, constantly reminding the
world that fifteen of the nineteen hijackers on 9/11 had been Saudi. The
Saudis would throw a fit and point back to Iran's support for groups like
Hezbollah and the Shia militias in Iraq, who had killed more than six hundred American soldiers since 2003.

When Baghdadi's men swept through Iraq and Syria in the summer of 2014, Iran did indeed come to the rescue. The Obama administration was still weighing whether to send jets to strike ISIS targets while Iraq begged for quicker delivery of the Apache helicopters and F-16s it had ordered from the US. But within hours of the fall of Mosul, Suleimani arrived in Baghdad to lead the counterattack. He coordinated the defense and called on Shias around the country to join militias to fight ISIS. Thousands volunteered. The ranks of the Mahdi army swelled with loyalists of the firebrand cleric Moqtada al-Sadr. Others joined the Badr Brigades, run by Iran's erstwhile friend Hadi al-Amiri. Various splinter factions attracted other fighters; more factions emerged. Prime Minister Nouri al-Maliki, who had already made use of such ruthless paramilitary groups to maintain his grip on power, legitimized them with a decree, branding them as the Popular Mobilization Force. The PMF's role should have been to support Iraq's floundering armed forces. That's what Ayatollah Ali Sistani had in mind when he issued a fatwa calling on all Iraqis, Shias and Sunni, to join the fight against ISIS. Instead, a parallel Shia army had emerged with anywhere between 60,000 and 140,000 men who mostly answered to Suleimani.

The "living martyr," also known as the shadow commander, was now in the limelight, posing as the hero of the war against ISIS. Pictures and video footage of him touring the front lines of the war against ISIS began to circulate on social media. At first, they were amateurish snapshots taken by his fans in the militias. Then professional photographers began to take shots of him on the battlefield, posing with fighters, a sign of how keen Iran was to advertise its role as the rampart against ISIS. When US air strikes against ISIS finally started in the fall of 2014, America and Iran were in the trenches together—or rather, the Iranians and their proxies were in the trenches, while the Americans provided air cover. In this bizarre alignment of interests, Saudi and Emirati fighter jets were also briefly in the sky as the kingdom vaunted its own role in fighting ISIS, trying hard to shake any comparisons to the zealots who had taken so many pages out of the kingdom's book. One of the pilots was Prince Khaled bin Salman, son of the man who was then still crown prince but would become King Salman within a few months, in January 2015.

The paradox wouldn't last. Iran and Saudi Arabia both feared ISIS, but they hated each other more. Secretly, many Arabs cheered ISIS on, hoping it would bring Tehran to its knees and put an end to Iranian dreams of hegemony in the region. And as Iran took the lead in fighting ISIS on the ground, it looked like Shias were out to kill any Sunnis, the latest brutal, sectarian mutation of the Saudi-Iran rivalry. Which came first: Iran's imperial sectarianism or the Sunni sense of exceptionalism? By now the dynamic was hard to unpack, but it was about to intensify with the rise of King Salman and his favorite son, prince Mohammad bin Salman. While Obama dismissed Iran's "destabilizing activity" as a "low-tech, low-cost activity," Saudi Arabia watched with alarm as Iran poured thousands of men and an estimated $35 billion into Syria to prop up Assad. Suleimani was turning into the king of Iraq. As the US-Iran nuclear negotiations inched closer to a deal in the spring of 2015, the Saudis grew unnerved by the prospect of cash flowing into Iran's coffers after the lifting of sanctions. They seethed as US secretary of state John Kerry and the Iranian foreign minister Javad Zarif exchanged pleasantries and smiled for the cameras during the negotiations.

In neighboring Yemen, the Houthi rebel group had seized the capital Sana'a in September 2014 and brought down the internationally recognized government. The Saudis accused the Iranians and Hezbollah of supporting and arming the Houthi rebel group whose fighters belonged to a Shia subsect known as Zaidi. When Sana'a fell, Prince Salman was defense minister and his son Mohammad was his aide. The young prince was incensed by what he perceived as the weakness of King Abdallah in dealing with the Houthis and Iran. Some Iranian politicians declared smugly that Iran now controlled four Arab capitals: San'aa, Baghdad, Damascus, and Beirut. Worse, Iran's sphere of influence had extended to Saudi Arabia's southern border. Soon, the Houthi rebels would start lobbing rockets into the kingdom.

On January 23, 2015, King Abdallah died and Salman became king. He appointed his son as defense minister. The duo and the coterie around them wanted to push back against Iran and step into the vacuum that America was creating. The Saudis wanted to beat their chests, restore Sunni pride, and bolster their leadership of the Muslim world. And so, for the first time in its recent history, on March 25, 2015, the kingdom went to war. The Saudi military operation, launched with barely a warning to the Obama administration, was called Decisive Storm. Within hours, bombastic Saudi analysts went on television claiming the campaign would be so successful it would be studied in history books. Airplanes from Saudi allies joined in, at least initially. The Sunni world watched the Saudi air strikes against the Houthi rebels and felt their pride restored. And Prince Mohammad bin Salman, two months into his job as defense minister, was certain this would make him king of the Middle East chessboard, a mastermind who could rival Suleimani. The days of King Abdallah's consensus politics were over, his penchant for compromise not part of Bin Salman's repertoire.

The military campaign would be anything but decisive. The Saudis had never fought a war in such a way; they had never deployed troops. They couldn't do precision strikes with their fancy fighter jets. They were now facing a guerrilla force in rugged, hilly terrain. The conflict would drag on for years; tens of thousands of civilians would die by 2019, in air raids by the Saudi-led coalition and ground fighting, but the worst impact would be the starvation and diseases. Ten million people were on the brink of famine because of the blockade the Saudis and the United Nations had imposed, and the country was battling a dangerous outbreak of cholera. Almost ninety thousand children died. It was the largest humanitarian crisis in the world, almost on par with Syria.

And so the Saudi rulers now also had the death of a country on their conscience. But neither they nor the Iranians seemed able to step back from their fight to the death—they were unable to reflect on how their quest for supremacy had been unmaking the region over decades, culminating in the destruction of Syria and Yemen. And the Saudis were not done. In January 2016, they executed a number of Sunni al-Qaeda militants as well as a Shia cleric, Sheikh Nimr al-Nimr. He had been sentenced to death for his role in antigovernment protests in the Eastern Province in 2011, when the winds of the Arab uprisings had reached the kingdom. Nimr was accused of having Iranian support. In its self-ascribed role as protector of all Shias, Iran warned the kingdom against carrying out the sentence. King Salman could have pardoned Nimr or delayed the execution indefinitely, but this was a new, assertive Saudi Arabia eager to show that it tolerated neither internal dissent nor outside criticism. Nimr's beheading provoked instant protests in Tehran, where a mob ransacked the Saudi embassy and set it on fire, while the Revolutionary Guards warned that "harsh revenge" would topple "this pro-terrorist, anti-Islamic regime." Ambassadors were recalled and diplomatic relations severed for the first time since 1987.

Beyond the mobs, many Iranians were tiring of the attention to causes that were not their own. The nuclear deal had not delivered tangible benefits for people, their lives had not improved, their pockets were still empty. But the regime was still spending blood and money in Iraq and Syria. In December 2017, protests erupted and spread quickly across the country. Thousands of Iranians chanted: "not Gaza, not Lebanon, my life is devoted to Iran." They called for the removal of the Supreme Leader. The response was, again, brutal. The protests were quelled within a month.

Meanwhile, the campaign against the mandatory veil accelerated. The women became more daring. One of them stood on a utility box, her veil hanging from a stick. She was arrested and later sentenced to a year in jail. Dozens more were arrested, but the women were not deterred. Increasing numbers protested across the country, in cities and villages, individual acts of resistance that were harder to contain than a crowd of protesters. Masih received dozens of videos every day from inside Iran of women walking without the veil, baring their face to the cameras, confronting the religious police and even clerics. Their husbands, fathers, and sons also joined in, helping with the filming or recording their own messages of support. This was not a minority movement: President Rouhani's own office had conducted a poll that found that half of Iranians opposed the mandatory veil. On the women-only section of the Tehran metro, on International Women's Day, March 8, 2018, three young women removed their veils. They had short hair—one of them was bottle-blond, another wore big silver earrings. They held hands and sang like they were marching.

> From the bruises on my body, I bloom,
> I'm wounded but I bloom by my very being
> For I am a woman, a woman, a woman.
> If we sing all along, shoulder to shoulder, if we walk
> Hand in hand and strong, we'll be freed from this wrong.

The song had been written and first sung in 2007, during a country-wide campaign to repeal discriminatory laws, including the mandatory veil. The campaign failed, and many of its members, men and women, were arrested. Now the women were singing the hymn again. Masih wished she was there, in Iran, on the streets, removing her veil, taunting the morality police, and helping to organize more protests. Still, she could do more from the United States to publicize the protests, thanks to social media and the freedom to speak without fear of arrest. But exile was not where she wanted to spend the rest of her life. Exile was also not where Mohsen thought he'd end up, but exile seemed to be the fate of any Iranian who didn't believe in the system anymore, any Iranian who wanted to breathe, remove the veil, or seek better opportunities. Mostly, it was the choice of those who could afford to leave and could find a way out. Ever since thousands of Iranians had rushed to get on a plane to escape the country that Khomeini was taking over, millions of Iranians have built or rebuilt their lives around the world, from Los Angeles to Paris to Istanbul. Despite all the ways that Iran and Saudi Arabia mirrored each other or competed with each other during the last four decades, exile has remained an Iranian experience (with few exceptions). Despite the kingdom's many shortcomings, the rulers showed magnanimity for their subjects. The absolute monarchy was suffocating, especially to its women, but still somewhat benevolent. But this, too, was changing. Exile was becoming a refuge for Saudis.

19

MURDER ON THE BOSPORUS

TURKEY, SAUDI ARABIA
2015–19

When you dare ask a question about the deteriorating situation
They silence you with slogans about all the conspiracies -
They brand you a traitor like sheep, every time you demand change
for the nation
They drive you to despair, so you sell your freedoms to save the nation.
—Mashrou' Leila, lyrics from "Lil Watan" (For the Nation) (2013)

Exile was not something that the Saudi journalist Jamal Khashoggi had ever contemplated. He had never considered it could be a location, a real place. To him, it was a word, an intangible idea. Even after he left his home in Jeddah with two suitcases and landed in the United States in the summer of 2017, he still pronounced the word with a disbelieving smile. Jamal's decision to leave the kingdom had been difficult, not only because it was destroying his family life but because he had always thought of himself as a loyal citizen, a subject of the king. Jamal had changed since his days as a student in Indiana in 1979. He had once embraced the idea of Islam as a political system, although he had never fully adhered to a political group like the Muslim Brotherhood. He now fervently believed in democracy and pluralism, the separation of religion and state. He admired Turkey as an example of how Islam and democracy could coexist—though his friend President Recep Tayyip Erdoğan was increasingly authoritarian.

Jamal cringed with deep shame when he thought back to how he had contributed to the spread of Surur's hateful book on Shias, and could not understand how he had once given away his own music LPs. He knew these acts could be partly explained away as the excesses of youth, the naive embrace of ideals that eventually fail you. He also understood that he was the product of a specific era and a country where he had embraced the culture around him. But he had moved on, where others had not.

He had traveled, moved between countries and continents, and now, in his late fifties, Jamal loved to reminisce about covering the war in Afghanistan in the 1980s. He still believed the kingdom had been politically and morally correct to support the mujahedeen against the Soviets. Then Saudi Arabia and America had both failed, each in its own way, to contain the consequences. Though he was loath to dull the shine of those heady days, he recognized that the war effort had been corrupted from the start by the arrogance of Salafist jihadists who imposed their puritanism everywhere they went, not to mention the funding that Saudi Arabia channeled only to specific groups. After his days as a reporter in the field, Jamal remained a truth teller as the editor of a newspaper and then as a columnist. He constantly bumped up against the boundaries of what was permissible in the kingdom, criticizing the ultraconservative Saudi clerical establishment, offering a mea culpa after 9/11, or calling for social reforms and openness in a stifling country.

When Jamal had angered the clerics and their ally Prince Nayef, the ultraconservative interior minister, he was fired as editor of *Al-Watan* newspaper in 2003. *Al-Watan* answered to a more progressive branch of the family, sons of the late King Faisal, so Jamal moved to London and then Washington, DC, as a media aide to the Saudi ambassador Turki al-Faisal, the former intelligence chief who had overseen the war effort in Afghanistan. There would be rumors that Jamal had ties to the intelligence services. He always denied it, but he also made clear that if he were asked to serve his country he would not hesitate—after all, he was at the service of the monarchy, even as a journalist.

Jamal was increasingly well connected, a non-royal who counted powerful princes among his friends, but he continued to push boundaries. After his time working in Saudi embassies, he returned to the kingdom and to *Al-Watan*. He was fired again. But he was becoming a towering media figure in the Arab world. He had an avid readership for his column in the Saudi-owned pan-Arab daily *Al-Hayat*, and after he joined Twitter in 2009, he amassed 1.7 million followers. Perhaps most crucially, he was a sought-after commentator for all things Saudi in the Western media. The kingdom remained a difficult place to report from, with all the layers of obfuscation. Jamal was the rare Saudi who was as well informed as he was candid, loyal to his country but never trying to excuse its many faults. He also believed that right and good would prevail. After the US invasion of Iraq in 2003,

he had briefly hoped that the removal of Saddam would shake up the ossi-
fied Arab political system. In 2011, he grew excited about the uprisings,
seeing in them an Arab renaissance that had been building for years and
was finally coming to fruition. Saudis tried to protest as well, demanding
more freedoms and better job opportunities, and some even called for a
constitutional monarchy. King Abdallah distributed $30 billion worth of
subsidies to silence the opposition. "We will never have freedom in the
Arab world without true democracy," wrote a depressed Jamal to a friend in
a text message in 2014 as conflict raged from Syria to Libya and dictatorship
returned to Egypt. He could not have foreseen that things would get even
worse with the accession to the throne of King Salman in January 2015 and
that this moment would also mark the beginning of his own slow march
toward exile. The new king was known as a ruthless enforcer and efficient
bureaucrat during his time as governor of Riyadh. He had also allowed the
most fundamentalist jihadists to take over the war against the Soviets in
the 1980s and continued to help fund fighters in other wars, like Chechnya
and Bosnia. Within months, a climate of fear descended on the kingdom.

King Salman had appointed his son Mohammad bin Salman, or MbS,
as he became known, as minister of defense and chief of the royal court—a
huge amount of power concentrated in the hands of a thirty-year-old. Saudis whispered about the "boy," spreading stories about his alleged drug use,
his recent, inexplicable weight gain, his rumored second wife. Tall and
energetic, he was his father's favorite son. Soon after graduating with a law
degree from King Saud University, he became his father's private adviser,
often accompanying him on visits around the kingdom, scribbling notes
about everything he saw and heard. He had a reputation for being ruthless
in pursuit of what he wanted. In one infamous incident, he sent a bullet in
an envelope to an official who refused to help him appropriate a parcel of
land. This earned him the street name Abu Rassassa, father of the bullet.
He clashed often with King Abdallah, who instructed Salman to keep his
son on a "short leash."

MbS supposedly felt like a second-tier royal, poorer than the sons of
King Abdallah and with fewer privileges. He had also come of age in the
shadow of the Iraq War, as Rafiq Hariri was assassinated, Saddam Hussein
was executed, and Iranian power was on the rise. MbS seemed predis-
posed to prove his and his country's worth. But until 2012, his means to
do so were confined to sending bullets in envelopes. In 2012, when Prince
Salman was suddenly elevated to crown prince, MbS began to see a path

to the top though there were still uncles and cousins in line ahead of him. When Salman became king, MbS felt the throne was within reach.

In many ways, except for his immense fortune, MbS was a truer reflection of the kingdom than other royals. While generations of well-to-do Saudis have lived and studied abroad, even more so under King Abdallah, who granted tens of thousands of scholarships to young Saudis, the country remained insular, stuck in a time warp. Unlike many royals, including his own brothers, MbS had never lived abroad, and he spoke English haltingly. With 70 percent of the Saudi population under thirty and almost half the country on Twitter, MbS's youth and tech savvy made young Saudis feel he was one of them. Half of the youth under thirty were unemployed, and many of them were frustrated by boredom in a country where music, theater, dancing, museums, and cinemas were all officially banned. MbS looked like someone who might understand their need for jobs and fun. But first the thirty-year-old prince wanted to prove himself and he had chosen to do so with the war in Yemen.

Jamal was enthusiastic at first. The somnolent kingdom was being shaken up. Perhaps this was the moment when Saudi Arabia could restore the pride of the Arab world not only by countering Iran but by helping to remove despots like Assad. A month into the war, Jamal tweeted: "Iran's craziness and insolence is growing, not only in Syria but they've reached our Yemen, after taking our Damascus." But there was no strategy and no exit plan. MbS, though minister of defense, had no military experience. Older Saudis scoffed that he had never read history. In the 1960s, Egypt and Saudi Arabia were on opposite sides during a civil war in Yemen that turned into Nasser's Vietnam. Egypt lost ten thousand men in the fighting. Saudi Arabia meanwhile was backing the Shia Zaidi tribes, yet more evidence that sectarian belonging did not matter then. The Saudis had even considered the shah of Iran's offer for assistance. Now the Saudis were fighting the Houthis and Iran in Yemen. And though jingoistic patriotism was swelling inside the kingdom, Jamal slowly began to see the hubris and the folly of the move. Washington was mostly a silent partner to the crime: trying to make up for the betrayal of the nuclear deal with Iran, the Obama administration assisted Saudi Arabia with refueling missions, intelligence sharing, and further weapons sales.

The ill-planned war had angered many of MbS's older cousins who headed some of the kingdom's security services, like the National Guard and the Interior Ministry. But MbS was on the warpath against them too, trampling all over royal traditions as he concentrated more power in his own hands. In April 2015, his father named him deputy crown prince—yet another step closer to the top. Then MbS went to war against the old way of doing things: he slashed subsidies, froze government contracts, reduced civil servants' pay. With oil prices at a low of $40 per barrel, the old model of the rentier state was no longer sustainable, but MbS was taking away too much too fast. In April 2016, he announced Vision 2030—a grand plan to wean his country off oil and fast-forward the economy and the people into the twenty-first century. Past kings had promised sweeping reforms but never managed more than incremental, minute changes.

MbS wanted to give the kingdom shock therapy, but there was something delusional about his Vision 2030, which came complete with a futuristic city in the desert and a Six Flags amusement park in a country where male-female segregation was still strictly enforced and shops were required to close whenever the call to prayer sounded. Glowing headlines were written about the young visionary, just as they had been written in the 1950s about King Saud (ARABIA PREPARING EXTENSIVE REFORM), and in the 1960s about King Faisal (PRINCE'S REFORM SAID TO GIVE REGIME NEW LIFE), and the reign of the cautious King Abdallah (KING TRIES TO GROW MODERN IDEAS IN THE DESERT). MbS was described as THE PRINCE WHO WOULD REMAKE THE WORLD and a YOUNG PRINCE IN A HURRY. Topping it all was a story characterizing the prince's efforts as the kingdom's top-to-bottom Arab Spring, a cheap dismissal of the sacrifices of millions of Arabs who had tried to rise up against dictatorships across the region. The West was always eager to believe its own orientalist trope: that what Arab countries really needed were enlightened despots to lift up the illiterate masses, an idea the despots entertained gladly to justify their rule, claiming their citizens were not ready for democracy. MbS played the part perfectly. His visits to the United States went well beyond the usual handshake at the Oval Office and visit to Camp David. The prince went to Silicon Valley and Harvard. He wore jeans and a blazer and talked about the future in terms that Americans could understand. He was a millennial, like Facebook founder Mark Zuckerberg, but with even more power and more cash. He dazzled with promises of billions of dollars in investments.

In Saudi Arabia, MbS had also met with intellectuals and journalists while devising his plans, and had reportedly asked Jamal to join his team. Instead, Jamal wrote a series of thoughtful columns in the Saudi-owned pan-Arab daily *Al-Hayat* outlining the more basic hopes of Saudi citizens: more jobs, yes, but also green spaces, better sidewalks, better health care.

Who needed a new robot city in the desert when suburbs of Riyadh and Jeddah were falling into disrepair? Jamal hoped that MbS, in his youthful enthusiasm, just needed some better advice. The young prince was saying and doing a lot of the right things: the feared religious police had their powers reined in; women were promised they would soon be allowed to drive; there was talk that the kingdom might soon have cinemas. But activists were pushing for more substantive changes.

In September 2016, fourteen thousand women signed a petition asking the king to lift the male guardianship system. With tweets and hashtags, with artwork, bracelets, and videos, the women led an extensive campaign that made a lot of noise. Twitter was the only public forum in which Saudis could talk and meet, albeit virtually. The king never responded. Some of the signatories were veterans of campaigns for women's rights, like Aziza al-Youssef, an academic and mother of five, who held salons in her living room and remembered the days when the guardianship system was still a loose arrangement. In 1980, when she first enrolled in university, women did not need a male guardian's permission to sign up. That changed within a year, as the Juhayman effect took hold on the kingdom. Her own father had always empowered her, and he sent her to the United States in her early twenties to finish her studies. Aziza believed it was important to go beyond women's driving rights or the issue of the guardianship system—all Saudis, men and women, needed to be granted their rights as full citizens. This could happen only in a constitutional monarchy. Another signatory, Loujain al-Hathloul, was barely twenty-seven and already a former convict. In 2014, armed with a driver's license she had obtained abroad, she had driven from the UAE into Saudi Arabia and was promptly arrested. She spent seventy-three days in jail. Loujain had the support of her father, who had once sat next to her in the car as she drove in Riyadh. They were breaking the law but were not caught. She had the support of the man she had wedded barely a week before being jailed, Fahad al-Butairi, a graduate of the University of Texas. Fahad, a stand-up comic, had earned a reputation as the Seinfeld of Arabia and had produced a video with friends mocking the ban on women driving, "No Woman No Drive," set to the music of Bob Marley's classic.

Loujain, Fahad, Aziza, Jamal, and countless others, men and women of different generations, were fearless and relentless in their pursuit of more freedoms, risking the ire of both the clerical establishment and the royal family. None of them stopped to consider why the election of Donald Trump on November 8, 2016, was a turning point not just for America but also for them and their country.

The Saudis had been eager to see the end of the Obama administration, and while they, too, had expected Hillary Clinton to win, they embraced the new man in the White House quickly and warmly. The Emiratis had assiduously courted Trump's son-in-law Jared Kushner during the campaign. Within days, Jamal published a column warning that Trump's positions on Middle East issues were full of contradictions that could work to the detriment of the kingdom. He said so again a week after the US election, as he video-conferenced into a public debate at a think tank in Washington, DC. Within days, he received a call from the royal court telling him to shut up: he was no longer allowed to write his column, speak to other journalists, or even tweet. He bided his time at home in Jeddah and waited for the ban to be lifted. Trump's first foreign trip was to the kingdom, where he was treated like royalty in May 2017. In Jeddah, still banned from speaking, Jamal observed in silence—a silence that was deafening to those who knew him and increasingly unbearable for Jamal.

On June 21, 2017, the kingdom woke up to the news that it had a new crown prince. The eighty-one-year-old king had rewritten all the laws of succession and appointed his son heir to the throne. Prince Mohammad bin Nayef, son of the former minister of the interior and minister of the interior himself, a man Washington trusted on all things counterterrorism, had been unceremoniously pushed aside. Worse, he had apparently been held in a palace against his will until he relented at dawn and agreed to make way for his young cousin. Jamal had begun to sense that beyond the hubris of war and the grandiose plans for Vision 2030, beyond even the Machiavellian intrigue of royal machinations, lay something more trenchant, more sinister.

Within a couple of weeks, Jamal left Jeddah and moved to Washington, DC, to begin his life in self-imposed exile, alone. His wife had divorced him, his children were upset with him—why couldn't he just fall in line? And yet, in his own way, Jamal remained loyal. Even with the Atlantic Ocean separating him from the kingdom, he still abided by the ban not to speak publicly, still loyal to his ruler, still waiting for permission to write. He messaged back and forth with the information minister and with Saud al-Qahtani, a close adviser to MbS. On August 17, 2017, Jamal was given permission to write again, and he tweeted his thanks to the young prince: "May no free pen be broken and no Twitter user silenced in the era of the crown prince."

Within a month, Jamal was silenced again, his column in *Al-Hayat* canceled as the publisher, Prince Khaled bin Sultan, very publicly announced that the paper was severing its relationship with him. Jamal's last column, published in early September, was titled "I Am Saudi, but I Am Different." In it he wrote about the time that King Abdallah had appealed to his citizens to embrace one another in all their diversity of thought and political leanings. Without ever mentioning the young prince in his column, he had shown him up as an authoritarian, simply by comparing him to a beloved old monarch who within the limits of his own worldview had attempted to reform and soften the country. There was always only one narrative acceptable in Saudi Arabia: the one that the House of Saud presented with the acquiescence of the clerical establishment. In the absolute monarchy in which the men wore white and the women wore black, shoots of color were always springing up as Saudis of all generations kept trying to carve out space to express themselves. But MbS was silencing men like Jamal, who had never considered himself a dissident. The prince was jailing men like Jamal's friend Essam al-Zamel, an economist who had traveled to the United States on an official Saudi delegation, then made the fatal mistake of pointing out flaws in Vision 2030. Liberal clerics who criticized Wahhabism were also jailed. There was still only one narrative allowed: the one offered by a charismatic yet deeply insecure prince who decreed that his vision of the kingdom's future was perfect and unassailable. "This kid is dangerous," Jamal texted a friend. "I'm under pressure . . . to be 'wise' and stay silent. I think I should speak wisely." But Jamal could not stay silent anymore. He took another decisive step away from his home country and published a column in the *Washington Post* about how Saudi Arabia was turning into a police state. "I left my home, my family and my job, and I am raising my voice. To do otherwise would betray those who languish in prison. I can speak when so many cannot," he wrote on September 18, 2017. "I want you to know that Saudi Arabia has not always been as it is now. We Saudis deserve better."

On November 4, 2017, the five-star Ritz-Carlton hotel in Riyadh was transformed into the most luxurious prison on the planet. A week earlier, the hotel had hosted an international investment conference; in May it had welcomed Donald Trump; before him, in 2014, Obama had been a guest. Now the ostentatious hotel had been commandeered by the government to host reluctant guests: hundreds of princes, businessmen, and current and former ministers had been rounded up overnight. The kingdom declared it was cracking down on corruption. One of the men in custody was the billionaire prince Al-Waleed bin Talal, one of Jamal's former employers, and one of Citigroup's and Twitter's largest single shareholders. Also detained

were the head of the National Guard, the minister of economy and planning, the chairman of a pan-Arab satellite broadcast company, and a phy-
sician who was a US citizen and the founder of a hospital in Jeddah. There
was a common theme: if the men weren't rich, they were connected to
the late King Abdallah or presented an intellectual challenge to MbS.
Billions of dollars were seized from bank accounts and other assets confiscated. Saudis cheered the campaign that punished the thieves who
had enriched themselves at the expense of the people and the country's
progress.

There was plenty of poverty in the oil-rich country: although the GDP
per capita was $20,000, more than half the country could not afford hous-
ing and a quarter of the population reportedly lived below the poverty line.
Saudi Arabia now had its own Robin Hood—never mind that he had just
bought himself a $500 million yacht. On November 6, the Lebanese prime
minister, Saad Hariri, son of the late Rafiq (both also holders of Saudi citizenship), was called to Saudi Arabia, forcibly detained, and made to resign
on television in a bizarre performance. In the eyes of Saudi Arabia, years of
patronage of the Hariri family and other allies in Lebanon were not paying
off, since Hezbollah and Iran still had so much power in the country—it
was time to bench Saad.

But Washington had begun to worry about the erratic ways of MbS
and signaled its support for Hariri, while the French president traveled to
Riyadh to extricate the Lebanese leader. Jamal was now writing a regular
column for the *Washington Post*, and in his next piece he compared MbS
to Russian president Vladimir Putin. Jamal kept undermining the crown
prince's narrative as a reformer, criticizing him from the one perch that
mattered most to the House of Saud: America.

———

In Jeddah, Sofana Dahlan wanted to believe that Mohammad bin Salman
was the hero that her generation had long been waiting for. The descendant of Mufti Dahlan, who as a schoolgirl had been made to draw black
lines through people's faces in art class, was now a grown woman—and a
trailblazer. She had relentlessly pursued the impossible dream of being a
lawyer in a country with no law schools for women and no female lawyers.
She had studied law in Cairo and then Islamic studies at Al-Azhar in the
hope that her degree would be recognized in the kingdom. She graduated
in 2003, but not until ten years later, in 2013, did the king finally declare
that women would be allowed to practice law. She applied for a license.

At the ministry of justice in Riyadh, they dismissed her: "You won't get your license, not for a thousand years." For weeks on end, Sofana traveled to Riyadh once a week and sat for hours on a chair staring at the bureaucrat who had the power to issue her a license. Eventually she wore him down—he even bought her a cake to celebrate her achievement.

Sofana wanted to believe that a new era was opening up in the kingdom, but again she felt excluded. She had felt excluded growing up, in the 1980s and 1990s, on the margins of a religious revival promoted by the House of Saud. The intense, exclusionary Islam she was taught at school did not mesh with her understanding of her religion or what her parents were teaching her. As descendants of the mufti, her family still followed the Shafi'i school of thought in Islam, as did many people in the Hejaz and in neighboring Yemen. Sofana was devout and embraced her religion with love; she found peace in prayer.

She could still barely listen to music, even though she knew, on an intellectual level, that nothing would happen to her if she did. The image of molten lead being poured into her ears on Judgment Day was difficult to forget. As a young girl, she had been expelled from school for three days for challenging a teacher at school who told her that the family portraits her parents kept at home were idolatrous. "Fine, then take the pictures of the king off the walls," the ten-year-old had retorted. As a teenager in the early 1990s, she and a friend had gone to the Hallmark shop in a mall looking for a card. The religious police walked in and began to scream at the vendors, tearing up all the cards. Though terrified, Sofana and her friend could not escape from the shop—the religious police had walked in just as prayer time began and the doors of the shop were locked. She could not forget the image of strange men with whips, destroying private property in the name of righteousness—and the contradiction of a shop operating legally but facing the ire of a religious police that was an arm of the state. Her desire to fight injustice stemmed partly from such episodes. She felt like a victim on the inside but never acted like one. She overcame the challenges with the systematic approach of critical thinking, dogged learning, and guts. And she loved a challenge.

But the limitations and restrictions placed on her for years were not something she could easily forgive. And that's what Saudis of her generation were now being asked to do—to forget and forgive the sahwa, the Islamic awakening, the one that the royals themselves had encouraged in the 1980s before denouncing its political activism in the 1990s. MbS wanted to erase the past by injecting fun into the lives of Saudis. Fun was much needed, but the entertainment plans of Vision 2030 were catering to Westernized millennials; they were the product of American consultants working for big companies like McKinsey who were adding a layer of Western life-style to a conservative kingdom. The events were all sold out and generated coverage in the Western media. But they left behind large swaths of the population who could not relate to the entertainment on offer. The future felt just as exclusionary as the past. For Saudis who had never had the means to travel or live abroad, the conservative context of the king-dom was all they knew. The sudden arrival of John Travolta, Cirque du Soleil, and American wrestlers was not what they'd had in mind when they had wished for more social freedoms. The most conservative Saudis and the ultra-orthodox clerics were incensed by the debauchery on display: women in cat suits dancing, men and women mixing freely on the seaside promenade in Jeddah watching the fireworks, rappers dancing in front of a mixed crowd. An ominous video circulated on social media warning that those who embraced Western ways were forsaking their religion. The warning seemed to be addressed as much to the man at the top who was making it all possible as to his subjects.

What bothered Sofana wasn't that jazz concerts and operas were now on offer; she welcomed those. But when she looked at the crowds attending such events, she was full of questions. Where were women who wear the full-face veil? They were a product of the system—what were they being offered in this new Saudi Arabia? Why was there talk of graffiti art on the walls of the old city of Jeddah, a UNESCO heritage site, instead of a project to restore the buildings and their intricate architecture and wood-work? And why was the kingdom building a national ballet theater when there wasn't even a ballet school? The country was going from one extreme to another. At the turn of the century, the House of Saud had vacuumed inclusive values and diversity out of the peninsula to impose Wahhabism; now it was vacuuming out the religion to impose fun. What was haram yesterday was permissible today, and Sofana's generation was confused. They were the product of the era of 1979, and their past was being rewrit-ten with no acknowledgment of the suffering they had endured.

In his quest to transform aspects of life in the kingdom, MbS was the first royal to acknowledge that 1979 had been a turning point, but he described it as a reaction only to events in Iran, ignoring the kingdom's own history. "What happened in the last 30 years is not Saudi Arabia . . . After the Iranian revolution in 1979, people wanted to copy this model in different countries, one of them is Saudi Arabia. We didn't know how to deal with it. And the problem spread all over the world. Now is the time to get rid of it," he claimed in an interview with the *Guardian* newspaper. "We are simply reverting to what we followed—a moderate Islam open to the world and all religions . . . 70% of the Saudis are younger than 30, honestly we won't waste 30 years of our life combating extremist thoughts, we will destroy them now and immediately."

But when he vowed to return the kingdom to moderate Islam, people in the Hejaz province scoffed. Which Islam was that? The unforgiving puritanism that the House of Saud had imposed on everyone when it founded the kingdom and then exported to the world? Or was it the Islam from the Hejaz built on centuries of inclusive interactions with the world, a choice of halaqas (study circles) in the Holy Mosque, and an embrace of the mysticism of Sufism? None of this diversity was being brought back to the holiest places of Islam, the beating heart of the religion. Even worse, when MbS was asked about Wahhabism, he feigned ignorance: "First of all, what is this Wahhabism—please define it for us. We're not familiar with it. We don't know about it," he told one American journalist.

It was true that strict adherents hated the term. They still considered it a derogatory way of referring to the creed practiced in the kingdom, a disrespectful way to refer to a man whose only fault, in their eyes, was to have tried to return Islam to its purest form. And he was still being celebrated in the kingdom: the desert settlement of Dir'iyah, birthplace of the alliance between Ibn Abdelwahhab and the founder of the first Saudi state, was being turned into a tourist attraction with a sleek glass, metal, and stone structure housing a foundation dedicated to the sheikh, his life and his mission. And when MbS decried the sahwa, he reduced it only to the political movement of the 1990s and placed the blame squarely on the Muslim Brotherhood for any extremism in Saudi Arabia. There was no mention of the blind sheikh Bin Baz's own efforts at a religious revival before 1979, no reference to Juhayman, no word about King Khaled himself publicly praising the sahwa in 1981 in Mecca.

Sofana oscillated between resentment, disbelief, and joy. She was excited when women were allowed into a football stadium for the first time ever—they were seated in a separate section for families and mixed groups, but they were there. In Iran, women had been banned from public stadiums since 1979, and they watched with some envy as Saudi women scored a win. Iran had just barred women from attending a World Cup qualifying match in Tehran between Iran and Syria, though, bizarrely, Syrian women had been allowed into the stadium. Although the abaya, the ankle-length cloak, was mandatory in Saudi Arabia, women could walk around without

covering their hair, unlike in Iran. When the religious police in Iran suddenly declared that women who were not properly veiled would simply
get a warning, it suddenly looked as though Iran and Saudi Arabia were
competing to improve women's rights.

On June 24, 2018, the stroke of midnight signaled another victory for
Saudi women. Thousands of them sat behind the wheel and drove off in
cities across the country. This was not a protest but a celebration. In 2017,
the king promised that women would be allowed to drive, and now he had
delivered—women were on the roads, legally, with driver's licenses issued
in Saudi Arabia in the previous days. Sofana was elated. This was something she could celebrate, not a luxury but a necessity. She posted a picture of
herself holding her brand-new Saudi driver's license on Facebook, issued
in her hometown of Medina. And on Twitter. And again, from a different
angle, on Facebook. And then a picture of herself getting behind the wheel
of a car outside her office in Jeddah. The world's media had descended on
the kingdom to cover the moment when the only country in the world
where women were not allowed to drive finally lifted the ban. Automakers
rolled out stunning television ads celebrating the moment, ready to market
their latest models to new, eager drivers. *Vogue* magazine produced a striking cover showing Princess Hayfa bint Abdallah, daughter of the late king,
leaning out of the driver's seat of a red convertible in the desert, dressed all
in white and wearing stiletto-heeled leather boots.

The women who had campaigned for years for this moment, such as
Lujain al-Hathloul and Aziza al-Youssef, and others who had taken the
wheel in protest back in 1991, like academic Aisha al-Mane'a, now a feisty
seventy-year-old grandmother, should have been celebrating the fruit of
their relentless efforts to overturn the retrograde ban. Instead, they were
in jail. Eleven activists had been picked up two weeks earlier, a way to
ensure they could not claim credit for this moment (four of the detained
were men, some of whom were known to have supported the women's
campaign). This moment could not be their victory, nor the result of
activism—in the absolute monarchy, everything good was the result of
the king's munificence. And to erase their decades of activism and their
standing in society, they were being branded as traitors in a vicious smear
campaign online and in newspapers.

When MbS had declared that the era of 1979 was over, he was right in
one sense: religion was no longer enough to motivate society and mobilize the masses. Across the Middle East, a majority of young people were
declaring that religion played too big a role in daily life. Even in a conser-

vative society like Saudi Arabia, national cohesion could no longer rely on religious ideology. MbS had understood this when he went to war in Yemen in 2015—nationalism could be the new ideology to rally young Saudis, and "traitor" could replace *kafir* as a rallying cry.

Around the same time, in the United States, Jamal tried to look up one of his old articles in *Okaz*, a local Saudi newspaper. What came up instead was "ERROR: 404 Page Not Found." He searched for other pieces he had written for the paper; there was nothing. He checked other publications he had written for, including the website of *Al-Arabiyya* television station. There was nothing. Although he had been officially banned from *Al-Hayat*, his columns were still online, perhaps because the paper was headquartered in London. But within the kingdom, he had been erased online.

In the early afternoon of October 2, 2018, just over a year into his life in exile, Jamal was chatting with his fiancée in a taxi in Istanbul, heading for the Saudi consulate. On the shores of the Bosporus, he had found love again and wanted to believe in the future. He had met Hatice Cengiz, a thirty-six-year-old Turkish doctoral student, at a conference in May. She knew his work and had asked a question after he spoke onstage. They talked more afterward. She spoke Arabic; his family had ancient Turkish roots. They stayed in touch and met again during his next visit to Istanbul. The emotional connection developed rapidly. As fearless as he appeared to those around him, Jamal was a teddy bear of a man, and he had been lonely in his big house in Virginia. Jamal could not speak of exile without tears in his eyes. He had tried to reconcile with his wife but had failed. On his bedside table was a picture of his children and grandchildren; they were the last thing he saw every night when he went to sleep; they greeted him when he opened his eyes in the morning. But the relationship was strained. One of Jamal's sons had been banned from leaving the kingdom and refused to speak to him. Jamal missed his family and the smell of home, the hustle of cities like his hometown of Medina; he dreamed of walking its streets again—Istanbul was the closest approximation. Washington had begun to feel too far from the world he knew, and he was working to launch an organization to promote democracy in the Arab world: Democracy for the Arab World Now (DAWN). He was on a mission to teach younger generations about pluralism and democracy—democracy was the solution, he kept telling his friends.

Hatice watched from behind the protective metal police barricades that surrounded the Saudi consulate as Jamal walked away from her, toward the two-story building. She was excited about their upcoming wedding. All that was missing was one piece of paper that Jamal was going to get inside the consulate. She held on to her fiancé's two phones. Security measures at the consulate meant he couldn't take them inside. He had told her to call a friend of his in the Turkish government if anything went wrong. He had been a bit hesitant about walking into the consulate. The Saudi embassy in Washington had directed him to the consulate in Istanbul for the legal document he was seeking. There was no clear reason why: this was a Saudi document certifying he was single so he could officially marry his fiancée. He should have been able to obtain it at any Saudi embassy. He had gone to the consulate in Istanbul the first time unannounced, just five days earlier, on September 28. He told Hatice the consular staff had been friendly and welcoming, but the paperwork required a few days and they had given him a return appointment. He had weighed the risks. There was no arrest warrant against him, he was not a wanted man. Though in exile, he still didn't consider himself a dissident; he had never called for the overthrow of the Saudi monarchy. He had nothing to hide if they wanted to interrogate him. He had been to the embassy in Washington, DC, plenty of times, and had even sat down a few times with the ambassador, Khaled bin Salman, MbS's younger brother. And he laughed at friends who worried and asked him to let them know before he walked into the austere, monumental marble-clad building by the Potomac River. "You are ridiculous," he had told one of his American friends. But he was in fact taking precautions. He had stopped going to prayers at a Saudi-affiliated mosque in Washington. He had resisted offers to return to the kingdom for a government job. But he had concluded that the Saudi authorities would not dare do anything to him in a foreign country, in their own diplomatic mission. Hatice still worried that it was a trap. She had skipped classes to accompany him back to the consulate.

She told Jamal she would be waiting for him, right there, in the same spot where she left him. "Fine, my darling," he had said with a smile. He walked past a black Mercedes-Benz Vito van and smiled to the Saudi consular employee in a light blue blazer standing by the door. The entrance door opened, a heavy metal door embossed in gold with the crossed swords and palm tree of the Saudi emblem. At exactly 13:14:37, Khashoggi walked past the threshold and into the Saudi consulate. Home soil. The metal door shut behind him.

Outside, Hatice waited, pacing. They had already furnished the apartment they would live in. "The house is beautiful, like its owner," he'd written to her in a message a few days ago. At three in the afternoon, Hatice was still waiting. Could the paperwork really be taking this long? Perhaps Jamal was chatting with Saudi officials inside. After all, he was well known and had worked in embassies himself. She asked the guards outside about her fiancé. The consulate was now closed, they told her. There was no one inside. Hatice panicked and dialed the number Jamal had given her in case of emergency. Yasin Aktay, the senior adviser to Turkish president Recep Tayyip Erdoğan, answered the phone and then made some calls. Hatice stayed outside the consulate until one in the morning. She returned later in the day. Still no sign of Jamal. The news began to spread that Jamal had vanished, perhaps abducted by his own government. Alarm bells rang from Istanbul to Ankara, all the way to the newsroom of the *Washington Post* and the Oval Office at the White House. The next day, his editor Karen Attiah wrote: "Jamal, if you have a chance to read this, please know that we at *The Post* are actively seeking to ensure your safety and freedom. I won't be able to rest easy until you appear safe and sound." On October 5, the *Washington Post* published a blank space where his column should have been—a poignant move that sent shock waves around the world. That same day, in Riyadh, MbS was sitting down for an interview with a team from Bloomberg News and was asked about Jamal.

"My understanding is he entered and he got out after a few minutes or one hour. I'm not sure. We are investigating this through the foreign ministry to see exactly what happened at that time," said the crown prince. The reporters followed up: "So he's not inside the consulate?" "Yes, he's not inside," MbS responded. In Istanbul, the Saudi consul organized an elaborate tour of the building for a few journalists, jokingly opening cupboards to prove Jamal was not hiding in them.

Jamal was long dead, murdered within minutes of entering the consulate. Hatice was a widow before even being a wife. For days, the Saudis continued to deny knowledge of Jamal's whereabouts. After two weeks, they admitted that Jamal was dead, claiming he had died in a fistfight that had gone wrong. But the Turks had it all on tape. The Saudi consulate was bugged, like most diplomatic missions—though it is a breach of diplomatic conventions, most countries engage in such espionage. Turkish officials could not publicly reveal where the recordings were coming from, so they leaked the stomach-churning details of Jamal's death to the media, slowly, bit by gruesome bit. Jamal's fatal mistake had been to agree to return to the consulate after a first visit. Someone inside had alerted the powers that be

in Riyadh—most likely Saud al-Qahtani. A team of fifteen men had traveled to Istanbul on private jets and lay in wait for him. The leader of the
squad was a colonel in the Saudi army who knew Jamal from the days they
both served at the London embassy. The men initially told Jamal they were
taking him back to Saudi Arabia. Jamal had resisted, saying there were people waiting outside for him. Several of the men set upon Jamal, apparently
suffocating him with a plastic bag. Within seven minutes, he was sedated,
then dismembered with a saw. A five-month-long UN investigation into
the killing later found that the team had discussed dismembering Jamal
just thirteen minutes before he entered the building. They referred to Jamal
as a "sacrificial lamb." There was a forensic doctor among the hit squad
who put on his headphones while he cut Jamal to pieces. "When I do this
job, I listen to music. You should do that too," he told the others. The Saudis
tried to cover up their crime. There was footage of a man walking out the
back door of the embassy that was meant to mislead people into thinking Jamal had left the building; this was a body double who had donned
Jamal's clothes, warm off his back, and walked around town, then entered a
building, discarded the clothes in a trash can, and walked back out wearing
different clothes to scramble the tracks. The UN investigation also found
that the crime scene had been thoroughly scrubbed by the Saudis.

After more than a year in exile, Jamal had underestimated how much
Saudi Arabia had hardened, how brazen and evil those at the top had
become. He had also underestimated his own importance. As had the
Saudis, in a monumental way, expecting that they could make him disappear without anyone noticing. But Jamal wasn't just any columnist, though
that's perhaps how he was perceived by some royals—he was their subject,
their property to dispose of as they wished. His body was never found.
But his disappearance and the news of his gruesome killing received wall-
to-wall coverage on television news worldwide, capturing the attention of
American audiences in a way that few foreign stories ever do. He was a
resident of Virginia, a columnist for a top American paper, and there was
something more immediate about his death than any distant war, more
gruesome and depraved in its horrific details.

The initial Saudi obfuscation and the details of the murder unleashed
global furor. European ministers, bankers, and businessmen canceled visits
to the kingdom. Investors suspended their plans for joint ventures. The
US-Saudi relationship was in limbo, training programs on hold, visits by
government officials postponed. There were talks of sanctions against the
kingdom. The immediate assumption was that such an intricate plot to kill

a Saudi citizen on foreign soil in a consulate could not have been hatched without the knowledge or tacit consent of the all-powerful crown prince. Republican senator Lindsey Graham called MbS a wrecking ball and said he had to go. Congress prepared to vote to end American support for the Saudi war in Yemen. Saudi Arabia's archenemy Iran rubbed its hands at this self-inflicted wound, the latest folly of a paranoid thirty-three-year-old prince. Young Saudis, hopeful about the future, suddenly awoke to the possibility that their country could become a pariah.

There was no undoing what had happened. For a few weeks, it looked as though MbS would not survive Jamal's murder. Rumors circulated that the king was bringing in another royal to replace the young crown prince. Promises were made that there would be accountability and a trial. But the ruling family was only circling the wagons. Nationalism peaked as Saudi journalists and commentators decried what they said was a plot to weaken the kingdom. Some issued veiled threats, warning that destabilizing Saudi Arabia would turn it into another Syria. Religion was deployed along with nationalism to shore up the crown prince. Barely two weeks after the killing, the officially appointed preacher of the Holy Mosque in Mecca stood at his pulpit and delivered a sermon heard by the millions of Muslims around the world who tuned in every Friday. The criticism of the kingdom in the wake of Jamal's killing was a conspiracy, and "the attack against these blessed lands" a provocation to a billion Muslims, he declared. But the reform program pursued by the "young, ambitious, divinely inspired reformer crown prince, continues to blaze forward guided by his vision of innovation and insightful modernism." The scripts of these sermons were always approved beforehand by Saudi security forces, and they always ended with a blessing for the royal family. But seldom had religion been bent so far for royal political expediency. Worse, the preacher had proclaimed that the crown prince was *divinely inspired*, thus sheathing him in an unassailable protective layer—as if he were a Supreme Leader.

MbS survived. Qahtani, his adviser, was momentarily pushed aside, as was another high-ranking officer. "I may have caused some of our people to love our kingdom too much," the crown prince would later say, trying to absolve himself of any responsibility and offering a justification for why some of those close to him might have wanted to kill Jamal. His words were met with disbelief. The UN special rapporteur who conducted the investigation, Agnes Callamard, would later declare that the murder had been premeditated and said there was credible evidence linking the murder to high-ranking state officials, including the crown prince. A year after the killing, in an attempt to rehabilitate his credibility, MbS would tell CBS News that "I take full responsibility as a leader in Saudi Arabia, especially since it was committed by individuals working for the Saudi government" but he denied he had ordered the murder. The statement was a layer of protection shielding him from direct accountability, as the crown prince pressed on with his Vision 2030. Investors and world leaders were flocking to the kingdom again. But the new authoritarianism went well beyond a desire to silence Jamal. Reports would surface of other dissidents, as far away as Canada, who had been targeted for possible abduction. Qahtani had formed a hit squad in 2015 to monitor and silence dissent, online and in real life. He had overseen the interrogations of those detained in November 2017 at the Ritz-Carlton. He had also overseen the torture of the women activists arrested in May 2018, according to their relatives. Loujain al-Hathloul's family had initially feared divulging details about her treatment, but after a year in prison and trials shrouded in secrecy, her brother spoke out, describing how his sister had been broken by waterboarding and electrocution, while Qahtani laughed and threatened her with rape. Loujain's husband, Fahad, the stand-up comic, had been abducted from Jordan and brought back to the kingdom, then forced to divorce his wife. There would be many more arrests.

The social changes continued, too. Clothing restrictions were loosened and women ventured out without an abaya. Music played in restaurants. Crucially, the guardianship system was changed, granting single mothers the right to be guardians of their children and all women the ability to get a passport and travel without permission from a male guardian (after the age of twenty-one). But a cloud still hung over many in the kingdom as they waited for relatives to be released from jail, and details of torture leaked from prisoners' cells. Gone were the days of fatherly kings sending women off with a warning. This was a new Saudi Arabia that instilled fear in its citizens, at home and abroad and beyond. The prince's initials were given a new meaning: Mr. Bone Saw. Arab dissidents, already wary of their own governments, became fearful of what could happen if they crossed the Saudi crown prince or criticized his regional policies. The kingdom's neighbors and nearby allies could see that MbS was reckless and vengeful, not hesitating to kidnap the prime minister of another country and send hit squads to kill his own citizens, but they also knew he would most likely be the next king, potentially for fifty years.

MbS was being compared to Saddam Hussein—a brutal dictator stoked and backed by America as long as he kept supplying oil and fighting Iran. But the young Saudi prince's ways were also the ways of the Islamic

Republic of Iran, hunting down its dissidents everywhere, imprisoning and torturing women, instilling fear in its neighbors. And this was what MbS wanted, something the kingdom had never quite managed to attain, despite the billions of dollars it had spent over decades to buy friends, something that revolutionary Iran had mastered with strategy and thuggery: he wanted to be respected and feared. Jamal may have been a bothersome critic for the thin-skinned crown prince, his elimination a domestic affair, but his death was also the latest, most unexpected, and macabre twist in the competition between Iran and Saudi Arabia. The rivalry was older than the crown prince, but he was not letting it go. And he was intent on making sure that, unlike the older generation of Saudi royals such as King Abdallah or the Saudi foreign minister Saud al-Faisal, he wouldn't be deceived by Iran's promises of engagement and moderation. He believed that the smiles of Iran's centrists and reformists were only a front for the radicals and that Iran's hegemonic designs knew no bounds.

"We know that the main goal of the Iranian regime is to reach and control the Holy Shrine of Islam," MbS once declared. "We won't wait for them to bring the fight to Saudi Arabia, we will make sure that it occurs there in Iran." There was even a war game video circulating online, probably produced by Qahtani's army of bots, showing the Saudi armed forces striking Iran after a provocation at sea. Saudi missiles hit an Iranian military air base and troops land to take over a position held by the Revolutionary Guards. At the end of the video, a defeated, haggard Qassem Suleimani falls to his knees and surrenders to the Saudi soldiers. This is perhaps the kind of victory MbS aspires to. In real life, the kingdom depends on the US for its protection and for scoring points against Iran and it was President Trump who ordered the surprise drone strike that felled the crown prince's nemesis. Just before one in the morning, on January 3rd, 2020, Suleimani was killed as he left Baghdad airport in a convoy, having just returned for a trip to Syria and Lebanon. In Iraq and Syria, thousands celebrated the death of a man who had caused such devastation and death in their countries. But the Iranian regime's regional power or certainly its ambitions outlive Suleimani. And here the kingdom remains unable to win an outright victory in Yemen or find a way to make peace in the devastated country. In September 2019, there had also been a drone attack on one of its major oil installations which briefly cut Saudi production by five million barrels, shaking the global energy markets and exposing yet another of the kingdom's vulnerabilities. Iran was accused of carrying out the attack. And so, the rivalry continues, the two countries still hostage to 1979.

CONCLUSION

They imprisoned us in the name of religion
They burned us in the name of religion
They humiliated us in the name of religion
They blocked us in the name of religion
Religion is innocent, Oh Mother.

—Sudanese folkloric poem, chanted during the 2019 Sudan uprising

Differences [of opinion] amongst my nation is mercy.
—Hadith of the prophet Muhammad

"What happened to us?" That question propelled my research. It was the North Star that guided me from one country to the next, unpacking layers of history and politics with the help of many people who in their own ways were also trying to understand the transformation of their lives and their countries. Each person offered clues to the larger puzzle; each brought me closer to understanding the question that loomed so large. Along the way I encountered another recurrent question, one that surprised me, one that young Saudis and Iranians in particular were asking of their parents: "Why didn't you do anything to stop it?" In the eye of the storm, in those countries from which the ripples had emanated and life had been blunted since 1979, there was resentment toward the generation that had allowed it to happen.

For Iranians, 1979 is an obvious turning point in the country's history. For them, it wasn't so much the slow realization of what had happened as the growing disbelief at the naivete of their parents and grandparents who had cheered on a revolution that replaced the tyranny of monarchy with the even worse tyranny of religion, one that was politically but also socially and economically repressive, effectively freezing the country in time and disconnecting it from the world seemingly forever. In December

2017, when demonstrations erupted across Iran, the weeks of unrest were the most serious threat to the Islamic Republic since the Green Movement of 2009. Angry at the blood and money spent overseas, Iranians chanted, "Let go of Syria, think about us!" In a video that circulated online, one young woman also addressed the older crowd of mostly men around her during a night protest with this remonstration: "You raised your fists [in 1979] and ruined our lives. Now we raise our fists [to fix your mistake]. Be men, join us. I will stand in front of you and protect you. Come represent your country."

In Saudi Arabia, awareness of what the year 1979 had meant for the kingdom was not as obvious. Juhayman's siege of the Holy Mosque in Mecca that year, though shocking, had not been a countrywide event, and the kingdom excels—then as today—at camouflaging internal dissent. Awash with cash during the 1980s, Saudis could travel anywhere to go to the cinema and the theater or to sit in cafés in Paris if they wanted to escape the darkness engulfing their country. There was no clear turning point to stand against; there were many smaller ones. But now their children want to know why. Why hadn't their parents protested when the music was silenced, when the male guardianship system was tightened, when the religious police started cracking their whips in public malls? How could they have let this happen without a word? This generation of Saudis do not know that Iranians are asking the same questions about 1979; nor do Iranians know that some in Saudi Arabia are fueled by similar feelings of betrayal. Iran and Saudi Arabia are echoing each other, once more, in subtle ways.

There was a brief moment in 2018 when it looked as though the two foes were going to compete to undo the damage of 1979: the Saudis from the top down, thanks to a crown prince opening up his country to the twenty-first century; and the Iranian people, thanks to their own determination to chip away at the system. Instead, the competition continued to be a race to the bottom, as though nothing and nobody was equipped to dissuade the leadership of either country from its own worst instincts. Syria, Yemen, and Iraq paid the price, as did those who raised their voices against their respective leaders in Iran and Saudi Arabia. The most dangerous opponents were those who spoke softly and who presented the most credible alternative to the absolutism of the leaders, such as Jamal Khashoggi. Or Nasrin Sotoudeh, an Iranian human rights lawyer sentenced to thirty-eight years in jail and 148 lashes for defending the women campaigning against the mandatory veil.

Traveling around the region to conduct my reporting for this book, I oscillated between despair and hope. The challenges are so immense, the dynamics seemingly so intractable, the players so entrenched, that it is easy to conclude there really is no way out. After four decades of rivalry between two foes in constant competition for influence, both abusing religion, both weaponizing sectarian identities, the past is no longer history for some. Rather, it is alive in the boiling rancor of the present, and there is no chance of forgiveness. Once obscure, forgotten historical wrongs have been turned into fresh memories in the collective consciousness, as a result of the relentless crescendo of sectarian spin created by Iran and Saudi Arabia. In 2018, Hezbollah did well in legislative elections in Lebanon while Saad Hariri's coalition suffered losses, even in Beirut. The sentiment of victory was expressed by a Hezbollah supporter in a statement on Facebook: "We will not vote for the candidates of the Yazidi state, the killer of the children in Yemen, the supporter of Daesh and Nusra, but most importantly, the destroyer of the tombs of the Imams, peace be upon them."

Yazid was the caliph who faced off with Imam Hussein in the battle of Karbala in 680 AD, and the term "Yazidi state" was being used to refer to Saudi Arabia, now seen as the ultimate embodiment of oppression of the Shias; the mention of the destruction of tombs was a reference to the cemetery of Jannat al-Baqi, leveled by the Al-Sauds at the turn of the twentieth century. The candidate of this Yazidi state was Saad Hariri, the Lebanese prime minister, who had made many compromises with Hezbollah and had been humiliated by his Saudi patrons precisely for this reason in his bizarre, televised forced resignation in November 2017. After the 2018 election results were announced, Hezbollah supporters on mopeds or hanging out of their cars drove through the city waving the yellow flag of the party, stamped with a fist raising a Kalashnikov. They chanted: "Beirut is Shia, Beirut is Shia"—an echo of the 1980s when young men with beards and women in chadors went on a rampage on Hamra Street, smashing liquor bottles and laying claim to that part of the city. The men on mopeds made a frenzied spectacle of pulling down posters of Saad. They drove up to the Saint George Hotel, site of the 2005 assassination of Rafiq Hariri, Mr. Lebanon. A bronze statue of him stood near the spot where the bomb had cratered the road and changed the political trajectory of the country. Hezbollah supporters attached their yellow party flag to it, declaring their final victory over a dead man.

For those no longer interested in religion, the leadership of both Iran and Saudi Arabia now resorts to nationalism. In the kingdom, the crown prince's Machiavellian aide Saud al-Qahtani deployed an army of Twitter trolls to defame the women activists who had been jailed, branding them traitors to the nation. When Saudi Arabia faced the ire of the international community after the killing of Jamal, social media and television portrayed the kingdom as a victim of an outside plot and called on citizens to close ranks. In Iran, the Supreme Leader has repeatedly entreated Iranians to support the state even if they don't support its Islamist ideology. The IRGC now promotes itself as the guardian of the nation. Nationalist sentiments run so high in some sections of society that those who rally around the flag in Iran or Saudi Arabia lack the perspective to reflect on what their governments are inflicting and imposing on the rest of the region.

Between despair and hope, I ultimately settled on hope. My journey across time and space was both humbling and exhilarating, as it reminded me of the incredible power of those of who continue their relentless, courageous fight for more freedoms, more tolerance, more light. Beyond the headlines about war and death, the region is alive with music, art, books, theater, social entrepreneurship, advocacy, libraries, cafés, bookshops, poetry, and so much more, as old and young push to reclaim space for cultural expression and freedom of expression. Their defiance is a source of hope, their steadiness contagious. Even when they go into exile, they don't give up. In 2019, the novelist Ahmed Naji was finally able to leave Cairo. The travel ban was lifted, and he traveled to the United States to be reunited with his wife and baby daughter. He continues to write, publish, and provoke. Ebtehal Younes remains in Cairo, the city of her youth, upholding the legacy of Nasr Abu Zeid, who continues to tower over all other thinkers to this day. Now in Berlin, Yassin al-Haj Saleh never stops publishing and speaking about Syria and the greater ills of the region. He also helped launch Al-Jumhuriyya, an online Arabic news platform that is one of the best sources of information and analysis in the region. He continues to hope he will be reunited with his wife, Samira, and their friends Razan Zaitouneh, Wael Hamada, and Nazem Hammadi, all four still missing since 2013. After the trauma of his father's and uncle's assassinations, Jawad al-Khoei returned to live full-time in Najaf in 2010. He expanded on his grandfather's al-Khoei foundation and launched an academy for interreligious studies that includes non-Muslim teachers and students. In Pakistan, the Salman family felt vindicated when Asia Bibi was acquitted of all charges of blasphemy and spirited out of the country. The governor's widow and children believe that perhaps the wave of intolerance has begun to recede. In Lebanon, Badia Fahs continues to poke holes in the aura of Hezbollah with her writings and by speaking out against the stranglehold of religion on the community. From Brooklyn, Masih Alinejad continues to spearhead the ever-growing campaign against the mandatory veil in Iran, which is turning into a war of attrition against the state. These people are the past and the future and they aren't alone. They are but a sample of a large majority, one which given the opportunity and the space will seize the occasion to rise against the forces of darkness that have impoverished the region economically. In October 2019, such a moment came in Lebanon and Iraq with extraordinary protests against corruption and poverty, but also against sectarianism. Hundreds of thousands demonstrated in both countries, almost in unison, for weeks on end, from Beirut to the Sunni city of Tripoli in the north to Shia Nabatiyeh in the south, from Baghdad to Karbala and Najaf. With music, dancing, and even a DJ, with flowers, humor, and poetry, they let out a cry for life, braving bullets and beatings. The protestors declared their unity, across all social and sectarian divides, against those in power. In Iraq, Iran was the direct target of the ire of the protestors for days, and even Shia clerics joined the marches to denounce Tehran's influence, while some protestors scaled the walls of the Iranian consulate in Karbala to hoist the Iraqi flag on its roof.

In trying to answer the question at the heart of the book, I attempted to render this region in all its diversity and cultural vibrancy, to remind those who look in from the outside that the headlines of today's insanity are not a reflection of who we are—they never have been. Although our countries have been changed by the hegemonizing influences of both Iran and Saudi Arabia, the headlines in the Western media have always reduced matters of extraordinary depth and complexity to a mere snapshot, which more often than not has catered to an orientalist audience that regards Arab or Muslim cultures as backward and to security-focused policymakers. Over time, those two groups have worked to reinforce each other, merging to such an extent that everything was viewed through the prism of the security of the West, especially after 9/11. Even now, as cities like Mosul in Iraq and Raqqa in Syria struggle to overcome the emotional and physical destruction wrought by ISIS, even as whole communities like the Yazidis, a Kurdish ethnic minority, have been decimated by genocide and rape at the hands of ISIS militants, even as Bashar al-Assad continues to kill, torture, and bomb his people, the headlines in the Western media seem focused almost exclusively on the Europeans and Americans who joined the ranks of the militants, on whether they should be allowed back home or stripped of citizenship and what should happen to their wives and children.

People in Europe or the United States often ask blithely, where are the Muslims and Arabs speaking out against extremism and terrorism? It is deeply troubling to expect that all Muslims should apologize or take responsibility for a minuscule fraction of those who share their faith. Furthermore, the question ignores the devastating sacrifices of those who have been fighting intolerance and its violent manifestations within their own countries long before anyone in the West even thought to pose the question. Far too many progressive minds in the wider Middle East have been left to fend for themselves for decades, as they and their countries were bludgeoned to death by forces of darkness, forces, such as Zia in Pakistan, that most often served Western interests. The largest number of victims of jihadist violence are Muslims themselves within their own countries.

In focusing mostly on the actions of Iran and Saudi Arabia and the multitude of local players, I did not intend to absolve America for the many mistakes it has made and the deadly policies it has often pursued. From invasions to coups and support for dictators, America's actions have fed and aggravated local dynamics. President Trump's decision in May 2018 to withdraw from the multilateral nuclear agreement with Iran, and the additional sanctions he imposed on the country, dramatically raised tensions in the region, almost bringing it to war. But Saudi Arabia and Iran have agency; they make decisions based on their interests and drive the dynamics, too. This endless self-reinforcing loop of enmity cannot easily be broken.

There are big geopolitical pieces of the puzzle, such as negotiations to end the war in Yemen, or curbing Iran's influence in Syria. But many of the people I spoke to, those who have not taken sides with either Iran or Saudi Arabia, believe there is no way to defuse the paranoid, vengeful insecurity of Saudi Arabia and to curb the militant ardors of those who feel threatened by Iran's expansionist designs without first altering the nature of Iran's regime. Nobel Peace Prize–winner and Iranian human rights activist Shirin Ebadi believes the regime can no longer be reformed and has suggested a UN-monitored referendum to change the constitution and remove the position of Supreme Leader. Removing the article about Iran being the defender of the oppressed everywhere could also help defuse anxiety about Iran's designs. Meanwhile, many Iranians and Shias will continue to see Saudi Arabia as the enemy as long as it does not moderate anti-Shia rethoric and teachings in the kingdom. Outside its borders, Saudi influence continues in the form of money spent on mosques and teachings that hone close to the kingdom's understanding of Islam.

Seventeen million Muslims are expected to visit Mecca in 2025, and the kingdom should reintroduce the diversity of teaching in Mecca to reverberate a kinder, softer tone out of the heart of Islam. None of this is on the horizon under the current leaders, but it's not impossible. Saudi and Iranian leaders found their way to détente once before. Before it was weaponized in the years following 1979, the Sunni-Shia schism lay mostly dormant.

I started this project with the full awareness that the extremist partisans on either side of the Saudi-Iran divide would find fault with everything I wrote—or perhaps they would pick apart the sections that depict them and applaud passages about their nemeses. I did not write this book for them. I wrote it for peers and colleagues and a wider audience of readers who want to understand why events in the Middle East continue to reverberate around the world. I wrote it for those who believe the Arab and Muslim worlds are more than the unceasing headlines about terrorism, ISIS, or the IRGC. Perhaps above all I wrote it for those of my generation and younger in the region who are still asking, "What happened to us?" and who wonder why their parents didn't, or couldn't, do anything to stop the unraveling. I hope the book provides them with some clues and helps them find a better path forward, separate from the one imposed by the leaders of Iran and Saudi Arabia. As the Danish philosopher Søren Kierkegaard wrote: "It is perfectly true . . . that life must be understood backwards. But they forget the other proposition, that it must be lived forwards."

NOTES

1: Cassette Revolution:

9   **The history of Lebanon's Shia:** Condensed from A. Hourani, "From Jabal 'Amil to Persia," in H. E. Chehabi, ed., *Distant Relations: Iran and Lebanon in the Last 500 Years* (London: I. B. Tauris, 2006).

9   **The struggle opposed two visions:** Condensed from F. Ajami, *The Vanished Imam: Musa al Sadr and the Shia of Lebanon* (Ithaca, NY: Cornell University Press, 1987), 139.

10   **"I have words harsher than bullets":** Ibid., 145.

12   **He once drew huge crowds:** N. Blanford, *Warriors of God: Inside Hezbollah's Thirty-Year Struggle Against Israel* (New York: Random House, 2011), chapter 1.

12   **paying homage to Christ:** Ajami, *Vanished Imam*, 134.

12   **Some historians dismissed:** Condensed from Ajami, *Vanished Imam*, 144–49.

13   **You could buy them from fat men:** H. E. Chehabi, "The Anti-Shah Opposition in Lebanon," in Chehabi, ed., *Distant Relations*, 187.

14   **Hundreds of young Iranians:** Ibid., 184.

14   **Marzieh, the daughter of a cleric:** A. S. Cooper, *The Fall of Heaven: The Pahlavis and the Final Days of Imperial Iran* (New York: Henry Holt, 2016), 372.

15   **the British High Commissioner reported:** H. Samuel, *United Nations Document: An Interim Report on the Civil Administration of Palestine, 1 July 1920—30 June 1921* (London: His Majesty's Stationery Office, 1921), https://www.un.org/unispal/document/mandate-for -palestine-interim-report-of-the-mandatory-to-the-league-of-nations-balfour-declaration -text/.

15   **a majority in Jerusalem:** Palestine Government, *Palestine: Report and General Abstracts of the Census of 1922,* available online at https://users.cecs.anu.edu.au/~bdm/yabber/census /PalestineCensus1922.pdf.

17   **Husseini explained:** Author interviews with Husseini, May 2016 and January 2018.

18   **"there is no point":** B. Moin, *Khomeini: Life of the Ayatollah* (London: I. B. Tauris, 2009), 143.

18   **"what sin I have committed":** Ibid., 147.

18   **he delivered in Persian:** Ibid., 153.

18   **"This is the juice of a sick mind":** Cooper, *Fall of Heaven*, 205.

19   **Husseini did not bring up:** Author interviews with Husseini, May 2016 and January 2018.

19   **He had met Khomeini:** Cooper, *Fall of Heaven*, 194–96.

20   **if he were not a Muslim:** L. Secor, *Children of Paradise: The Struggle for the Soul of Iran* (New York: Riverhead Books, 2016), 14.

20   **"A futureless past is a state of":** Ali Rahnema, *An Islamic Utopian: A Political Biography of Ali Shari'ati* (London: I. B. Tauris, 2000), 107.

20   **He was inspired by Frantz Fanon:** Secor, *Children of Paradise*, 13.

21   **a discourse for emancipation:** S. Saffari, *Beyond Shariati: Modernity, Cosmopolitanism, and Islam in Iranian Political Thought* (New York: Cambridge University Press, 2017), 10.

21   **"offspring of the Exalted Leader":** A. Taheri, *The Spirit of Allah: Khomeini and the Islamic Revolution* (Washington, DC: Adler & Adler, 1986), 184.

21   **Shia cleric Sayyed Hani Fahs:** K. al-Rashd (presenter), "Sheikh Hani Fahs" [television series episode], *Memory Lane,* RT Arabic, February 8, 2013.

23   **the shah was in the middle of a banquet:** Cooper, *Fall of Heaven*, 387–88.

23   **The meeting, organized by the anti-Western Libyan leader:** Condensed from Ajami, *Vanished Imam,* 182–87; Cooper, *Fall of Heaven*, 386; K. Bird, *The Good Spy* (New York: Broadway Books, 2015), 205.

23   **"The Call of the Prophets":** M. Sadr, "L'Appel des Prophètes" [The call of the prophets], *Le Monde*, August 23, 1978.

23   **Sadr was planning to travel:** Condensed from Ajami, *Vanished Imam,* 182–87; Cooper, *Fall of Heaven*, 386; Bird, *Good Spy*, 205.

24   **One of Sadr's traveling companions:** *The Imam and the Colonel* (documentary), Al-Jazeera, July 24, 2012.

24   **Sadr had asked him:** Author interview with Hussein al-Husseini, Beirut, January 2018.

24   **Khomeini's zealots had already burned:** Cooper, *Fall of Heaven*, 376.

25   **described as "a holocaust":** Ibid.

25   **Thousands of Iranians had stayed:** R. P. Mottahedeh, *The Mantle of the Prophet: Religion and Politics in Iran* (New York: Simon & Schuster, 1985), 375.

25   **The crowd of mostly men:** Cooper, *Fall of Heaven*, 399–403.

25   **he had decided to go into exile:** Ibid.

25   **a popular, progressive:** Ibid., 410.

26   **"a frail and crazy old man":** M. R. Pahlavi, *Answer to History* (New York: Stein and Day, 1980), 163.

26   **Mohsen Sazegara was one of the youngest:** All details of Mohsen Sazegara's story are based on an interview with the author in Washington, DC, March 2018; *Iran and the West: From Khomeni to Ahmedinejad: Part 1*, BBC television broadcast, July 20, 2009; and D. Patrikarakos, "The Last Days of Iran under the Shah," *Financial Times,* February 7, 2009.

27   **had cultivated relationships:** Cooper, *Fall of Heaven*, 196–97.

27   **the house's redbrick garage:** E. Sciolino, *Persian Mirrors: The Elusive Face of Iran* (New York: Free Press, 2000), 48–52.

27   **"spend the rest of his days":** Cooper, *Fall of Heaven*, 449.

27   **Khomeini had been admonished:** Ibid., 424.

27   **Khomeini never again discussed:** Moin, *Khomeini*, 195.

28   **"The Shah is holding the oil":** Reza Baraheni, *God's Shadow: Prison Poems* (Bloomington: Indiana University Press, 1976).

28   **described as political spirituality:** M. Foucault, "À Quoi Rêvent les Iraniens?" *Nouvel Observateur*, October 16–22, 1978.

28   **"Khomeini was a moderating influence":** Cooper, *Fall of Heaven*, 469.

28   **a "Soviet onslaught":** Embassy Jidda, "Saudi Press Comment on Iranian Situation: Arab News Discusses Shah's Probable Departure," Wikileaks Cable: 1979JIDDA00015_e, dated January 2, 1979, http://wikileaks.org/plusd/cables/1979JIDDA00015_e.html.

28   **Crown Prince Fahd expressed Saudi support:** "Al-Fahd: We Are with the Legitimate Rule in Iran," *Al-Riyadh*, January 7, 1979.

29   **Members of Sunni Islamist movements:** A. Mansour, "Witness to an Era with Youssef Nada" [television series episode], *In Shahed Ala Al-Asr*, Al-Jazeera, August 2002.

29   **On January 16, 1979:** Cooper, *Fall of Heaven*, 487–89; W. Branigin, "Bakhtiar Wins Vote," *Washington Post*, January 17, 1979.

30   **wild scenes of joy:** J. C. Randal, "Dancing in Streets," *Washington Post*, January 17, 1979.

2: Today Tehran, Tomorrow Jerusalem

31   **Tickets were issued for $500 each:** Sciolino, *Persian Mirrors*, 47.

32   **"Ayatollah, would you be so kind":** Ibid., 55.

32   **Reza Pahlavi, the exiled shah's son:** Patrikarakos, "Last Days of Iran under the Shah."

32   **playing the role of the shah:** Moin, *Khomeini*, 2.

32   **Confident of his relationship with God:** Ibid., 52.

33   **"It seemed that the duty":** Ibid., 200.

33   **Bakhtiar tender his resignation:** J. Buchan, *Days of God: The Revolution in Iran and Its Consequences* (New York: Simon & Schuster, 2012), 219.

34   **"no reason to stay":** Author interview with Mohsen Sazegara, Washington, DC, March 2018.

34   **Walking back to the hotel:** Ibid.

34   **"Ayatollah Khomeini is right":** Ibid.

34   **as though Khomeini were the Mahdi:** Moin, *Khomeini*, 199.

35   **"I will decide the government":** *Iran and the West: From Khomeni to Ahmedinejad, Part 1* [Television broadcast], BBC, July 20, 2009.

35   **Sadeq Khalkhali, once a pupil of Khomeini:** Buchan, *Days of God*, 228, citing Khalkhali in *Khaterat-e Ayatollah Khalkhali* (Tehran: Nashr-e sayeh, 2000), 277.

35   **Safavi and his devotees:** M. Prazan (director), *La Confrérie, Enquête sur les Frères Musulmans* [The Brotherhood: an investigation on the Muslim Brotherhood] [documentary], 2013, quoting Ladan Boroumand.

35   **The devotees turned to Khomeini:** Moin, *Khomeini*, 223.

36   **"Revolt against God's government":** Ibid., 204, citing Khomeini, *Sahifeh-ye Nur* (Tehran: The Institute for Publication of Imam Khomeini's Works, 2008).

36   **The executions began:** Ibid., 207.

36   **"I killed over 500 criminals":** N. Fathi, "Sadegh Khalkhali, 77, a Judge in Iran Who Executed Hundreds," *New York Times*, November 29, 2003.

37   **In PLO offices in Lebanon:** E. Cody, "PLO Now Dubious About Iranian Revolt It Once Hailed," *Washington Post*, December 15, 1979.

37   **early hours of February 17:** G. Khoury (presenter), "The Scene: Sheikh Hani Fahs" [television series episode], *Al-Mashhad*, BBC Arabic, September 18, 2014; further details from *An-Nahar* front-page reportages by Nabil Nasser, February 18–22, 1979.

39   **this was a triumph:** Embassy Beirut, "Pro-Khomeini Demonstrations in Lebanon," Wikileaks Cable: 1979BEIRUT00977_e, dated February 19, 1979. http://wikileaks.org/plusd /cables/1979BEIRUT00977_e.html.

39   **"Can you believe that the Palestinian revolution":** Associated Press, *Yasser Arafat Hails Iranian Revolution*, video, available online at https://www.youtube.com/watch?v =65xpvmCsm-c.

39   **"The victory of the people of Iran":** Quotes translated from Arabic in *An-Nahar* reportages by Nabil Nasser, February 18–22, 1979.

39   **fifteen hundred Israeli citizens:** Cooper, *Fall of Heaven*, 313.

41   **as "real nut cases":** Cody, "PLO Now Dubious."

42   **angry phone call:** J. Al-e Ahmad, *The Israeli Republic: An Iranian Revolutionary's Journey to the Jewish State*, translated edition (New York: Restless Books, 2017), 7.

42   **He had stayed in a kibbutz:** L. Sternfeld, "Pahlavi Iran and Zionism: An Intellectual Elite's Short-Lived Love Affair with the State of Israel," *Ajam Media Collective*, March 7, 2013.

42   **Persian and Shia culture:** Secor, *Children of Paradise*, 8.

43 **The meeting in Jerusalem recommended:** A. al-Ouywaysi, "The General Islamic Conference: 1953–1962" (Jerusalem: n.p., 1989), available online at https://www.slideshare.net/islamicjerusalem/the-general-islamic-conference-for-jerusalem-19531962.

43 **No one in official circles:** *"Nawab Safavi La Yazal Fi al Qahera"* (Navvab Safavi is still in Cairo), *Akhbar El-Yom*, January 16, 1954.

43 **The man who paid for the plane:** Mansour, "Shahed Ala Asr with Youssef Nada."

44 **"we felt like members of the same family":** S. Fuchs, "Relocating the Centers of Shi'i Islam: Religious Authority, Sectarianism, and the Limits of the Transnational in Colonial India and Pakistan," PhD diss., Princeton University, 2015, available online at https://pdfs.semanticscholar.org/e6ab/53a27fd3a8a2d90f78701edb48a552301cec.pdf, quoting Sayyid Murtaẓā Ḥusayn, *Ayatullāh Khumaynī Qum se Qum tak* (Lahore: Imāmiyyah Publications, 1979), 535.

44 **According to some accounts:** Author interview with Rashed Ghannoushi, leader of Tunisian party Ennahda, Tunis, March 2018; M. Rassas, *Ikhwan al-Muslimin wa Iran al-Khumayni–al-Khamina'i* [The Muslim Brotherhood and Khomeini–Khamenei] (Beirut: Jadawillil-Nashr was al-Tawzi, 2013); Mansour, "Shahed Ala Asr with Youssef Nada."

45 **listened to Hawwa's plea:** S. Hawwa, *Hathihi Tajroubati wa Hathihi Shahadati* [This is my experience, this is my testimony] (Cairo: Wahba, 1987).

45 **North Tehran looked like Beverly Hills:** A. Sooke, "The $3 Billion Art Collection Hidden in Vaults," BBC television news report, aired December 7, 2018.

45 **Husseini had joked with Bazergan:** Author interview with Husseini, Beirut, January 2018.

47 **"once more fall back into the hands":** J. Kifner, "Ayatollah Taleghani Backs Away from a Showdown with Khomeini," *New York Times*, April 20, 1979.

47 **"Disrespect to Taleghani is disrespect to the nation":** Ibid.

48 **Hezbollah, or the Party of God:** Moin, *Khomeini*, 211.

48 **still dominated the streets:** This section is based on M. Ayatollahi Tabaar, *Religious Statecraft: The Politics of Islam in Iran* (New York: Columbia University Press, 2018), chapter 5.

49 **broad powers:** J. Kifner, "Iran's Constitutional Vote Overshadows News of the Shah," *New York Times*, December 3, 1979, 1.

50 **The Brothers who had visited Khomeini:** Mansour, "Shahed Ala Asr with Youssef Nada."

3: Bleeding Heart

51 **Sami Angawi overslept:** Author interview with Angawi, Jeddah, February 2018.

52 **Saudi Arabia's oil revenues:** S. Mackey, *The Saudis: Inside the Desert Kingdom* (New York: W. W. Norton, 2002), 7.

52 **Every major American hotel chain:** A. Vassiliev, *King Faisal of Saudi Arabia: Personality, Faith and Time* (London: Saqi Books, 2016), 418.

54 **five hundred feet long with a carved square stone:** R. Burton, *Personal Narrative of a Pilgrimage to Al-Madinah and Meccah*, vol. 2 (New York: Dover, 1964), 273–75.

54 **he ordered the destruction:** "Arabia: Tomb of Eve," *Time*, February 27, 1928.

55 **as Wahhabism:** Z. Sardar, *Une Histoire de La Mecque: De la naissance d'Abraham au XXIe siècle* [A history of Mecca: from Abraham's birth until the 21st century] (Paris: Payot, 2014), 272.

55 **"And fight not with them":** Quran, 2:191, from *English Translation of the Holy Quran*, M. M. Ali, trans., and Z. Aziz, ed. (Wembley, UK: Ahmadiyya Anjuman Lahore Publications, 2010).

56 **The call to prayer:** In addition to interviews with Sami Angawi and Turki al-Faisal, I relied extensively on and merged details from various sections of the following works for my descriptions of events in this chapter: Y. Trofimov, *The Siege of Mecca: The 1979 Uprising at Islam's Holiest Shrine* (New York: Anchor Books, 2007); R. Lacey, *Inside the Kingdom: Kings, Clerics, Modernists, Terrorists, and the Struggle for Saudi Arabia* (New York: Viking, 2009); L. Wright, *The Looming Tower: Al-Qaeda and the Road to 9/11* (New York: Alfred A. Knopf, 2007).

58 **"Ahmad al-Luhaybi! Up to the roofs":** N. Al-Huzaymi, *Ayyam Ma' Juhayman* [My days with Juhayman] (Beirut: Arab Network for Research and Publishing, 2012), 132.

59   **redistribution of oil wealth:** T. R. Furnish, *Holiest Wars: Islamic Mahdis, Their Jihads, and Osama bin Laden* (Westport, CT: Praeger, 2005), 62.

59   **This was the first time:** M. Al-Rasheed, *A History of Saudi Arabia* (Cambridge, UK: Cambridge University Press, 2010), 139–40.

60   **managed to escape to his nearby office:** Lacey, *Inside the Kingdom*, 27.

60   **the Al-Sauds had also set out to homogenize:** M. Yamani, "Changing the Habits of a Lifetime: The Adaptation of Hejazi Dress to the New Social Order," in N. Lindisfarne-Tapper and B. Ingham, eds., *Languages of Dress in the Middle East* (New York: Routledge, 2013).

61   **with gray stone replacing:** Z. Sardar, *Desperately Seeking Paradise: Journeys of a Skeptical Muslim* (London: Granta Books, 2004).

62   **"Beware! (Mecca is a sanctuary)":** M. Khan, *The Translation of the Meanings of Sahih Al-Bukhari* (London: Darussalam Publications, 1997), vol. 9, book 83.

62   **a mere "domestic incident":** Trofimov, *The Siege of Mecca*, 117.

63   **"Mecca Mosque Seized by Gunmen":** P. Taubmannov, "Mecca Mosque Seized by Gunmen Believed to Be Militants from Iran," *New York Times*, November 21, 1979.

63   **"It is not farfetched":** "Khomeyni's Office Says U.S. May Be Behind Attack in Mecca," Foreign Broadcast Information Service, November 21, 1979.

64   **"Death to the American dogs":** Trofimov, *The Siege of Mecca*, 109.

64   **Writing in his diary:** J. West, "John West: In His Own Words," South Carolina Political Collections, available online at https://delphi.tcl.sc.edu/library/digital/collections/jwest .html.

64   **"key industrial plants, airports":** "Gunmen Still Hold Mecca Mosque," *New York Times*, November 22, 1979.

65   **The grand sheikh of Al-Azhar:** Trofimov, *The Siege of Mecca*, 120; H. Tannernov, "Attack in Mecca Attributed to Khomeini Influence," *New York Times*, November 22, 1979.

65   **"The moment I met this guy":** "Iranian Pilgrim Tells of Mecca Attack," *New York Times*, November 22, 1979.

66   **in Pakistan, the headlines stated:** "Haram Sharif Under Full Control of Saudi Forces," *Dawn*, November 23, 1979.

66   **had taken theology and turned it:** W. Wahid Al Ghamedi, *Hekayat al-Tadayyon al-Saudi* [The story of Saudi piousness] (London: Tuwa Media & Publishing Limited, 2015), 66.

67   **and tried to kill him:** C. Allen, *God's Terrorists: The Wahhabi Cult and the Hidden Roots of Modern Jihad* (Boston: Da Capo Press, 2007), 51.

67   **One virulent critic . . . was a young:** Condensed from Trofimov, *The Siege of Mecca*, 20.

67   **they described Juhayman's men:** Ibid., 151, citing *Arab News*, November 26, 1979.

68   **Juhayman . . . broke away from:** Trofimov, *The Siege of Mecca*, 35–42.

68   **barely one Saudi riyal:** Al-Huzaymi, *Ayyam Ma' Juhayman*, 67.

68   **added approving remarks to the pamphlets:** T. Hegghammer and S. Lacroix, "Rejectionist Islamism in Saudi Arabia: The Story of Juhayman Al-'utaybi Revisited," *International Journal of Middle East Studies* 39, no. 1 (February 2007): 111.

68   **Bin Baz stepped in to support:** Trofimov, *The Siege of Mecca*, 42.

69   **with three hundred kilograms:** Ibid., 207.

69   **The king circled the Ka'aba seven times:** Ibid., 225.

70   **For centuries, scholars from the four different schools:** Sardar, *Une Histoire de La Mecque*, 353–54.

70   **from several hundred to around thirty-five:** Interview with Sami Angawi, Jeddah, February 2018.

4: Darkness

72   **They chanted "Death to Al-Saud":** Trofimov, *The Siege of Mecca*, 17–18 and 199–200.

72   **There was a little-known history of protest in the Eastern Province:** T. Matthiesen, "Migration, Minorities, and Radical Networks: Labour Movements and Opposition

Groups in Saudi Arabia, 1950–1975," *International Review of Social History* 59, no. 3 (December 2014): 473–504.

72 **al-Sa'id described it as a people's revolt:** Hegghammer and Lacroix, "Rejectionist Islamism in Saudi Arabia," 103–22.

72 **the tiny Saudi Communist Party:** Matthiesen, "Migration, Minorities, and Radical Networks," 473–504.

73 **the Saudi government tried to address:** T. Matthiesen, *The Other Saudis: Shiism, Dissent and Sectarianism* (New York: Cambridge University Press, 2014), 110–11.

73 **"If we did this . . ."** "Naif Briefs Journalists on Renegades," *Arab News*, January 14, 1980.

73 **foreign women eating in public:** Embassy Jidda, "Public Morality in Riyadh," Wikileaks Cable: 1979JIDDA04261_e, dated June 6, 1979, http://wikileaks.org/plusd/cables /1979JIDDA04261_e.html; Embassy Jidda, "Saudi Ulema Ban Table Soccer: Paper Criticizes Decision," Wikileaks Cable: 1979JIDDA00058_e, dated January 1, 1979, http://wikileaks.org /plusd/cables/1979JIDDA00058_e.html.

74 **"the boy from the Al-ash-Sheikh family":** Vassiliev, *King Faisal of Saudi Arabia*, 59.

74 **Women presenters were yanked off television:** E. Cody, "Saudis, Shaken by Mosque Takeover, Tighten Enforcement of Moslem Law," *Washington Post*, February 5, 1980.

74 **They felt so empowered:** Private anecdote from Saudis interviewed in Riyadh and Jeddah, February 2018.

75 **the king quietly asked him:** Anonymous Saudi source speaking to author in Saudi Arabia, February 2018.

75 **King Khaled would praise the sahwa:** King Khaled, speech given during 1981 Islamic Summit in Mecca, available online at https://m.youtube.com/watch?v=35R5jPlSHt4.

75 **"no different from opium":** J. Kifner, "Khomeini Bans Broadcast Music, Saying It Corrupts Iranian Youth," *New York Times*, July 24, 1979.

75 **crates of vintage champagne:** Associated Press, "Iranian Guards Dump Costly Wines, Liquor," *Globe and Mail*, June 14, 1979.

76 **"naked women":** G. Jaynes, "Bazargan Goes to See Khomeini as Iran Rift Grows," *New York Times*, March 9, 1979.

76 **"In the dawn of freedom, there is an absence of freedom":** G. Jaynes, "Iran Women March Against Restraints on Dress and Rights," *New York Times*, March 11, 1979.

76 **the *hijab* (headscarf) would never become mandatory:** E. Sadeghi-Boroujerdi, "The Post-Revolutionary Women's Uprising of March 1979: An Interview with Nasser Mohajer and Mahnaz Matin," *Iran Wire*, June 12, 2013.

76 **they were depicted as the work of monarchists:** Ibid.

76 **Some women were so angry:** J. C. Randal, "Militant Women Demonstrators Attack Khomeini Aide Who Heads Iran," *Washington Post*, March 13, 1979.

77 **Foucault recognized Islam as a "powder keg":** J. Afary and K. B. Anderson, *Foucault and the Iranian Revolution: Gender and the Seductions of Islamism* (Chicago: University of Chicago Press, 2005), 107.

77 **Seven hundred qualified scholars:** Secor, *Children of Paradise*, 69–71.

77 **Sciences were left alone:** Ibid.

78 **"More than 7,900 Iranian political prisoners":** Ibid., 91.

79 **After his stop in Tripoli:** Condensed from Cooper, *The Fall of Heaven*, 352, 371; and Bird, *The Good Spy*, 206. Both books relied on personal interviews and declassified CIA documents.

79 **deeply distressed:** Ibid.

79 **US intelligence files . . . implicated:** Bird, *The Good Spy*, 226.

81 **referred to King Faisal as *Amir el Mu'meneen*:** H. Fürtig, *Iran's Rivalry with Saudi Arabia Between the Gulf Wars* (Reading, UK: Ithaca Press, 2006).

81 **little girls and boys draped in the Saudi and Iranian flags:** D. A. Schmidt, "Shah of Iran and Saudis' King Seek Persian Gulf Cooperation," *New York Times*, November 14, 1968.

81 **Sent Prime Minister Bazergan a congratulatory message:** "Wali al-Ahd Youhani Bazergan" [Crown Prince congratulates Bazergan], *Al Nadwa* (Mecca), February 14, 1979.

81 **"making Islam, not heavy armament, the organizer":** N. Safran, *Saudi Arabia: The Ceaseless Quest for Security* (Cambridge, UK: Belknap Press, 1985), 308, citing Foreign Broadcast Information Service (FBIS), April 25, 1979.

82 **"the camel grazers of Riyadh":** R. Khomeini, *Kashf al-Asrar*, as translated in Moin, *Khomeini*, 62.

82 **The overtures of all the Gulf countries:** M. Heikal, "'Mini-Shahs' Trust Evolution to Avert Revolution in the Gulf," *Dawn*, December 30, 1979.

82 **"demote the Iranian Revolution":** Ibid.

82 **Saudi funding for WAMY:** Pew Research Center, Religion and Public Life, "Muslim Networks and Movements in Western Europe," September 15, 2010, available online at https://www.pewforum.org/2010/09/15/muslim-networks-and-movements-in-western-europe/.

83 **At five o'clock on the morning of December 25:** United States Embassy Afghanistan Office of the Defense Attaché, "Soviet Airlift to Kabul," declassified cable, December 26, 1979.

83 **military training:** P. Niesewand, "Guerrillas Train in Pakistan to Oust Afghan Government," *Washington Post*, February 2, 1979.

83 **The Saudis had also been pushing the US:** H. Haqqani, *Pakistan: Between Mosque and Military* (Washington, DC: Carnegie Endowment for International Peace, 2005), 199.

83 **Saudi intelligence chief Turki al-Faisal:** Wright, *Looming Tower*, 114.

84 **The Muslim Brotherhood organized protests:** R. Lefevre, *Ashes of Hama: The Muslim Brotherhood in Syria* (New York: Oxford University Press, 2013), 48.

85 **hit-and-run acts:** P. Seale, *Asad: The Struggle for the Middle East* (London: I. B. Tauris, 1989), 317.

85 **The violence was not all Islamist:** The analysis of the events surrounding the Aleppo incident and the Brotherhood uprising is based on M. Seurat, *Syrie, l'État de Barbarie* [Syria: the state of barbarism] (Paris: Presses Universitaires de France, 2012), 89–90 and 134–36. Written before his death in 1985, these articles were compiled in a book posthumously.

85 **"The people die like rain":** S. Pickering Jr., "Pedagogica Deserta: Memoir of a Fulbright Year in Syria," *American Scholar* 50, no. 2 (Spring 1981): 163–77.

85 **Sa'id Hawwa:** Lefevre, *Ashes of Hama*, 48.

86 **Shia-Alawite geographical axis:** Seurat, *Syrie, l'État De Barbarie*, 134.

87 **He rounded some of them up:** Author interviews in Baghdad, March 2018, with former Islamist and counterterrorism expert Husham Hashmi and with Mahmoud Mashhadani, organizing member of al-Muwahidoun, jailed in 1979 and 1989.

87 **a surprise twenty-four-hour visit:** "Tafahum tam bayna al Saudia wal Iraq ala daam masa'i tawhid al saf al arabi" [Total understanding between Saudi Arabia and Iraq on closing Arab ranks], *Asharq al-Awsat*, August 7, 1980.

88 **Crown Prince Fahd called for a holy war:** "Saudi Prince Issues Call for Holy War with Israel," *Globe and Mail*, August 15, 1980.

88 **a $14 billion loan:** "Al-qard al-kuwaiti lil-iraq jiz' min qard khaliji dakhm" [Kuwait loan to Iraq is part of massive Gulf loan], *Al Ra'i al-A'am* (Kuwait), April 16, 1981.

5: I Killed the Pharaoh

94 **He disapproved of cinema:** All descriptions and details of Ibrahim's journey from student life to prison are based on author interview with Nageh Ibrahim, Alexandria, Egypt, October 2017; and with G. Khoury (writer), posed online April 9, 2014; "Al-Mashhad: Nageh Ibrahim" [television series episode], *Al-Mashhad*, BBC Arabic.

95 **Friday on university campuses:** Author interview with Nageh Ibrahim; R. Solé, *Sadate* (Paris: Tempus Perrin, 2013), 263.

96 **the focus of many jokes:** Ibid., 241.

96 **calling him "my friend Kissinger":** Ibid., 132.

97 **he had a Swiss watch:** Ibid.

97 **for his children and grandchildren:** Ibid., 264.

98   **allowed Islamist groupings to run:** Ibid., 112; interview with Emad Abu Ghazi (former socialist, imprisoned in 1981, later minister of cultural affairs in 2011), October 2018.

98   **sense of belonging in the city:** S. Ibrahim, *Egypt, Islam, and Democracy* (Cairo: American University in Cairo Press, 1996), chapter 1.

98   **socialist summer camps were renamed:** Author interview with Emad Abu Ghazi, leftist activist and former minister.

99   **rage had quickly replaced the initial:** Solé, *Sadate*, 171; and "Al-qahira: al-sadat najaha mi'a fil mi'a. 'Ada'oul thalathouna 'aman 'ouzila fi thalathin sa'a" [Sadat's victory: 30 years of hostility erased in 30 hours], *An-Nahar*, November 22, 1977; "Al-sadat yabda'u rihlatil 'ari wal khiyanah" [Sadat begins his trip of shame and treachery], *Al-Thawra*, November 20, 1977; "Khutwatul sadat khurujon 'ala 'iradatil 'umat il-arabiyya" [Sadat's move a departure from the Arab nation's will], *Tishreen*, November 19, 1977.

99   **"trip of treachery and shame":** "Dimashq tastaqtibu al-'amala al-'arabiy didda khiyanat al-sadat" [Damascus to lead Arab action against Sadat's treason], *Tishreen*, November 21, 1977); and "Al-sadat yabda'u rihlatil 'ari wal khiyanah" [Sadat begins his trip of shame and treachery].

99   **secretly King Khaled had prayed:** M. Heikal, *Autumn of Fury* (London: Andre Deutsch Limited, 1983), 98.

99   **billions of dollars:** T. W. Lippman, "Post-Camp David Split Sours Egypt's Ties to Saudi Arabia," *Washington Post*, December 9, 1978.

100   **"empty out-bidding":** "Saudi Arabians Stand Firm: Arabs in Disarray on Punishing Sadat," *Globe and Mail*, March 30, 1979.

100   **He dismissed the leaders of Gulf monarchies:** Solé, *Sadate*, 237.

100   **who had "turned Islam into a mockery":** "Al-'islamu din-ul hob wal samahat wal 'ikha' wa laysa abadan ahqada al-khomeiny" [Islam is a religion of love, forgiveness and compassion, and not Khomeini's hatred], *Al-Ahram*, December 26, 1979.

100   **"The success of the Islamic revolution":** Y. M. Ibrahim, "Iranian Leaders Consider Egypt Ripe for Islamic Uprising," *New York Times*, February 25, 1979.

101   **Khomeini went further:** M. Wallace, *20th Century with Mike Wallace: Death of the Shah and the Hostage Crisis*, Arts and Entertainment Network, History Channel (television network), 2002.

102   **raised many questions for Islamists:** Embassy Cairo, "Some Further Egyptian Reactions to Khomeini's Return," Wikileaks Cable: 1979CAIRO02483_e, dated February 3, 1979, http://wikileaks.org/plusd/cables/1979CAIRO02483_e.html.

102   **control of its finances:** T. Moustafa, "Conflict and Cooperation Between the State and Religious Institutions in Contemporary Egypt," *International Journal of Middle East Studies* 32, no. 1 (February 2010): 3–22.

102   **while in prison Qutb had read:** Heikal, *Autumn of Fury*, 126.

104   **"going about like black tents":** Ibid., 241.

104   **"and no religion in politics":** "Waqfatu hisaben ma'il nafs wa muhasabat kol 'abith bi 'amni misr" [Self-accountability for those who endanger Egypt's security], *Al Ahram*, September 6, 1981.

104   **the autumn of fury:** Title of Mohammad Heikal's book about Sadat's assassination.

104   **Farag had broken his leg:** Heikal, *Autumn of Fury*, 251.

104   **this was a question of survival:** Author interview with Nageh Ibrahim.

105   **"rise as the Iranian masses":** Heikal, *Autumn of Fury*, 252.

106   **"death of the traitor mercenary":** "Al-sadat shaheedan fi rihabi-llah" [Sadat a martyr in God's care], *Asharq al-Awsat*, October 7, 1981.

106   **the nucleus of the new order:** Heikal, *Autumn of Fury*, 262.

106   **armed forces to stay neutral:** Ibid., 263.

107   **a calm sense of achievement:** G. Khoury (presenter), "Al-Mashhad: Sheikh Hani Fahs" [television series episode], *Al-Mashhad*, BBC Arabic, September 18, 2014.

107   **the investigators' wrath:** Ibid.

108   **By 1985, he was in Jeddah:** Wright, *Looming Tower*, 69–70.

108 **the silence was eerie:** W. E. Farrell, "Sadat Is Interred at Rites Attended by World Leaders," *New York Times*, October 11, 1981.

108 **Syria's official newspaper,** *Tishreen*: "Misr tadfunu al-yawm wa ilal abad ramz al-khiyanah" [Egypt today bids farewell forever to the ultimate traitor], *Tishreen*, October 11, 1981; "Janazaton amrikiya-isra'iliyya lil sadat" [An American-Israeli funeral for Sadat], *Al-Thawra*, October 11, 1981.

6: No Dupatta

110 **"My sole aim":** L. M. Simons, "Pakistani General Pictured as Reluctant Coup Leader," *Washington Post*, July 12, 1977.

112 **"Who can say there is no freedom here?":** S. Ayaz, *The Storm's Call for Prayers: Selections from Shaikh Ayaz* (New York: Oxford University Press, 2001), 26.

112 **Muhammed Ali Jinnah, the father of the nation:** F. Ispahani, *Purifying the Land of the Pure: A History of Pakistan's Religious Minorities* (Noida: HarperCollins India, 2016), 8.

112 **His first law minister:** Ibid., 27.

113 **"you are free to go":** M. A. Jinnah's speech on August 11, 1947, in "Constituent Assembly of Pakistan Debates," Government Printing Press, 1948.

113 **brandished Pakistan as a citadel:** Ispahani, *Purifying the Land of the Pure*, 28.

113 **Mawdudi was dismayed by the fall:** N. F. Paracha, "Abul Ala Maududi: An Existentialist History," *Dawn*, January 1, 2015.

113 **Mawdudi's ideas about Islam:** based on V. Nasr, *Mawdudi and the Making of Islamic Revivalism* (New York: Oxford University Press, 1996); and P. Jenkins, "Clerical Terror," *New Republic*, December 24, 2008.

114 **"Give to the drinkers, O wine bearer":** Nasr, *Mawdudi and the Making of Islamic Revivalism*, 141.

115 **The Pakistani scholar and Khomeini met:** V. Nasr, *The Vanguard of the Islamic Revolution: The Jama'at-i Islami of Pakistan* (Berkeley: University of California Press, 1994), 254 n29.

115 **the intervention of Saudi Arabia:** J. M. Dorsey, "Pakistan's Lurch Towards Ultra-Conservativism Abetted by Saudi-Inspired Pyramid Scheme," *Eurasia Review*, April 23, 2017.

115 **During the elections of 1970:** Nasr, *Mawdudi and the Making of Islamic Revivalism*, 45.

115 **Mawdudi was suddenly useful:** Ibid., 46.

115 **Even when Zia spoke:** *Pakistan Horizon* 31, no. 2/3 (Second and Third Quarter, 1978): 232–74.

116 **connections in Mecca and Medina:** Nasr, *Vanguard of the Islamic Revolution*, 60, 236 n23.

116 **Pakistan's biggest English-language daily:** "Dawalibi Coming to Advise Ideology Body," *Dawn*, September 25, 1978; "Renowned Muslim Jurists to Assist Pakistan," *Dawn*, October 5, 1978.

116 **He had also served as:** Dawalibi's life story is reconstructed from interviews with his sons Hisham and Nofal in Riyadh; and Vassiliev, *King Faisal of Saudi Arabia*, 272.

116 **reason with retrograde clerics:** Vassiliev, *King Faisal of Saudi Arabia*, 272.

116 **Dawalibi despised Bin Baz:** Author interview with Nofal Dawalibi, Riyadh, February 2018.

117 **there was grandiose talk:** Embassy Islamabad, "Saudi Religious Advisor Visits Latest Manifestation of 'Islamania,'" Wikileaks Cable: 1978ISLAMA09483_d, dated October 2, 1978, https://wikileaks.org/plusd/cables/1978ISLAMA09483_d.html.

117 **Zia had made a forty-eight-minute speech:** "Measures for Nizam-i-Islam," *Dawn*, February 10, 1979.

118 **King Khaled of Saudi Arabia:** "Islamic Laws," *Dawn*, February 28, 1979.

118 **a Pakistani jurist doing a review:** Interview with Syed Afzal Haidar, former member of the Council of Islamic Ideology.

118 **bars, brothels, and breweries:** "Ighlaq kol l-barat wa buyuti l-bagha' fi Pakistan" [Closure of all bars and brothels in Pakistan], *An-Nahar*, February 14, 1979.

118 **Zia spoke to CBS television:** "Zia to Consult Military Council, Cabinet," *Dawn*, February 17, 1979.

119 **A week later, Mawdudi received:** "Shah Faisal Award for Maudoodi," *Dawn*, February 20, 1979.

119 **should the young thief of a mosque:** W. Claiborne, "Zia's Islam Metes Strict Tolls," *Washington Post*, December 6, 1982.

120 **Women screamed "Death to Zia":** P. Niesew, "Pakistan Stunned by Bhutto Execution," *Washington Post*, April 5, 1979.

121 **Pakistani television had shown ballet:** S. Kothari, "From Genre to Zanaana: Urdu Television Drama Serials and Women's Culture in Pakistan," *Contemporary South Asia* 14, no. 3 (2005): 289–305.

121 **She told her co-presenter:** Author interview with Mehtab Rashdi, Karachi, October 2017.

121 **When Zia banned makeup:** N. F. Paracha, "The Heart's Filthy Lesson," *Dawn*, February 14, 2013.

123 **Benazir and her mother lived:** F. Prial, "Pakistan Keeps Bhutto Family Behind Barbed Wire," *New York Times*, November 15, 1980.

123 **They sent orders to the provincial government:** Author interview with Mehtab Rashdi, Karachi, October 2018.

123 **Pakistanis were starting to suffocate:** This characterization is based on descriptions from a number of Pakistanis who were young teens or adults in that period.

124 **tensions grew within families:** N. F. Paracha, *End of the Past* (Lahore: Vanguard Books, 2016), 19–20.

124 **Clerics were gaining influence everywhere:** Haqqani, *Pakistan: Between Mosque and Military*, 169–70.

124 **History was also being rewritten:** Ispahani, *Purifying the Land of the Pure*, 97–98.

125 **During the 1960s and early 1970s:** The description, statistics, and laws on the position of women in Pakistan are taken from A. Weiss, "Women's Position in Pakistan: Sociocultural Effects of Islamization," *Asian Survey* 25, no. 8 (August 1985): 863–80.

125 **The uncompromising attitudes:** "Entertainers in Pakistan: Mehtab Channa," *Dawn*, December 3, 1979.

126 **They faced off with the police:** J. Stokes, "Pakistani Women Stage Protests Against Proposed Islamic Laws," *Globe and Mail*, March 3, 1983.

126 **But the polling stations had been deserted:** "Pakistani Leader Gets 98% of Referendum Vote," *New York Times*, December 21, 1984.

127 **For ten long minutes:** R. Massey, "Obituary: Iqbal Bano," *Guardian*, May 11, 2009. Recordings of the concert are also available online.

7: Karbala in Beirut

130 **At eleven in the morning:** C. Collins, "Chronology of the Israeli Invasion of Lebanon, June–August 1982," *Journal of Palestine Studies*, special issue, vol. 11, no. 4–vol. 12, no. 1 (Summer/Autumn 1982): 135–92.

131 **several thousand Shias:** Blanford, *Warriors of God*, chapter 1.

131 **Israeli soldiers would walk around:** Ibid., prologue.

131 **a hunting rifle and shot:** F. Ajami, *The Dream Palace of the Arabs: A Generations Odyssey* (New York: Vintage, 1999), 99.

132 **in his 1957 poem "The Bridge":** Ibid., 27, quoting a translation by Issa Boulatta.

132 **"Where are the Arabs?":** Ibid., 26.

132 **leaving behind a love letter:** R. Rahim, *In English, Faiz Ahmed Faiz: A Renowned Urdu Poet* (Bloomington, IN: Xlibris, 2008), 358–59.

133 **When Sheikh Sobhi Tufayli:** Blanford, *Warriors of God*, chapter 2.

134 **and his "radiant presence":** P. Claude, "Mystery Man Behind the Party of God," *Guardian*, May 13, 2005.

134 **five thousand Iranians:** Chehabi, *Distant Relations*, 213.

135 **The statue of President Nasser:** H. Saghieh and B. Al-Sheikh, *Shu'ub al Sha'ab al Lubnani* [Peoples of Lebanese people] (Beirut: Dar al Saqi, 2015), 72–79.

135 **out of precaution:** Chehabi, *Distant Relations*, 218.

135 **Some reports talk of families:** Saghieh and Al-Sheikh, *Shu'ub al Sha'ab al Lubnani*, 72–79.

136 **wearing military fatigues under their clerical robes:** Blanford, *Warriors of God*, chapter 2.

137 **Montazeri was a typical:** Chehabi, *Distant Relations*, 193.

137 **three hundred volunteers:** "Ready to Fight, Iranians Wait in Vain for Trip to Lebanon," *Globe and Mail*, December 11, 1979.

137 **closed the airspace:** Chehabi, *Distant Relations*, 207.

137 **declared Montazeri mentally deranged:** Ibid.

137 **he did make it:** "Iranian Volunteers Seen in Lebanon," *Globe and Mail*, January 5, 1980.

138 **thousands marched in the streets:** R. Wright, *Sacred Rage: The Wrath of Militant Islam* (New York: Touchstone, 1985), 159.

138 **Their recruiters were more canny:** Blanford, *Warriors of God*, chapter 2.

139 **people like Sheikh Tufayli:** Ibid.

139 **a band of a hundred women:** B. Graham, "Islamic Fundamentalism Rises," *Washington Post*, October 5, 1984.

140 **"And whoever takes Allah":** Quran, 5:56, from *English Translation of the Holy Quran*, Ali and Aziz.

140 **They wanted to show:** C. Dickey, "Young Lebanese Seek New Martyrdom: Suicide Bombers Emerge as Martyrs," *Washington Post*, May 12, 1985.

141 **"I am a future martyr":** Ibid.

141 **Wearing red headbands:** T. Smith, "Iran: Five Years of Fanaticism," *New York Times*, February 12, 1984.

141 **a celebrated open letter:** F. Ajami, "Iran: The Impossible Revolution," *Foreign Affairs* 67, no. 2 (Winter 1988): 135–55.

142 **Karbala cannot be used to justify "war":** Ajami, *Dream Palace of the Arabs*, 152.

143 **Fahs was shaken:** Author interview with Badia Fahs, Beirut, March 2018.

8: Shia Kafir

146 **The two men met only once:** A. Rieck, *The Shias of Pakistan: An Assertive and Beleaguered Minority* (New York: Oxford University Press, 2016), 441 n373.

147 **one of the first Pakistani religious students:** Ibid., 221.

148 **$225 million in seed money:** "Historic Announcement," *Dawn*, February 11, 1979. The fund was 2,250 million Pakistani rupees in 1979, which was equivalent to $225 million according to the exchange rate then.

148 **would next distribute punch cards:** S. Auerbach, "Pakistan's Official Turn to Islam Collides with Tradition," *Washington Post*, September 8, 1980.

149 **Sunni groups in Karachi:** Rieck, *Shias of Pakistan*, 204.

149 **banks across the country:** D. Denman, "Zia's Tax Opposed," *Guardian*, June 28, 1980.

149 **they had called on outside support:** M. Abou-Zahab, "The Politicization of the Shia Community in Pakistan in the 1970s and 1980s," in A. Monsutti, S. Naef, and F. Sabahi, eds., *The Other Shiites: From the Mediterranean to Central Asia* (Bern: Peter Lang, 2007), 103; and citing S. A. Tirmazi, *Profiles of Intelligence* (Lahore: Fiction House, 1995), 272, 283.

149 **Pakistan had looked to Iran:** A. Vatanka. *Iran and Pakistan: Security, Diplomacy and American Influence* (London: I. B. Tauris, 2015), 6.

150 **the ISO would be directly linked to:** Ibid., 241.

150 **four thousand students:** Abou-Zahab, "Politicization of the Shia Community in Pakistan in the 1970s and 1980s," 101.

150 **He went to visit Khomeini:** Author interview with Hussaini companion Shia Allama Iftikhar Naqvi, Islamabad, October 2017.

150 **Pakistan became a huge source:** Abou-Zahab, "Politicization of the Shia Community in Pakistan in the 1970s and 1980s."

150 **He thought Khomeini was blessed:** Fuchs, "Relocating the Centers of Shi'i Islam," 504.

151 **new tradition of "Jerusalem Day":** Rieck, *Shias of Pakistan*, 223.

151 **"Wahhabis who wrap themselves":** S. W. Fuchs, "Third Wave Shi'ism: Sayyid 'Arif Husain al-Husaini and the Islamic Revolution in Pakistan," *Journal of the Royal Asiatic Society* 24, no. 3 (July 2014): 493–510.

152 **"cold black eyes" peering:** R. Tempest, "City of Evil Countenances," *Gazette* (Montreal), May 17, 1986.

153 **establishing a small Arabistan:** "Asharq al-Awsat Interviews Umm Mohammed: The Wife of Bin Laden's Spiritual Mentor," *Asharq al-Awsat*, April 30, 2006.

153 **the unity of the Islamic nation:** J. Khashoggi, "Arab Mujahideen in Afghanistan—II: Maasada Exemplifies the Unity of the Islamic Umma," *Arab News*, May 14, 1988.

153 **give the Soviets their own Vietnam:** S. Coll, *Ghost Wars: The Secret History of the CIA, Afghanistan, and Bin Laden, from the Soviet Invasion to September 10, 2001* (London: Penguin, 2005), 50–51.

154 **the American Club, which opened in 1985:** K. Brulliard, "Khyber Club's Bartender Had Front-Row Seat to History in Pakistan," *Washington Post*, February 7, 2012.

154 **Jamal sat in the garden:** Author interview with Khashoggi in Washington, DC, July 2017.

155 **why was Jamal helping the *kuffar*:** B. Rubin, "The Jamal Khashoggi I Knew," *War on the Rocks*, October 26, 2018, available online at https://warontherocks.com/2018/10/the-jamal-khashoggi-i-knew/.

155 **was Abdallah Azzam:** The descriptions of Azzam, his relationship with Bin Laden, and their joining forces with money and a fatwa are condensed from Wright, *Looming Tower*, 109–11 and 117–19. The author also relied heavily on the work of Thomas Hegghammer, including T. Hegghammer, "Abdallah Azzam and Palestine," *Die Welt des Islams* 53, nos. 3–4 (January 2013): 353–87.

155 **by raising a fortune:** Wright, *Looming Tower*, 117.

155 **religious edict that turned modern tradition:** T. Hegghammer, "The Rise of Muslim Fighters: Islam and the Globalization of Jihad," *International Security* 35, no. 3 (Winter 2010/2011): 53–94.

156 **a quarter of a million:** Wright, *Looming Tower*, 452 n122.

156 **estimated total of thirty-five thousand over the course of the war:** A. Rashid, *Taliban: Militant Islam, Oil and Fundamentalism in Central Asia*, 2nd ed. (New Haven, CT: Yale University Press, 2010), 129.

156 **So was his chief of staff:** Wright, *The Looming Tower*, 119–20.

156 **Saudi Airlines gave huge discounts:** T. Hegghammer, *Jihad in Saudi Arabia: Violence and Pan-Islamism Since 1979* (Cambridge, UK: Cambridge University Press, 2010), 21.

156 **Azzam's salary was paid:** Ibid., 41.

156 **In Cairo, the office:** Wright, *The Looming Tower*, 112.

156 **Saudi individuals raised:** Coll, *Ghost Wars*, 83–84.

156 **The governor of Riyadh:** B. Riedel, *The Prince of Counterterrorism* (Washington, DC: Brookings Institution Press, 2015).

157 **he made his views known:** Rubin, "The Jamal Khashoggi I Knew."

157 **the number of registered Afghan refugees:** M. Safri, "The Transformation of the Afghan Refugee: 1979–2009," *Middle East Journal* 65, no. 4 (Autumn 2011): 587–601.

157 **Saudi charities built hundreds of religious *madrassas*:** Coll, *Ghost Wars*, 86.

157 **rise in the number of graduates:** J. Malik, *Colonization of Islam: Dissolution of Traditional Institutions in Pakistan* (Delhi: Manohar, 1998), 230–32; Fuchs, "Relocating the Centers of Shi'i Islam," 269.

157 **The quality of teaching could not keep up:** V. Nasr, "The Rise of Sunni Militancy in Pakistan: The Changing Role of Islamism and the Ulama in Society and Politics," *Modern Asian Studies* 34, no. 1 (February 2000): 139–80.

159 **no publisher in the Arab world:** Mohammad Zayn al Abidine Suroor interview, Al-Hiwar TV, July 31, 2008.

159 **he ordered three thousand copies:** Ibid.

159 **the most influential cleric:** B. Haykel, "Al-Qa'ida and Shiism," in A. Moghadam and B. Fishman, eds., *Fault Lines in Global Jihad* (New York: Routledge, 2011), 191.

160 **amply fulfilled the hopes:** Fuchs, "Relocating the Centers of Shi'i Islam," 256.

160 **not only encouraged such vitriol:** Nasr, "Rise of Sunni Militancy," 160.

160 **Saudi embassies from Islamabad:** Nasr, *The Shia Revival*, 163–66; interview with former militant Mansour Nogeidan, Dubai, April 2017.

160 **As a secular Baathist:** S. Helfont, "Saddam and the Islamists: The Ba'thist Regime's Instrumentalization of Religion in Foreign Affairs," *Middle East Journal* 68, no. 3 (Summer 2014): 352–66.

160 **The Pakistani delegation was the largest:** Ibid.

160 **"Those people only understand":** Ehsan Elahi Zaheer, speech available online at https://www.youtube.com/watch?v=06Lo-CxhGrI.

161 **with the tacit approval of Zia:** K. Ahmed, *Sectarian War: Pakistan's Sunni-Shia Violence and Its Links to the Middle East* (New York: Oxford University Press, 2012), 116–17.

161 **In 1986, the sectarian poison:** Ahmed, *Sectarian War*, 116–17.

161 **The local tribes mobilized:** Rieck, *The Shias of Pakistan*, 229; M. Abou-Zahab, "Sectarianism in Pakistan's Kurram Tribal Agency," *Terrorism Monitor* 7, no. 6 (March 2009).

161 **Both Saddam and King Fahd:** Details surrounding the circumstances of Zaheer's death, transfer to Saudi Arabia, and funeral are from an interview with his son Ebtessam Elahi Zaheer, Lahore, August 2018.

162 **protests erupted over his death:** "Blood for Blood, Anti-Zia Rioters Yell," *Gazette* (Montreal), April 1, 1987.

163 **the Saudis became wary of Shia soldiers:** R. M. Weintraub, "Saudis to Send Pakistani Unit Back Home," *Washington Post*, November 28, 1987; "Gulf War: Shifting Sands," *Economist*, December 12, 1987.

163 **massing six hundred thousand troops on the border:** "Military Escalation Continues Amidst US-Soviet Consultations," *Asharq al-Awsat*, August 15, 1986.

9: Mecca Is Mine

164 **On this day, July 31, 1987:** Interview with Sami Angawi, Jeddah, February 2018.

165 **rose a Hilton Hotel:** D. Howden, "Shadows over Mecca," *Independent*, April 19, 2006.

165 **1.8 million pilgrims participated:** S. M. Badeeb, *Saudi-Iranian Relations 1932–1982* (London: Centre for Arab and Iranian Studies (1993).

166 **King Fahd launched:** D. B. Ottaway, "Fahd Adjusts Step to March of Islam," *Washington Post*, November 27, 1984.

166 **The Saudi-endorsed translations:** K. Mohammad, "Assessing English Translations of the Qur'an," *Middle East Quarterly* 12, no. 2 (Spring 2005): 58–71.

167 **The arched gateway, known as:** M. N. Mirza and A. S. Shawoosh, *The Illustrated Atlas of Makkah and the Holy Environs* (Center of Makkah History, 2011), 218.

167 **$10 billion up to December 1981:** Fürtig, *Iran's Rivalry with Saudi Arabia Between the Gulf Wars*, 64–65.

168 **They once offered the Iranians $25 billion:** Ibid., 66.

168 **a cease-fire through backroom deals:** M. Sieff, "New Ties with Iran Aim of Saudi Role," *Washington Times*, December 18, 1986.

168 **No caliph had reigned:** Sardar, *Une Histoire de La Mecque*, chapter 3.

168 **there were violent clashes:** Fürtig, *Iran's Rivalry with Saudi Arabia Between the Gulf Wars*, 43–45.

169 **The leaders assigned to guide:** M. Khalaji, "Iran's Ideological Exploitation of the Hajj," Washington Institute, September 12, 2016, available online at https://www.washingtoninstitute.org/policy-analysis/view/irans-ideological-exploitation-of-the-hajj.

169 **First introduced by Saladin:** G. Fakkar, "Story Behind the King's Title," *Arab News*, January 27, 2015.

169 **the title had never been officially used:** King Faisal once referred to himself as Custodian of the Two Holy Mosques but never adopted the title officially.

169 **turn it into a "battlefield":** E. Sciolino, "Mecca Tragedy: Chain of Events Begins to Emerge," *New York Times*, September 6, 1987.

169 **"with as much ceremony as possible":** "Excerpts from Khomeini Speeches," *New York Times*, August 4, 1987.

169 **denied that such an agreement:** Author interview with Turki al-Faisal, Riyadh, February 2018.

170 **The crowd of sixty thousand:** I. Leverrier, "L'Arabie Saoudite, le Pèlerinage et l'Iran" [Saudi Arabia, the pilgrimage and Iran], *Cahiers d'études sur la Méditerranée orientale et le monde turco-iranien* 22 (1996): 111–48.

170 **"Shots could be heard":** M. Hussain, "Eyewitness in Mecca," *Washington Post*, August 20, 1987.

170 **275 of them Iranian:** The death tolls varied depending on accounts; these are both the official Saudi death toll and the tolls reported in ibid.

170 **in the face of the "Iranian mob":** "Ta'yeed islami shamil lil 'ijra'at al-saudiyya al-hazimah" [Complete Islamic support for Saudi Arabia's decisive actions], *Asharq al-Awsat*, August 4, 1987.

170 **"uproot the Saudi rulers":** Associated Press, "Tehran Urges Faithful to Attack Saudis," *Orlando Sentinel*, August 3, 1987.

171 **The Saudis gathered six hundred supporters:** M. Kramer, *Arab Awakening and Islamic Revival* (New Brunswick, NJ: Transaction Publishers, 1996), 161–87.

171 **expel the Al-Sauds from the Hejaz:** Ibid.

172 **invited delegations from Persia:** Badeeb, *Saudi-Iranian Relations 1932–1982*, 80–81.

172 **"the remains of great saints":** O. Beranek and P. Tupek, "From Visiting Graves to Their Destruction: The Question of Ziyara Through the Eyes of Salafis," Crown Center for Middle East Studies, Brandeis University, July 2009, available online at https://www.brandeis.edu /crown/publications/cp/CP2.pdf.

172 **killing two thousand people:** H. Redissi, *Une Histoire du Wahhabisme: Comment l'Islam Sectaire Est Devenu l'Islam* (Paris: Editions du Seuil, 2007), 63.

172 **"killing 300 Wahhabis":** M. Ajlani, *History of Saudi Arabia: The First Saudi State*, vol. 2, *Era of Imam AbdelAziz Bin Muhamad* (Beirut: Dar al-Nafaès, 1994), 128–29.

10: Culture Wars

175 **a four-engine C-130 . . . crashed:** E. Sciolino, "Zia of Pakistan Dies as Blast Downs Plane," *New York Times*, August 18, 1988.

175 **The US secretary of state:** Ibid.

176 **Shias celebrated loudly:** T. Weaver, "Zia's Death Sparks Intra-Moslem Feud," *Washington Post*, August 24, 1988.

176 **This was God's wrath:** Author interview with Mehtab Rashdi, Karachi, October 2017.

176 **"I do not regret the death of Zia":** Sciolino, "Zia of Pakistan Dies as Blast Downs Plane."

176 **He maintained the ban on political parties:** T. Mehdi, "An Overview of 1988 General Elections: Triumph but No Glory," *Dawn*, April 11, 2013.

176 **Benazir would be days away from delivering her:** M. Fineman, "Timing Puts Pregnant Foe at Disadvantage: Zia Sets Pakistan Election for November," *Los Angeles Times*, July 21, 1988.

177 **sixty-six infants and children:** Associated Press, "30 Years Later, US Downing of Iran Flight Haunts Relations," *Voice of America*, July 3, 2018.

178 **The country could take no more:** Moin, *Khomeini*, 268.

178 **"Happy are those who have departed":** Khomeini's full statement is available online at https://www.nytimes.com/1988/07/23/world/words-of-khomeini-on-islam-the-revolution -and-a-cease-fire.html?searchResultPosition=1.

179 **At headquarters, they popped the champagne:** Coll, *Ghost Wars*, 185.

179 **the headlines in . . . *Asharq al-Awsat*:** "Iran tuhadidu al-mujahideen wa tatadakhal li-maslahati a-lshi'a" [Iran threatens the mujahedeen and intercedes in favor of shiites], *Asharq al-Awsat*, February 13, 1989.

179 **On Valentine's Day 1989:** K. Malik, *From Fatwa to Jihad* (London: Atlantic Books, 2017), 8.

179 **"I inform the proud Muslim people":** P. Murtagh, "Rushdie in Hiding After Ayatollah's Death Threat," *Guardian*, February 15, 1989.

180 **"migration, metamorphosis, divided selves":** S. Subrahmanyam, "The Angel and the Toady: Twenty Years Ago Today Ayatollah Khomeini Issued a Fatwa Against Salman Rushdie for The Satanic Verses," *Guardian*, February 14, 2009.

180 **Ahmad had previously worked:** D. H. Clark, "Syed Faiyazuddin Ahmad Obituary," *Guardian*, September 24, 2014.

180 **which received funding from Saudi Arabia:** Malik, *From Fatwa to Jihad*, 3.

181 **five were shot dead:** P. E. Tyler, "Khomeini Says Writer Must Die," *Washington Post*, February 15, 1989.

181 **came out against Khomeini's fatwa:** "Al-azhar yukhalif fatwa al-khomeini bi 'ihdar dam salman rushdi" [Al-Azhar opposes Khomeini's fatwa on killing Rushdie], *Asharq al-Awsat*, February 16, 1989; Y. M. Ibrahim, "Saudi Muslim Weighs Rushdie Trial," *New York Times*, February 23, 1989.

181 **"Muslims should curse the tyrants":** Moin, *Khomeini*, 305.

11: Black Wave

183 **"was against Islam. Far from it":** N. H Abu Zayd and E. R. Nelson, *Voice of an Exile: Reflections on Islam* (Westport, CT: Praeger, 2004), 11.

183 ***inshallah,* he would die a Muslim:** Ibid.

183 **in October 1992 the pope:** A. Cowell, "After 350 Years, Vatican Says Galileo Was Right: It Moves," *New York Times*, October 31, 1992.

184 **"scientific reasoning and solid methodology":** "Dr. Nasr Abu Zeid: fi bayan 'ila l'ummah: al-7aqiqa aw il-shahada" [Dr. Nasr Abu Zeid in a statement to the nation: a testimony], *Rose al-Youssef*, June 19, 1995.

184 **"the earth does not move":** "Qadiyat Nasr Abu Zeid" [The Nasr Abu Zeid case], *Al-Ahram*, March 31, 1993.

184 **"in the garb of religion":** Ibid.

184 **"Liberalism till victory or martyrdom":** A. Buccianti, "Les Obsèques de l'Écrivain Farag Foda Se Sont Transformées en Manifestation Anti-Islamiste," *Le Monde*, June 12, 1992.

184 **"the Quran needs to be reconsidered":** Abu Zayd and Nelson, *Voice of an Exile*, 57.

184 **how could anyone understand it?:** Ibid.

185 **purest form of the original faith:** M. Hoexter, S. N. Eisenstadt, and N. Levtzion, *The Public Sphere in Muslim Societies* (Albany: State University of New York Press, 2002), 41.

185 **"kind of 'Sunni inquisition'":** W. Muir and T. H. Weir, *The Caliphate, Its Rise, Decline, and Fall: From Original Sources* (Edinburgh: J. Grant, 1915), 570–71.

186 **"to destroy Egypt's Muslim society":** Abu Zayd and Nelson, *Voice of an Exile*, 2.

186 **"who had lost his way":** Ajami, *Dream Palace of the Arabs*, 214.

187 **Islamists were using to hurt Nasr:** Abu Zayd and Nelson, *Voice of an Exile*, 128.

187 **dressed up as a political act:** Author interview with Ebtehal Younes, Cairo, October 2017.

187 **the Islam of riches:** F. Fodah, *Before the Fall*, 2nd ed. (Cairo, Egypt: F. A. Fawda, 1995), 151.

188 **supposedly more righteous ways:** Ibid., 156.

188 **could earn $3,000 per month:** J. Miller, "The Embattled Arab Intellectual," *New York Times*, June 9, 1985.

188 **"But leave us our culture, our letters":** N. Qabbani, "Abu Jahl Buys Fleet Street," 1990. Author's translation. Poem is available online in Arabic at http://www.nizariat.com/.

189 **"I cannot accept that Islam be insulted":** Full video of debate can be found online at https://www.youtube.com/watch?v=ubF2jHuHN1w.

190 **as the martyr of the nation:** "Janazat farag foda tahawalat ila muzaharah wataniyyah tandud al-irhab" [Farag Foda's funeral turned into a national demonstration denouncing terrorism], *Al-Ahram*, June 11, 1992.

190 **"long live the cross"**: Ibid.

190 **"divide us between Muslims and infidels?"**: "'I'tirafat al-muttahem 'an khutuwat al-'amaliyyah" [Confessions of the accused about the different steps of the operation], *Akher Saa'a*, June 18, 1992.

191 **"hounding them with war"**: K. Murphy, "Egypt's 'Unknown Army' Wages War in Islam's Name," *Los Angeles Times*, July 12, 1992.

191 **enemies "of everything that is Islamic"**: Mohammad Kamal El Sayyed Mohammad, *Al Azhar Jami'an wa Jami'atan* [Al-Azhar, the mosque and the university], book 4 (Cairo: Majma' Al Bohouth al Islamiya, 1984).

191 **carry out this deadly duty**: C. Murphy, "Killing Apostates Condoned," *Washington Post*, July 2, 1993.

191 **was feeding intolerance and playing with fire**: "Silenced: Egypt," *Economist*, June 13, 1992.

192 **condemning women who didn't cover their hair**: J. Lancaster, "Top Islamic University Gains Influence in Cairo," *Washington Post*, April 11, 1995.

192 **considered Wahhabism to be a deviation**: Author interview with Al-Azhar expert Amr Ezzat, Cairo, October 2017.

193 **Egyptian women wore the headscarf**: T. Osman, *Egypt on the Brink: From Nasser to Mubarak* (New Haven, CT: Yale University Press, 2010), 89.

193 **decided to the veil on the spot**: "Muhadarat al-sheikhah hanaa tharwat" [Sheikha Hanaa Tharwat's Lectures], *Rose al-Youssef*, March 1, 1993.

193 **and a monthly salary of $150,000**: K. Van Nieuwkerk, *Performing Piety: Singers and Actors in Egypt's Islamic Revival* (Austin: University of Texas Press, 2014), 131.

194 **"to their account if they stop dancing"**: Ibid., 130.

194 **and traditional religious forces**: A. Cooperman, "First Bombs, Now Lawsuits: Egypt's Vibrant Cultural Life Is the Target of a New Legal Assault by Islamic Fundamentalists," *U.S. News & World Report*, December 23, 1996.

195 **at the Cairo book fair were religious**: Van Nieuwkerk, *Performing Piety*, 115.

195 **came off the walls and mantels**: Details gathered from conversations with several Egyptian intellectuals and journalists describing how social norms changed within a generation.

195 **In front of his usual massive crowd**: A section of Nasser's speech is available online at https://www.youtube.com/watch?v=TX4RK8bj2W0.

197 **coursed through his veins**: Abu Zayd and Nelson, *Voice of an Exile*, 2.

197 **It was a village of believers**: Reset DOC (producer), *Nasr Abu Zayd: My Life Fighting Intolerance*, part 1 [video uploaded September 2, 2010], available online at https://www.youtube.com/watch?v=_d7WGgHKfXc.

197 **"throwing a few pebbles into it"**: Ajami, *Dream Palace of the Arabs*, 225.

198 **"has now been transplanted into the university"**: A. Bakr, E. Colla, and N. H. Abu Zayd, "Silencing Is at the Heart of My Case," *Middle East Report* 185 (1993).

198 **had already died inside her**: Associated Press, "Egypt: Separated Muslim Scholar Faces Death Threats," video, June 26, 1995, available online at https://www.youtube.com/watch?v=Chup196QNt4.

198 **declared his marriage to Ebtehal null and void**: Abu Zayd and Nelson, *Voice of an Exile*, 8.

198 **"a murtad is a dead man"**: Associated Press, "Egypt: Separated Muslim Scholar Faces Death Threats."

198 **from Cairo University's library**: Abu Zayd and Nelson, *Voice of an Exile*, 155.

199 **Zawahiri had approved**: Wright, *Looming Tower*, 211.

199 **Palestinian militants had opted**: Associated Press, "Suicide Car Bomb Kills Two Near West Bank Restaurant," *Sarasota Herald*, April 17, 1993.

12: Generation 1979

201 **At 11:40 a.m., a car bomb exploded**: Descriptions of the incident are taken from E. Sciolino, "Bomb Kills 4 Americans in Saudi Arabia," *New York Times*, November 14, 1995; and

J. Lancaster, "Five Americans Killed by Car Bomb at Military Building in Saudi Capital," *Washington Post*, November 14, 1995.

201 **"This was not something you think would":** Sciolino, "Bomb Kills 4 Americans in Saudi Arabia."

202 **some fifteen thousand American troops:** M. R. Gordon, "Bush Sends US Force to Saudi Arabia as Kingdom Agrees to Confront Iraq," *New York Times*, August 8, 1990.

202 **"organizing battalions of righteous Islamic":** Coll, *Ghost Wars*, 222–23.

202 **"We will fight him with faith":** Ibid., 223.

203 **Saddam convened a repeat of:** Helfont, "Saddam and the Islamists."

203 **Against the advice of some:** "Obituary: Sheikh Bin Baz," *Economist*, May 22, 1999; J. Miller-jan, "Muslims; Saudis Decree Holy War on Hussein," *New York Times*, January 20, 1991.

204 **seventy Saudi women gathered:** Y. M. Ibrahim, "Saudi Women Take Driver's Seat in a Rare Protest for the Right to Travel," *New York Times*, November 7, 1990.

204 **made to sign pledges:** Ibid.

204 **denounced the protesters as:** J. Miller, "The Struggle Within," *New York Times Magazine*, March 10, 1991.

205 **"It is not the world against Iraq":** M. Fandy, "The Hawali Tapes," *New York Times*, November 24, 1990.

205 **Audah had been deeply influenced by Surur:** H. Saleh, "A Contemporary of the Founder of the Syrian Muslim Brotherhood Reveals Muhammad Surur's Secrets," *Al-Arabiya*, November 20, 2016.

206 **had an explicit mission:** Description of the role and scope of the Islamic University of Medina and the role of the Muslim Brotherhood in the teaching are summarized from M. Farquhar, *Circuits of Faith: Migration, Education, and the Wahhabi Mission* (Redwood City, CA: Stanford University Press, 2016).

206 **Assailed by doubts:** Mansour's journey is summarized from M. Al-Mansour, "Losing My Jihadism," *Washington Post*, July 22, 2007; and E. Rubin, "The Jihadi Who Kept Asking Why," *New York Times Magazine*, March 7, 2004.

207 **The Saudis supported the growth:** Coll, *Ghost Wars*, 296–97.

207 **a twenty-four-year-old Saudi, Abdelaziz Mu'atham:** M. Fandy, *Saudi Arabia and the Politics of Dissent* (New York: Palgrave Macmillan, 1999), 3–4.

208 **such extremism needed to be fought:** A. Y. Shaheen, "Riyadh Explosion: The Full Confessions and the Afghan Link," *Al-Hayat*, April 29, 1996.

209 **and Sheikh Huthaifi was removed:** B. Rubin, "Escaping Isolation," *Jerusalem Post*, April 2, 1998; author interview with Mansour al-Mansour.

209 **resuming diplomatic ties within forty-eight hours:** T. Wilkinson, "Saudis, Iran Settling Bitter Dispute over Mecca Pilgrimage, May Soon Resume Ties," *Los Angeles Times*, March 19, 1991.

209 **were also paying off:** W. Drozdiak, "Iran Reasserts Influence in Gulf," *Washington Post*, March 24, 1991.

210 **Rafsanjani believed that keeping it off-limits:** Author's interview in May 2018 with Hossein Mousavian, former high-ranking Iranian official who conducted secret negotiations with Crown Prince Abdallah on behalf of Rafsanjani in 1995 and 1996.

210 **made sure that Jannat al-Baqi was opened:** "Rafsanjani yazuru fadk wa yaltaqi shiah al-madinah wa yushahidu raksat al-'ardah" [Rafsanjani visits Fadak, meets the Shias of Medina and watches the arda dance], *Al-Wasat*, June 10, 2008.

210 **Even after an indictment in June 2001:** D. Johnston, "14 Indicted by U.S. in '96 Blast," *New York Times*, June 22, 2001.

212 **"We still ask ourselves":** T. Mostyn, "Crown Prince Nayef bin Abdul-Aziz Al Saud Obituary," *Guardian*, June 21, 2012.

212 **few had made it to an actual battlefield:** T. McDermott, *Perfect Soldiers: The 9/11 Hijackers: Who They Were, Why They Did It* (New York: Harper, 2005), 219, 295.

213 **channeled $300 million worth of weapons:** M. Dobbs, "Saudis Funded Weapons for Bosnia, Official Says," *Washington Post*, February 2, 1996.

213 **attacks against the House of Saud:** Wright, *Looming Tower*, 181.

213 **He began to focus his newspaper articles:** Al-Mansour, "Losing My Jihadism."

214 **had pronounced him an infidel:** Ibid.

214 **three hundred private Saudi charities:** Z. Abuza, "Funding Terrorism in Southeast Asia: The Financial Network of Al Qaeda and Jemaah Islamiya," *Contemporary Southeast Asia* 25, no. 2 (August 2003): 169–99.

214 **acting as a kind of unofficial intermediary:** Wright, *Looming Tower*, 227.

214 **as living in a fantasyland of terror:** N. Boustany, "Bin Laden Now a Target in Arab Media," *Washington Post*, November 23, 2001.

215 **of some three hundred sites, only ten remained:** H. Pope, "Iconic Clash: Saudi Fights to End Demolition Driven by Islamic Dictate," *Wall Street Journal*, August 18, 2004.

215 **If there was any trauma in his life:** Author interview with Sami Angawi, Jeddah, February 2018.

215 **Saudi officials dismissed:** Pope, "Iconic Clash."

216 **"The sky's the limit":** Iranian Press Service, "Saudi Defence Minister Visit to Iran Good for Persian Gulf Peace and Security," May 3, 1999.

13: Cain and Abel

220 **survived the initial impact:** As told to author by Jawad al-Khoei in an interview in Najaf in March 2018. The Khoei family stated that details of the arranged car accident were contained in files of the Baath Party that were uncovered after 2003.

220 **Jawad loved the city:** Author interview with Jawad al-Khoei, Najaf, March 2018.

221 **hosted him for a week:** Ibid.

221 **the senior clergy in Najaf:** Moin, *Khomeini*, 158.

221 **empress of Iran had visited:** Ibid.

221 **He thought the Iranians were crazy:** Author interviews in Najaf with senior clerics and scholars from the Najaf hawza.

222 **Abdulmajid understood:** Interview and private correspondence with Hayder al-Khoei, son of Abdulmajid, in Najaf, March 2018.

222 **if Shias had come to see the state:** F. Haddad, "Shia-centric State-Building and Sunni Rejection in Post-2003 Iraq," in F. Wehrey, ed., *Beyond Sunni and Shia: The Roots of Sectarianism in a Changing Middle East* (New York: Oxford University Press, 2017), 133.

223 **"But the Shia of Iraq are not happy":** C. Clover, "Warm Homecoming for Exiled Clergyman," *Financial Times*, April 6, 2003.

223 **"I must go because the risks":** F. Alam and M. Bright, "Murdered Cleric's Family Vow to Continue His Work," *Guardian*, April 13, 2003.

223 **camping on the outskirts of Najaf:** Clover, "Warm Homecoming for Exiled Clergyman."

223 **He wore a bulletproof vest:** Private correspondence with Hayder al-Khoei.

223 **"I have never felt so safe":** Clover, "Warm Homecoming for Exiled Clergyman."

224 **Moqtada's black turban had barely settled:** H. Al-Amin, "Moqtada Sadr: Leader of Orphans," *Al-Ahram Weekly*, May 27–June 2, 2004.

224 **Those were his men shouting:** Although it was initially unclear whether this was a planned assassination and who had carried it out, later investigations revealed the Sadr movement's involvement and an arrest warrant was issued for Moqtada al-Sadr and a dozen of his lieutenants. See also H. Al-Khoei, "Moqtada al-Sadr Should Not Be Above the Law," *Guardian*, January 6, 2011.

224 **A window was smashed:** P. Cockburn, "Death in the Temple," *Independent*, May 8, 2003.

225 **"Don't let them sit":** Ibid.

225 **One man killed by religious violence:** Author interview with Jawad al-Khoei, Najaf, March 2018.

225 **call on Iraqis to rise up:** Reuters, "War in the Gulf: Bush Statement," *New York Times*, February 16, 1991.

225 **the Saudis invited exiled Iraqi politicians:** E. Sciolino, "Saudis Gather Ousted Iraqi Officials," *New York Times*, February 22, 1991.

226 **an estimated ten thousand Shias:** P. Koring, "Iraqi Opposition Anti-Hussein Factions Fragmented, Repressed," *Globe and Mail*, March 8, 1991.

226 **founding commander Hadi al-Amiri:** Original footage available online at https://www.youtube.com/watch?v=RQY4NqUJ4vg.

226 **an Iraqi tank commander:** "Flashback: The 1991 Iraqi Revolt," *BBC News*, August 21, 2007.

226 **"Iran help us":** Original footage filmed by Iraqis available online at https://www.youtube.com/watch?v=F7wZL_MqPGg.

227 **"In the following weeks":** N. Schwarzkopf, *It Doesn't Take a Hero: The Autobiography of General H. Norman Schwarzkopf* (New York: Bantam Books, 1993), 566.

228 **"We'll give our lives":** K. Sim (director), "Pilgrimage to Karbala" [television series episode], in *Wide Angle*, PBS, March 26, 2007.

228 **Ayatollah al-Hakim, leader of SCIRI:** Description of his return and killing come from P. J. McDonnell and T. Wilkinson, "Blast Kills Scores at Iraq Mosque," *Los Angeles Times*, August 30, 2003; and P. J. McDonnell, "Mosque Blast Suspects Arrested," *Los Angeles Times*, August 31, 2003.

229 **The sky rained blood:** B. Ghosh, "Twelve Years On, Remembering the Bomb That Started the Middle East's Sectarian War," *Quartz*, August 28, 2015.

229 **"The Sayyed is dead":** Ibid.

229 **Their leader stood out:** This section is a summary from ibid., with additional details provided to author by Ghosh in email correspondence.

229 **"Don't you see?":** Ghosh, "Twelve Years On."

230 **start-up money from al-Qaeda:** J. Warrick, *Black Flags: The Rise of ISIS* (New York: Doubleday, 2015), 67.

230 **"Iraq today harbors a deadly":** Transcript of Powell's UN Presentation, *CNN*, February 6, 2003.

230 **young men lined up:** Firsthand reporting by author from Damascus during the 2003 US-led invasion of Iraq.

231 **to smuggle Wahhabi religious propaganda:** S. Helfont, "Compulsion in Religion: The Authoritarian Roots of Saddam Hussein's Islam," PhD diss., Princeton University, 2015, 143.

231 **to counter the spread of Wahhabism:** Author interview in March 2018 in Baghdad with Abdullatif al-Humayyem, appointed by Saddam Hussein to oversee Faith Campaign.

232 **More than half a million Iraqis:** P. Bump, "15 Years After the Iraq War Began, the Death Toll Is Still Murky," *Washington Post*, March 20, 2018.

233 **half the foreign fighters:** N. Parker, "The Conflict in Iraq: Saudi Role in Insurgency," *Los Angeles Times*, July 15, 2007.

233 **a resurgence of fundamentalism:** "Saudis Warn US over Iraq War," *BBC News*, February 17, 2003.

234 **The pious father taught Quranic recitation:** W. McCants, *The Believer: How an Introvert with a Passion for Religion and Soccer Became Abu Bakr Al-Baghdadi, Leader of the Islamic State* (Washington, DC: Brookings Institution Press, 2015).

235 **one of three women in a newsroom:** M. Welsh, "Atwar Bahjat: A Believer in Iraq," Al-Jazeera, February 27, 2006.

236 **"We want the correspondent":** Reuters, "Journalists Killed in Iraq Attack," Al-Jazeera, February 23, 2006.

236 **twenty-seven Sunni mosques:** R. F. Worth, "Blast at Shiite Shrine Sets Off Sectarian Fury in Iraq," *New York Times*, February 23, 2006.

14: Fracture

240 **Nasrallah said he offered:** Partial speech, translated by the author from video titled "Nasrallah victory speech, Bint Jbeil, Lebanon, 26 May 2000," available online at https://www.youtube.com/watch?v=0YnH7qhENDQ.

241 **Hezbollah was only gaining in stature:** This section is based on personal reporting;

anonymous interviews with Shias; and H. Saghiyeh and B. El Cheikh, "Nabatiyeh Is Hez-bollah's Fortress–Part I," *NOW Media*, June 14, 2013.

242 **a cultural bastion of Jabal Amel:** Saghiyeh and El Cheikh, "Nabatiyeh Is Hezbollah's Fortress–Part I."

243 **"break Lebanon over [Hariri's] head":** R. Bergman, "The Hezbollah Connection," *New York Times Magazine*, February 10, 2015.

243 **in the company of visitors:** Private conversation between author and Rafiq Hariri in January 2005 at his private office in Qoraytem.

245 **"to cut off the head of the snake":** R. Colvin, "'Cut Off Head of Snake' Saudis Told U.S. on Iran," Reuters, November 29, 2010.

246 **Several members of parliament:** "Pro-Zarqawi MPs Anger Jordan," Al-Jazeera, June 12, 2006.

246 **a thousand more Zarqawis:** "Al-Zarqawi Relatives See a Martyr for Islam," NBC News, June 8, 2006.

246 **a man in a black suit:** Video of the execution titled "Saddam Execution Full Video!" (uploaded December 31, 2006), available online at https://www.youtube.com/watch?v=IljDpUxPmi8. Additional details from M. Bazzi, "How Saddam Hussein's Execution Contributed to the Rise of Sectarianism in the Middle East," *Nation*, January 15, 2016.

247 **"We have become Saddam":** Author interview with Jawad al-Khoei in Najaf, March 2018.

15: Surrender

250 **"I am a slave of the Prophet":** S. Masood and C. Gall, "Killing of Governor Deepens Crisis in Pakistan," *New York Times*, January 4, 2011. Descriptions of events of that day are also taken from Pakistani TV footage.

250 **Aamna Taseer was now a widow:** Description of events and reactions of Aamna Taseer are based on interview with the author, Lahore, October 2017.

251 **Bibi's story began:** A. Bibi and A. Tollet, "Sentenced to Death for a Sip of Water," *New York Post*, August 25, 2013.

252 **its victims were minorities:** M. Qadri, "Pakistan's Deadly Blasphemy-Seeking Vigilantes," *Guardian*, February 3, 2011.

252 **From 1927 to 1985:** Agence France Presse, "The History of the Blasphemy Law," *Express Tribune*, January 5, 2011.

252 **More than thirteen hundred Pakistanis were formally:** "What Are Pakistan's Blasphemy Laws?," *BBC News*, November 6, 2014.

252 **he saw it as an existential threat:** Author interview with Aamna Taseer, October 2017.

253 **"liberal, modern-minded president":** "Pakistan's President Will Pardon Christian Woman, Official Says," *CNN*, November 23, 2010.

253 **even burning Taseer's effigy:** Masood and Gall, "Killing of Governor Deepens Crisis in Pakistan."

253 **Taseer quoted Faiz's most beloved:** "The Day Salman Taseer Fell Silent," *Dawn*, January 4, 2011.

254 **saluted "the bravery and valor":** S. Shah, "Pakistani Religious Groups Cheer Killing of Governor," *McClatchy Newspapers*, January 5, 2011.

254 **Munawar Hasan, the head:** Ibid.

254 **a garland of flowers:** C. Galljan, "Assassination Deepens Divide in Pakistan," *New York Times*, January 5, 2011.

254 **scattered pamphlets on the scene:** D. Walsh, "Pakistan Minister Shahbaz Bhatti Shot Dead in Islamabad," *Guardian*, March 2, 2011.

255 **was heading to work:** S. Taseer, "How I Survived Four and a Half Years in Captivity," *New York Times*, May 17, 2016.

255 **Thousands more traveled:** J. Boone, "Thousands at Funeral of Pakistani Executed for Murdering Governor," *Guardian*, March 1, 2016.

256 **The minister of religious affairs:** Ibid.
256 **cost almost a million dollars:** A. Hashim, "In Pakistan, a Shrine to Murder for 'Blasphemy,'" Al-Jazeera, February 10, 2017.
256 **Barelvis had long promoted themselves:** S. Hashmi, "The State of Barelvi Islam Today," *Daily Times*, June 15, 2018.
257 **Saudi organizations were still paying:** "Saudi Arabia, UAE Financing Extremism in South Punjab," *Dawn*, May 21, 2011.
257 **The Ahl-e Hadith movement had grown:** Summarized from M. Abou Zahab, "Salafism in Pakistan: The Ahl-e Hadith Movement," in Roel Meijer, ed., *Global Salafism: Islam's New Religious Movement* (New York: Columbia University Press, 2009), 126–42.
257 **The Saudi ambassador requested that:** K. Ghattas, "The Saudi Cold War with Iran Heats Up," *Foreign Policy*, July 15, 2015.
257 **"Servility to rich Arabs":** P. Hoodbhoy, "The Saudi-isation of Pakistan," *Newsline*, January 2009.
258 **In 1994, she'd established:** The details about the Al-Huda Foundation, its funding, and its graduates are from Dorsey, "Pakistan's Lurch Towards Ultra-Conservativism Abetted by Saudi-Inspired Pyramid Scheme"; and F. Mushtaq, "A Controversial Role Model for Pakistani Women," *South Asia Multidisciplinary Academic Journal* 4 (2010).
258 **Mehtab walked into the Regent Plaza:** Author interview with Rashdi, Karachi, October 2017.
260 **one in two Pakistanis:** H. Murtaza, "Who Gets to Be a Muslim in Pakistan?," *Dawn*, August 15, 2012.
260 **Shias were still more fortunate:** J. Bell, "The World's Muslims: Unity and Diversity," Pew Research Center, Pew Forum on Religion and Public Life, August 9, 2012, available online at https://www.pewresearch.org/wp-content/uploads/sites/7/2012/08/the-worlds-muslims-full-report.pdf.
261 **sent an open letter to the Shia community:** B. Peer, "The Shiite Murders: Pakistan's Army of Jhangvi," *New Yorker*, March 9, 2013.
261 **even officers were shot:** Ibid.
261 **Shia professionals left the country:** Ibid.

16: Counterrevolution

263 **more alive than ever:** Author interview with Ebtehal Younes, Cairo, October 2017.
264 **three hundred channels to choose from:** M. El-Sayed, "Religious Islamic Satellite Channels: A Screen That Leads You to Heaven," Reuters Institute Fellow's Paper, University of Oxford, 2009, 7, available online at https://reutersinstitute.politics.ox.ac.uk/our-research/religious-islamic-satellite-channels-screen-leads-you-heaven.
264 **the channels were split almost equally between:** "'An qorb: watha'iqi athir alkarahiyya 'anel tahreed alta'ifi fil e'lam" [A documentary about hatred of sectarian incitement in the media], BBC Arabic, available online at https://www.youtube.com/watch?v=DUJfzv6oXKI.
265 **Lewis saw everything as a clash of civilizations:** D. Martin, "Bernard Lewis, Influential Scholar of Islam, Is Dead at 101," *New York Times*, May 21, 2018.
265 **his personal ordeal paled:** "Nasr hamed abu zayd dayf barnamaj albayt baytak takdeem mahmood saad" [Nasr Hamed Abu Zayd, guest of the program al-Bayt Baytak, presented by Mahmoud Saad], video uploaded August 29, 2016, retrieved from https://www.youtube.com/watch?v=YugMjBi773k&t=1s. No longer available.
266 **though he cared little about religion:** Interview with author, Cairo, October 2017.
267 **painted the walls with verses:** M. Abdalla, "Ahmed Fouad Negm: Writing a Revolution," Al-Jazeera, March 15, 2014.
268 **same fate as the shah:** S. Tisdall, "Egypt Revolt Has Iran in a Spin," *Guardian*, February 1, 2011.
269 **publicly mourned him:** "Al-ikhwan wal khilafatu al-khomeini" [The Brotherhood and Khomeini's caliphate], *Al-Majallah*, February 16, 2013.

270 **"spreading the Shiite sect"**: Associated Press, "Egyptian cleric upbraids Iranian leader on string of issues," video, available online at https://www.youtube.com/watch?v=R6wO-d6EgVg.

270 **"This is not what we agreed"**: "Dispute between Ahmadinejad and Al-Azhar University in the press conference," video, available online at https://www.youtube.com/watch?v=kblv0MhjOD4.

271 **Ebtehal and her late husband:** Author interview with Ebtehal Younes, Cairo, October 2017.

271 **calling on him to draw:** "Iranian Elites, Scholars Urge Morsi to Foster Unity, Implement Islamic Law," *BBC Monitoring Middle East*, February 15, 2013.

271 **Egyptian newspapers quickly repeated:** "Iranian Letter to Egypt's Morsi Draws Fire from Islamist Critics," *Al-Ahram Gate*, February 21, 2013; D. El-Bey, "A Martyr Every So Often," *Al-Ahram Weekly*, February 19, 2013.

272 **"infiltrate" Al-Azhar:** All leaked Saudi diplomatic cables can be found online at WikiLeaks, The Saudi Cables, https://wikileaks.org/saudi-cables/db/.

272 **The Saudi intelligence services:** Ibid.

272 **publicly and forcefully spoken about the dangers:** W. Abdul Rahman, "Shayhku lazhari yastankiru muhawalati nashri almazhhabi al-shi'iyyi bijiwari ma'azhini "qal'atu ahli alsunnati" [Al-Azhar's sheikh condemns the attempt to spread the Shiite doctrine near Ahl al-Sunna's muezzin], *Asharq al-Awsat*, September 30, 2011.

272 **Al-Azhar launched a campaign:** WikiLeaks, The Saudi Cables.

272 **anti-Shia posters went up:** Description of the incident from: MBC, "Shahidu 'ayanin 'ala qatli abu al-nimras yabki 'alal hawa'I" [Eyewitness to the killing of Shiites in Abu Al-Nimras cries on air], video, available online at https://www.youtube.com/watch?v=arJYv8303NU.

273 **one hundred twenty religious stations:** "'An qorb: watha'iqi athir alkarahiyya 'anel tahreed alta'ifi fil e'lam," BBC Arabic.

273 **"to expose the Safavid enterprise":** Y. Feldner, "Fitna TV: The Shi'ite-Bashing Campaign on Salafi TV Channels and Social Media," Middle East Research Institute, November 30, 2015.

273 **"I'm very happy he died":** Wesal TV, "Tahta al-majhari halakatu 75 'ala maktali hassan shahata wa thana' al-maliki 'ala al'ilhadi," video, available online at https://www.youtube.com/watch?v=PsHrFdFezuw.

274 **"This is not our fight":** Author interview with Younes, October 2017.

274 **the largest killing of demonstrators:** Human Rights Watch, "Egypt: Rab'a Killings Likely Crimes Against Humanity," August 12, 2014.

275 **"Cairo's not what you'd expect":** A. Naji, *Using Life* (Austin: Center for Middle Eastern Studies, University of Texas at Austin, 2017), 44.

276 **of shivering cold and sweats:** J. Guyer, "Inside the Strange Saga of a Cairo Novelist Imprisoned for Obscenity," *Rolling Stone*, February 24, 2017. Other parts of Ahmed's story are also summarized from the *Rolling Stone* article.

276 **Former officials spoke in his favor:** Author interview with Ahmed Naji, Cairo, October 2017.

276 **perhaps he wouldn't even have been exiled:** Ibid.

277 **Some journalists did knock on the Saudi mission's door:** H. Bahgat, "Wikileaks: Egyptian Media and Journalists Go to Saudi for Financing," *Mada Masr*, July 5, 2015.

277 **paying him $200,000:** Ibid.

17: Between ISIS and IRGC

281 **in August 2011, Abu Bakr . . . sent a scouting mission:** This passage relies on reporting done in Warrick, *Black Flags*, 251.

281 **traveled west from Iraq:** Ibid.

282 **hundreds of Lebanese and Syrian men:** This passage relies on reporting done in B. Daragahi, "Inside Iran's Mission to Dominate the Middle East," *BuzzFeed*, July 30, 2017.

282 **operatives had been tried in The Hague:** A. Fielding-Smith, "Hizbollah Man Named Over Hariri Murder," *Financial Times*, July 29, 2011.

284 **its top fighters into Syria:** N. Blanford, "The Battle for Qusayr: How the Syrian Regime and

Hizb Allah Tipped the Balance," *Combating Terrorism Center Sentinel* 6, no. 8 (August 2013): 18–22.

284 **Suleimani declared:** D. Filkins, "The Shadow Commander," *New Yorker*, September 30, 2013.

284 **to help their Syrian brothers, by all means:** A. Zelin, "The Saudi Foreign Fighter Presence in Syria," *Combating Terrorism Center Sentinel* 7, no. 4 (April 2014): 10–14.

284 **They berated women who didn't veil:** R. Spencer and D. Rose, "Under the Black Flag of al-Qaeda, the Syrian City Ruled by Gangs of Extremists," *Telegraph*, May 12, 2013.

286 **A huge new structure was rising:** Information from this passage comes from M. Ababsa, "Les Mausolées Invisibles: Raqqa, Ville de Pèlerinage Chiite ou Pôle Étatique en Jazîra Syrienne?" [Invisible mausoleums: Raqqa, city of Shiite pilgrimage or a pole for the state in Syrian Jazira?], *Annales de Géographie* 110, no. 622 (November–December 2001): 647–64; M. Ababsa, "Significations Territoriales et Appropriations Conflictuelles des Mausolées Chiites de Raqqa (Syrie)" [Territorial significances and conflictual appropriations of Raqqa's Shiite mausoleums (Syria)], in S. Chiffoleau and A. Madoeuf, eds., *Les Pèlerinages au Maghreb et au Moyen-Orient: Espaces Publics, Espaces du Public* (Damascus: Presses de l'Ifpo, 2005); and a detailed picture and video essay on Flickr curated by the scholar Martin Kramer, "The Shiite Crescent Eclipsed," available online at https://www.flickr.com/photos/martin _kramer/galleries/72157630819437940/with/2343449697/.

289 **Jamal looked at ISIS and he saw Wahhabism untamed:** Author interview with Jamal Khashoggi, Washington, DC, August 2017.

289 **in the footsteps of Ibn Abdelwahhab:** C. Bunzel, "The Kingdom and the Caliphate: Duel of the Islamic States," Carnegie Endowment for International Peace, February 18, 2016, available online at https://carnegieendowment.org/2016/02/18/kingdom-and-caliphate-duel-of -islamic-states-pub-62810.

290 **a few months later in a newspaper:** R. Ghazzawi, "Yassin Haj Saleh on Samira Khalil" (translation), August 11, 2014, available online at https://douma4.wordpress.com/2014/08 /11/yassin-haj-saleh-on-samira-khalil-translation/.

18: Achilles' Heel

293 **Masih Alinejad had long since removed her veil:** All sections about Masih Alinejad are based on two interviews with the author in Washington, DC, and New York in March 2018 and follow-up email exchanges. I also relied extensively on her memoir, *The Wind in My Hair: My Fight for Freedom in Modern Iran* (Boston: Little, Brown, 2018).

300 **"You're provoking the regime":** M. Alinejad (@AlinejadMasih), "Brave woman risk arrest in order to make awareness about anti compulsory hijab movement in Tehran' public bus," Twitter, May 16, 2018, https://twitter.com/AlinejadMasih/status/996694870302523392.

302 **six hundred American soldiers:** J. Schogol, "Report: Iran Killed 600 U.S. Soldiers in the Iraq War," *National Interest*, April 3, 2019.

303 **Suleimani arrived in Baghdad to lead the counterattack:** M. Chulov, "Qassem Suleimani: Can This Man Bring About the Downfall of Isis?," *Guardian*, December 7, 2014.

303 **they were amateurish snapshots:** S. Kamali Dehghan, "Qassem Suleimani Photo Makeover Reveals Iran's New Publicity Strategy," *Guardian*, October 14, 2014.

303 **Prince Khaled bin Salman:** J. Vela, "Saudi Prince Flew Jet in Syria ISIL Attacks," *National* (Abu Dhabi), September 24, 2014.

304 **Iran's "destabilizing activity":** K. Ghattas, "Why Saudi Arabia Has Lost Faith in the US," *BBC News*, May 18, 2015.

305 **Iran warned the kingdom against:** "The Sword Unsheathed," *Economist*, October 18, 2014.

19: Murder on the Bosporus

308 **never fully adhered:** "Jamal khashoggi: men yasar hekmatyar ila yamin turkil faysal ahenn ilal sahafa" [Jamal Khashoggi: from Hekmatyar's left to Turki al-Faisal's right], *Asharq al-Awsat*, March 11, 2005.

310 **one infamous incident:** D. Filkins, "A Saudi Prince's Quest to Remake the Middle East," *New Yorker*, April 9, 2018.

310 **on a "short leash":** K. House, "Profile of a Prince: Promise and Peril in Mohammed bin Salman's Vision 2030," Belfer Center for Science and International Affairs, Harvard University, April 2019, available online at https://www.belfercenter.org/publication/profile-prince-promise-and-peril-mohammed-bin-salmans-vision-2030.

310 **a path to the top:** Ibid.

311 **had angered many of MbS's older cousins:** M. Mazzetti and B. Hubbard, "Rise of Saudi Prince Shatters Decades of Royal Tradition," *New York Times*, October 15, 2016.

312 **in the 1950s about King Saud:** W. Hangen, "Arabia Preparing Extensive Reform," *New York Times*, December 11, 1953.

314 **been held in a palace:** B. Hubbard, M. Mazzetti, and E. Schmitt, "Saudi King's Son Plotted Effort to Oust His Rival," *New York Times*, July 18, 2017.

314 **in self-imposed exile:** Private communication between author and Khashoggi in June 2017, in which Khashoggi stated he was in self-imposed exile in the United States.

315 **"I'm under pressure":** D. Ignatius, "Jamal Khashoggi's Long Road to the Doors of the Saudi Consulate," *Washington Post*, October 13, 2018.

316 **reportedly lived below the poverty line:** K. Sullivan, "Saudi Arabia's Riches Conceal a Growing Problem of Poverty," *Guardian*, January 1, 2013.

316 **Sofana Dahlan wanted to believe:** Author interview with Sofana Dahlan, Jeddah, May 2018.

318 **"What happened in the last 30 years":** M. Chulov, "I Will Return Saudi Arabia to Moderate Islam, Says Crown Prince," *Guardian*, October 24, 2017.

319 **"this Wahhabism—please define it for us":** J. Goldberg, "Saudi Crown Prince: Iran's Supreme Leader 'Makes Hitler Look Good.'" *Atlantic*, April 2, 2018.

320 **Eleven activists had been:** K. Ghattas, "Saudi Arabia's Dark Nationalism," *Atlantic*, June 2, 2018.

320 **religion played too big a role:** ASDA'A Burson-Marsteller, "Arab Youth Survey 2018."

321 **democracy was the solution:** *TRT World*, "In Remembrance of Jamal Khashoggi," video, available online at https://www.trtworld.com/video/social-videos/in-remembrance-of-jamal-khashoggi/5bccb605315f18291a6c78f4.

322 **The Saudi embassy in Washington had directed him:** K. Jovanovski, S. Smith, F. Bruton, and D. De Luce, "Jamal Khashoggi Was Fearful of Saudi Government Before Disappearing, Friends Say," *NBC Palm Springs*, October 8, 2018.

322 **he laughed at friends:** B. Hubbard and D. Kirkpatrick, "For Khashoggi, a Tangled Mix of Royal Service and Islamist Sympathies," *New York Times*, October 14, 2018.

322 **"Fine, my darling":** S. Mekhennet and L. Morris, "Missing Journalist's Fiancee Demands to Know: 'Where Is Jamal?'" *Washington Post*, October 8, 2019.

323 **"My understanding is":** S. Flanders, V. Nereim, D. Abu-Nasr, N. Razzouk, A. Shahine, and R. Hamade, "Saudi Crown Prince Discusses Trump, Aramco, Arrests: Transcript," *Bloomberg*, October 5, 2018.

324 **fifteen men had traveled to Istanbul:** Details of Jamal Khashoggi's killing are taken from D. Ignatius, "How the Mysteries of Khashoggi's Murder Have Rocked the U.S.-Saudi Partnership," *Washington Post*, March 29, 2019; D. Ignatius, "The Khashoggi Killing Had Roots in a Cutthroat Saudi Family Feud," *Washington Post*, November 27, 2018.

324 **"I listen to music":** M. Chulov, "Jamal Khashoggi: Murder in the Consulate," *Guardian*, October 21, 2018.

325 **"young, ambitious, divinely inspired reformer":** K. M. Abou El Fadl, "Saudi Arabia Is Misusing Mecca," *New York Times*, November 12, 2018.

325 **"I may have caused some of our people":** S. Samuel, "Trump's Evangelical Advisers Hear from the Saudi Crown Prince on Khashoggi," *Atlantic*, November 9, 2018.

326 **her brother spoke out:** F. Gardner, "'Shrouded in Secrecy': Saudi Women Activists' Trial Hearing Delayed," *BBC News*, April 17, 2019.

ACKNOWLEDGMENTS

This book took longer to research and write than I expected and was a much tougher project than I anticipated, but I made it to the finish line thanks to the incredible constellation of people in my life and on this journey: longtime friends, amazing colleagues and mentors, total strangers who provided crucial support or shared their stories with me, serendipitous encounters that brought me pieces I didn't even know were missing from the puzzle of this book—their trust and faith in my work, their unwavering support, and their love carried me forward and brought light to the darkest hours of writing.

For my second book, I am incredibly grateful to have had the same stellar team by my side again, at both Henry Holt and William Morris Endeavor. At Holt, my editor, Serena Jones, pulled out all the stops to make sure I would publish with her again and took a chance on yet another unusual project. I am thankful for her wise guidance shepherding the project from start to finish, her prodding questions while reading my drafts, her constant encouragement and patience, all of which she delivers with incredible calm even when I'm weeks behind and her workload has skyrocketed because she's received a massive and well-deserved promotion. Madeline Jones read and reread the manuscript and answered my inane questions about Word, footnotes, and schedules. I am, once more, so grateful for the patience and support of the production editor Chris O'Connell. Maggie Richards and Patricia Eiseman have been there for me from the minute I walked into their offices back in 2011. I could not ask for better champions of my work. With Declan Taintor, they make sure that when the tree falls in the forest, someone is around to tell the story and the books get an audience. Many trees were felled to make this book; in exchange, I have contributed to a reforestation project of cedars in Lebanon. Please consider doing the same at www.adoptacedar.org. Thank you to Stephen Rubin and Ben Schrank for making me feel that I have a home at Henry Holt. At WME, my agent, Dorian Karchmar, is the best in the business, and I am so lucky to have her in my corner. She's both visionary and relentlessly detail oriented; she pushes me so much further than I think I can go while also protecting me from the pressures that go with writing a book. She goes beyond the call of duty herself and her high standards keep me on my toes. She also has an incredible knack for coming up with the best title for a book. She gets credit again for this one.

Whom does a writer call in her darkest hour of need? Domenica Alioto. Between pasta and Perugia, Domenica provided a pair of fresh eyes and a constant presence while her expert hands helped polish my prose. Joy Johanessen came through on a very tight deadline to provide a crucial fine comb. At the BBC, I thank Paul Danahar, Andrew Roy, and Jonathan Munro for giving me the time off to write this book; and to all my former colleagues at the BBC, thank you for an incredible twenty years.

I am indebted to several institutions that gave me critical support, space to write, and intellectual freedom to create. At Carnegie Corporation, I must thank Hilary Weisner, Nehal Amer, and especially president Vartan Gregorian. At the Rockefellers Brothers Fund, my thanks go to Ariadne Papagapitos, Karen Karnicki, and president Stephen Heintz. Henri Barkey was the first to alert me to the possibilities of fellowships at the Woodrow Wilson Center for International Scholars, where I spent six months. Robert Litwak's enthusiasm for my project and his help in sorting out some of the logistics meant a lot while I was buried under my books in a cubicle. I miss the wonderful library staff and the resourceful Arlyn Charles. I had the privilege of being a senior visiting fellow for fifteen months at the Carnegie Endowment for International Peace, where Ambassador Bill Burns welcomed me like a member of the family and gave me all the latitude (and longitude from DC to Beirut and beyond) I needed to get the research and writing done. His feedback and comments on my work, but especially his kindness, were a true gift. The inimitable Elizabeth Dibble worked out all the behind-the-scenes arrangements so I could just focus on the work; Hilary McGraw, Jin Wang, and Yu-Chieh Chou administered the grant, and I am so grateful for their patience. At Carnegie Beirut, Maha Yahya and Mohanad Hage Ali were wonderful colleagues and sounding boards.

It's no exaggeration to say that I could never have achieved this impossible task in the time I had without my two incredible research assistants and their complementary roles: Zeead Yaghi, with his master's in neuroscience and keen interest in the topic of collective memory, and Micheline Tobia, with her master's in international affairs and her love of all things cultural and artistic. They pored over hundreds of newspapers, books, and academic publications; they dug deep and found hidden gems; they assembled an incredible library of documents that represent forty years of the region's history. We relied extensively on the world-class Jafet Library at the American University of Beirut—an unbelievable resource that deserves more recognition. Thank you, Lokman Mehio, Mona Assi, and Carla Chalhoub, for putting up with our endless requests for months on end. Thank you as well to Ali el-Yasser and Jane Olin-Ammentorp who were there at the genesis of this project and helped me believe it was possible to pull it off.

There were many "last miles," moments when I thought I could see the finish line only to slump back in my chair. The absolutely very last mile would have been a painful slog were it not for the incredible timing of a residency I was awarded at the Civitella Ranieri Foundation in the spring of 2019. Surrounded by the lush green hills of Umbria and fed a steady diet of magnificent pasta and *secondi piatti*, I ended the isolation of the working day with dinner in the company of the brilliant minds of the other fellows—writers, poets, composers, and visual artists. They changed my understanding of language, writing, and creating. Civitella is a magical place and I will never forget the people who make it so: Dana Prescott, Diego Mencaroni, Ilaria Locchi, Sam Lloyd-Knauf, and all the staff. I left a few pounds heavier, but I have forgiven the fantastic chef, Romana Cubini, and her duo of Patrizia sous-chefs. A huge thank-you to Tom Fletcher for connecting all the right dots.

I also spent many weeks on the road, interviewing people and researching the countries I chose to focus on in these pages. Some of my sources prefer to remain anonymous, and I thank them for their trust. In Egypt, I found an oasis filled with love and good food in the home of Tamara al-Rifai and Khaled Mansour. Hamada Adwan was my driver, bodyguard, big brother, and all-around excellent companion from Cairo to Alexandria. Ahmed Naji was a hoot to hang out with and a mine of information. Both he and Khaled read my Egypt chapters and provided much-needed feedback. I'm grateful to Ebtehal Younes for welcoming me into her home and telling me her incredible story. Thanks as well to Emad Abou Gad, Amro Ali, and Amr Ezzat for their expertise and kindness. In Iraq, I was in the company of the larger-than-life Khaled Ali and Haidar Abboud, who arranged all the logistics and interviews and drove me around from Baghdad to Najaf. In Najaf, I had the privilege of being in the company of the wonderful, smart Hayder al-Khoei, who not only shared the story of his father but introduced me and facilitated access to clerics from the hawza and experts who spent hours talking to me about the intricacies of the holy city and Shiism. In Baghdad, Husham Hashmi and Hana' Edward filled in important pieces of the puzzle. I am also grateful to Ambassador Fareed Yasseen for his help and insights. In Pakistan, my wonderful friend Shaban Khalid was the most generous host and made the trip a success. No trip to Pakistan is complete without Shaan and Wajahat Khan. From Islamabad to Peshawar, Lahore to Karachi, my trip was filled with incredible people who all contributed in invaluable ways to my research and reporting: Ahmad Rashid, Haroon Rashid, Hoori Nourani, Rahimullah Yousefzai, Sheema Kermani, and Farid Ghul Mohammad. Aamna and Shehrbano Taseer spent hours talking to me about their lives and their country; Mehtab Rashdi welcomed a total stranger into her home and told the best stories. Alia Chugtai and Khudai Noor provided essential logistical support. My thanks also go to Hussain Haqqani, Farahnaz Ispahani, Bina Shah, and Raza Rumi, who read and commented on my pages. In Saudi Arabia, several of the people I spoke to wished to remain anonymous. I had many conversations with Jamal Khashoggi before his gruesome killing. Jamal was incredibly generous in sharing his story, imparting knowledge, and responding to endless follow-ups over email and messaging. He is missed but his memory lives on. Thanks to Ahmad Badeeb and Mohammad al-Sulami as well for their time. In DC, New York, and Tunis, I am also indebted to Rashed Ghannoushi, Andrew Scott Cooper, Hassan Hassan, Hassan Abbas, Ambassador Abdallah Al-Saud, Prince Turki al-Faisal, Prince Faisal bin Farhan, Mohammad al-Yahya, and Saoud al-Kabli. I could not have written my chapters on Iran and all things Iranian without Mohsen Sazegara, Masih Alinejad, and Kambiz Foroohar. In Beirut, in specific connection to the book, I thank Hazem Saghieh for Saturday morning breakfasts served with endless wisdom and knowledge; Badia Fahs, who fed me and taught me all she knew about Iran and Shiism; Hussein al-Husseini and his sons Ahmad and Hassan al-Husseini, who shed light on an essential but forgotten period of history and whose friendship is precious and unwavering across continents; Saoud al-Mawla, who provided the stepping-stones for several of the chapters; and Elias Khoury, who shared his unique perspective. I wish I could have devoted more pages to Syria and Yemen—two humanitarian disasters that are a stain on our collective conscience. I'm glad others have taken on this essential task and can do it much better than I could. I am in awe of Yassin al-Haj Saleh's unwavering commitment to freedom, pluralism, and democracy, and I owe him a huge debt of gratitude for allowing me to tell his story and reminding me of what really matters. The story of how I secured permission to use the lines of poetry and lyrics in this book is worthy of a book in itself. For now, my immense gratitude to Omar Kabbani, the Faiz Foundation Trust and Salima and Moneeza Hashmi, Joumana Hawi, Abla al-Ruwaini, Arsalan Baraheni, Asif Farrukhi, Farzaneh Milani, Fayrouz as well as Fawzi Moutran, Mashrou' Leila, Vali Nasr, Farid Gul Mohammad, and Maziar Samiee.

To tell this story and the stories of the people on its pages, I knew I had to get away from Washington, DC, and immerse myself in the Middle East, its history, politics, music, poetry, and food, so I moved back to Lebanon for a year. In the process, I decided to stay in Lebanon, adopted a dog, and left full-time journalism. Washington remains my other home, and I am ridiculously fortunate to have two tribes, on both sides of the Atlantic, friends who provide encouragement, comic relief, spirited conversations, drinks, and gourmet dinners. Most of all, they give me space to disappear and write for weeks on end—it's a miracle that they're always there when I reemerge.

Kate Seelye, Lamia Matta, Joyce Karam, and Lynn Chia kept me sane, happy, and alive. I could not have done this without them by my side. Muna Shikaki tried hard to keep me fit, then fed me steak. Yuri Kim, Sonia Dridi, Vivian Salame, Reema Dodin, and Hannah Allam are the smartest, coolest gang a girl could wish for in DC. Dani Isdale and Toby Holder were heaven-sent guardians of everything. An extra-special thank-you goes to Randa Slim, who like me divides her life between the United States and Lebanon—without her incredible wisdom and analysis about the Middle East, we would all be the poorer. She has been a friend, a mentor, and a role model. In 2014, when I first came up with the idea at the heart of this book, I envisioned a magazine piece. David Rothkopf gets the credit for convincing me that I was onto something that deserved a whole book. He pestered me for weeks until I began to write a proposal to submit to my agent. Lissa Muscatine is a powerhouse, a fellow writer, a friend, and a writer's best friend, and such fun to hang out with. Dana Milbank read the proposal, played wordsmith with the subtitle, gave reactions to the cover design, and checked in on a regular basis—a list of self-assigned duties that come with his wonderful friendship. Marwan Muasher is my intellectual mentor and sparring partner, my favorite sounding board and partner in the crime of continuous hope that our region will have a better future. He was there when the idea for this book was born, guided me along the way, kept me wise, and saved me from many errors. Karim Sadjadpour, forever known as DC's handsome sheikh, was a constant presence along the way—his friendship and intellect make me richer. Emile Hokayem is one of the smartest and kindest people I know, and our friendship travels where he goes. Both he and Karim know more about this subject than I do, and their feedback to the draft made it so much better. Thanks as well to Shadi Hamid and Daniel Levy for their essential comments. Mark Landler, Angela Tung, Adam Brookes, Susan Lawrence, Jennifer Ludden, Gerry Holmes, Nicole Gaouette, and Flore DePreneuf are my extended family in DC. I wish I could hang out with them more often.

The list of people to thank in Beirut is simply too long. This is a city where the social network is vast and strong and where emotional support comes from close friends but also from neighbors who ring the doorbell with homemade food and the newspaper vendor who cuts out articles he thinks will be useful. Key to the Beirut tribe are Karim and Michele Chaya—they remain my anchors and their home is my haven. Raya and Michel are always next door, and Claudia and Kris provide the island extension of the happiness bubble. Jad Salhab remains part of the Beirut tribe even while in DC. I'm grateful that Loubna Dimashqi cares little about politics. Nada Abdelsamad, Maya Beydoun, Diana Moukalled, and Hazem al-Amine endured endless conversations, questions, and absences but never gave up. Christine Codsi provided lunches and escapades. Kamal Mouzawak and Rabih Keyrouz are my source of all things beautiful. Jehanne Phares, Tony Yazbek, Amira Solh, and Carine Chebli are always there, even when they're far. My mother and my sisters remain at the heart of everything.

INDEX

ABOUT THE AUTHOR

Kim Ghattas is an Emmy Award–winning journalist and writer who covered the Middle East for twenty years for the BBC and the *Financial Times*. She has also reported on the US State Department and American politics. She has been published in *The Atlantic*, *The Washington Post*, and *Foreign Policy* and is currently a nonresident scholar at the Carnegie Endowment for International Peace in Washington. Her first book, *The Secretary*, was a *New York Times* bestseller. Born and raised in Lebanon, she now lives between Beirut and Washington, DC.